Governing from the Centre

Core Executive Coordination in France

JACK HAYWARD

and

VINCENT WRIGHT

OXFORD

UNIVERSITY PRESS

OXFORD
UNIVERSITY PRESS

Great Clarendon Street, Oxford OX2 6DP

Oxford University Press is a department of the University of Oxford.
It furthers the University's objective of excellence in research, scholarship,
and education by publishing worldwide in

Oxford New York

Auckland Bangkok Buenos Aires Cape Town Chennai
Dar es Salaam Delhi Hong Kong Istanbul Karachi Kolkata
Kuala Lumpur Madrid Melbourne Mexico City Mumbai Nairobi
São Paulo Shanghai Taipei Tokyo Toronto

Oxford is a registered trade mark of Oxford University Press
in the UK and in certain other countries

Published in the United States
by Oxford University Press Inc., New York

© Jack Hayward, 2002

British Library Cataloguing in Publication Data
Data available

Library of Congress Cataloging in Publication Data
Hayward, Jack Ernest Shalom.
Governing from the centre: core executive coordination in France / Jack Hayward
and Vincent Wright.
p. cm.
Includes bibliographical references.
1. Government executives–France. 2. Executive power–France. 3. Government
executives–France–Case studies. 4. Executive power–France–Case studies.
I. Title: Governing from the centre. II. Wright, Vincent. III. Title.
JN2738.E95 H39 2002   320.944–dc21   2002025020
ISBN 0-19-925601-2   ✓

1 3 5 7 9 10 8 6 4 2

Typeset by Newgen Imaging Systems (P) Ltd., Chennai, India
Printed in Great Britain
on acid-free paper by
Biddles Ltd., Guildford & King's Lynn

Contents

Preface and Acknowledgements

This study of core executive policy coordination in France was part of a comparative study, that was intended to yield both a cross-national comparative volume, as well as specific country volumes. Although formally part of the ESRC Whitehall Programme headed by Professor Rod Rhodes, we deliberately chose to exclude Britain from our study to acquire the necessary detachment. So, this investigation might have been called 'Not Just the Whitehall Programme'.

In undertaking the comparative study of policy coordination, our principal aim was to describe the traditional core executives and their networks and processes, as well as their responses to the various challenges. To secure sufficient longitudinal grasp of their procedural and behavioural characteristics, we initially set a timescale of fifteen years that eventually became twenty years. Four major states of the European Union (EU), with distinctive constitutional, cultural, political, and institutional arrangements and traditions, were initially studied: France, Germany, Italy, and the Netherlands, to which Austria and Spain were subsequently added. More especially, the project focused on the policy ambitions of the core executives which have been triggered by the challenges, as well as on their political and institutional capacity to translate policy ambitions into coordinated programmes. Four contrasting sectors were selected: EU policy-making, budget-making, immigration, and privatisation.

Given the lack of even basic information on core executive coordination with which we were confronted, we had to concentrate initially on fact-finding within a conceptual framework by way of mapping exercises as a preliminary to the case studies undertaken. While we started out by testing three interlinked theories—historical institutionalism, convergence, and network approaches—the first of these emerged as the most useful for our purposes. The case studies, in particular, showed that the broadly 'new institutionalism' research approach which we adopted was partly confirmed by the fact that issue coordination was mediated by prevailing policy frames and national or sectoral institutional arrangements. These determined the parameters of decision-making, the constellation of actors, procedures and structure of arenas, the types and style of coordination. Historical institutionalism was also useful in explaining persistent national differences: convergent pressures do not always lead to convergent institutional responses, as EU policy coordination most markedly demonstrated. The 'stickiness' of national institutional arrangements also helped to explain persistent differences in coordination ambitions, in the salience of particular issues, in coordination needs, actors, and mechanisms.

However, our research also pointed to the limits of institutionalism for two main reasons. First, it understates the degree of fluidity in traditional institutions. Our study reveals a great deal of instability and malleability, particularly in institutional arrangements narrowly conceived (ministries have been created, amalgamated, and dismembered with surprising ease), and it points to the importance of contingent factors of a political and even personal nature. Coordination processes are not politically neutral: who coordinates in which arena has powerful political implications. Coordination processes may be reshaped by the changing political salience of an issue (e.g. EU policy-making and immigration), by electoral change, or even designating a different lead ministry (e.g. Foreign Affairs instead of Finance Ministry for EU policy, Justice or Social Affairs in the place of Interior, or vice versa for immigration policy). Personalities also matter: the coordination ambitions and style of successive prime ministers have differed widely. In France, the President–Prime Minister relationship has been determined by the results of the most recent elections or the personal wishes of the incumbents. The coordinating role of the French presidency between 1981 and 1995 was determined by changing political circumstances to which the personal decisions of François Mitterrand had to be adjusted. Second, historical institutionalism underestimates the profound impact of exogenous shocks to traditional systems. Policy frames, ambitions, needs, actors, institutions, and processes have all been remoulded, although not necessarily in convergent fashion, by the cumulative impact of these changes.

Five salient conceptual and methodological issues emerged, which posed problematic preliminaries. In the first place, the concept of the core executive proved to be more elastic in empirical practice than anticipated. We used the Dunleavy and Rhodes definition of the core executive which includes '*all those organizations and structures which primarily serve to pull together and integrate central government policies, or act as final arbiters within the executive of conflicts between different elements of the Government machine*'.[1] In our research, issues could be coordinated by a variety of core executives from the President down to interdepartmental committees (comprising key civil servants) of a permanent or *ad hoc* nature—or often a combination of some or occasionally all of them. In practical terms, it would have been easier to focus on one actor (probably the President or Prime Minister) in order to simplify the dependent variable. This is usually done[2] but at the crippling cost of other-actors-being-neglected oversimplification which we were determined to avoid. We, therefore, opted to cope with the consequent additional complexities.

Second, we confronted the problem of how to define coordination. The purposes of governmental coordination are well known: facilitating organizational spread; protecting members of the core executive by providing a formal sharing of the responsibility for any particular decision (thus obfuscating the real source of responsibility); disguising the inevitable divisions and tensions of government by presenting an image of unity; managing policy externalities, and the problems of duplication and redundancy. However, what at first sight is a simple and straightforward activity turns out on closer investigation to raise questions of a conceptual nature. First, it was not always easy to draw a distinction between decision-making

---

[1] R. A. W. Rhodes, 'From Prime Ministerial Power to Core Executive', in R. A. W. Rhodes and P. Dunleavy (eds.), *Prime Minister, Cabinet and Core Executive* (London, Macmillan, 1995), p. 12. His italics.
[2] See, for example, J. Blondel and J.-L. Thiébault (eds.), *The Profession of Government Minister in Western Europe* (London, Macmillan, 1991).

in general and coordination. Second, coordination emerges as a multi-dimensional activity involving both process and objectives, and it takes many forms.

Third, having adopted a 2×2 matrix, using the categories political/non-political, routine/non-routine for selecting our case studies, we discovered—given our extended timespan—that there was a blurring of the matrix categories, most notably with respect to the politicized/non-politicized distinction. Several case studies underlined the fact that a particular issue could oscillate between the two. Thus, the BSE crisis study revealed an issue that moved from a non-politicized quadrant to a politicized one as a largely technical issue blew up into a major political scandal. The privatisation of France Télécom, on the other hand, moved over time from being a politicized issue into a depoliticized one. It was also clear that each of the key distinctions such as politicization could mean very different things, thus triggering very different coordination needs. Our matrix risked, therefore, being rather static, failing to capture the dynamics of certain coordination processes. Fortunately, our timespan of nearly two decades allowed us to introduce a dynamic corrective to the matrix used, which would have been a bad master but proved a useful servant.

Fourth, obliged to restrict the fields to be investigated, we faced the problem of generalization. Having selected four sectors or major policy areas, we were aware that a study of other sectors—notably defence and foreign policy—might yield quite different conclusions. So, information from secondary sources or previous work by the authors on other sectors was incorporated to provide a more comprehensive analysis.

Fifth, we were also compelled to restrict the policy stages investigated. To render the project feasible, it was reluctantly agreed to analyse coordination at only the initiation, agenda-setting, and formalization stages of policy-making, and to ignore the implementation, monitoring, and evaluation stages, except where they impinged directly on the early stages. In several of the case studies this distinction proved to be rather artificial because of constant feedback loops.

Readers of this volume will make their own assessment of whether the choices made in dealing with these problems were wise.

We are indebted in several directions for help in making this study possible. Generous support under the ESRC Whitehall Programme (Award No. L124251013) and the advice from its Director, Professor Rod Rhodes, are acknowledged with thanks. A very large number of people were interviewed as part of the research for this volume, either by its authors or those associated with its preparation, notably Dr Robert Elgie, Professor Anand Menon, and Dr Patrick Weil, as well as by Dr David Howarth, one of the two Research Officers. Our gratitude goes to them for allowing their work to be used in some of the case studies that make up Part II of the book. Stephanie Wright at Nuffield College helped Vincent Wright administer the project which involved numerous workshops and conferences. She did so with superlative efficiency and equanimity. Drafts of the typescript were successively prepared for publication by Jane Wyatt and Sue Wiles. Sally Harris prepared the bibliography. They have our thanks for the care with which they did so. While the project was conducted in Oxford, much of the writing was done in Hull, to which one of the authors retired in autumn 1998. Professor Ed Page read the whole of the typescript and made useful suggestions leading to some modifications of presentation.

Finally, it is with immense personal sadness that an enterprise that was conceived, planned, and researched jointly became the sole responsibility of one of the progenitors owing to the untimely death of Vincent Wright in July 1999. All those who knew him and his work will recognize his imprint at certain points in this volume, although he did not live to make the contribution we had projected.

Jack Hayward

Abbreviations

BSE	bovine spongiform encephalopathy
CAP	Common Agricultural Policy
CC	Constitutional Council
CFDT	Confédération Française Démocratique du Travel
CGE	Compagnie Générale d'Electricité
CIMEE	Comité Interministériel des Moyens de l'Etat à l'Etranger
CJD	Creutzfeldt–Jakob Disease
CNAL	National Committee for Secular Action
CNEC	National Committee of Catholic Education
COREPER	Committee of Permanent Representatives
DAFAG	Financial Affairs and General Administration Division
DGSE	General Direction of External Security
DGT	General Direction of Telecommunications
EC	European Commission
ECB	European Central Bank
ECOFIN	Council of Finance Ministers
EMS	European Monetary System
EMU	European Monetary Union
ENA	Ecole Nationale d'Administration
EU	European Union
EUT	European Union Treaty
G7	Group of Seven
GATT	General Agreement on Tariffs and Trade
GEM	Study and Mobilization Group
GIGN	Groupe d'Intervention de la Gendarmerie Nationale
GISTI	Support Group for Immigrant Workers
IGC	Intergovernmental Conference
ILO	International Labour Organization
IMF	International Monetary Fund
INSEE	Institut National de la Statistique et des Etudes Economiques
NATO	North Atlantic Treaty Organization
NF	National Front
NGOs	non-governmental organizations
OECD	Organization for Economic Cooperation and Development
OFPRA	French Office for the Protection of Refugees and Stateless Persons
PCF	Parti Communiste Français
PS	Socialist Party
PTT	Post and Telecommunications

RPR	Rassemblement Pour le République
SGCI	General Secretariat of the Interministerial Committee for European Economic Cooperation
SGDN	Secretariat General of National Defence
SGG	Government General Secretariat
SGP	Secretary General of the Presidency
SGPP	Secretariat General for Public Policies
SID	Service d'Information et de Diffusion
SIS	Schengen Information System
SLF	Service de la Législation Fiscale
TMM	Thomson Multimedia
UDF	Union pour la Démocratie Française
UNAPEL	National Union of Parents of Private Schoolchildren
UNESCO	United Nations Educational, Scientific, and Cultural Organization
VAT	value added tax
WTO	World Trade Organization

PART I

THE COMPLEXITIES OF FRENCH CORE EXECUTIVE COORDINATION

1

The French Context of Coordination: A Fractured Indivisible Republic

Due to its inordinate impulse to impart a state-organized monolithic unity to an inherently diverse and conflict-ridden society, achieving cohesion and cooperation in France has posed problems to those officially in power that few have successfully resolved in a sustained way. The persistent temptation has been to impose top-down comprehensive solutions, provoking periodic upsurges of resistance against ill-informed failures to understand the complexity of specific problems and the need to secure at least the acquiescence if not the enthusiastic support of the subjects of such authoritative intervention. While the ensuing difficulties are not peculiar to France, it is the overweening self-confidence of the political and administrative directorate in its capacity to command that raises false expectations about its ability to attain its objectives.

This confidence is fostered by a belief in the directorate's own cohesion, which on closer inspection turns out to be largely an illusion. Those who purport to unify the activities of others do not themselves share the same purposes. The nucleus of state power turns out to be a soft core, susceptible to fragmentation. To counteract this endemic fragility and propensity to centrifugal dispersion, those in authority have sought to coordinate their own activities which became an ever more difficult task as these activities have proliferated and ceased to be subject to control within penetrable state boundaries. In France, which prided itself on the highly integrated and cen-tralized state structure which had been superimposed upon French society, the contrast between the aspiration to unity and the actuality of disunity has elevated the need to achieve coordination into a constant challenge to statecraft. Before we can examine how far the state core executives have demonstrated the necessary skills, we need to take the measure of the difficulties they face, first in the specific French context (Part I) and then in the general context of policy interdependence (Part II).

VICISSITUDES OF THE STATE INTERVENTIONIST IMPERATIVE

The French aspiration for a state-sustained unity has, until recent years, been all the more intense because of the bitterly divided nature of French society. These divisions have been religious versus secularist, the regional identities of peripheral France versus the Parisian centre, rural versus urban conflicts, class conflicts between small and big business, and between both of them and the working classes. The growth of public employment added a further division between those enjoying the security and prestige of working for the state and those in the private sector. These conflicts, ineffectively mediated by weakly organized political parties and interest groups, periodically destabilized the working of government, which sought to assert its authority by centralizing and expanding its power. Democratic recourse to the 'people' did not evoke unity so much as a multiplicity of cross-cutting cleavages, while the pre-democratic institutions of state power lacked the legitimacy that required public support manifested in elections. Substituting a Republic for the Monarchy, it was hoped, would impart a new legitimacy to state power.

In place of the personified state unity of the monarch, the French endeavoured to establish a 'one and indivisible republic'.[1] However, precisely because of the past abuse of arbitrary power by absolute monarchy, the new administrative and representative institutions sought to create a uniform system that would ensure equal treatment to all French citizens, as well as predictability of public action. While the pursuit of administrative integration could be seen as continuing and completing the work of monarchy, the successive republics were unable successfully to manage the conflicts in French society. The would-be unity of state power was frustrated by the fissiparous consequences of ideological rifts and adversarial politics, preventing the establishment of an effective republican synthesis.

While appealing to 'the Republic' as the founding consensus institution attracted increasingly universal acceptance and enthusiasm for at least a century, it acquired this status on condition that what it meant was not investigated too closely. It became the sacred ark of the covenant, secluded in the holy of holies, frequently invoked as unifying, celebratory rhetoric but threatening to disintegrate if exposed to close investigation. At the dawn of the Third Republic, and in the wake of the civil war of the Paris Commune of 1871, the pragmatic recognition by Thiers that the republican form of government was the one that 'divides us least' subsequently gained a more or less reluctant acquiescence. However, was it to be a minimal, elitist Republic as conceived by the Opportunists or the maximum, secular, social, and egalitarian Republic of the Radicals and more especially the Socialists? The slow transformation of 'peasants into Frenchmen'[2] was partly a process of economic modernization, assisted by the socializing forces of compulsory education and conscription. However, the controversy over church versus state schools perpetuated divisions in a society, where practising Catholicism continued to be a better indicator of voting behaviour than occupation and social class. Nationalism, which had been associated with the Left, was taken over by the Right, while the Socialists and then the Communists adopted an internationalist stance.

State power in economic and social affairs was conceived as protective of various special interests in practice, despite the claim that it was being deployed in the

---

[1] J. Hayward, *The One and Indivisible French Republic* (London, Weidenfeld & Nicolson, 1973).
[2] E. Weber, *Peasants into Frenchmen: The Modernization of Rural France, 1870–1914* (London, Chatto & Windus, 1977).

service of the general interest. Once again, legitimizing principle was far removed from day-to-day intervention, which was determined by the need to placate vociferous clienteles piecemeal rather than used in the service of a farsighted strategy. This was true both of what purported to be a planned industrial policy and a comprehensive welfare state. Industrial *dirigisme* took the form of piecemeal intervention in collusion with industrialists, particularly those in competitive difficulties, although support was also provided in foreign trade and certain major projects were launched principally in high technology sectors. Despite grandiloquent appeals to social solidarity, French social security was largely left to separately organized occupational funds, particularist practice predominating over generalist rhetoric. The state's function was to subsidize the resulting deficits out of taxation. As this has proved fiscally unbearable, recourse to market solutions has led to the privatisation of former national champion public industrial enterprises and the provision of some public welfare services. Such retreats from direct state involvement are only accepted with difficulty because of the French allergy to liberalism.

The pluralist and federalist implications of an 'Anglo-Saxon' liberalism are regarded as antithetical to an indivisible Republic, democratic but looking back to classical Rome. The fear that countervailing power in the form of Montesquieu-style checks and balances will paralyse the effective expression of the 'popular will'—one of those collective fictional abstractions for which the French have a fatal predilection—has condemned liberalism to the status of a suspect doctrine, an alien import. Its supporters found it difficult to become politically more than marginal or peripheral. The price of territorial centralization was to create the phenomenon of what has been hyperbolically and condescendingly called 'Paris and the French desert',[3] while the attempt to improve a top-down functional bureaucratic uniformity slowed up decision-making without preventing the need to adapt to local circumstances and pressures. The would-be irresistible will of the state authorities has been distorted by the resistance of societal forces which can mobilize their political allies or engage in direct action to frustrate the ambitions to unify and standardize.

The chief instrument of the unity and continuity of state power was an administration built on a Napoleonic model that perfected its absolute monarchy predecessor. The hierarchical command structure presupposed a simplicity and uniformity of functional purpose requiring comprehensive mobilization of resources and subordination of all actors to achieve efficient execution of top-down decisions. Centralization of power in Paris ministries was intended to ensure maximum structural integration to complement the functional integration so that all agents of state activity marched in step. The Fifth Republic, which initially identified the general will with the will of General de Gaulle, shared the Napoleonic concern to minimize 'external' interference by either the elected legislature or an independent judiciary in the discretionary power of the political and administrative executive, using Napoleon's Council of State for a measure of internal control.

---

[3] J.-F. Gravier, *Paris et le désert français* (Paris, Le Portulan, 1947).

While this Napoleonic approach has provided 'a model attractive to tidy minds in untidy countries'[4] elsewhere (especially states needing to consolidate new regimes), in no country other than in outright totalitarian states has it been propounded in principle with such fervour, even if the repeated reassertions indicate that there have been frequent divergences from it in practice.

However, now that the French state was less concerned with preparing for, waging, and recovering from war and mainly preoccupied with expanding its regular peacetime activities, the would-be uniformity, which a regulatory outpouring of decrees and instructions has sought desperately to preserve, has proved impracticable. The administration that was meant to achieve unity has itself become fragmented between and within different ministries and corps so that 'The French administration became like a huge Balkan empire, full of squabbling cliques... Conflicts were displaced rather than resolved. The neat pyramidal power structures which underpin the model gave way to the conflictual and ill-coordinated world of competitive groups' of politicized and partisan officials rather than impassive public servants of an unquestionable public interest.[5] The consequent discredit suffered by the senior officials, who can no longer plausibly pose as personifications of a public good from which they derive the legitimacy of their power, has further weakened their capacity to coordinate state intervention and reversed its previous propensity to proliferate. Excessive and ineffective regulation has prompted a top-down recourse to deregulation in a country where Catholic precepts had associated markets with sin and intervention by authority with virtue. An increasing incapacity to coordinate administratively has led many of the very guardians of authoritative state power to renounce its prerogatives and instead seek their fortunes in the private sector.

Successive attempts to simplify and coordinate the multiplicity of local politico-administrative bodies in France have not merely preserved but increased them, superposing new on old ones and supplementing the inadequacies of some by adding others. Repeated efforts to reinforce the 'horizontal', territorial control of the prefects over the 'vertical', functional field services of the ministries have proved ineffective within the departments. The attempts to do so through the regions has made very limited impact. This is because of the refusal to choose between the historic department and the modern region, itself motivated partly by a fear of promoting centrifugal regionalism instead of the integrating regionalization of central policies and preferences. So the 1980s decentralization benefited principally the departments and the large towns. Democratization having added political to administrative conflicts, the ambition of ensuring greater coherence of government action has been frustrated. Similarly, the objective of drastically reducing the 36,779 communes by encouraging mergers has been almost a complete failure, so that unlike other European states, France has been conspicuously unable to modernize

---

[4] V. Wright, 'The Administrative Machine: Old Problems and New Dilemmas', in P. Hall *et al.* (eds.), *Developments in French Politics*, revised edn. (London, Macmillan, 1994), p. 116.
[5] Ibid., pp. 120–1.

its most basic territorial structures. Instead, it has been necessary to fall back on promoting intercommunal piecemeal collaboration, which has added to the confusion. Schemes for organizing 400 *pays*, 100 conglomerations, and some six inter-Regions are further forlorn attempts at restructuring. The 'one and indivisible Republic', always more a project than a reality, has encountered hitherto insuperable resistance to the pressures to adapt to the demographic and technological changes that have triumphed elsewhere. The linkage between centre and periphery formally through the Senate and informally achieved by the cumulation of local and central office (currently being reduced) both helped the system to function but constrained its ability to innovate. Continuity has been preserved at the cost of reducing the capacity to coordinate from the centre, although the prefects have retrieved some of the power they lost in the 1980s reforms.

The French state has actively pursued a conspicuously self-conscious cultural public service mission for centuries, to integrate at home and extend its influence abroad. Having lost its imperial civilizing mission through the process of decolonization in the mid-twentieth century, France's cultural imperative has since adopted a more inward-looking and defensive stance. Whereas the Third Republic saw its domestic role as promoting universal and compulsory public education as a means of unifying the nation over and above its overt pedagogical function, the Fifth Republic innovated by establishing a Ministry of Cultural Affairs in 1959, the first democratic state to do so. Mitterrand declared at an early Cabinet meeting, 'There can be no great policy for France without a great architecture',[6] in a way that recalled Louis Napoleon's personal involvement in Haussmann's mid-nineteenth-century remodelling of Paris. We shall return later to the way in which these projects were coordinated because, however personal the ambitions of President Mitterrand were, he needed the support of others for what a critic has called a 'tyrannical neurosis' consisting of 'a little mythomania, plenty of megalomania, even more paranoia and very little real culture'.[7] The audiovisual defence of French language and culture remained an ambition, which like so many others has had only limited success because of the weakened capacity of state power to achieve its objectives. Such anachronistic efforts to project a comprehensive control over mass communication were rendered technologically futile during the Mitterrand presidency. Pluralism became unavoidable, whatever the mental reservations of those who were compelled to tolerate what they could not prevent. Decentralization, Europeanization, and internationalization ensured that a would-be monolithic and monolingual culture had to concede defeat. A more self-assertive and self-confident journalism, working informally with a less subservient judiciary, ensured that the core executives could

---

[6] F. Chaslin, *Les Paris de François Mitterrand: Histoire des grands projets architecturaux* (Paris, Gallimard, 1985), p. 21.

[7] M. Fumaroli, *L'Etat Culturel: Essai sur une religion moderne*, Livre de Poche edn. (Editions de Fallois, 1992), p. 393. See also M. Harrison, 'The President, Cultural Projects and Broadcasting Policy', in J. Hayward (ed.), *De Gaulle to Mitterrand: Presidential Power in France* (London, Hurst, 1993), pp. 191–5. On Beaubourg, see ibid., pp. 269–72, 326. On Lang's role, see Fumaroli, pp. 189–91, 213–18, 222–3, 226, 249–53, and Harrison, p. 201.

not keep their activities as secluded from investigation as they had done previously. What emerged in the public domain was no longer merely what had been selected from above for public consumption. Leaks defied the attempts at their suppression and accountability began to take on more than formal significance. It is within this new context that the formal and informal parameters of coordination in the 1980s and 1990s shaped core executive activities.

What may we provisionally conclude from this brief survey? The traditional omnipresence of the state was perpetuated at sectoral level and at territorial level, and at all stages of the decision-making process. The French state helps to initiate policies, to set the policy agenda, to formalize, implement, monitor, and evaluate policies. It also harbours a scale and quality of technical (and generalist) expertise rivalled in few countries of the world. And these experts have never lacked a taste for exploiting the massive potential leverage of the state, often garbing themselves in the cloak of 'the public interest' when doing so. Coordination costs are naturally higher in any large organization—because of the multiplication of potentially conflicting interests, because information flows are more problematic, because opposition is often easy to carry off and to escape the control from the top. Nevertheless, the traditional French picture, with its enhanced coordination costs, harboured a degree of flexibility in its coordinating potential. It could resort to a whole battery of different coordinating styles, ranging from imposition (by itself or an insulated policy unit chosen for the task), to negotiated delegation, to outright surrender to a power group. French state coordination, when faced by strong societal resistance (by farmers, road hauliers, even fishermen) readily shifts from the authoritarian to the pusillanimous, behaving like the legendary army of Offenbach, 'trained to surrender'.

The Divisive Politics of Ministerial Government

The arrival in office of a government is a particularly important context in which to identify the consequences for core executive coordination of electoral programmes, coalition constraints, and ministerial ambitions. The organizational implications of policy innovations are seldom anticipated and are improvised hectically in the days that follow the formation of a new government. The allocation of ministerial portfolios is accompanied by the *décrets d'attribution* fixing the precise distribution of departmental responsibilities, the formal attempt to avoid or at least minimize interdepartmental turf guerrilla warfare. Clearly, if the number of ministers can be kept down, there are fewer boundaries between ministries, although this may relocate the problems of coordination by internalizing the conflicts between divisions of the same ministry. Frequent structural reorganizations and redistributions of functions can disrupt coordination arrangements, particularly when they are motivated more by the need to ensure political equilibrium rather than the reduction of coordination difficulties.

The composition of the French ministerial core executive—the political, regional, and sex balance—is determined by the President and Prime Minister (although during periods of cohabitation the President's role becomes highly circumscribed).

The silence of the Constitution allows them a large measure of discretion of which they avail themselves. Ministries are created, amalgamated, and dismembered, functions are transferred without much change in the lower ministerial echelons, suggesting a strong undertow towards departmental government. Recourse to coordinating ministers without portfolio has not been favoured in France, the core executives—and the prime ministerial, and presidential staffs in particular—preferring to avoid creating such a level of coordination which may exacerbate conflicts by the intervention of too many rival coordinators and would detract from their role of oversight.

The personal standing, personality, and role interpretation of the leading figures injects an idiosyncratic element into the policy coordination processes. That this may change over the same person's tenure of office is clear from the successive Mitterrand presidencies. Even during the 1981–86 period of unchallenged Socialist dominance, the changing context and the replacement as Prime Minister of Mauroy by Fabius modified the style and extent of presidential intervention. After the drastic shift in power of 1986–88 to Prime Minister Chirac, the contrast between the Rocard, Cresson, and Bérégovoy Governments, prior to the cohabitation with Balladur from 1993–95, shows that even if we merely focus upon relations with the Prime Minister there were major shifts of behaviour with the same President.

Coordination is a more subtle matter than the habitual references to strong or weak leadership imply. A good coordinator needs the qualities of a good chairman. An overly assertive, impositional style risks losing the support that a more conciliatory, consensual style would provide when the political context becomes turbulent. (The contrast between Juppé as Prime Minister before 1997 and Jospin subsequently exemplifies this.) However, it is necessary to impart a clear sense of direction if the government is not to seem like a dead dog drifting downstream, pushed hither and thither by the waves made by others. Mitterrand's style by the last years of his presidency became much less assertive, especially when he lost control over the National Assembly and the government in 1993, as well as being enfeebled by illness and his 'lame duck' status, although his loss of grip—particularly over his party—preceded these developments. President Chirac's de facto delegation of much overall policy coordination to authoritarian and hyper-interventionist Prime Minister Juppé from 1995 to 1997 proved disastrous.

As we shall see, it is not only in their choice of ministers—especially the Prime Minister—but in the selection of their personal entourage that French Presidents show their personal capacity and judgement because great reliance will be placed on these ministers in matters of coordination. If one includes those directors of the central administration with a claim to membership of the core executive and whose appointments are at the mercy of a change of government, the task of coordination takes on a more impersonal character, although they are frequently former members of the personal staff of political executives. What appears to the public as a highly personalized office in practice becomes somewhat depersonalized as the plural character of the institutions and procedures of coordination asserts itself. The tensions produced by increasing issue interdependence and dispersal of authority results in a dysfunctional urge to excessive coordination which exacerbates the disparity between aspirations and achievements by simultaneously inflating ambitions and inhibiting capacities to exert overall state control.

French Aspirations and Achievements

For many years the French have tended to close their eyes to the contradiction between their principles and many of their practices, their aspirations and achievements. As these contradictions became more flagrant, the endeavour to reiterate abstract claims in the face of actual experience was increasingly impractical and difficult to sustain. Quite apart from whether the French could logically claim that their country was both exemplary and exceptional, and if the reduction in its exceptionalism could enable it at least in part to preserve its pretension to exemplarity, which will be clearer by the end of our investigation, how have they responded to the uncomfortable facts that could no longer be ignored? To continue asserting general principles one is compelled to violate piecemeal by pragmatic improvisations is not intellectually respectable and less politically feasible once the divergences between what is supposed to happen and does happen are subjected to embarrassing public exposure. If conduct is increasingly dictated by insuperable pressures, then it is the precepts that have to be adapted or abandoned. The presumption that the French state in fact had the unity and strength which the model of an indivisible Republic painted, having been shown to be unsustainable, its capacity to pursue consistent policies with continuity becomes problematic.

The notion that there is 'one best way' of attaining public purposes, that this can be ascertained by those exercising state authority and that it can be imposed by hierarchical government control, is deeply embedded in French political and administrative culture. It has been widely shared by both the elected executives and the citizens, by the selected administrators and the administered, by the government and the governed. The great mistake has been to assume that what is a prescriptive norm—whose desirability can in any case be questioned—could still be equated with practice at a time when, whatever services it rendered in the past, it is not merely inaccurate but unserviceable. The refusal to recognize the new context of state action has led to a somewhat disorderly retreat, with past proclivities only being abandoned reluctantly, out of defeatism and a humiliating sense of repudiating admirable traditions.

The collision between the aspirations to achieving comprehensive consistency and cohesion in the attainment of state objectives and the conflicts between competing centres of both state and extra-state power is especially evident in the endeavour to coordinate public action. Anticipating so as to prevent such conflicts, as well as repressing them when they emerge, has increasingly had to give way to managing and manipulating actors over whom the formal hierarchical structures often cannot exert effective control. Rather than the court politics of an absolute Republican monarch and despite survivals of past practice, it is the committee politics of a plurality of core executives who seek convergence when consensus is unattainable that characterizes French policy-making. A context in which complexity and inter-dependence usually prevail renders ineffective the simplicity of a unilateral sovereign asserting a singular will, apart from specific exceptional circumstances. As the implica-tions of particular policies for each other need to be dealt with in ways that involve several centres of authority and their associated networks, it is not sufficient to exchange information or engage in consultation, important as these are. (The refusal to share information is one of the besetting sins of French senior officials, so that a precondition of effective coordination is frequently absent.) The process of securing agreement on mutually compatible overall policy objectives and ways to implement them is complicated by an increasing plurality of actors involved. Achieving a positive sum interaction between the policy-makers by imparting an added value to their several inputs represents a formidable challenge when those to be coordinated tend to see the process as zero sum, reducing their freedom of action and therefore to be resisted.

Within the ministries making up government, the tendency to departmentalism and even sub-departmentalism is as old as government itself. However, resistance to coordination becomes more difficult to overcome as boundary conflicts of respons-ibility increase. Neither ministers, conscious that they make and lose their reputa-tions mainly on the strength of their performance as departmental ministers, nor senior officials in charge of the divisions within ministries, regard achieving a coordinated decision as their prime concern. Extending their functions and increas-ing their budgets are major preoccupations of spending ministers and their officials. The tendency for individual seclusion to predominate over collective cooperation is reflected in the preservation of the autonomy of each part of the government machine leading to fragmentation. To counteract the dysfunctional consequences that result for the cohesion of government requires assertive countervailing action by the core executives who carry the ultimate responsibility for the collective success or failure of public policy.

However, it is crucial to appreciate that because coordination is a highly complex, multi-level, and sequential series of processes, confronted by a compartmentalized and introvert set of bureaucracies, as well as personal and partisan rivalries and ambitions, it cannot in practice be the prerogative of any single authority. This presents especially great problems in France where the normative presumption is that authority should be pyramidal, with a clear, hierarchical chain of command. So, we are once again confronted by the disjunction between what ought to be and what is. The implication is that partial coordination may and often will occur at levels well below the core executive, although the issues may be reopened and appealed to a higher level, either formally or informally. As we shall see when we consider specific cases, a filtering process seeks to prevent overload on the core executives. This will vary as between policies, notably whether they are or are not politicized, matters of routine or precipitated onto the policy agenda by a crisis. We must first take a closer look at both coordination and the coordinators to see why the French self-image of statecraft loses much of its heroic status when confronted with how coordination is variously conducted in practice.

COMPLEXITY, CONTINGENCY, AND COORDINATION: CORE EXECUTIVES CONFRONT INTERDEPENDENCE

'Coordination' and 'core executive' are quintessentially question-begging concepts. Empirically, they are characterized by complexity and contingency, coming in all shapes and sizes, with very variable durabilities. Coordination is proposed as the solution to a wide range of problems but on closer examination is revealed as itself a frequently intractable and sometimes an insuperable problem. While the term 'core executive' was certainly an advance on the simplistic conceptions of Cabinet, prime ministerial and presidential government, even when further elaborated to cover ministerial government, bureaucratic coordination, and segmental decision-making, it implies a too monocratic, top-down statecentric concept. It asserts that somewhere at the summit there are final, overall arbiters capable of integrating the interdependent policies of central government. If the plural is substituted for the singular, the term 'core executive' reflects more accurately the internal dynamics of a plurality of actors and processes seeking to resolve conflicts and promote consistency between the interdependent objectives pursued, and the interlinked executive networks of the pursuers. It brings out more explicitly the hazardous, overweening, and problematic nature of the enterprise, inherently prone to contradiction because the purported protagonists of conflict resolution are themselves often antagonists who pull the steering wheel in divergent directions as they are buffeted by sideways and bottom-up turbulence.

Some thirty years ago, the predicament was forcefully presented by American political scientists Harold Seidman and Aaron Wildavsky. With the insight that came from being an experienced administrative infighter in a federal system, Seidman asserted: 'The quest for coordination is in many respects the twentieth century equivalent of the medieval search for the philosopher's stone. If only we can find the right formula for coordination, we can reconcile the irreconcilable, harmonize competing and wholly divergent interests, overcome irrationalities in our government structures and make hard policy choices to which no one will dissent.'[8] An integral component of the confusion surrounding the term is due to the fact that 'Coordination describes both a process—the act of coordination—and a goal: the bringing together of diverse elements into a harmonious relationship in support of common objectives'.[9] Since the goals of a pluralistic polity are frequently contradictory, the superimposition of 'Layers of coordination can conceal but not cure the defects and contradictions' of core executive objectives, while further 'Problems are created when multiple lead agencies share responsibility for coordinating the implementation of similar and

---

[8] H. Seidman, *Politics, Position, and Power: The Dynamics of Federal Organization* [1970], third edn. (Oxford, OUP, 1980), p. 200.   [9] Ibid., p. 205.

overlapping policies'.[10] Seidman warned that 'Coordination is rarely neutral . . . inevitably it advances some interests at the expense of others', thus reorganizing the coordination mechanisms—a favourite pastime of governments—is often futile because it does not resolve the basic incompatibility of objectives.[11]

Wildavsky sought to impart some analytical clarity to a term that could naively be deemed to resolve many policy problems of unresolved conflict because four possibly contradictory separate meanings had not been distinguished. These can be grouped into two pairs, according to whether or not there is an agreed purpose. If there are common objectives, then coordination seeks efficiency and reliability through the elimination of duplication and overlapping. What seems obvious is shown counter-intuitively not to be true. 'We ensure against failure by having adequate reserves and by creating several mechanisms to perform a single task in case one should fail. Coordination of complex activities requires redundancy. Telling us to avoid duplication gives us no useful instruction at all; it is just a recipe for failure. What we need to know is how much and what kind of redundancy to build-in to our programs. The larger the number of participants in an enterprise, the more difficult the problem of coordination, the greater the need for redundancy.'[12] As we shall see, President Mitterrand fully appreciated this counter-intuitive insight and practised it adroitly by duplicating his sources of information and advice.

If it is not assumed that the policy actors share an agreed purpose, 'To coordinate one must be able to get others to do things they do not want to do.'[13] Such coordination may be secured either by consent or coercion. Consent is achieved by consultation and bargaining, which usually involves compromising the original policy purpose, while coercion requires the imposition of preferences usually by the assertion of hierarchical power. As the matters dealt with by core executives are likely to be issues where purposes are either not agreed or there is divergence in how to attain them, the choice is usually made by some combination of consent and coercion. The former clearly has prudential advantages. For example, coordination by consent means that the issue 'should be cleared with other official participants who have some stake in the matter. This is a way of sharing the blame in case things go wrong [each initial on the documents being another hostage against retribution]'.[14] Such diffusion of responsibility—formal and informal—will be commonplace in the French interministerial and interdepartmental processes of coordination that we shall encounter, although the conflicting claims of personal responsibility for success render even more inextricable the task of allocating praise where it is due than of blame. Success has many parents; failure is an orphan.

---

[10] Ibid., pp. 227, 219.   [11] Ibid., p. 204, cf. p. 203.

[12] A. Wildavsky, 'If Planning is Everything, Maybe it's Nothing', *Policy Science*, 4 (1973), p. 143; cf. p. 142. He refers also to M. Landau, 'Redundancy, Rationality and the Problem of Duplication and Overlap', *Public Administration Review*, 29 (July 1969), pp. 346–58.   [13] Wildavsky, p. 143.

[14] Ibid.

Intragovernmental Coordination

As the provocative title of the Wildavsky article quoted, 'If Planning is Everything, Maybe it's Nothing', suggests, a shift was beginning away from the 1960s emphasis upon centralized rationalist planning—particularly important in France—weakening in the 1970s, to incrementalist organizational and interpersonal interaction of core executives of the 1980s and 1990s. Five salient features of pre-1980s planned coordination can be identified, residues of which still persist. First, there was a misleading 'conceptualisation of policy as a coherent, relatively self-contained, complete and authoritative guide to future action'.[15] Second, it was assumed that consensus on problems, goals, methods, and priorities existed or were attainable, whereas organizational and personal interdependence normally lead not to harmonious collaboration but to either conflictual bargaining or coercion[16]—as Wildavsky had pointed out. Third, the existence of an effective centralized authority was assumed capable of implementing the consensus. Fourth, the assumption was made that routine operating procedures would assist rather than frustrate coordination, whereas 'formal machinery may have no relevance where the preconditions for bargaining are absent, but it may play a real role in giving permanence to networks and lowering transaction costs'.[17] Fifth, the adoption of a system-wide rather than a sectoral perspective led to a neglect of the complex variety of contexts in which policy-makers operated, resulting in an overconfidence in the predictability and generalizability of policy innovations whose interdependence posed intractable coordination problems. As Glyn Davis has put it, 'Specialised policy processes may make the State no more than a loose confederation of separate policy domains or subsystems.'[18] Since the 1980s, the reversal of all these assumptions provides the context for a more modest approach to coordination.

Davis (writing from Australian experience as Director General of the Queensland Cabinet Office) described coordination as the means by which core executives exert control over the government's activities. While 'coordination is secondary to the key task of defining policies and ensuring their dissemination . . . Through coordination information is obtained, agendas set, and policies made consistent.'[19] The core executive must decide how far diversity can be accommodated and whether the benefits of consistency are great enough to warrant the costs of imposing coordination.[20] To do so it has at its disposal two instruments: government structures and procedural routines, through whose institutional interplay it seeks to ensure cohesion between

---

[15] L. Challis et al., *Joint Approaches to Social Policy, Rationality and Practice* (Cambridge, CUP, 1988), p. 36; cf. p. 37.   [16] Ibid., p. 39; cf. p. 24.
[17] Ibid., p. 41; cf. p. 40.
[18] G. Davis, *A Government of Routines: Executive Coordination in an Australian State* (Melbourne, Macmillan Australia, 1995), p. 13. See also G. Davis, 'Executive Coordination Mechanisms', in P. Weller et al. (eds.), *The Hollow Crown* (Basingstoke, Macmillan, 1997), pp. 128–31. For a perceptive theoretical review of the literature of complexity, contingency, and coordination, see Y. Papadopoulos, *Démocratie Directe* (Paris, Economica, 1998), part 4, ch. 3 on public policy negotiation, especially pp. 237–75; cf. pp. 153–5, 232.   [19] Davis, *Government of Routines*, p. 2.
[20] Ibid., pp. 16, 18.

the organizational structures. We shall have frequent occasion to refer to these structures in France as they were reorganized to suit core executive purposes (both policy priorities and political expediency). However, as the presence or absence of routine was a criterion together with politicization/non-politicization on the basis of which we selected our case studies, it is necessary to give it preliminary consideration.

Davis sets out an unattainable ideal of generalized routine coordination preceding core executive decisions. 'The unity of political purpose, policy objectives and administrative action that characterises a successful government is the dividend of well crafted coordination systems: by insisting on such systems, power is made routine.'[21] (Note the word 'insisting', implying that one cannot presume upon agreed purpose.) Davis then links it to making core executive objectives operational. 'Shared procedures set down rules about who can make choices and in what sequence. They tie each official to an organisational and governmental wide agenda. Routines become systems of control, marshalling decisions toward those offices in which authority resides. They establish channels for policy making and make power relationships explicit.'[22] Davis suggests of routines that 'unless some extraordinary event occurs, they are self-sustaining.'[23] However, such 'events' that assume the proportions of a crisis are by no means as infrequent as he implies, so that they are the other side of the matrix used in the selection of cases to study core executive coordination in action. We cannot so readily depersonalize government or accept that 'Coherence emerges not from heroic personal feats of integration but from the continuous application of standard operating procedures . . .'[24] This would reduce the political process to a uniformly humdrum level of stifling, interlocking, rule-bound routines, a bureaucratic ideal that will seem a nightmare to others. While core executives cannot impart an irresistible impetus, they are not necessarily faced by immovable institutions, immune to the skills of statecraft. We shall see that this is especially true in France, where in virtue of the fact that practice habitually does not conform with the principles enunciated, rules are a poor guide to the conduct of core executives.

Intergovernmental Coordination

The boundary between intragovernmental and intergovernmental coordination is an increasingly permeable one because of the interdependence between them as well as outright dependence of internal upon international actors and policies, rendering the prized independence of the past largely illusory. While national governments have sought to reduce domestic public policy interdependence by privatization, contracting out, and decentralization—and thereby reducing the need for coordination—'At

---

[21] Ibid., p. 21., cf. I. Sharkansky, *The Routines of Politics* (New York, Van Nostrand Reinhold, 1970), p. 3.
[22] Davis, *Government of Routines*, p. 23.   [23] Ibid., p. 25.
[24] Ibid., p. 3; cf. pp. 140–1. See the penetrating analysis of crisis and complexity by M. Dobry, *Sociologie des crises politiques* (Paris, Presses de la Fondation nationale des sciences politiques, 1986).

the international level, increasing interdependence is creating a need to improve and upgrade policy coordination capacities', formally through numerous specialized international organizations (such as the International Monetary Fund (IMF), World Bank, World Trade Organization (WTO), International Labour Organization (ILO), and United Nations Educational, Scientific, and Cultural Organization (UNESCO)) and informally through concerted bilateral and multilateral activities.[25]

If domestic policy core executive actors are jealous of their autonomy, how much more difficult is international coordination likely to be between nominally or would-be sovereign states. However, before that stage is reached, 'a very large part of the work that goes into international negotiations involves negotiators negotiating with their own side to reconcile internal differences, clarify objectives and priorities, and agree strategies and tactics'.[26] The ambitious objective of achieving coherence and consistency in comprehensive and compatible policy outcomes requires not only simple policy coordination between core executives but between the interacting policies of the lead organizations. In the international and domestic arenas, pervasive market forces are increasingly intruding on de facto external coordination, with whose consequences national core executives are having to cope when they have not been able to anticipate them. However, this complicates rather than reduces the need for coordination among the national core executives. Such externally induced coordination is especially true for European Union (EU) countries, the process of integration necessitating continuous and increasing coordination of the interacting policy negotiations as positions are adapted to changing contexts. We shall see that this process led France to establish permanent oversight coordination between the many ministries involved in EU negotiations.

The Policy Coordination Scale

The diverse nature of coordination when investigated in a comparative perspective requires establishing 'empirical regularities among particular cases'. As Metcalfe goes on to argue: 'Part of the complexity of public management is that spheres of high and low interdependence co-exist; governmental activities involve both tight and loose coupling among organizations. One of the tests of a useful method of measuring and comparing coordination processes in government is whether it is flexible enough to cope with the diversity of coordination tasks that arise . . . As this suggests, co-ordination is not an all or nothing matter, it involves the choice of combinations of processes and methods appropriate to the problems to be solved. The same set of organizations may be able to act quite independently on some occasions while in other circumstances their activities are closely interdependent and require intensive co-ordination efforts.'[27]

---

[25] L. Metcalfe, 'International Policy Coordination and Public Management Reform', *International Review of Administrative Sciences*, 60 (1994), p. 271.　　　　　　　　[26] Ibid., p. 277.
[27] Ibid., p. 279.

Metcalfe's policy coordination scale is helpful in distinguishing the 'qualitatively different components of co-ordination capacity' of a 'national government conceived as a network of interdependent ministries'.[28] 'The components of co-ordination capacity are cumulative in the sense that the higher level of co-ordination functions depend on the existence and reliability of the lower ones.'[29] While our sectoral and case studies will demonstrate that the usual generalizations are ephemeral and fragile at best and seriously misleading or erroneous at worst, for purposes of preliminary illustration let us provide institutional examples of who usually coordinates in France at each of the nine levels distinguished by Metcalfe.

1. *Independent decision-making within ministries.* Already, this level subjects coordinating capacity to stern tests because not only does the national government consist of interdependent ministries; ministries themselves are structured into all too appropriately named divisions and sub-divisions, often having a self-centred commitment to their intraministerial autonomy. The propensity to engage in 'turf wars' poses severe problems to the division *directeurs* and the *directeur* of the minister's *cabinet*, the latter playing in part the role of the Permanent Secretary at the head of a British ministry. Ultimately, while it may be the minister who is the coordinator, he has many other preoccupations and is likely to leave what *seem to be* routine and non-politicized matters to senior line and staff officials.

2. *Formal and informal communication of information to other ministries.* While there are deliberate as well as inadvertent denials of information to other parts of the same ministry, as a way of protecting oneself from intrusion by others, such uncommunicative practices are much more evident when we move to interorganizational communication or the lack of it. This behaviour takes place both horizontally and vertically because the capacity to exert hierarchical control is much weaker and the propensity to engage in power struggles for the position of lead executive actor is much greater. Although interdepartmental committees provide a formal channel of regular communication, they are often less reliable than informal interpersonal networks of those who are inclined to trust each other through sharing a common *grand corps* background or political sympathies. Internet technology does facilitate the communication especially of more routine information but recourse to the confidential official telephone system remains indispensable to core executive communication of sensitive information.

3. *Bilateral consultation with other ministries.* Such two-way communication between executives of the same status (both line or staff officials as well as ministers) is a crucial means of sounding out those who are in a position to provide useful advice or might seek to block proposals on which they have not been consulted or which were not modified to accommodate their reservations

---

[28] Ibid., pp. 281, 280.
[29] Ibid., p. 281. Metcalfe sets out his scale as Figure 1 on p. 281 and explains it on pp. 282–4. We have slightly modified his designations of the nine points in the scale.

or objections. Written minutes of such consultations provide a record that can be shared with those that are deemed suitable to know what has transpired.

4. *Avoiding public divergence between ministries* is important both to avoid providing opportunities to domestic political opponents to exploit dissensions and to protect the national negotiating position in dealings with foreign governments. So prior discussions to clarify ministerial positions in advance of public commitments is a vital 'closed politics' prelude to publicizing government policy through the media. Investigative journalism and the propensity of core executives to leak information when it suits them, has rendered such endeavours to speak with one voice much less effective in France in recent years.

5. *The interministerial search for agreement* involves negotiation and bargaining in joint working parties, and interdepartmental and interministerial committees to resolve policy differences. Interdependence must be translated into positive sum coordination if the interested parties are not to be tempted to revert to zero sum intransigence. The lead ministry will play a crucial role at this stage, requiring on its part a consensus-promoting capacity, notably through the role of the chairman, in steering the participants towards mutually acceptable compromises. *Ad hoc* recourse to such formal mechanisms fluctuates, notably at the behest of the French President and Prime Minister. However, there are a small number of permanent standing committees that are institutionalized, although their significance has varied over time. The Secretariat General of Government and the Secretary General of the Presidency play pivotal roles in ensuring respectively the formal and informal respect of coordination procedures.

6. *Arbitration of interministerial policy differences.* When it is clear that either the policy purposes or the ways of attaining them cannot be agreed, coercion replaces bargaining. We are now at Wildavsky's stage of coordination, of getting others to do things they would prefer not to do. Vertical assertion of imperative authority replaces horizontal negotiation of voluntary consent. What a minister or his *directeur de cabinet* might have imposed within a ministry is now subject to imposition by the Prime Minister or President and at a lower level, as appropriate, by their staffs. This does not mean that the 'arbitration' does not achieve some measure of agreement but imposition remains the final option, which may be preceded by the threat and followed (much less frequently) by the reality of ministerial resignation. During periods of cohabitation between a President and Prime Minister of Left and Right, the Prime Minister's coordinating predominance is strengthened by the fact that ministers are very unlikely to appeal to the President to override his arbitrations.

7. *Setting limits for ministerial discretion* is very much the prerogative of the Finance Minister and Prime Minister, once the structural allocation of responsibilities has been made between ministerial portfolios, in which the President will play a major role. Budget constraints will restrict what ministries can do, while the government programme—by excluding what it does not

include—will provide negative coordination of government activities. The staffs of the President, Prime Minister, and Finance Minister will police respect for the imposed limits, which may lead to discord.

8. *Establishing core executive priorities* takes the form of an election manifesto, coalition agreement, or government programme, setting the guidelines of ministerial activities. The President and Prime Minister, together with a select group of party and expert advisers, including certain ministers, set the commitments to be carried out, which are kept up to date by weekly meeting to make tactical adaptations of the overall strategy.

9. *Determining and adjusting overall government strategy* is very much a presidential prerogative as long as his supporters have a majority in the National Assembly. If the French President has to 'cohabit' with a political opponent as Prime Minister because there is a hostile parliamentary majority, his coordinating role is largely confined to defence, EU, and foreign policy and even there it is shared with the Prime Minister. However, at other times the legitimacy conferred by his direct universal suffrage election gives the President the authority to fix the initial framework within which the government's specific programme is fitted and to make the tactical adjustments—including government reshuffles—during the course of his tenure of office. His Elysée staff and trusted external advisers can be drawn upon in policy-making but his staff is pivotal to coordinating policy.

The Structured Plurality of Core Executives Confront the Coordination Predicament

The post-planning awareness of increasing policy overload on governments has meant a recognition that coordination was a problem rather than a solution. In a context in which decisions have to be made quickly, with inadequate information and unanticipated consequences, core executive capacity to keep control over those whose actions are to be coordinated is a risky mixture of hit and miss. Dealing effectively with intrinsically awkward problems is compounded by being ill equipped to handle them. Government policies, from the start, are seldom properly thought through. Their full implications only become clear after the commitment to proceed has irreversibly been made. This is partly due to the lack of prior consultation or defective expert advice, so that there is a failure to anticipate how those affected by the decisions will react. While precipitate action during a crisis may be unavoidable, such action is often unnecessary, especially when inexperienced ministers take office, as was the case of the 1981 Mauroy Government.

When overload is combined with the increasing interdependence of government activities, unintended consequences spilling over from complex interactions frustrate the unilateral, top-down coordination of actors, who thereby succeed in achieving mutually recognized greater autonomy. In the late 1970s it became fashionable to write about 'ungovernability' and in the 1990s, less apocalyptically, of 'governance'. As the composition of the core executive changes over time, the preferences of its members modify policy objectives. Where the turnover is rapid, this instability further complicates internal and external core executive coordination by reopening issues previously settled and the associated reciprocal commitments made. By disrupting path dependence, core executive coordinators lose the inertial benefits of routinized continuity. They have to cope with the costs of abandoning previously agreed arrangements, resulting in major reform proposals often being sacrificed or scaled down into modest incremental adjustments dictated by short-term, expediential improvisation.[30] Reaction to internal and external pressures, rather than agenda-setting initiatives by the core executives, become the salient feature of the coordination process in practice, whatever the pretentious posturings to impress the public.

Before proceeding to examine in detail how French core executives have sought to deal with the coordination predicament both in general and in the four policy sectors of the EU, budget, privatisation, and immigration, it may be helpful to stipulate in general terms and as succinctly as possible the way in which the key terms, starting with 'coordination', have been used here and why it is a major preoccupation. Coordination is the management of anticipated/actual conflict in a context of systemic relations of interdependence, through the mobilization of available resources of hierarchical control and/or the manipulation of networks to achieve greater consistency and cohesion in the attainment of cross-cutting policy objectives, subject to the prevailing normative, structural, and procedural constraints.

Coordination may be both an outcome of the policy process and a procedural objective that may be pursued to achieve greater consistency and cohesion between the separate purposes of competing centres of authority. Our emphasis will be on procedures rather than outcomes. As a process, it seeks to manage the conflicts that may be anticipated or do actually emerge in a context of interdependence between the policy actors which necessitate the search for convergence even if consensus is unattainable.[31] This process takes place within a system of formal and informal relationships that operate subject to prevailing normative, structural, and procedural constraints. Within these limits, the process of coordination is conducted through the mobilization of available resources of a vertical and horizontal nature: hierarchical control and the manipulation of networks.

From the 1980s there has been a paradoxical combination of both increased pressures from a variety of sources for greater coordination and a 'downsizing' of the resources of government to perform its traditionally central role in the policy coordination process. This readjustment and reduction in central capability may tend to shift the emphasis from a centralized resort to hierarchical control towards

---

[30] See P. Pierson, 'The Path to European Integration: A Historical Institutionalist Analysis', in W. Sandholtz and A. Stone Sweet (eds.), *European Integration and Supranational Governance* (Oxford, OUP, 1998), pp. 39–41, 46–7.

[31] K. Hanf, in K. Hanf and F. W. Scharpf (eds.), *Interorganizational Policy Making: Limits to Coordination and Central Control* (London, Sage, 1978), pp. 1–2.

greater reliance on decentralized networks but it is not likely to reduce the demand for greater coordination.

Who is responsible for taking the initiative in seeking to meet the ambitious challenge of policy coordination? As already mentioned, we adopted with reservations the Rhodes formulation of the term 'core executive', although we stated at the outset that we prefer to use core executives to emphasize the plurality of inner core authorities. Although they have other important duties, core executives work within a system of governance in which it is unusual for any single actor to enjoy an unlimited capacity to impose a policy decision upon others. There is seldom one centre of authority but rather several competing centres, whose potential or actual conflicts it is the task of coordination to preclude or overcome, with a view to using this convergence for the achievement of collective policy objectives. The summit of core executive coordination is occupied by the holders of a small number of offices, with the Prime Minister/President occupying a central position, often acting in conjunction with the Finance Minister and other leading Cabinet ministers (notably the Foreign and Interior Ministers) and relying upon a small staff that undertakes much of the non-routine work of policy coordination. Despite ritual references to collective Cabinet responsibility, the work of coordination occurs elsewhere in France. Inner cabinets, where they exist, are usually informal and related to the need for the coordination of the policy views of parties to a coalition government.

It is not easy to reduce styles of leadership to categories that would enable us to compare how particular Prime Ministers have gone about the task of coordination in ways that are not specific to the individual concerned. The personal standing, personality, and role interpretation of the leading figures play an important part in the policy coordination process, which injects an idiosyncratic element into the analysis. This may change over the same person's tenure of high office, especially when this is an extended one, with conjunctural ups and downs that reflect the changing context over which the leader frequently has little control. It is a more subtle matter than the usual reference to strong or weak leadership; a good coordinator needs the qualities that make for a good chairman. An overly assertive, impositional style may risk losing the support that a more conciliatory, consensual style would provide when the political context becomes turbulent. However, it is necessary to impart a sense of direction if the government is not to be pushed hither and thither by the waves made by others. So, despite the constraints upon the would-be coordinator's discretion, usually exerted by the need to operate according to the prevailing norms and procedures, there is an opportunity for each leader to display personal capacities and judgement.

The separation of overall policy coordination between formal and informal arenas may seem rather artificial because, although they are distinguishable, they overlap in practice. The Cabinet, which is the principal formal arena of coordination, has become a body for ratifying policies coordinated elsewhere. In France, a highly developed system of interministerial and interdepartmental coordinating committees is of three kinds: ministers meeting without officials; ministers meeting with officials and—much the most numerous—officials meeting without ministers. The latter are chaired by a member of the Prime Minister's staff with the authority to attempt coordination without involving ministers directly. Regular meetings of the *directeurs de cabinet* in France provide another informal channel for overall coordination. There are likely to be too many rival coordinators, resulting in tension not only between the staff of the President and Prime Minister but from competition for the role of 'lead' minister in particular policy sectors, which increases rather than reduces policy conflicts.[32]

By contrast with interest groups, which may sometimes be expected to reinforce fragmentation between policy communities, political parties do seek to develop an overall view of public policy in electoral programmes and so should contribute towards policy coordination. However, in multi-party contexts resulting in coalition government, parties create problems of partisan coordination. Where the Prime Minister is the leader of one of the coalition parties, this duality of roles can cause additional problems. Regular meetings of party leaders, with or without the presence of ministers, are a feature of the attempt to coordinate party and government policy positions. France has a distinctive reliance upon informal coordination through the *corps* old boy networks. However, even here an overlap exists with party affiliation, so there is not a neat separation between partisan and corps coordination. In routine and non-politicized policy issues, one would naturally expect bureaucratic coordination to be predominant, as against politically controversial and non-routine issues when partisan linkages will come to the fore. For example, the budgetary process provides a coordination mechanism that has both routine and non-routine features which usually places the Finance Minister in a pivotal position. However, in financial crises, that position can be threatened as emergency action may have to be improvised, as we shall have occasion to discuss later. The Prime Minister can usually be expected to arbitrate on appeals in favour of the Finance Minister but there are inevitably tensions between them and not just when they belong to different political parties.

The capacity to coordinate reflects the resources and constraints of each of the policy actors. These are often two sides of the same coin. The most obvious structural resource/constraint is the Constitution, which both empowers and restricts the power of major actors. The constraints on the executive as interpreted by judicial review of constitutionality has been a significant phenomenon especially since the 1980s. The legal rules on the drafting of legislation provide another formal constraint on executive discretion. Recourse to consultative and advisory bodies is a resource for coordination but may accentuate fragmentation if linked only to one ministry, as they usually are, rather than having an interdepartmental character. A major constraint on the capacity of the core executive to coordinate its legislative programme has generally been the time it takes to win the agreement of those whose parliamentary support will be necessary to secure its passage without amendments

---

[32] On 'Staffing the Summit', see the first chapter by B. G. Peters, R. A. W. Rhodes, and V. Wright in their *Administering the Summit: Administration of the Core Executive in Developed Countries*, (Basingstoke, Macmillan, 2000).

that would destroy the coherence of the policy package on which the legislation is based.

Shifting the focus from the political to the sectoral aspects of policy coordination, these allow policy networks and (where they exist) policy communities to come to the fore. Here, the style of coordination is likely to be less hierarchical and the range of variation between sector-specific policy areas will be especially great. For example, policy-making in the EU is a resource in matters of overall coordination by using its package deals as a *fait accompli* constraint upon those sectoral actors within the national policy process who resist the proposed changes. However, the need to achieve EU agreement does impose constraints upon the core executive as well by restricting the policy options available. The unavoidable complexities in the coordination process will be explored in case studies through the four selected sectors: budgeting, European Union, immigration, and privatisation. Our findings will enable us to diversify our understanding of French policy-making culture, through cross-sectoral and cross-case-study comparisons.

Before we do so, we must place these studies of partial coordination within the context of the ambitious aspirations to overall coordination as a concomitant of the French state imperative. Without going as far as Russell Hardin, who reduces constitutions essentially to coordination devices,[33] the role of the written and unwritten constitution in setting the normative framework for political and administrative coordination will need to be discussed. In doing so, we should bear in mind a cautionary assessment: the French state 'is a world composed of entrenched traditions, half-remembered rules and conveniently forgotten stipulations of complicity and conflict, ideological clashes and masonic collusions, political chicanery and petty administrative corruption, personal rivalries and political alliances, unabashed self-interest and embarrassing idealism, compromising commitments and watchful opportunism, unforgivable cowardice and praiseworthy courage, naked ambition and calculated disinterest. It is a highly *personalized* complex and confused world, rendered difficult to analyse and defiant of comparison by the unceasing play of irritating imponderables.'[34] Swallowing hard, let us consider how a state that prided itself on its centralized power has responded to increasingly unwelcome demands on its adaptive capacities through the rival centres whose activities need to be reconciled. We shall need to ascertain, in particular cases, from which centre France seeks to govern.

---

[33] R. Hardin, *Liberalism, Constitutionalism, and Democracy* (Oxford, OUP, 2000).
[34] V. Wright, 'Politics and Administration in the Fifth French Republic', *Political Studies*, 22/1 (March 1974), p. 65.

2

The Normative, Political, and Administrative Frameworks

In the previous chapter, we have emphasized the problems that the French conception of the superordinate role of the state has posed to the protagonists of integrated government activity. The difficulties encountered in sustaining such an elevated image in contemporary conditions have led to the development of mechanisms to overcome the ensuing dissensions. This chapter will describe what these coordinating mechanisms are in general terms, indicating the disparity between the orderly presuppositions and the messy realities. It will be the task of subsequent chapters to show how these coordinating institutions fare in a variety of specific contexts.

Enduring dualities and the ensuing tensions, conflicts, and instabilities have been deep-seated impediments to French governments seeking cohesion and consistency in action. The regal absolutism of state power, buttressed by a Gallican Church that preached the divine right of kings, asserted that personified political authority was not merely legitimate but sovereign. It proclaimed itself unlimited and irresistible, the majestic manifestation of state unity. This fiction—that the diversity of loyalties and interests of individuals and groups could be subsumed under the singular will of the monarch—underpinned the pretence that the law emanating from this sublime source was the expression of the general interest of the people living within the French state. Decapitated and partially delegitimized and discredited by the French Revolution, the 1790s attempts to depersonalize political authority, first substituting government by assembly with, successively, a twelve-member Committee of Public Safety, a Directory of five, and a Consulate of three, ended in one-man rule by Napoleon Bonaparte. However, although the 'one and indivisible Republic' had simply transferred absolute power and not abolished it, that power was no longer irresistible. Popular sovereignty had emerged as the new basis of legitimate political authority, with which the state imperative had to achieve an uneasy accommodation. It was to take France two monarchical restorations, two Empires, and a further four Republics to overcome an incapacity for any ruler to ensure a peaceful succession after 1791. Such were the vicissitudes of re-establishing state power on an agreed foundation. Before this could be achieved, a party system allowing a diversified public opinion to be effectively expressed through domestic representation had to come into existence.

By the time the Fourth Republic was created in 1946, political parties were seeking to govern France through the National Assembly. This latest swing of the pendulum away from the authoritarian state power embodied in the Vichy regime of 1940–4, however, proved incapable of dealing with the challenge that decolonization posed to the indivisibility of France, of which Algeria was deemed to be part. The institution of the Fifth Republic under the aegis of General de Gaulle deliberately made a virtue of the duality of French state traditions by embodying them within a new constitution. The monarchical tradition of sovereign state power was harnessed to the democratic tradition of parliamentary representation. Instead of a dichotomy between an exorbitant concentration of arbitrary power in a single ruler and a paralysing dispersion of accountable power among hundreds of deputies loosely associated in multi-party intermediaries between them and fragile governments, the Fifth Republic has provided a normative institutional framework for government based upon the dynamic duality of shared power. The directly elected President is a 'Republican Monarch' who, despite his partisan origins, is expected as head of state to be both largely an arbitrator above political conflict when deprived of the support of a partisan Assembly majority and an arbiter-in-chief when he does enjoy such support. Pre-democratic state power and democratic party power have been embodied in the President of the Republic as partisan statesman, powers which he shares with the Prime Minister and their respective staffs, supported by the permanent officials of the state.

The written and unwritten constitutional frameworks within which French governments seek to coordinate their activities are superimposed upon two sets of institutions distinguished by their mode of recruitment: selection or election. Each needs the other but there is a built-in rivalry between them. Of those that are selected to staff the machinery of government, the senior administrative officials are our main concern. The military have intervened decisively from time to time—notably in bringing de Gaulle back to power in 1958—but he put them in their subordinate place in the 1960s, although we shall encounter them in matters of defence policy. The judiciary, notably administrative lawyers of the Council of State led by Michel Debré, played a key role in drafting the Constitution of the Fifth Republic and its subsequent interpretation, but fear of 'government by judges' has induced prudence in extending the role of judicial review by the Constitutional Council (CC). However, a salient feature of the Fifth Republic's attempt to overcome the divergences between the democratic and bureaucratic modes of access to state power has been the colonization of the former by the latter. Instead of the liberal separation of politics from administration, they have increasingly been merged by the number of administrative officials who become ministers before or after they seek election, having previously served a political apprenticeship on the *cabinet* staff of a minister. The National School of Administration, set up by Michel Debré in 1945, has provided the unified politico-administrative elite with most of its leaders as Presidents and Prime Ministers, as well as those who form the nucleus of the interlocking political and administrative state directorate. Many of the strengths and weaknesses of the distinctive French style of policy coordination derive from this impulse to unify.

THE NORMATIVE JURIDICO-POLITICAL FRAMEWORK

The sovereignty of law had been considered in France to be the supreme normative principle since the Revolution. As a corollary, under the Third and Fourth Republics, parliament as the maker of law was accepted as the sovereign expression of the general will. Although this principle was not always respected in practice, the abandonment of legislative primacy in 1958 was a constitutional revolution. The new duality between enumerated matters reserved to law made by parliament and the rest, the discretionary realm of statutory instruments, meant that the government acquired an autonomous regulatory power. This might appear to reproduce the political and administrative split that the desire for unity had sought to overcome. While this is formally correct, in practice Fifth Republic governments have largely achieved command over the legislative process, thanks to a combination of procedural devices laid down in the Constitution with the customary emergence of stable Assembly majorities. This has meant that while it is necessary to coordinate legislative and regulatory activities, those who do so are parts of the same decision-making constellation. Furthermore, the reaction against 'government by assembly' led the authors of the Constitution to provide through article 11 for a number of important matters (increased in 1995) to be decided by referendum if the government so requested and the President agreed. Thereby, greater recourse to direct democracy as well as representative democracy provided for in article 6 of the 1789 Declaration of the Rights of Man and the Citizen has been made possible, but the initiative is exclusively in the hands of the government. French citizens are confined to the administered, passive role of responding to their political masters even when they are occasionally invited to decide themselves.

While de Gaulle is supposed to have said that 'In France, the Supreme Court is the people', and it is true—as was demonstrated in 1993—that a referendum can reverse a decision of the CC, the latter virtually always has the last word. Having decided in 1962 that it was not competent to overrule the approval by referendum of a violation of the Constitution because it was the direct expression of national sovereignty, the CC nevertheless declared in 1985 that laws passed by parliament 'only express the general will if they respect the Constitution'.[1] The CC is the judge of such conformity in general and in particular those designated 'organic laws' by the Constitution.[2] A feature of the 1958 Constitution is that it provides for three other kinds of law that have led the CC to adjudicate. To implement its programme, the government can make ordinances (article 38) which are in effect regulations having the validity of law.

---

[1] Quoted by Guy Carcassonne, *La Constitution* (Paris, Seuil, 1996), p. 247; cf. pp. 89, 251. Carcassonne argues that the 1962 violation of the procedure for constitutional amendment (article 89 by recourse to article 11) was essential to overcome a veto by the Senate and should be available for this purpose in future (ibid., pp. 92, 321).

[2] The relevant articles of the Constitution designating the matters covered by 'organic laws' are listed in ibid., p. 195. More generally, see A. Stone, *The Birth of Judicial Politics in France: The Constitutional Council in Comparative Perspective* (Oxford, OUP, 1992).

The Finance Law is subject to special provisions (article 40) restricting the time at parliament's disposal for its discussion as well as its capacity to amend or tack on additional provisions. The frequency with which legislation has been censured by the CC—most Finance Laws from 1983 to 1993 were censured in part—encourages governments to find ways of bypassing law. The ratification of European Union (EU) treaties—those of Maastricht in 1992 and Amsterdam in 1997—have required constitutional amendments at the insistence of the CC under article 54. Thus, not merely has the sphere of parliamentary legislation been circumscribed but its identity has become more diffuse and subordinated to a higher constitutional law.

With the abandonment of the dogma of the normative omnicompetence of the legislature, the judiciary has almost inadvertently emerged from its subordinate position to government, resulting in selectively 'excessive zeal' and 'myopic docility', to become a watchdog over it. Making the President of the Republic guarantor of judicial independence (article 64) amounted to putting the wolf in charge of the sheepfold's security because 'until recently, absolutely all political authorities have sought to dispose of as docile a judiciary as they could imagine in their most insatiable dreams'.[3] However, exasperation at the inability to hold ministers judicially to account for their actions while in office led in 1993 to amendment of the Constitution. By article 68, the Court of Justice of the Republic tries such offences. The issue that brought matters to a head was the scandal of contaminated blood, which occurred when Laurent Fabius was Prime Minister in 1985 and is discussed in Chapter 4. He maintained that his trial for 'complicity in poisoning' cast him as a scapegoat for a matter which he had initially not dealt with and on which he took the correct decision once it was drawn to his attention.[4] The requirement of ministerial countersignature of decisions has led to the de facto submersion of individual ministerial into protective collective responsibility. Notwithstanding the almost inextricable problem of personalizing responsibility for a complex process of ineffectively coordinated public decision-making, the demand for simple and clear accountability has proved irresistible. The change in the climate of opinion has meant that mutual tolerance for their failings by the politicians has yielded to the emergence in the 1990s of a convention of enforcing ministerial resignations when charged by the courts with judicial offences, even when these do not directly relate to their ministerial activities. This practice began under Socialist Prime Minister Bérégovoy and continued with Rassemblement Pour le République (RPR) Premier Balladur.

---

[3] Carcassonne, Constitution, p. 264; cf. p. 263. In the October 1981 Assembly debate on the Mauroy Government's Nationalization Bill, a socialist deputy, André Laignel, put the legislative case for parliamentary sovereignty, in reply to a RPR former minister with his remark: 'The legislator is entitled to judge sovereignty. M. Foyer accordingly is legally in the wrong because he is politically in the minority' quoted by P. Favier and M. Martin-Roland, *La Décennie Mitterrand* (Paris, Seuil, 1990), i, p. 133.

[4] L. Fabius, *Les Blessures de la Vérité* (Paris, Flammarion, 1995), pp. 215–25, 237. Fabius was exonerated. The resentment of some ministers at increasing judicial and investigative journalistic 'intrusion' to enforce ministerial accountability is conveyed in Michel Charasse's comment: 'henceforth judges engage in journalism and journalists hand out justice' (M. Charasse, *55 Faubourg St. Honoré: Entretiens avec Robert Schneider* (Paris, Grasset, 1996), p. 303).

The encroachment of a French and EU constitutional *Etat de Droit* upon traditional sovereign *Raison d'Etat* has imposed legal constraints upon the actions of
French governments. When this has not dissuaded governments from acting or
slowed them down, it has required them to coordinate in anticipation of the risks of
partial or total annulment of their acts, as well as dealing with the consequences when
they nevertheless occur. The main burden of such coordination falls on the shoulders
of the Council of State, the Government General Secretariat (SGG) and, for EU
affairs—insofar as they can still be separated from domestic activities—the General
Secretariat of the Interministerial Committee for European Economic Cooperation
(SGCI) and the Secretariat General for European Union Affairs. But before discussing
their role, it is necessary to appreciate the dimensions and complexity of their task.

The average size of the *Journal Officiel* has increased by 51 per cent between 1958
and 1992, amounting to an annual average 108 laws from 1982 to 1991 and 680
decrees in 1991 alone. The government has accumulated a total of some 7,500 laws
and 82,000 regulations, whose volume and constant increase means that by the time
that new legal norms have been introduced, abrogation or modification of past norms
render the legal order inconsistent. This makes coordination through codification a
vital and permanent task. The less government is capable of ensuring the coherence
of its output of edicts, the more it is inclined to have recourse to norm inflation,
resulting in a vicious circle *fuite en avant*.[5] While lower level statutory instruments
(circulars and *arrêtés*) are the responsibility of ministerial judicial specialists, the
more important decrees, ordinances, and draft legislation are verified by the SGG,
Council of State, and SGCI. Since a 1990 Clausade Report, 'The Adaptation of French
Administration to Europe', ministries have either created European units within
their vertical structures (as in the ministries of Finance, Agriculture, and Industry) or
a horizontal Service des Affaires Européennes et Internationales in the Justice
Ministry.[6]

Since the mid-twentieth century, European integration has increased its normative
legal impact to the point that by the early 1990s 'more than half the texts (operational
in France) originate in Brussels'.[7] In 1992, 22,445 EU regulations were directly applicable in member states; 1,675 directives had to be transposed into domestic legislation; plus 1,198 agreements or protocols, 185 Commission or Council of Ministers
recommendations, 291 Council resolutions and 678 Commission communications.
The Maastricht Treaty alone had seventeen protocols and thirty-three declarations
appended to it, all of which complicate the task of those that have to respect EU
treaty provisions.[8] The Treaties contained some 700 articles by the end of the millennium, not to mention the appendices. It was the need to amend the French

---

[5] 'Les Contraintes Juridiques qui pèsent sur le travail gouvernemental', in Ecole Nationale
d'Administration, *Le Travail Gouvernemental*, i (La Documentation Française, 1996), pp. 251–2.

[6] Ibid., pp. 254–5. See J. de Clausade, *L'Adaptation de l'administration française à l'Europe* (La
Documentation Française, 1991).

[7] *Etudes et Documents du Conseil d'Etat*, no. 44 (La Documentation Française, 1992), p. 17, quoted by
V. Nicolas, 'Le Désordre Normatif', in *Pouvoirs*, 69 (April 1994), p. 37.

[8] Ibid., pp. 36–7.

Constitution to bring it into line with the Maastricht Treaty in 1992 that led to the acquisition by the EU of constitutional status. As a result, all future EU power-sharing decided by treaty can be presumed to be constitutional according to article 88-1, whilst article 88-2 transfers (not shares) monetary powers under Economic and Monetary Union to an independent European Central Bank (ECB). Article 88-4 provides that parliament can vote resolutions on proposed EU legislation but these only have the status of advice to the French government's negotiators.[9]

When, in its landmark 1989 Nicolo judgement, the Council of State belatedly followed the Court of Appeal which since 1975 had accepted that French legislation could be overruled by European Treaty provisions, the legal risks to which government action was subject were significantly expanded. A 31 July 1992 circular from the Prime Minister insisted that all draft European directives and regulations received by the SGCI should be submitted to the Council of State to decide whether they had a legislative or regulatory character according to the French Constitution. While the Council of State's part in the coordination process is mainly an advisory one, through its widespread network of officials in core executive positions, more especially in the SGG, its four administrative sections—Interior, Finance, Social, and Public Works—review the massive output of decrees from the ministries, notably Interior and Social Affairs. Such statutory instruments provide the government with flexibility in the implementation of its policies without recourse to parliament. Far from being centralized, both laws and decrees are drafted in France by the lead ministry consulting other ministries concerned, verification by the Council of State helping to standardize their varied juridical practices.[10] The quality of the texts submitted from the ministries is often poor and they require numerous changes of form, substance, and expression. It has to work at high speed to keep up with the government's political calendar. Political considerations may modify its confidential judicial advice, notably through amendments made later in the decision-making process. The Council of State's advice sometimes deals with the desirability but always the legality and constitutionality of drafts to avoid the risks entailed before and the interpretative reservations following CC judicial review. Its advice is less reliable on constitutional than on strictly administrative law matters. However, its members enjoy an enviable reputation for their independence of judgement, encouraging less docility in other branches of the judiciary.

Although it is not mentioned in the Constitution, we shall repeatedly return to the work of the SGG, whose top officals are recruited from the Council of State (post-poning until later, in this chapter, discussion of its extensive politico-administrative coordination work), because of its pivotal role in the coordination of government activies. It is also its function to give legal advice to the government generally and to the Prime Minister in particular. Out of a total staff of a hundred, fourteen have specifically the task of checking the formal legality of proposed government

---

[9] Carcassonne, *Constitution*, pp. 302–9. See also D. Chagnollaud and J.-L. Quermonne, *Le Gouvernement de la France sous le Ve République* (Paris, Fayard, 1996), pp. 714–16.

[10] J. Fournier, *Le Travail Gouvernemental* (Paris, Dalloz, 1987), pp. 240–50. See also Jean-Paul Costa, *Le Conseil d'Etat dans la société contemporaine* (Paris, Economica, 1993).

legislation and statutory instruments. One senior official is specifically concerned with constitutionality matters, while seven deal with the work of groups of ministries. A legislative service tracks the progress of each text until its publication in the *Journal Officiel*, ensuring that all formalities have been observed. The head of the SGG and a member of the Prime Minister's *cabinet* jointly chair the meeting to finalize drafts before they are submitted to the Cabinet. While the President and Prime Minister are having their Wednesday morning pre-Cabinet meeting, the SGG's *directeur de cabinet* prepares the post-Cabinet press release! When legislation is referred to the CC, the SGG coordinates the written presentation of the government's case. Its best endeavours have not prevented an increasing number of cases in which judicial review has compelled the government to rectify constitutional infringements before its legislation is promulgated.

The SGCI plays the pivotal role in coordinating the French government's handling of the interaction between EU and domestic legal affairs. It has a team of five to deal with the anticipated impact of draft EU directives and regulations while they are being considered. An updated note is prepared by the lead ministry and circulated to the SGCI, the Council of State, and all interested ministries, so that the SGCI can decide what further consultations are necessary. It also increasingly takes part in interdepartmental preparatory meetings concerned with domestic matters to check on the consistency of the draft proposals with EU law, as well as the implementation of EU directives and regulations. France had the unenviable record from 1989 to 1993 of having usually to face the largest number of EU Commission 'presumed infractions' (complaints, petitions, questions by MEPs, and cases detected by the Commission staff), being outdistanced only by Italy in 1989 and by Spain in 1992. However, the number of cases in which the Commission took the French government before the European Court of Justice has declined, from a high point in 1984 and 1985 (14 cases) to 6 cases in 1990, 4 in 1991, 1 in 1992, and 2 in 1993.[11] We shall return in Chapter 5 to the wider question of the constitutional impact of the EU Treaties upon the task of coordinating French policy. Having considered the implications of limiting French legal sovereignty and the fragmentation of legal norms, we must now turn more specifically to the inspiration underlying the Constitution and how it has been modified by custom and practice.

PRESIDENTIAL–PRIME MINISTERIAL POWER-SHARING: COORDINATING COHABITENSIONS

In answering the question whether constitutions matter, Sammy Finer admitted that they were 'highly incomplete, if not misleading, guides to actual practice' and often ineffective constraints on those determined and powerful enough to violate their provisions.[12] They are idiosyncratic, autobiographical summations of a country's

[11] ENA, *Le Travail Gouvernemental*, i, p. 263; cf. p. 258 and ii, p. 804.
[12] S. E. Finer, V. Bogdanor, and B. Rudden, *Comparing Constitutions* (Oxford, Clarendon Press, 1995), p. 1; cf. pp. 2–3, 6–7.

experience, with an emphasis on counteracting weaknesses revealed in any recent crisis encountered, as was the case with the Constitution of the Fifth Republic. So, it is necessary to identify what the constitutional framework was reacting against, how it has evolved over its forty-year existence and the extent to which European integration has modified the normative framework within which coordination takes place.

The 1958 Constitution was intended to correct the failings of a political system that was democratically legitimate but operationally ineffective. The main weakness was identified as a government at the mercy of a parliament that was itself at the mercy of fragmented and undisciplined political parties. The new constitution was deliberately crafted to reinforce government against parliament, without anticipating that the parties would be subjected to a bipolarizing pressure such that governments could usually rely upon the support of a parliamentary majority coalition. The reassertion of state power in the person of the President of the Republic, with reinforced democratic legitimacy from 1965 by direct popular election (the second ballot ensuring that the winner would have the support of more than half of those voting), was intended to impart the positive impetus once government was released from the inhibitions of the party–parliamentary restraints.

Georges Clemenceau, who championed the Jacobin belief that one should dispense with a head of state, famously declared, 'there are two things in the world for which I have never seen any use: the prostate gland and the president of the republic'. The normative antithesis to this view was put at a 1964 press conference by de Gaulle, even if the tone was more regally absolutist than the reality of presidential power warranted. Emphatically denying that there was a duality of state authority, de Gaulle asserted that 'the indivisible authority of the state is wholly confided to the President by the people who elected him, and that there is no other authority, be it ministerial, civil, military or judicial, which is not conferred or maintained by him. Finally, he adapts his own supreme sphere of action to those whose execution he delegates to others. Nevertheless, normally, it is essential to preserve the distinction between the function and sphere of action of the Head of State and that of the Prime Minister.'[13] The last sentence in this oracular pronouncement alludes to a key problem of coordination because [the powers shared between President and Prime Minister may be distinct but they are frequently not separable.]This coordination is especially problematic during formal periods of cohabitation (1986–88, 1993–95, and 1997–2002) in which the duality at the summit of the French state which de Gaulle denied is particularly clear, because without the support of an Assembly majority the primacy of the President is not indivisible in most spheres of public policy. However, it can be argued that the 1958 Constitution has in practice institutionalized continuous cohabitation between President and Prime Minister, although there have been periods when the former appeared to exercise undisputed dominance. As this is a crucial contextual factor in the working of government coordination, its fluctuating impact must be considered.

[13] C. de Gaulle, *Discours et Messages*, iv (Paris, Plon, 1970), p. 168.

While one can argue that far from having a semi-presidential system, France has alternately a predominantly semi-presidential or a predominantly semi-parliamentary system of government, such labels are an illusory simplification of ambiguous relationships that are complex and shifting. President Mitterrand sought to clarify matters in a message to parliament on 8 April 1986, following the election of a hostile Assembly majority and his appointment of Jacques Chirac as Prime Minister. The only reasonable guide to this unprecedented situation was 'the Constitution, nothing but the Constitution, all the Constitution'.[14] He explained that this would mean reverting to its provisions from the discretionary practices that had developed under his predecessors, whereby the President had usurped powers that, according to the letter of the Constitution, belonged to the Prime Minister and government. The coexistence of two heads of the executive would mean that the President would not have a free hand to interpret his powers at will because he could not rely upon a subservient Prime Minister and secure Assembly majority. However (as we shall consider in detail later), this was an oversimplification of the pre-Mitterrand years, as well as of his own incumbency.

There have been attempts to mark out a clear division of labour between President and Prime Minister. The debate about a presidential 'reserved sector'—an attempt to distinguish an exclusive sphere of presidential prerogative—which was generally rejected during de Gaulle's period in office, resurfaced in 1986. Prime Minister Chirac quoted article 20 of the Constitution to Mitterrand, to establish his claims to decide foreign policy matters, with the president quoting back five other articles because 'the Constitution is a whole'. As we shall see, the attempts at dual control were confusing at home and abroad.[15] The dismissal of Prime Ministers Debré and Pompidou while they enjoyed the confidence of the Assembly, of Chaban-Delmas by Pompidou despite an Assembly vote of confidence, and the 1976 resignation of Chirac in disagreement with President Giscard d'Estaing, were earlier examples of an uneasy cohabitation that sooner or later came to grief. The disputed claim that de Gaulle demanded undated letters of resignation from his Prime Ministers on taking office—which Chirac repeated unprompted by Giscard in 1974[16]—is indicative of a persistent lack of mutual confidence that is structural to the relationship. In anticipation of a possible left-wing victory in the 1978 Assembly elections President Giscard warned of the consequences, while Mitterrand explicitly used the term cohabitation.[17]

---

[14] See the text in Chagnollaud and Quermonne, p. 883.

[15] J. Attali, *Verbatim, ii: 1986–1988* (Paris, Fayard, 1995), p. 38; cf. pp. 101–2. See ch. 3, pp. 66–73.

[16] See the account in V. Giscard d'Estaing, *Le Pouvoir et la Vie*, ii (Livre de Poche, 1991), p. 30.

[17] Giscard's Verdun-sur-le-Doubs speech of 27 January 1978 is appended to his *Le Pouvoir et la Vie*, i (Livre de Poche, 1989), pp. 402–3. For references to Mitterrand in *Le Monde* (4 March 1978), articles by P. Avril and J.-C. Colliard, and M. Duverger, *Echec au Roi* (Paris, A. Michel, 1978), pp. 227–8, see M.-A. Cohendet, *La Cohabitation: Leçons d'une expérience* (Paris, PUF, 1993), pp. 11–12, 24, 30, 48, 51. See also M. Duverger's later *Bréviaire de la cohabitation* (Paris, PUF, 1986).

The 1986–88 cohabitation was from start to finish a period of bitter and persistent attrition between President Mitterrand and Prime Minister Chirac, with the former as de facto leader of the Opposition from the Elysée in preparation for the 1988 presidential election at which they expected to face each other. The guerrilla warfare began with Mitterrand's veto of Chirac's proposed nominations for the foreign, defence, and justice ministries, and continued with his refusal to sign ordinances which slowed down the government's programme. Chirac got his own back by rapidly replacing Jacques Fournier as Government Secretary General and denying the presidency receipt of some diplomatic telegrams by classifying them as 'messages', while the telephone-tapping reports were restored only after presidential protests. Dismissals and appointments were tenaciously negotiated. Mitterrand restricted meeting with the Chirac ministers to five members of his Elysée staff, notably his Secretary General, Bianco, to ensure an indispensable minimum of coordination. The weekly Cabinet meetings became an even more formal rubber stamp of the government's prior decisions, although the pre-Cabinet tête-à-tête between President and Prime Minister took longer. The President's spokesperson could voice reservations, only to be subjected to a rival communiqué from the Prime Minister's spokesperson.[18] While powers were shared in some policy sectors, the senior of the two reluctant partners was usually the Prime Minister, the President often being able only to prevent some decisions and delay others.

The 1993–95 cohabitation was much smoother than its predecessor for several reasons. The Socialists had suffered a crushing electoral defeat, unlike the narrow 1986 result. The President's increasingly debilitating prostate cancer deprived him of his earlier pugnacity. Knowing that he would not be standing for re-election, he took a more resigned view of his differences with the Balladur Government. Mitterrand accepted Balladur's choice of ministers without demur. For his part, Balladur had been closely associated, as his Secretary General of the Presidency (SGP) twenty years before, with the dying President Pompidou. He was by temperament less inclined to aggressiveness than Chirac, whose repeated 1986–88 confrontations with Mitterrand, he believed, had been more damaging to the Prime Minister. His real rivalry was with Chirac because both wished to be candidates for the presidency in 1995.

The internal cohesion of the Balladur Government was undermined by the fratricidal split in the RPR, with Interior Minister Pasqua supporting Balladur and Foreign Minister Juppé championing Chirac. The *modus vivendi* reached with Mitterrand was that the Prime Minister would largely control domestic affairs, they would share control of foreign affairs, whilst nuclear deterrence was the President's responsibility. They were in broad agreement on European policy, while the tough

---

[18] Cohendet, pp. 103–5, 158–9, 163–7, 190–8, 202–7. See also Charasse, pp. 137–43, and Fabius, pp. 147–8. Mitterrand disliked 'cohabitation''s connotation of connivance, preferring the neutral term 'institutional coexistence' (Favier and Martin-Roland, ii, p. 587). For an insider's running commentary on the early months of the 1986–8 cohabitation, see Attali, *Verbatim*, ii, pp. 10–11, 19–24, 33–5, 97, 107, 114, 152–7, 161–2.

General Agreement on Tariffs and Trade (GATT) negotiations with the USA were left to Balladur and his EU *cabinet* adviser, Yves Thibault de Silguy. He accepted Mitterrand's veto on nuclear tests but appropriated the money for them, so that in the event Chirac as President could carry them out in 1995. Only three ministers— Foreign Affairs, Defence, and Cooperation—had regular meetings with the President, the others requiring the Prime Minister's permission to do so. What ensured satisfactory coordination between President and Prime Minister was that Hubert Védrine as the Presidency Secretary General and Nicholas Bazire as Balladur's *directeur de cabinet* remained in close contact by telephone and had frequent meetings.[19] However, the third cohabitation from 1997 took yet a different form.

The first two cohabitations worked in their rocky or smooth ways because neither the President nor the Prime Minister pushed their constitutional prerogatives to the ultimate point of paralysing conflict. Brandishing article 5 (the President's power of *arbitrage* (arbitrator or arbiter?)) against articles 20 and 21 (the Prime Minister directs the government which decides and carries out national policy) is a recipe for deadlock. To preserve the delicate balance between presidential and prime minis-terial power when the Assembly majority changed partisan hands required feats of coordination. However, in 1981 and 1988, President Mitterrand brought the Assembly into line with him by successfully using his power of dissolution. The result was two five-year periods of presidential predominance, followed by two periods of cohabitation each lasting two years. During the first of these the President, acting like a Roman Tribune of the People, prepared the way for his return to predominance, a tactic that Mitterrand could not employ from 1993. Announcing in May 1986 that he had no intention of dissolving the Assembly, Mitterrand declared: 'Dissolution is only effective after a presidential election, not before one. Why fight a battle in 577 constituencies rather than a single one?'[20] Fearing loss of his Assembly majority in 1998, President Chirac dissolved it in 1997 only to lose the subsequent election, opening up the prospect of five years of cohabitation. Unlike the previous periods of coexistence, when the resolution of the contradiction between President and Prime Minister would take place within two years, a more prolonged and uncertain cohabitation exacerbates the incentive for each to seek a tactical advantage and precipitate a confrontation. The crucial role of ensuring an indispensable measure of coordination between them was played by Chirac's SGP (Dominique de Villepin) and Jospin's *directeur de cabinet* (Olivier Schrameck) who frequently tele-phoned each other (avoiding putting compromising matters in writing) and had a discreet monthly lunch together. The longer the President was confined to a minimal role, the greater was the likelihood of a permanent shift of power in favour

---

[19] N. Bazire, *Journal de Matignon* (Paris, Plon, 1996), pp. 92, 102–3, 145–6, 159–69, and B. Brigouleix, *Histoire indiscrète des Années Balladur: Matignon durant la seconde cohabitation* (Paris, A. Michel, 1995), pp. 80–6. Bazire reports (pp. 85–8) that after the 1993 PS electoral defeat, Mitterrand's SGP Védrine had a precautionary meeting with Balladur to find out how he intended to operate cohabitation, prior to his appointment as Prime Minister.

[20] Quoted by Jean Massot, *L'Arbitre et le Capitaine: Essai sur la Responsabilité Présidentielle* (Paris, Flammarion, 1987), p. 268; cf. pp. 266–7.

of the Prime Minister.[21] Thus, French constitutional provisions have made a major contribution to increasing the problems of intra-core executive coordination, which EU membership was exacerbating.

THE POLITICAL AND ADMINISTRATIVE FRAMEWORK OF COORDINATION

Much of French history since the Revolution can be written in terms of the attempts to subordinate administration to politics or to depoliticize politics by subsuming it under administration. This corresponds in part to our earlier distinction between partisan and state power. In the matter of core executive coordination, while partisan politics and state administration can be distinguished, they are interconnected in practice. So, this institutional description of coordination will deal successively with its more specifically electoral and parliamentary features, then the interlocking politico-administrative superstructures, and finally the specifically administrative structure, it being understood that these distinctions amount more to differences of emphasis within an interrelated process. While the first deals with the programmatic aspect of coordination, the second and third focus upon the mechanisms and agencies through which it is attempted.

Partisan Coordination

The guidelines of government action, proceeding from the general to the specific, are provided, first by the President or Prime Minister's medium-term electoral programme; second, by the priority programme usually set out in a general policy declaration to parliament by the Prime Minister after the government's formation, usually supported by a motion of confidence; third, the twice-yearly policy and legislative programme for matters to be considered by Cabinet and requiring coordination with parliament.

Although Mitterrand had been First Secretary of the Socialist Party (PS) for a decade, he did not think the PS should decide on the content of his 1981 campaign programme. At his two previous presidential candidatures, Mitterrand had first offered seven 'fundamental options' and twenty-eight propositions (1965), while in 1974 he had confined himself to five 'fundamental options' to 'change life'.[22] In January 1981, he telephoned the Secretary of the PS Parliamentary Group, Michel Charasse, to say that, the Communist candidate having presented a 'struggle plan' in 131 points, it was necessary to produce something similar in about 100 proposals. They should be derived from the PS–Parti Communiste Français (PCF) Common Programme and the Socialist Project. Charasse quickly compiled some 300 proposals.

---

[21] For a subtle exploration of the prospects for the third cohabitation, see G. Vedel, 'Variations et cohabitations', *Pouvoirs*, 83 (November 1997), especially pp. 113–25. For a revealing comparison of the personal styles of Villepin and Schrameck, see P. Labro, 'Le Hussard et l'Horloger', *Le Monde* (19 September 2000), pp. 14–15.   [22] Massot, pp. 193–4.

They then reduced them to the 110 proposals which Mitterrand announced later in January when formally launching his campaign.[23] These proposals were to become the objectives of Mitterrand's first presidential term, so even before the election, Mitterrand's future deputy Presidency Secretary General and then SGG, Jacques Fournier, prepared a timetable for carrying out the programme. In a message to parliament on 8 July 1981 President Mitterrand declared that, following the election victories of May and June, he expected his parliamentary majority to fulfil the 'contract' between him and the French people.[24] The deliberately unspecific *Lettre à tous les Français* of 1988 was prepared by three members of Mitterrand's presidential *cabinet* (including his actual and future SGP) and Charasse was consulted again.[25] It was the President rather than his party that was being re-elected.

The partisan coordination of presidential majority, parliamentary majority, and the leadership of the parties that support the government, has presented problems that impinge on the strategy and especially the tactics of members of the core executive. Especially in the early years of his presidency, Mitterrand still thought of himself as the PS First Secretary as well as the head of the presidential and parliamentary majority, the PS having an unprecedented absolute Assembly majority. Prime Minister Mauroy and the new First Secretary Lionel Jospin were inexperienced executants of a dominant presidential will. Partisan coordination took place at weekly Tuesday breakfast meetings at the Elysée, with the Prime Minister, First Secretary, the SGP, and, from 1982, special adviser Attali always present. Discussions were informal but the matters to be discussed had been settled the previous day between the staffs of the President and the Prime Minister, the latter usually initiating the matters that he wished to try out on the others. At post-Cabinet Wednesday lunches, Mitterrand regularly met the President of the PS Parliamentary Group and the President of the Assembly, three PS leaders, the Prime Minister, and several other ministers, as well as Attali. Mitterrand used these informal lunches to settle specific issues, iron out intra-party dissensions, trail new initiatives, or reflect at large.[26]

The composition of the Mauroy Governments of 1981–84 reflected a balance between PS factions, as well as representatives of its Communist and Left Radical allies. His general policy declaration conveyed the excitement of rapidly translating into action as many as possible of Mitterrand's 110 options, its only equivalent in the Fifth Republic being the 'New Society' programme of Chaban-Delmas in 1969. Mauroy met groups of deputies once a month, always arriving late because he could seldom leave Matignon before 10 p.m. This did not satisfy the PS parliamentary party leaders, who saw themselves as the guardians of the party priorities and sought to exercise control over the activities of the government. Mauroy met them on Tuesday afternoons together with any ministers whose policies were being

---

[23] Charasse, pp. 21–2, and Favier and Martin-Roland, i, p. 108.

[24] Chagnollaud and Quermonne, p. 599; cf. pp. 879–80 for the full text.

[25] H. Védrine, *Les Mondes de François Mitterrand: A l'Elysée, 1981–95* (Paris, Fayard, 1996), p. 401.

[26] T. Pfister, *A Matignon au Temps de l'Union de la Gauche* (Paris, Hachette, 1985), pp. 149–52. See also Favier and Martin-Roland, i, pp. 536–7, where testimony to Mitterrand's role as de facto PS party leader who gave its nominal leaders instructions is presented.

finalized.[27] So determined was the Prime Minister to show how loyally his government had set about implementing Mitterrand's 110 propositions that he appended to the book on his first year in office a check-list of progress made.[28] Although inclined to be carried away by an old-fashioned lyrical rhetoric, Pierre Mauroy, while dangerously duplicating François Mitterrand's economic illiteracy, reassured everyone by his transparent honesty and solid working-class credentials.

The lame duck President avoided overtly getting into party conflicts after 1988. His intense dislike of his reluctant choice of PS Prime Minister—Michel Rocard—led him to support former Prime Minister Fabius to succeed Jospin as First Secretary in 1988. However, rivalry between Fabius and Jospin to take over control of the Mitterrand faction—foreshadowed in their 1985–86 clash over who was to lead the PS campaign in the general election, with Mitterrand deciding in Jospin's favour—led to Mauroy being chosen as First Secretary. The 1990 Rennes Congress led to an open split in the Mitterrand faction, from which the PS took five years to recover. From 1990 to 1995 the party was without an effective leader and had lost any sense of direction.[29] It was only the unexpected emergence of Jospin as the PS presidential candidate in 1995, deliberately distancing himself from some aspects of the Mitterrand record, which prepared the way for his control of the PS and accession in 1997 to the prime ministership.

Jospin could plausibly be described as an efficient leader when PS First Secretary from 1981 to 1988, 'responsible, courageous and the enemy of all demagogy' and, by contrast with Chirac, as someone who 'took time to reflect before acting'.[30] Founder-leader of the RPR, Chirac broke with Gaullist principle in 1986 not merely by continuing as party leader while Prime Minister but by recruiting as ministers the leaders of his coalition parties: François Léotard (Republican Party), Pierre Méhaignerie (Centrists), and André Rossinot (Radicals). Chirac also held weekly meetings with representatives of his coalition parties, as he derived his legitimacy from an Assembly majority, not from the President. However, Chirac relied most heavily on his Finance Minister, Balladur, with whom he had worked during the Pompidou presidency. Virtually a Deputy Prime Minister, Balladur was accustomed to receiving several telephone calls each day from Chirac, and this dependence was to lead in 1993 first to a naïve Chirac encouraging Balladur to become Prime Minister and then discovering that Balladur was preparing the ground for his own presidential candidacy in 1995, not Chirac's.[31] Regular Tuesday lunches for leaders of the majority parties, most of whom were ministers, served a coordinating function but by the summer of 1994 Chirac stopped attending them. Their fratricidal battle gravely weakened the RPR without preventing Chirac's election, but

---

[27] Pfister, *A Matignon*, pp. 153–4; cf. Chagnollaud and Quermonne, pp. 597–8.

[28] P. Mauroy, *C'est ici le chemin* (Paris, Flammarion, 1982), pp. 220–47.

[29] Favier and Martin-Roland, ii, pp. 400–5; iii, pp. 21–9, 343–6, 352. See also Fabius, pp. 124–6, 149–54, 185–6.

[30] Charasse, pp. 271–8.

[31] P. Bauchard, *Deux ministres trop tranquilles* (Paris, Belfond, 1994), pp. 96–9, 103–4, and N. Domenach and M. Szafran, *Le Roman d'un Président* (Paris, Plon, 1997), pp. 28–9, 35–6.

by tying his fortunes too closely to those of his unpopular Prime Minister Juppé (who succeeded him as RPR leader) and dissolving the Assembly by tactical miscalculation, he not only gravely weakened his presidential power but his control over the RPR. While Jospin, the victor in the 1997 Assembly election, temporarily held on to the post of PS First Secretary, the position quickly passed on to his hand-picked nominee François Hollande, ensuring a trustworthy link between Prime Minister and the PS.

Coordinating Parliamentary Activities

Although the Prime Minister, unlike the President, can participate in parliament, he seldom bothers to attend or to stay long after he has made a speech. He attends Wednesday Assembly question time (since 1995 Tuesdays and Wednesdays) much more frequently, with Socialist Prime Ministers tending to be more assiduous in answering questions. Since 1961, the Prime Minister has been content to leave coordinating the government's dealings with parliament to a relatively junior minister, although in 1997 the Minister for Relations with Parliament's *directeur de cabinet* was also the Prime Minister's adviser on parliamentary affairs. (We shall see that this kind of linkage has been systematically developed by the Jospin Government as an aid to intra-ministerial coordination.) He has no staff of his own other than a small *cabinet*, relying upon the SGG. He needs to work closely with the Prime Minister's parliamentary adviser and the Presidents of the Parliamentary Groups, who endeavour to act as Whips. While he seeks to cultivate friendly relations with the Opposition to minimize legislative obstruction (especially likely in the Senate for left-wing governments) his main task is to ensure that the government remains in close touch with his backbenchers.[32] It helps if he is approachable, well informed about their concerns, and can include them in the early stages of legislative preparation. This requires regular attendance at the meetings of the parliamentary group. His task is to maximize persuasion rather than use the coercive powers that the Constitution has placed at the government's disposal.

Before each session, the minister meets the Prime Minister's parliamentary adviser and the SGG to plan the legislative timetable, contacting the chairmen of the six standing committees of both Chambers to reach agreement on when the bills will be considered. (Only 30 to 40 per cent of the bills from the ministries can be fitted into congested programmes.) He arranges weekly meetings during the session with the chairmen of the standing committees and parliamentary groups. He decides which minister presents each bill in parliament but will stand in for the minister during the debate when necessary. When parliament is in session, there is almost daily contact between his *directeur de cabinet* with that of the Prime Minister and with the SGG. The preparatory work on the legislation has been done in the line divisions of the lead ministry, with interdepartmental consultation and legal advice prior to its approval by the Cabinet. The lead minister's *cabinet* prepares the minister's speech, and plays a key role in the parliamentary discussion, improvising

---

[32] M. Mopin, 'Diriger le Parlement', *Pouvoirs*, 83 (November 1997), pp. 42–3, 47–8, and interviews.

responses to amendments (which may necessitate rapidly calling an interministerial committee meeting) and to the compromises struck between the two Chambers. The Budget Ministry always has a member present to avoid ministers agreeing to amendments involving unacceptable financial commitments. Jospin's future *directeur de cabinet* wrote that 'the precise dispositions voted are generally the result of a long, detailed, informal discussion between the committee president and rapporteur, the few parliamentarians really interested in the legislation's content, and the minister's *cabinet* under its director's supervision'.[33] The Prime Minister's *cabinet* keeps an eye on ministers making concessions on matters on which they did not get their way in Cabinet, so that the SGG can take steps to reverse the point at the next reading. Since many ministers and junior ministers (ten out of twenty-seven in the 1997 Jospin Government) have either never been members of parliament or only just been elected and had to resign their seats because of the incompatibility rule, it is especially necessary for Prime Ministers to send out frequent circulars reminding them of their need to work closely with parliament, which is indicative of their limited impact.[34]

Of the mass of Assembly amendments presented—12,499 in 1994 during the Balladur Government—those that were predictably most successful were presented by the government (474 out of 575) and the standing committees (1,195 out of 1,684), with government backbenchers presenting fewer amendments with more success than Opposition backbenchers.[35] In the 1995–96 session, of 108 bills adopted, four were amended more than a hundred times, the 1996 Finance Law 233 times.[36] Committee amendments usually make up half the total. The government, through the 'package vote' *en bloc* procedure, can counteract indiscipline in its own ranks, Opposition obstruction, or attempts to go back on compromise agreements. In the 1980s, the government invoked the 'package vote' on 15 per cent of bills sent to the Finance Committee, twice that for other committees.[37] The government is more inclined to use this article 44 weapon than demanding a confidence vote (article 49). The latter is deemed to have passed if an Assembly absolute majority does not vote a censure motion, which has only occurred once—in 1962. The draconian procedures of the package and confidence vote usually strengthen the government's capacity to conceal from public view dissensions among its backbenchers and facilitates their cohesion, especially important for the Rocard, Cresson, and Bérégovoy Governments of 1988–93, without an absolute Assembly majority. When the government's backbenchers push it too far by passing unwelcome amendments— as occurred over the Savary education bill in 1984 and the Devaquet education bill in 1986—it can lead to the abandonment of the legislation and to the resignation of the minister concerned.

[33] Olivier Schrameck, *Les cabinets ministériels* (Paris, Dalloz, 1995), p. 74; cf. pp. 72–5.

[34] Mopin, pp. 50–1. He notes the circulars of 14 June 1983, 15 June 1987, 25 May 1988, 2 January 1993, and 6 June 1997.

[35] See Chagnollaud and Quermonne, p. 414, for details from 1981 to 1994.

[36] Mopin, p. 52.

[37] J. D. Huber, *Rationalizing Parliament: Legislative Institutions and Party Politics in France* (Cambridge, CUP, 1996), p. 92; cf. pp. 72–6, 93–5, and Carcassonne, *Constitution*, pp. 188–9, 208–13.

A comparison of the budget debates in 1988 and 1989 shows the danger of generalizing about the Rocard 'minority' Government's capacity to preserve its proposals from parliamentary amendment. In 1988, determined to show that his government could survive without a majority or frequent use of coercive procedures, Rocard—thanks to the negotiating skills of his budget negotiator Guy Carcassonne—secured the abstention of either or both the Union pour la Démocratie Française (UDF) and the Communist deputies by submitting government amendments modifying, at their request, various ministerial budgets. By contrast, the 1989 budget made heavy use of the article 49 confidence vote to overcome opposition from both its own backbenchers and the Communists, to whom few concessions were made. Huber emphasizes that quite apart from the Rocard Government's motivations, some of its opponents were concerned to avoid confrontation in 1988—the Communists because of impending municipal elections and the UDF who wished by 'constructive opposition' to demonstrate independence from the RPR—and so made negotiable demands, whereas the changed 1989 political situation led them to make non-negotiable demands.[38]

THE INTERLOCKING POLITICO-ADMINISTRATIVE SUPERSTRUCTURE

From the elevation of being President of the Court of Accounts, Pierre Joxe, with the experience of having been Minister of the Interior and of Defence, declared that 'there is no fundamental difference between being a minister or a senior civil servant'.[39] In Britain, the clearer separation of politics and administration has meant that the minister relies upon the support of a number of junior ministers, while his administration is under the control of a permanent secretary. In France the *Ancien Régime* practice, developed in the early nineteenth century, of combining politico-administrative functions in a political secretariat or *cabinet ministériel*, became particularly important in the Fifth Republic. Until then, they were few in number and emphasized partisan recruitment. Since then, the political penetration of higher civil servants, increasing as one moves into positions of state power, from parliament to government and Prime Minister (ten out of sixteen in the Fifth Republic) has meant that the *cabinet* has been the main path to politico-administrative preferment. Such rapid political promotion has been utilized particularly by those recruited through ENA, established in 1945.

Ministerial Staff

Of the 1,276 official *cabinet* posts held by 762 people between 1984 and 1996, over a quarter were *énarques*, ranging between a low of 22 per cent in the Cresson Government and a high of 36 per cent in the Juppé Government (two of the least

---

[38] See Huber, pp. 144–70, for a detailed comparative account.

[39] P. Joxe, *A propos de la France: Itinéraire I. Entretiens avec Michel Sarrazin* (Paris, Flammarion, 1998), p. 275.

popular and successful French governments since 1981). Although the number of senior civil servants has fallen to an average 70 per cent since 1984 (after rising to over 90 per cent from 1958 to 1972), among civil servants the proportion of *énarques* has increased. This is especially true of the senior posts of director and assistant director of the *cabinet* (28 per cent on average) and in the most important ones: 41 per cent in Matignon and 48 per cent in the Finance Ministry on average, with significant fluctuations between governments. The majority of *énarques* in the *cabinets* are not from the *grands corps* (Finance Inspectorate, Council of State, and Court of Accounts) but from the interministerial corps of civil administrators.[40] The shift within this hybrid from political to administrative recruitment reflects the changing nature of the political regime and the increasing importance of providing informed advice to ministers and policy coordination within and between ministries. As a result, 'all matters considered important or sensitive must, at one stage or another, normally be raised, dealt with or evaluated by the *cabinet*'.[41]

Ministers devote more time to receiving deputations, dealing with the media and (frequently) the affairs of the town of which they are mayor, although Jospin reduced the cumulation of ministerial and local office from 1997. As a result, the minister often contents himself with ratifying the initiatives of his *cabinet*. As most of a minister's administrative decisions are taken by his subordinates, there is a competition for power between the line division directors and the staff *cabinet* members. If each line director is under the supervision of a single *cabinet* member, his authority is undermined. However, if he is accountable to several ministers and their staffs, coordination becomes much more difficult. It is generally acknowledged that line officials should be involved more frequently in meetings run by the *cabinets*, which would have the advantage of reducing the need for large *cabinet* staffs. Their official numbers (fixed by prime ministerial circular) vary between large governments—over 600 for Rocard, Cresson, and Bérégovoy—and small ones, such as Balladur's with 449, to which must be added numerous clandestine or unofficial members.[42] The latter are usually young officials and are not authorized to sign on behalf of the minister. The *cabinet* should enjoy the confidence of the minister but are often selected on the advice of the *directeur de cabinet* or of the President or Prime Minister's *cabinet*, wishing to influence the minister through his close advisers. (Michel Charasse had the role under Mitterrand of 'advising' inexperienced ministers on who they should choose).[43] There is sometimes a 'special adviser to the minister', who can be at least as important as the *cabinet* director. He is usually an experienced

---

[40] L. Rouban, 'Les Enarques en Cabinet: 1984–1996', *Les Cahiers du CEVIPOF*, no. 17 (Centre d'Etudes de la Vie Politique Française, 1997), pp. 8–25. More generally, see Chagnollaud and Quermonne, pp. 624–48.

[41] P. Pougnaud, *Les Rouages de l'Etat: Voyage à l'intérieure de l'exécutif français* (Paris, Eska, 1994), p. 58; cf. p. 57.

[42] Schrameck, *Les cabinets ministériels*, pp. 27, 31–2, 86–7. In 1983, 7 per cent of the 1980 ENA *promotion* illegally occupied *cabinet* posts with impunity (T. Pfister, 'L'usurpation du pouvoir des cabinets ministériels', *Le Débat*, 52 (November–December 1988), p. 33.)

[43] Favier and Martin-Roland, i, p. 521.

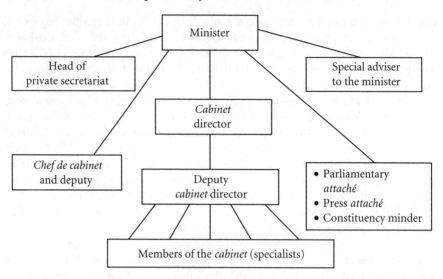

Figure 2.1   *The structure of a typical ministerial* cabinet

Source: Translated and adapted from O Schrameck, *Les Cabinets Ministériels* (Paris, Dalloz, 1995), p. 25.

confidant, dealing with strategic policy thinking or sensitive, high level contacts which warrant his status.[44] The *chef de cabinet* and the head of his private secretariat are generally longstanding political associates of the minister, having to organize his day-to-day activities, dealing with his political and confidential correspondence and parliamentary questions, as well as with the allocation of the 'special funds' which each minister receives.[45]

Figure 2.1 sets out the typical structure of a minister's *cabinet* but it is misleading if it is conceived too statically because influence and authority vary with circumstances and the personalities concerned.

The parliamentary *attaché* should not be confused with the person who maintains contact with the deputy who took over the minister's Assembly or Senate seat, a function usually combined with constitutional matters. In the case of the President, Prime Minister, and Defence Minister, there is also a military *cabinet*, which will be considered later, as will the key role of *cabinet* director.

The internal coordination of the *cabinet* requires avoiding a split between the primarily political and the relatively 'specialist' members of the *cabinet*, a task that falls particularly on the shoulders of the director. Since its work is concerned especially with the justification of government policy rather than its implementation, it is very important to create an integrated team of politically sympathetic 'specialists' and partisans with some specialist skills. The advice given to ministers depends on receiving information from the line officials, which is sifted and annotated, and sometimes partially rewritten prior to submission to the minister via the *directeur de*

---

[44] Pougnaud, pp. 60–3; cf. Fournier, pp. 106–9.   [45] Schrameck, *Les cabinets ministériels*, pp. 21–3.

cabinet. The *cabinet's* task is to shape the ministry's activities to suit their minister's priorities, which will generally include innovating in comparison with his predecessor. However, the *cabinet* 'specialists'—who work with particular ministry divisions—are tempted to become involved in detailed decision-making as well as engaging in coordination. The virtual disappearance of the Secretary General (apart from the Foreign, Defence, and, since 2000, Finance Ministries) has led to a strengthening both of individual divisions and of the *cabinet's* attempts to avoid conflicts between them, which may involve bypassing the line directors.[46] This has created bottlenecks and coordination overload.

Such intra-ministerial coordination is not so overtly political as the work of the parliamentary and press *attachés*. The parliamentary *attachés* keep the minister informed of the political temperature in the two Chambers by collecting information informally from members of parliament. The *cabinet* deals with the mass of parliamentary and other requests for government intervention in particular cases, which is a major distraction from the task of coordination. Thus, the Finance Minister's *cabinet* director deals daily with some sixty such requests, rising to a hundred if the Budget Ministry is added. In 1986, the latter's *cabinet* created a unit to respond to tax solicitations alone, dealing with 40 per cent of the ministry's correspondence.[47]

The *cabinet* spends a lot of time being lobbied by interest groups and with journalists. The latter cannot be left to line officials, who do not have a sufficiently political overview of the ministry's work or authority to react with due speed. Nor can the media be left to the press *attaché*, the more important meetings having to be the responsibility of the *directeur de cabinet*, who also needs to coordinate with the Prime Minister's *cabinet* and the Government Spokesman.[48]

Nearly a third of *cabinet* members (31 per cent) had made an explicit political commitment in the period 1984–96, which varied in its nature, as well as between parties and governments. Membership of the PS (22.7 per cent) and election to local office (20.7 per cent) led the way, with RPR membership only half as frequent (9.7 per cent). Those who had been associated as 'experts' with a party made up 10.6 per cent; 5.4 per cent had personal links with a minister. Trade unions and left-wing clubs were a lesser source of recruitment, but right-wing associations were much more strongly represented among *énarques*. While the overall level of commitment has not varied very much since 1984, the Fabius and Balladur Governments had the highest level of partisan recruitment to *cabinets*. As we would expect from their need to combine partisan and administrative experience, *directeurs de cabinet* and their deputies were 10 per cent more likely to have been directly involved in a political party. The general verdict is that 'politicisation has gained ground at the expense of technocracy', which has been the object of so much criticism throughout the life of the Fifth Republic.[49]

[46] 'Le role des cabinets ministériels', in ENA, *Le Travail Gouvernemental*, i, pp. 180–2.
[47] Ibid., p. 179.   [48] Ibid., p. 183; cf. Pougnaud, p. 65.
[49] Rouban, p. 87; cf. pp. 44–53.

French Presidents and Prime Ministers have fought a forlorn battle to restrict the size of *cabinets*. For example, Prime Minister Balladur sought to reduce their size to between ten and fifteen, according to the minister's status, but these limits have been exceeded with impunity. The estimate that between 20 and 30 per cent 'unofficials' should be added to the official figures makes it clear that more stringent methods of dissuasion would be necessary, for example, by giving the SGG control over numbers, firmly enforced by the Prime Minister.[50] President Mitterrand's *cabinet* had a slight tendency to increase but did not vary much from fifty. Prime Ministers have varied far more, ranging from modesty under Fabius to plethora under Rocard. In the case of the Finance Ministers, a fall in the Delors years (1981–84) was followed by a sharp increase in the Balladur years (1986–88) and then a decline in the Bérégovoy years (1988–92). Jospin's future *directeur de cabinet* summed up the composition of the insider core executive policy community by writing that 'A dense interministerial network, bringing together a hundred or so of the most important ministerial staff oversee the preparation, presentation and implementation of the most important decisions, as well as the day to day work of the ministries'.[51] They come predominantly from the staffs of the Elysée, Matignon, and Bercy.

Disagreements that cannot be resolved between the ministerial staffs or by their ministers ascend for 'arbitration' by the Prime Minister's *cabinet* or by him personally in interdepartmental and interministerial meetings, whose preparation is a major task of his staff. Due to the increasing upward pressure of interministerial coordination, the number of cases requiring Matignon's intervention has augmented the influence of the Prime Minister's *cabinet*. As an illustration, the structure of Balladur's 1993–95 *cabinet* was as follows:

- a *directeur de cabinet*, two deputy directors, and a *chef de cabinet*;
- five advisers for economic, diplomatic, European (also the head of the SGCI), interior and social affairs, under whom were grouped sectors drawn from
- fourteen special advisers dealing with: agriculture and fisheries; budget (usually from the Budget Ministry); communication; culture, youth, and sports; decentralization; education; financial and international economic affairs; health and family; industry and trade; infrastructure and housing; justice; legal affairs; macroeconomics and pensions; relations with parliament;
- three members dealing with the press, the private secretariat, and the military *cabinet*.

These twenty-six staff were responsible for coordinating the work of eighteen ministries and twenty-nine ministers.[52]

The importance of mutual trust and experience means that Prime Ministers tend to bring their team with them from their previous appointments, Fabius from the Industry Ministry in 1984 and Bérégovoy from Finance in 1992. One of the sources of Cresson's weakness in 1991 was that she relied on President Mitterrand to

---

[50] ENA, *Le Travail Gouvernemental, Les cabinets ministériels*, i, pp. 184, 205, 210, 227.
[51] Schrameck, *Les cabinets ministériels*, p. 64.   [52] Pougnaud, p. 69.

constitute her *cabinet*. It is important to have the right balance of mobile *grands corps* members, notably from Ecole Nationale d'Administration (ENA) and Poly-technique (*Corps des Mines*), if one is to succeed in using their networks to facilitate coordination. However, despite the need to create a strong team spirit, pressure of work means that the *cabinet* often operate as isolated individuals, even when, as was the case with Mitterrand, there is not a deliberate attempt to prevent them developing a collective view that might unduly constrain him.

One effect of the greater stability of governments (although by no means always of ministers) has been that *cabinet* members are increasingly likely to be in post longer than the line officials with whom they are dealing. Although the duration of French ministers is not as great as German, Austrian, and Dutch or even Italian ministers, the fact that they more frequently have a bureaucratic background means that they can work more easily with their officials as well as their *cabinet* intermediaries.[53] However, one must bear in mind that the appointment of ministers and *cabinet* have little to do with their knowledge of the ministry whose activities they are to guide. It has more to do with chance and contacts. Unprepared, they only discover on arrival what their new responsibilities will be, a situation exacerbated by the fact that their predecessors will remove on departure most or even all of the files with which they were dealing. If the untried minister has had the sense to appoint an experienced *directeur de cabinet*, the latter's task will include educating his political master. If an official follows his minister when he changes post, one can assume that he is prov-iding mainly political assistance, whereas if he serves different ministers in the same ministry his contribution is primarily his administrative capacity. The presumption is that what are primarily required are not specialists (although there always are some) but generalists with a network of core executive contacts which will enable them to coordinate effectively.[54] So 'The interministerial telephone is *par excellence* the attribute of power, restricted to 150 nomenklaturists', wrote Prime Minister Rocard's *directeur de cabinet*. In particular, 'the telephone is the typical instrument of the Prime Minister's *directeur de cabinet*, the pivot around which radiate the presid-ency, ministers, their *cabinets*, the ministries, and the other political, parliamentary, judicial or media powers'.[55]

The Head of the Ministerial Staff

The *directeur de cabinet* broadly corresponds to the British permanent secretary, in that he coordinates the work of the ministry's divisions. However, he does so through the *cabinet*, most of whose members he will have chosen. His political functions—formulating and presenting his minister's policy, as well as dealing with

---

[53] See W. E. Bakema, 'The Ministerial Career', and M. Cotta, 'Conclusion', in J. Blondel and J.-L. Thiébault (eds.), *The Profession of Government Minister in Western Europe* (Basingstoke, Macmillan, 1991), pp. 74–5, 182–4.

[54] C. Grémion, *Profession: décideurs. Pouvoir des hauts fonctionnaires et réforme de l'Etat* (Paris, Gauthier-Villars, 1979), pp. 361–3; cf. pp. 345, 370. See also G. Carcassonne, 'Typologie des cabinets', in a special issue of *Pouvoirs*, on 'Le Ministre', 36 (1986), pp. 88–90.

[55] J.-P. Huchon, *Jours Tranquilles à Matignon* (Paris, Grasset, 1993), pp. 111–12.

others—allow him, even though assisted by a Deputy Director, little time for intra-ministerial coordination. The diversity, even confusion of roles of the *directeur de cabinet*, makes it an especially exhausting post, usually held by a mid-career official of 35 to 45 years of age. The post's main prerequisites are political skill and administrative authority, although in some ministries like Finance and the Budget specialist skills are also necessary. Centralization of the ministry's activities through control over the circulation of correspondence and the attribution of tasks allows the *directeur de cabinet* to exercise general supervision of the work of both line and staff officials. As the minister's chief of staff, he often deputizes for him. Ministers sometimes meet their division directors but more frequently leave it to their *directeur de cabinet* to hold periodic meetings with them. Particularly in 'weak ministries', the *cabinet* are inclined to supplant the line staff, rather than simply intermediating between the division directors and the minister, with the *directeur de cabinet* becoming the hierarchical *directeur des directeurs*.[56] The ideal of combining a strong *cabinet* staff and strong line administration is hard to attain because power conflicts between them frequently frustrate their cooperation.

Cabinet cohesion is best achieved when there are regular meetings. Few ministers do this and Interior Minister Gaston Defferre was exceptional in meeting his *cabinet* daily while preparing his decentralization reforms of the early 1980s. In the Ministries of Foreign Affairs and of Cooperation the urgency of day-to-day matters means that the *directeurs* meet their *cabinet* each morning. Some ministers and *directeurs* prefer to rely upon written minutes. Usually the *cabinet* meets their *directeur* on Wednesday mornings when the minister is attending Cabinet. If either the minister or his chief of staff rely primarily on bilateral dealings with individual *cabinet* members, this can cause a loss of cohesion. It may substitute court politics for team spirit and sacrifice a full discussion of all the alternatives, with decisions being made that are 'a parody of central administration, without being as rigorous or professional'.[57]

Jospin's *directeur de cabinet* favoured the idea of *cabinet* seminars with the minister, held away from the ministry, to reflect on the guidelines of policy such as Jospin practised as Education Minister from 1988. (Such seminars have been regularly held between ministers by the 1997 Jospin Government, doubtless suggested by Schrameck.) Coexistence within a ministry of several ministers and staffs always leads to rivalries, partly because the ministers have been chosen to counterbalance each other politically and their staffs competitively seek to maximize their role. The coordination problems that arise can be mitigated in three ways: interlocking their *cabinets*; the minister holding regular meetings with the junior ministers and their principal collaborators; his *directeur de cabinet* keeping his opposite numbers regularly informed.[58] Where ministers are frequently abroad (Foreign Affairs) a post of Secretary General has survived, and it was adopted in the Finance Ministry, to ease

---

[56] Schrameck, *Les cabinets ministériels*, pp. 44–6; cf. pp. 20, 84.   [57] Ibid., p. 36; cf. p. 35.
[58] Ibid., pp. 37–8. See the report on the November 1997 seminar organized by Olivier Schrameck (*Le Monde* (13 November 1997), p. 5). In the Juppé Government, a single adviser on budgetary matters was a member of the *cabinets* of both the Finance and Budget Ministers.

the burden on the *directeur de cabinet*. Where the functions of ministries overlap substantially, for example, Foreign Affairs and European Affairs or Social Affairs and Health, weekly meetings between *cabinets* may sometimes be organized.

Prime Minister Jospin institutionalized 10 a.m. Monday morning meetings, specifically for coordination purposes, of all his *cabinet* under the chairmanship of his *directeur de cabinet*. At 11.30 Schrameck met a smaller group to deal with the communication of government policy, followed by a 12.30 meeting on relations with parliament. At 3 p.m. with the SGG in attendance, he spoke to all the *directeurs de cabinet* and answered their questions.[59] Formal interministerial coordination is left to the SGG, while informal coordination is done as the need arises because the Prime Minister would regard anything else as a challenge to his authority. During the 1982–83 economic crisis, when a crucial struggle was taking place between those who wished to give priority to the Mauroy Government's Socialist programme over European integration, there were Monday luncheons between Prime Minister Mauroy and Finance Minister Delors together with their *directeurs de cabinet* to concert the strategy which was to play a decisive part in the final outcome.[60]

The Finance Ministry presents a potentially difficult problem of coordination, both internal and with the Budget Ministry. In the 1986–88 period when Jean-Claude Trichet was Finance Minister Balladur's *directeur* and Daniel Bouton was Budget Minister Juppé's *directeur*, they were able to work together particularly closely, thanks to their previous collaboration during the Barre Government. As they could rely on strong line divisions and directors, effective leadership was possible, with *directeur de cabinet* Trichet organizing weekly meetings of directors and their principal collaborators. It was possible to drive through the Chirac Government's ambitious programme of privatization, reform of credit, price, and exchange control, following Balladur's clear political and economic strategy.[61]

The key relationship between the Prime Minister and his *directeur de cabinet* is a very personal one, so it may be best to contrast some instances from 1988 to 1997. Rocard's *directeur*, Huchon, was virtually a vice-Prime Minister, able to speak with authority on his behalf. They were complementary in character: 'Rocard is quite content with the administration of things, Huchon with the government of men.'[62] Handicapped by a cumbrously large government, Huchon organized weekly or fortnightly meetings of all the *directeurs de cabinet*, the SGG, and the deputy SGP to improve coordination, speed up decisions, and provide advance warning of difficulties. More explicitly political coordination occurred at the Tuesday Matignon breakfasts at which the PS leaders met Rocard for coffee and croissants, together with a representative of the Elysée, Huchon, and Guy Carcassonne, Rocard's

---

[59] Ibid.; cf. P. Avril, 'Diriger le Gouvernement', *Pouvoirs*, No. 83, November 1997, p. 34. For a later description, see B. Victor, *Le Matignon de Jospin* (Paris, Flammarion, 1999), pp. 203–8.

[60] Interviews and Pfister, *A Matignon*, op. cit. pp. 143–4.

[61] Interviews. In the 1990s, Jean-Claude Trichet became Governor of the Bank of France and Daniel Bouton head of Société Générale, a leading deposit bank.

[62] J.-L. Andréani, *Le Mystère Rocard* (Paris, Laffont, 1993), p. 437; cf. Favier and Martin-Roland, iii, p. 45.

parliamentary troubleshooter. 'With rare exceptions, there was neither solidarity or willingness to listen to each other and sometimes there was an atmosphere of hatred' was Huchon's bitterly frank verdict on these Tuesday breakfasts.[63]

A disgruntled member of Prime Minister Balladur's *cabinet* from 1993 to 1995 expressed his amazement that so experienced a person (who had served in Prime Minister Pompidou's *cabinet* from 1964 to 1968, as his deputy SGP and then SGP when President, and as Finance Minister from 1986 to 1988) should have appointed a young, totally inexperienced member of the Court of Accounts, Nicholas Bazire, first as his *directeur de cabinet*, then as the director of his presidential campaign team—with disastrous consequences. It is an example of the 'court politics' danger of choosing someone with whom one is comfortable rather than who is competent. Bazire was 'the Prince's confidant much more than the head of a team which hardly existed as such: he was not the animator of this group of brilliant and competent individuals (as Jean-Claude Trichet had been with Balladur at Rivoli)'.[64] Bazire held meetings of all twenty-nine *directeurs de cabinet* each Monday morning and on Wednesday met the Prime Minister's *cabinet*, the only time both its civil and military members encountered each other. They avoided discussing electoral politics in the Balladur *cabinet*, because some of them supported Chirac while others favoured Balladur as presidential candidate.[65]

In the Juppé *cabinet* of 1995–97, the heads of the groups of advisers met twice weekly under the chairmanship of the *directeur de cabinet* to review developments and prepare the Prime Minister's forthcoming programme of activities. Each of the heads held a weekly meeting with their groups of advisers. All members of the *cabinet* met for an hour at 8.30 a.m. three times a week to identify matters on which memos would need to be prepared or intra-ministerial disputes settled and for advice on how ministers should answer parliamentary questions. On Wednesday mornings, the whole *cabinet* discussed the Prime Minister's programme two months in advance on a 'rolling' basis. *Ad hoc* meetings took place as required by circumstances. Curbing expenditure was always a top priority in the discussions of the Juppé *cabinet*. Contributing to the preparation of the Prime Minister's speeches was a regular task. Juppé made few changes apart from adding a partisan emphasis. In line with Juppé's determination to ensure a centralized form of coordination through control over appointments, he replaced the usual practice of vetting ministers' proposed selection of *directeurs de cabinet* by imposing his own choices. This undoubtedly accentuated the introverted tendency to think that there was no alternative to the Prime Minister's standpoint, his preferences being substituted for the resolution of differences.

Jospin's fifty-five-member *cabinet* was very much the creation of his *directeur de cabinet*, Olivier Schrameck, Secretary General of the Constitutional Council, who

[63] Huchon, p. 193; cf. pp. 146, 192. On the working of Mauroy's *cabinet* from 1981 and the departure of his *directeur de cabinet* because they did not see eye to eye, see Pfister, *A Matignon*, pp. 15–17, 108–9, 179.   [64] Brigouleix, p. 52; cf. p. 51, and Bazire, pp. 23–51.
[65] Ibid., pp. 113–15, 119–20.

had been his *directeur* for four years from 1988, when Jospin was Education Minister. When it became clear that he was to be Prime Minister, Jospin asked him to reflect on the structure of his government, choose his *cabinet*, and decide how they were to be organized. (They jointly supervised the choice of the *directeurs de cabinet* of some ministers). Schrameck chose from personal knowledge or on the advice of friends nineteen team leaders, who in turn chose those who would work with them. On Fridays there was a meeting of team leaders, followed by one with the SGG and his principal collaborators, chaired by Schrameck. Jospin habitually turned to Schrameck for advice in public and in private; they frequently went into each other's adjacent rooms each day. Schrameck's proximity to the Prime Minister and his comprehensive grasp of governmental activity did not lead him to depart from a sense of his subordinate status inculcated by a lifetime's public service: 'I have no legitimacy apart from his confidence and my utility.'[66] The contrast with Villepin, the President's flamboyant SGP, with whom the unobtrusive Schrameck had frequent contact during the post-1997 cohabitation years, could hardly be sharper. Their collaboration sought to prevent the cohabitation of their political masters degenerating prematurely into explosive cohabitension.

Conflict between Line and Staff Officials

In turning from the *cabinets ministériels* and their directors, who are linchpins that help the wheels of French government function, to the 216 division directors who head the line administrations, we are confronted by a paradox. Although at least half of the latter have served at least once in a *cabinet*, their relations with the minister's collaborators are characterized by both their interdependence and their endemic conflict. Part of the reason for the conflicts may be the political differences between officials in overtly political staff posts and nominally apolitical line posts, although because these central administrative line posts are at the government's discretion, the likelihood of conflict is reduced. Nevertheless, some senior officials are allied to the parties out of office, awaiting their turn, often retreating to their *corps* post meanwhile. The impact of the spoils system is indicated by the fact that by the end of 1982, 57 per cent of central administration directors had been replaced by the Mauroy Government, while the 1986 Chirac Government replaced thirty-two out of nearly 170 within three months.[67]

The line administration tries to overcome the problem of potential conflict despite interdependence by influencing the composition of their minister's *cabinet*. The most successful are the powerful traditional ministries, such as Finance and the Budget, with strong divisions who virtually delegate high-flying younger officials to serve as their *cabinet* interlocutors. These officials become doubly subordinate: politically to the minister's team and administratively to their ministry division, on which their future promotion will depend on their return. This administrative

---

[66] Quoted by Victor, p. 159; cf. pp. 145–214.
[67] ENA, *Le Travail Gouvernemental*, i, pp. 191–2, 196.

capture helps to explain why, despite changes of minister and government, there is continuity in budgetary, fiscal, and monetary policy.[68] Capture undoubtedly facilitates a freer circulation of information and closer cooperation. However, the situational ambivalence of such officials leaves open the question of how far the compromises they make lean in the minister's political direction or towards their ministry's departmental viewpoint. When the distribution of *cabinet* responsibilities reproduce the ministry's divisions, it can as easily lead to the *cabinet* reflecting their conflicts as in coordinating and overcoming them.

Prime Ministers have repeatedly tried, unsuccessfully, to overcome the propensity of *cabinets* to interpose themselves between the minister and the line division directors, by stressing the need for frequent personal contact. The line directors do not receive the information sent to the *cabinet* by correspondence and have to go through the *cabinet* to present their views to the minister, which has an inhibiting effect. While they may use their greater knowledge of the rules or substance to stall or keep decisions in their own hands, especially when uncertain about the political implications, they can appeal directly to the minister or even to the *cabinet* of the Prime Minister and President if they have a personal friend there. Attempting to bypass the *directeur de cabinet* by a minute to the minister will be seen and commented on by him. Much more frequently, *cabinet* members bypass the division directors by directly contacting their subordinates. The line directors may also find that members of several antagonistic *cabinets* are intervening which, far from increasing coordination, adds to the confusion, especially when some of them are functionally subordinate to each other. Resenting their restriction to routine administration, the line directors are tempted—out of a mixture of prudence and resentment—to resort to bureaucratic inertia in the face of unpredictable instructions.[69] If ministers made a practice of seeing all their line directors weekly, as Juppé successfully did at Foreign Affairs from 1993 to 1995, they could share in a strategic reflection about their piecemeal activities. Coordination within the ministry and with governmental and non-governmental outsiders would be greatly improved.[70]

THE ADMINISTRATIVE FRAMEWORK

For over two hundred years, all attempts to regulate the number and functions of French ministries have failed to impart to them the continuity that comes from the stability of government structures. At the installation of each new government, a combination of political and circumstantial improvisation with the French optimistic aspiration to achieve reform by manipulating structures threatens to dislocate the machinery of government. It hampers the capacity to coordinate in the short term and to develop a medium-term strategy. The boundaries of traditional

---

[68] Schrameck, *Les cabinets ministériels*, p. 48.

[69] Ibid., pp. 46–53; cf. pp. 26, 44, 67–8. Circulars were issued notably by Rocard on 25 May 1988 and by Balladur on 1 April 1993 requiring ministers to keep in close contact with their division directors.

[70] ENA, *Le Travail Gouvernemental*, i, p. 213; cf. 112, 198–9, 211–14.

ministries such as Foreign Affairs, Interior, Justice, and Defence have changed little, while most of the others have expanded and contracted at the whim of President and Prime Minister. Due to the inflexibility of existing administrative structures and the desire to promote and publicize policy innovations, new and frequently ephemeral ministries are established such as the Ministry for Leisure in 1981 or Privatization in 1986. The conflicts of competence embodied in preparing the *décrets d'attribution* for each portfolio are often bitter, and compromises such as placing some divisions 'at the disposal' of other ministers may create more interministerial coordination problems than they resolve. These decrees specifying ministerial functions may take the SGG a month to sort out, even operating incrementally by dealing only with changes. 'The loss of memory, the imprecision and overlap of competences, the demotivation of officials, make such nomadism a major source of administration dysfunction.'[71] As it is very rare for a single ministry to have sole responsibility for a government decision, improvising structural reorganizations may precipitate 'turf wars', requiring resolution by appeal up the hierarchy.

President Mitterrand favoured large governments because they allowed greater political control over the administration and facilitated completing the political jigsaw puzzle of constituting a government.[72] To keep the size of the Cabinet down, junior ministers were appointed, sometimes autonomous or frequently attached either to the Prime Minister or another minister. (Balladur in 1993 exceptionally decided to keep his government small by appointing no junior ministers.) Reducing the number of ministers can only lead to partial coordination and does not necessarily facilitate overall political coordination. However, too many ministers increase fragmentation and identification with special interests at the point at which policy coordination is necessary. The official ranking of ministers is based on a combination of three factors: the traditional prestige of a ministry, for example, Justice; the personal standing of a minister (which may fluctuate according to their standing with the Prime Minister and President); the ministry's place in the government's priorities. Bureaucratic networks play an important part in overcoming the organizational irrationalities created by political improvisation, leaving it to ministers to sort out the matters they have been unable to resolve.

The problems of interministerial coordination are compounded by those of intraministerial coordination, given the large number of introvert administrative units and the weakness of general as against specialist divisions and bureaux. 'A French ministry is like a confederation of autonomous states .... Not only are the divisions autonomous, but bureaus within a division, too, often refuse to cooperate on common projects .... The tendency is for files to go up and down, but not across.'[73] The last thing that they wish is to be coordinated, particularly when this is presented

---

[71] 'La Structure gouvernementale et l'organisation des administrations centrales', ibid., p. 105; cf. pp. 102–8, 214–15; cf. Fournier, pp. 24–36.

[72] Védrine, p. 29; cf. p. 30, and Charasse, p. 118. For a proposal to reduce the size and stabilize the structure of government, see the Picq Report, *L'Etat en France: Servir une nation ouverte sur le monde: Rapport au Premier ministre* (La Documentation Française, 1995), pp. 112–13.

[73] G. Lord, *The French Budgetary Process* (Berkeley, University of California Press, 1973), p. 127; cf. p. 128.

as being done in a more general, higher interest. Hence the jealous resistance to the creation of an administrative head of the ministry, such as the Whitehall Permanent Secretary, both by politicians and line bureaucrats.

Both ministers and division directors have played an important part in the elimination of the coordinating post of secretary general from most ministries where they existed in pursuit of political primacy and bureaucratic autonomy, respectively. So-called 'general divisions' do not in practice coordinate several divisions. General Secretariats have survived in the Foreign Ministry because the frequent absence of the minister has necessitated a strong secretary general, who meets the line directors several times a week or even daily. Juppé—a much more successful Foreign Minister in 1993–95 than Prime Minister from 1995 to 1997—strengthened (as we shall see) the position of the secretary general, which has meant that the *cabinet* has a weaker role in matters of coordination. Since 1989, the Defence Ministry has had an administrative secretary general who is important as a counterweight to the military–industrial complex of the General Staff and the General Delegation for Armaments. Elsewhere, the lack of interministerial coordination is reflected in the example of sponsor ministry representatives on the boards of state enterprises adopting conflicting standpoints because they have received divergent instructions.[74] However, a decree of 23 May 2000-49 created the post of secretary general in the Finance Ministry to counteract compartmentalization in the ministry that, with Matignon, seeks to maintain a comprehensive oversight over all French government and needs especially to coordinate its own activities.

Interministerial Procedural Coordination: The SGG

The institution that above all counteracts administrative fragmentation and instability, regulating the procedural coordination of government, is the SGG. It was established in 1935 at Matignon, the year in which the Prime Minister moved there. Although it was the Third Republic's only innovative response to the need to strengthen administrative support for the Prime Minister, pioneered by the creation of the Cabinet Office in Britain, it was under the Vichy regime—where parliamentary and party politics was replaced by executive power—that its functions were institutionalized. De Gaulle, having acquired an admiration for the Cabinet Office during his London exile, ensured its subsequent survival as a stabilizer within the Fourth Republic's fitful politics, becoming the embodiment of the French ideology of state continuity. Headed by administrative lawyers, it does so with the Council of State's ambivalent emphasis on service yet preservation of a measure of independence from government. The Government Secretary General's reputation for competence and impartiality has been threatened by his need to work closely with more politicized individuals such as the SGP and the Prime Minister's *directeur de cabinet*, with general staff responsibilities. However, whereas they are concerned above all with

---

[74] See the remarks of a former Finance Minister from 1995 to 1997, Jean Arthuis, in *Dans les Coulisses de Bercy: Le Cinquième pouvoir* (Paris, A. Michel, 1998), pp. 105–6.

ensuring that the government's immediate policies come forward, the SGG's priority is their consistency over time and procedural and legal rectitude. Combining formal rigour with pragmatic flexibility, it is the institutional guardian at the crossroads of government activity.[75]

Precisely because of its central location within the machinery of government, we shall see that the institutions of the Fifth Republic have deprived it of the monopoly it used to exercise. The 1986 cohabitation in particular emphasized the crucial importance of the SGG. It challenged the apolitical nature of the post of Secretary General because the first nomination by the incoming Chirac Government was to replace Jacques Fournier, who had held the post from 1982 to 1986. While his predecessor had remained in post from 1981 to 1982, Fournier, although a member of the Council of State, had stood for election as a Socialist, held party office, advised Mitterrand during his 1981 campaign, and served from 1981 to 1982 as deputy SGP in the Elysée. So one might say that the post had apparently been politicized, although Fournier discharged his functions in the apolitical tradition of his office. However, once the Prime Minister ceased to be the President's man and became his principal rival, it was much more difficult to retain someone who did not have his confidence in a post providing access to the government's secretive activities. Having survived four regimes, the SGG institutionally survived the 1986 cohabitation and resumed its discreet, prudent, apolitical role of administrative servant of government.[76] Whereas changes of President and Prime Minister result in total replacement of their staffs, the SGG—with the 1986 exception—is an epitome of state continuity. As incomers do not have access to their predecessor's files, the SGG is the government's memory.

The Secretary General's proximity to and frequent contact with the few who occupy the summit of the core executive places him in a more intimate relationship with them than most ministers. He is in almost constant touch with the Prime Minister's *directeur de cabinet*. He sees the Prime Minister daily to obtain his signature for official documents and the President at least once a week ahead of Cabinet meetings where he takes the minutes. He has been described as the person who telephones the most and is the most telephoned on matters of government business,[77] so he is especially well informed. In periods of cohabitation, he eases relations between the President and Prime Minister, preparing minutes on less controversial matters for both of them. On delicate issues, such as important appointments, he may informally suggest a package deal to resolve disputes. To help him, he has the services of a 'counsellor for economic affairs', proposed by the Finance Ministry but working under the SGG's authority, who coordinates all economic and financial matters on the instructions of the Prime Minister's *cabinet*. 'His role is particularly important

[75] F. Bonini, *L'Histoire d'une institution coutumière: le Secrétariat Général de la République Française (1934–1986)* (Doctoral thesis, Institut d'Etudes Politiques de Paris, 1987), pp. 298, 320–32, 337. An early champion of an SGG was Léon Blum (Council of State) who, as Popular Front Prime Minister in 1936, strengthened Flandin's 1935 creation, IFSA, *Le Secrétariat Général du Gouvernement* (Paris, Economica, 1986), pp. 16–22; cf. pp. 24, 50.

[76] Bonini, pp. 256, 283–5, 297, 317; IFSA, pp. 26–31.   [77] Interview.

during the budgetary arbitrages, when, in collaboration with the economic and budgetary advisers to the Prime Minister, he prepares the Prime Minister's files for the meetings.'[78] Each of the SGG's senior officials works to two or three members of the Prime Minister's *cabinet* but are much longer in post than they or the line directors in the ministries with whom they deal.[79]

Of the mass of interdepartmental meetings organized each year, which increased from 1,002 in 1978 to 1,279 in 1992, particular significance is attached to the twice-yearly census of what all the ministries have in the pipeline. These meetings are chaired jointly by the relevant SGG official and a member of the Prime Minister's *cabinet*. Ministries are usually represented by two officials, one from the *cabinet* and a line specialist. About a third of all meetings are devoted to the advance examination of legislative texts, whose work is not facilitated by the preference of ministries to leave problems to be sorted out there rather than by negotiation. The SGG influences to which Chamber the legislation will be presented but thereafter largely loses sight of it unless it is challenged before the CC, possibly because of amendments that were adopted without consulting the SGG. Much more serious, the real reference points for the work of the ministries are the ten to fifteen thousand circulars issued each year under their sole responsibility. As the SGG merely receives and publishes them, it is all the more unfortunate that the ministries make little use of the SGG's Centre for Legal Documentation.[80]

EU Procedural Coordination: The SGCI

Unlike Britain, where the coordination of EU relations is done within the Cabinet Office, in France the SGG is separate from the SGCI. Even if this was justified in 1948—when it was established to overcome conflicts between the Finance and Foreign Affairs Ministries over the management of Marshall Aid—the interdependence of domestic and EU affairs has become such that it is now less defensible. National administrations are increasingly the field services of the EU. (It has been estimated that between 1984 and 1988, 102 out of 230 French laws voted reflected prior EU decisions.[81]) After decades in which control shifted between the Finance Ministry and Prime Minister, with the head of SGCI being a close collaborator of either the President or the Prime Minister, it has become the practice that it is directly under the latter's authority, while working closely with the Presidency, Finance, and Foreign Affairs. Although much of its work replicates for the EU that of the SGG within France, membership of the Prime Minister's *cabinet* makes its head the holder of a more political and precarious post. The legal division of labour involves the SGCI identifying the implications for French law of the EU law proposals, so that they can be taken into account in interministerial discussions, prior to incorporating the necessary changes into French law. This involves their collaborating in the forward planning of government activities.

[78] Lord, p. 79; cf. pp. 83–4.   [79] Bonini, pp. 276, 312.
[80] ENA, *Le Travail Gouvernemental*, i, pp. 273–5.
[81] 'Le travail gouvernemental et l'Europe', in ENA, *Le Travail Gouvernemental*, ii, p. 765.

The SGCI is like the SGG in size and type of activity, although the unsynchronized tempo of their work is determined in Brussels and Paris. The SGCI is a small body (150 staff, forty of them senior officials) organizing 1,100 meetings annually, on average eight interdepartmental meetings daily. It manages to achieve agreement in 90 per cent of cases at that stage. The remainder go for decision to a meeting at Matignon, the Prime Minister's *cabinet* receiving an advisory *note d'arbitrage* from the SGCI. The Secretary General's standing with the Prime Minister gives him the necessary authority to settle matters but occasionally they go for final decision to the Prime Minister or President. With the partial exception of 'second pillar' foreign and defence matters, which continue to operate on an intergovernmental basis and involve coordination with these ministries, the SGCI centralizes relations with the French Permanent Representatives in Brussels. All dealings with the European Commission (EC) formally transit through this channel. (However, it cannot centralize communication by telephone and fax.) A weekly coordination meeting, chaired by the Secretary General, takes place each Wednesday morning to settle disagreements and review the state of ongoing negotiations in Brussels. The SGCI coordinates the ministry officials attached to the European Parliament since the Maastricht Treaty. Coordinating police and judicial 'third pillar' policies, including the Schengen Convention (a particular concern of the Interior Ministry), are attempted more directly by the SGCI. Whereas most ministries only have modest European units, in Finance and Agriculture European affairs play a much more central role in the work of the line divisions. Each minister's *cabinet* has a European 'specialist', who coordinates within the ministry and attends meetings at Matignon to defend the ministry's standpoint.[82] We shall return to the SGCI in Chapter 5.

While the SGCI can deal with lower profile European matters, once they reach political level, the President, Prime Minister, Foreign Minister, and Finance Minister and/or Budget Minister are involved. The European Affairs Minister has seldom carried much weight, being subordinate to the Foreign Ministry, although Roland Dumas, thanks to his longstanding personal links with President Mitterrand, did impart importance to the post in 1983–84. In January 1984, Mitterrand said to Delors à propos of the British EC contribution: 'During the preparation of the French presidency, there must be no advance negotiation between experts and especially not several negotiations. Whatever their rank, ministers are only executants. The only person with authority in this matter is Roland Dumas.'[83] However, the President relied principally on Elizabeth Guigou, who headed the SGCI and was the European 'specialist' in his *cabinet*, both before and during the 1986–88 cohabitation. From 1985, his former Finance Minister Delors (who played a key role in 1982–83 with Guigou in shaping his 'European choice', along with Prime Minister Mauroy) as President of the EC was a well-placed ally in Brussels. Before the six-monthly

---

[82] Ibid., pp. 748–52, 778, 782, 797. See also M. C. Kessler, *La Politique Etrangère de la France: Acteurs et Processus* (Paris, Presses de Science, Po. 1999), pp. 204–7.

[83] Reported by Attali, *Verbatim i*, p. 865. In 1995–7 the European Affairs Minister, Michel Barnier, was relied upon in a similar way by President Chirac. On the role of Elizabeth Guigou, see Attali, *Verbatim, ii*, pp. 29, 55, 90, and Ch. 5 of this volume.

European Councils, preparatory coordination meetings between the staffs of President and Prime Minister were held at Matignon to work out a common French position and iron out possible clashes between the Finance and Foreign Affairs Ministries.[84]

Prime ministerial styles vary—Chirac delegating a great deal, while Balladur kept in close touch. At interministerial meetings on Europe, Foreign Affairs, European Affairs, Finance, and the Budget were always represented, with other ministers present as required. Ministers usually attended with their *directeurs de cabinet* but in the hectic GATT negotiations of 1993–94, only ministers attended the weekly meetings. Day-to-day coordination between the Prime Minister's leading economic adviser and the head of SGCI was facilitated by their membership of Balladur's *cabinet*. The SGCI always expected the Budget Ministry to adopt an extreme position—advocating maximizing the Common Agricultural Policy (CAP) revenues that on balance accrued to France and minimizing expenditure on structural funds and the EU budget where France was a net contributor. The director of the Budget Division and the head of SGCI try to settle matters of potential dispute in advance and concert viewpoints, helped by the fact that their approach was general rather than sectoral.[85]

Attempts to Mitigate Coordination Overload

Defence policy coordination on behalf of the Prime Minister is organized by the Secretariat General of National Defence (SGDN), as distinct from military coordination by the Chiefs of Staff attached to the Defence Ministry. A 1978 decree placed the SGDN (but not the SGCI, where conflicts were more likely) under both the President and the Prime Minister owing to the fear that cohabitension would threaten the former's primacy in defence policy (an eventuality that did not materialize until eight years later), formalizing the fact of power-sharing and the need to coordinate. While the abandonment of conscription was very much a personal initiative of President Chirac, during periods of cohabitation the SGDN can be used by the Prime Minister to shift control over defence policy somewhat in his direction. Authorization of arms exports involves SGDN–SGCI collaboration, with the Foreign Ministry taking the lead when political considerations have priority over commercial ones.[86]

A former head of the SGDN, Jean Picq, presented a report on reforming the machinery of government in 1995, having partially succeeded in slimming down the SGDN. He identified three major defects. First, there were too many ministers doing too much. This led, second, to an increase in the need for interministerial coordination by inflated *cabinets*. Third, too many unresolved conflicts needed to be settled by the Prime Minister and his staff. To help overcome these defects, Picq favoured strengthening the Prime Minister's coordinating capacity by adding to the SGG,

---

[84] On the continuing rivalry between Finance and Foreign Affairs, see the testimony of Jean Arthuis, pp. 242–4.   [85] Interviews.
[86] Interviews.

SGCI, and SGDN a Secretariat General for Public Policies (SGPP). The latter might help overcome the short-termism of the SGG and SGCI. Its proposals would be concerned with the benefits as well as the costs of government intervention and it would be better able to coordinate decisions between the centre and the periphery. The fundamental purpose would be to achieve a truly interministerial overview that was systemically frustrated by a public service divided and sub-divided by ministry and by the existence of some 1,700 *corps*.[87] (The Picq recommendations were not implemented.) In its 1960s halcyon days, the Planning Commissariat had performed a prospective, interministerial function for the government. It has since suffered from neglect, surviving more out of inertia than because Prime Ministers have sought to utilize its capacity to offer strategic advice on the basis of forward-looking consultation across the range of public policies. However, the Jospin Government has used it as a think tank on issues such as pensions and the reform of EU institutions.

Despite the instability of structures as each new government is formed, they have not been adapted to the 1980s retreat from detailed public control in favour of market regulation, of increasing European integration, and of domestic decentralization. After the Treasury Division largely abandoned control of monetary policy to the Bank of France in 1993 (with deposit and merchant banks, and insurance companies achieving greater autonomy, and privatisation reducing the size of the public sector), there has been no correlative contraction in that bastion of the Finance Ministry. Attempts from the late 1980s to bolster the intergovernmental Council of Finance Ministers (ECOFIN) by creating a countervailing 'economic government' to the monetary power of the European Central Bank seem destined to be as unavailing as the rearguard action to support traditional public services. The loss of control over EU affairs has also created an identity crisis in the Foreign Ministry, whose network of ambassadors are usually not the source of useful advice they may once have been. The Minister of European Affairs has not found an effective role between the Foreign Affairs Ministry, the SGCI, and the President, and might only do so if based as minister resident in Brussels, as he could replace lead ministers at meetings in Brussels they cannot attend.[88] Despite the decentralization of functions to local and regional authorities, the central administration—notably the Interior Ministry—has remained largely unaffected.[89] Yet all three developments (to the first two of which we shall return in Chapter 5) have accentuated the incapacity of individual ministries to deal with their consequences, resulting in coordination overload upon the interministerial and *cabinet* mechanisms. While there has been an increase in the National Assembly and Senate EU committee intervention in decision-making, French governments have jealously protected themselves from further complications to complex coordination processes.[90]

[87] Picq Report, and interview. See also ENA, *Le Travail Gouvernemental*, i, pp. 128–31.

[88] Ibid., i, p. 125; cf. p. 118, and ii, pp. 764–5, 769.

[89] Ibid., pp. 119, 126. For good examples of the failure to overcome coordination problems, see the comments on urban policy (pp. 120–1) and maritime policy (pp. 161–2).

[90] See J. Hayward, 'France and the United Kingdom: The Dilemmas of Integration and National Democracy', in J. Anderson (ed.), *Regional Integration and Democracy: Expanding on the European Experience* (Boulder, Colorado: Rowman and Littlefield, 1999), pp. 156–60.

The desire to learn from experience has taken the form of dispersed efforts at the evaluation of complex public policies. An attempt in 1990 to coordinate them was made under the aegis of an Interministerial Evaluation Committee chaired by the Prime Minister and serviced by the Planning Commissariat. However, evaluation has remained a marginal, piecemeal, and experimental venture, with limited impact on government activity. The few examples are confined to a single ministry, for example, the Evaluation and Prospective Division of the Education Ministry, established in 1987, whose estimates of the increase in the number of pupils and inadequate number of secondary school teachers rapidly led to substantial budget increases in successive years. Exceptionally, Prime Minister Rocard's 1988 creation of Minimum Income for First Time Employment provided for an evaluation report to be presented to the government and parliament. When this 800-page report was submitted in 1992 it led to significant changes of both procedure and substance.[91]

The predictable reason for the ineffectiveness of the evaluation initiative has been that although the Budget Division has frequently made proposals, the spending ministries have resisted, anticipating that these were motivated by the intention to cut their budgets. Neither the spending ministers concerned, the Prime Minister, nor their *cabinets* have provided the impetus which alone would overcome this cause of paralysis. As a result, budget allocation continues to be done quickly and bilaterally each year, without sufficient concern with how the spending ministry's estimates fit into the government's overall programme.[92] A former Chairman of the Evaluation Scientific Council, Professor Jean Leca reassuringly claimed that 'to evaluate is not to accuse', but one of his listeners replied that evaluation led to rewards or punishments,[93] which might not be only financial ones. If this inhibits sectoral, *ad hoc* activity, how much more does it deter ambitious medium-term, cross-sectoral planning.

Ironically, the resistance from the spending ministries was supported by parliament, whose capacity for financial control would have been increased by evaluation. Finance Minister Arthuis's proposal of a Public Expenditure Evaluation Office on the model of the US Congress Budget Office was rejected by the parliamentary Finance Committees, jealous of their ineffective prerogatives.[94] The de facto abandonment of quinquennial planning has meant that, apart from specific sectoral exceptions such as military expenditure, the general prospective coordination of public policy has proved to be beyond reach.

Having identified the normative, political, and administrative constraints upon government attempts at the central coordination of public policy, it remains to consider how the core executive actors seek to master these constraints and assess the comparative success with which they have done so since 1981. We shall do so by examining successively horizontal coordination by the central executives and vertical coordination between the spending ministries.

---

[91] 'L'Etat de l'evaluation des politiques publiques', in ENA, *Le Travail Gouvernemental*, i, pp. 339–40; cf. pp. 325–6, 330–7.   [92] Ibid., pp. 350–3.

[93] 'La Réforme de l'Etat', *Les Cahiers de l'ENA*, 3 (March 1998), p. 49; cf. p. 69.

[94] G. Ottenheimer, *Le Fiasco* (Paris, A. Michel, 1996), pp. 114–16.

3

Hierarchical and Horizontal Coordination: The Central Actors

Having considered the institutional mechanisms and procedures that exist to facilitate the achievement of cohesion in a vast state domain with an innate propensity to proliferate, we now turn to the central actors on whose shoulders fall the main burden of overall coordination. In many political systems, the Cabinet—where all the senior ministers meet each week—exercises more than a formal coordinating oversight of government policies. As we shall see, this is not the case in France. There are three clusters of actors who attempt comprehensive coordination, acting severally or together: the President and his staff at the Elysée, the Prime Minister and his staff at Matignon, and the Finance Minister and his staff at Bercy. While the Finance Minister has the responsibility for achieving the coordination of ministerial budgetary expenditure and the Prime Minister for coordinating the everyday work of government, it is the President of the Republic who—except in periods of cohabitation—makes the final decision when he chooses to do so. Although formally the President is the hierarchical superior of the Prime Minister, who in turn is the head of the government of which the Finance Minister may be the most powerful member, in practice their relative positions are much more complicated.

The pivotal normative principle regulating the coordination of French core executive action is a profoundly ambiguous one: arbitration. In the 1958 Constitution de Gaulle sought to ensure that his successors would live up to his elevated conception of the presidential function. Article 5 asserts that the President 'ensures, through his arbitration, the regular working of the public authorities as well as the continuity of the State'. In practice, a great deal of arbitration is done by the Prime Minister or in his name by the director of his *cabinet* or even by a *cabinet* member. However, outside periods of cohabitation it is possible for the President to arbitrate *ad hoc* over an extensive range of matters. So what does this crucial term mean?

When the Fifth Republic's Constitution was being drawn up, there was a deliberate obfuscation of which of the two main senses of this normative principle was the operative one. De Gaulle's meta-constitutional view that the President's judgement of what the circumstances required should always take precedence over legalistic constraints pointed to arbitration meaning the ultimate, monocratic taking of controversial political decisions. Those imbued with the spirit of parliamentary and constitutional restraints upon executive power conceived of the arbiter as a politically neutral and impartial referee who ensured that the rules were respected. If the latter view prevailed, the President need not be politically accountable, at the risk of weakening him in the fashion of the Third and Fourth Republics. However, while de Gaulle insisted that the President should not be accountable to parliament (as was the Prime Minister) he and his successors have adopted the broad, discretionary interpretation of the term arbitration. As we shall see, this has imparted a great adaptability to the working of the Fifth Republic's institutions in matters of core executive coordination. However, such flexibility has been achieved at the expense of the predictability that unequivocal rules provide.

Chairmanship of the Cabinet is the formal manifestation to the President's role as arbiter (although during cohabitation he retreats to a more neutral role) but it is in the preparatory interministerial meetings that the essential work of resolving conflicts occurs. Most of these are held at Matignon but a limited number are chaired by the President at the Elysée (*conseils restreints*). These were infrequent under de Gaulle from 1960 but increased under his successors to about fifty a year until 1983, when, even before cohabitation in 1986–88 made them infrequent, Mitterrand's preference for informal bilateral meetings with ministers led to their decline, with the exception of Defence Council meetings.

Excessive reliance upon 'arbitration' by the President and Prime Minister has been identified as a peculiarity of French core executive government,[1] rather than leaving ministers and officials to resolve most of their differences in interdepartmental meetings under the leadership of the lead ministry. The result of such concentration of power is to allow the staffs of the dyarchs at the summit of the French state to engage in a proliferating interventionism. What began as the right of appeal to the Prime Minister (or much more infrequently the President), in the case of budgetary disputes between spending ministers and the Finance Minister, has spread to almost all spheres of government activity, so that the Prime Minister and his staff are estimated to make 2,000 to 3,000 'arbitrations' annually, often improvised at short notice.[2] While this way of resolving conflicts may suffice for the bulk of more or less routine matters, the President's power as ultimate arbiter comes into its own in crisis situations. Since the President is not responsible to parliament, he can continue in office, easing some problems of coordination and exacerbating others in his dealings with the Prime Minister. It is a striking demonstration of the fact—with or without cohabitation—that the President only has circumscribed, not uninhibited power, and has to manoeuvre to achieve his objectives.[3]

---

[1] Chagnollaud and Quermonne, pp. 311, 637. More generally on arbitration, see Jack Hayward (ed.), *De Gaulle to Mitterrand. Presidential Power in France* (London, Hurst, 1993), pp. 46–9.

[2] ENA, *Le Travail Gouvernemental*, ii, p. 607. Matters for arbitration go upward from *cabinet* member to the *directeur de cabinet* and only the most important matters go to the Prime Minister personally (Fournier, p. 211).

[3] P. Joxe, *A propos de la France. Itinéraires I. Entretiens avec Michel Sarrazin* (Paris, Flammarion, 1998), pp. 195–6.

COURT POLITICS: THE PRESIDENT OF THE REPUBLIC AND HIS STAFF

Hubert Védrine, future Foreign Affairs Minister in the Jospin Government, had a privileged observation post at the inner court of President Mitterrand throughout his fourteen-year presidency, notably as Secretary General of the Presidency from 1991 to 1995. He recollects that there was not one court but several, corresponding to the plurality of inner and outer circles of Mitterrand's entourage. This was deliberate, the President refusing to become exclusively dependent on a very few confidants in the way that his successor, Chirac, has done. These court circles formed a diffuse 'nebula, more external than internal to the Elysée, of groups, circles, networks, created and activated separately by the President in the evening or at the weekend to preserve the variety of his sources of information, his contacts and his freedom of action, or simply to amuse himself'.[4]

Védrine acknowledged that while decisions were not mainly, still less only, taken within this inner circle, an influential core executive existed. The members of this '*governing group*, as a result of mulling over the same information and considering the same scenarios, meeting at all hours of the day and night . . . end up by acquiring reflexes and a very special common culture'.[5] Their response to events is the result of 'a series of very rapid interactions between the members of this group, whose relative influence is in constant flux', which, mediated by spokesmen and press spin doctors, mutually adjusted by the ministers concerned, is ultimately settled by the President.[6] Due to the importance of public opinion, the core executives seek to detect the short- to medium-term inclinations of the electorate as measured by the pollsters. Elite journalists are not so much an external countervailing power as associates deriving information, prestige, and legitimation from each other.[7] Such is the court life of the French core executive, with its combination of divisive personal intrigue and discretionary favouritism with unifying groupthink that risks eliminating non-conformist views from discussion. Mitterrand exploited to the full the scope for exciting hopes, disarming discontents, and flattering vanities, making the distribution of favours and decorations conditional and unpredictable so that the assertion of his arbitrary personal power promoted fidelity.[8] When one considers that some 500 senior posts were at the discretion of the government in the early 1980s—about 200 in the central administration, 150 ambassadors, 120 prefects, and 28 rectors—the scope for presidential patronage extended well beyond his personal entourage.[9]

[4] H. Védrine, p. 68. On 'Presidential Court Politics', see ch. 8 of Hayward, *De Gaulle to Mitterrand*. On this type of polity, see E. Finer, *The History of Government From the Earliest Times* (Oxford, OUP, 1997), i, pp. 38–43.   [5] Védrine, p. 53.

[6] Ibid., p. 54.   [7] Ibid., pp. 60–6.

[8] Ibid., pp. 69–70. Mitterrand consulted Michel Charasse on all proposed nominations (Charasse, pp. 102–3, 109–12, 275).

[9] On prefectoral appointments see Gilles Ménage, *L'Oeil du Pouvoir. Les affaires de l'Etat, 1981–86* (Paris, Fayard, 1999), pp. 42–6, 68.

Mitterrand was at the centre of a complex web of face-to-face contacts and con-versations supplemented by extensive and rapid reading of memoranda from his staff and from ministers (usually sent with a copy to the Prime Minister). Michel Charasse and Jack Lang inundated him with one- or two-page memos. He liked to reach his own opinion after the confrontation of alternative oral and written views, as well as from his reading of the press. Mitterrand was determined to control the beginning and end of all initiatives as far as this was humanly possible.[10] The mass of Elysée mail—2.35 million letters in the first ten years of Mitterrand's presidency or 1,000 on average per working day—keep a staff of ninety fully employed, a third of them responding with the help of a hundred standard replies. Such feedback sup-plements opinion poll information about the state of public opinion and reflects the mass public misperception that the President can resolve all problems and right all wrongs.[11]

While the work of the President's staff, headed by the Secretary General of the Presidency (SGP), is modelled on that of the Secretary General of Government (SGG), it is much more concerned with providing informal political impetus and partisan guidance and less with formal administrative coordination and cohesion. His staff are personal to the President and do not survive in the way that the SGG does despite the change of President. The Elysée staff are probably the best and most rapidly informed people in France. They often receive copies of the memoranda prepared by the staff of each minister.[12] However, they operated bilaterally with the President, not as a team, reflecting Mitterrand's rejection of committee politics. (Védrine quotes the barbed comment of Mitterrand's first *directeur de cabinet* in 1981, André Rousselet: 'Gatherings of more than two people will be dispersed'.[13]) Mitterrand's suspicion of technocrats meant that initially he chose politically reliable partisans. Half of his official collaborators in October 1984 were directly associated with him before his 1981 election, the others being recommended by people he trusted, fifteen out of thirty-seven being Socialist Party (PS) members.[14] Thus, his first SGP was a PS 'trusty', Pierre Bérégovoy, exceptionally a non-*énarque*. He and his successors have all become ministers.

Mitterrand's manner of working made coordination difficult as, apart from him, only the SGP and his deputy had an overall view of Elysée activity. They did so because they commanded the gateway to the President, both in the memoranda he received, and in his contacts with other members of the Elysée staff and with out-siders. The SGP sees the President several times daily and is in frequent telephone

[10] M. Schifres and M. Sarrazin, *L'Elysée de Mitterrand. Secrets de la Maison du Prince* (A. Moreau, 1985), pp. 109–24, 199–200, 217–18. See also Favier and Martin-Roland, i, pp. 543–5. On the preparation of Mitterrand's important speech in Bonn in January 1983 on the use of French nuclear weapons in defence of Germany, involving four collaborators and two ministers (defence and foreign affairs) see Attali, *Verbatim*, i, pp. 582–4.

[11] Schifres and Sarrazin, pp. 244–50. See also the informative article by E. Dupin, 'M. le Président, je vous fais une lettre', *Libération* (12 March 1991), pp. 10–11.

[12] Schifres and Sarrazin, p. 163; cf. 161.   [13] Védrine, p. 33; cf. 30–1.

[14] Schifres and Sarrazin, pp. 141–3.

contact with him. Ministers, parliamentarians, journalists, businessmen, and trade unionists telephone or visit him to learn the President's views at second hand. Whilst most specialist staff send concise and precise memos through the deputy SGP, the diplomatic unit, military unit, press service, and presidential spokesmen send their memos through the SGP, who adds his comment before passing them on to the President. The speed with which these memos circulate is in marked contrast with the customary bureaucratic sluggishness of line administration. The SGP works 10 to 12 hours a day and 60 to 70 hours a week to keep the President informed, preparing decision-making by him and seeing that his decisions are carried out.[15]

Védrine describes Bérégovoy as having been an ideal SGP, combining the qualities of 'speed, clarity, negotiation skills, conciseness, coolness, authority and loyalty'.[16] His replacement in 1982 was achieved by Prime Minister Mauroy, who resented his influence over the President. Mitterrand's first inclination was to appoint Jacques Attali as SGP but his reputation as a disorganized ideas man, incapable of team work, led most of the President's staff to gang up against him, leading to the appointment of the more emollient Jean-Louis Bianco.[17] An unflattering portrait is offered by a journalist of Chirac's first SGP, Dominique de Villepin, who is described as 'the most powerful unknown in France'.[18] His experience as a diplomat and as *directeur de cabinet* with Chirac's Prime Minister, Juppé, before going to the Elysée facilitated coordination with Matignon from 1995 to 1997. Dealing directly with ministers, his concern to monopolize Chirac's ear—'I am the President's entourage'—and to centralize power in his own hands was pushed to extremes.[19] He held a short *cabinet* 'synthesis meeting' each morning (except Wednesdays) at which all were forced to stand. He kept out Chirac's Paris Town Hall team, importing his Quai d'Orsay colleagues, at the risk of entrusting to them domestic affairs that were largely foreign to their professional experience.[20] His main rival on Chirac's Elysée staff was Jacques Pilhan, who had previously been Mitterrand's communications and image-making specialist. Pilhan saw the President every Monday and enjoyed the powerful support of Chirac's daughter Claude.[21] Chirac met the seven members of his inner circle on Sunday afternoons. They included Villepin and Pilhan, as well as the Prime Minister and his *directeur de cabinet*, Gourdault-Montagne. Chirac attached more importance to loyalty and courage than to political skill in his choice of staff.[22] After the

---

[15] Ibid., pp. 132–3; Védrine, pp. 38–41.

[16] Ibid., p. 32. Attali reports Mitterrand as saying to him on 30 June 1982: 'The government should govern and the Elysée should take a back seat. Bérégovoy is becoming bored because I am increasingly giving Mauroy a free hand'. (*Verbatim i*, p. 402).

[17] Favier and Martin-Roland, i, pp. 432–3; cf. 510. Attali complained that 'Bérégovoy showed me nothing. My influence increased after his departure' as SGP (interview quoted, ibid., p. 433 note). See also Attali, i, pp. 309, 403.

[18] A. Fulda, *Un Président très entouré* (Paris, Grasset, 1997), p. 20. See also N. Domenach and M. Szafran, *Le Roman d'un Président* (Paris, Plon, 1997), pp. 185–92.

[19] Quoted Fulda, p. 27; cf. 26. Juppé frequently being absent as Foreign Minister, Villepin made himself indispensable, answering Chirac's incessant telephone calls and using his office as the 'clandestine headquarters' of Chirac's presidential campaign in 1994–95 (ibid., pp. 28–35).

[20] Ibid., pp. 40, 43–4 and interview.   [21] Ibid., pp. 21, 70–82, 88–92.

[22] G. Ottenheimer, *Le Fiasco*, p. 76; cf. 62, 240.

defeat of the Juppé Government in 1997, following the disastrous decision to dissolve the Assembly, Villepin became the virtually exclusive point of contact with Prime Minister Jospin's *directeur de cabinet*, Olivier Schrameck, in the institutional management of the third cohabitation. Chirac had frequently, if insufficiently, to restrain the combative proclivities of Villepin, the retention of whom showed poor judgement.

During the Mitterrand presidency, the only occasion on which all Mitterrand's staff met was on Wednesday morning. As the SGP was attending the Cabinet meeting, it was his deputy who chaired this collective opportunity to hear about the Cabinet business, exchange information, and coordinate their activities. The SGP handled foreign affairs, while domestic policy—especially economic and social policy—was the prime responsibility of the deputy SGP. They met every morning to coordinate their activities but the holders of these positions often tended to be at loggerheads. The preparation of memos on nominations, also a concern of the SGG, required frequent meetings with him.

Jacques Attali and Michel Charasse exercised less institutionalized functions. Attali had at first headed a forecasting unit but his intellectual agility allowed him a role as a quickfire source of unconventional ideas, even if most of them were impractical or worse. Mitterrand also used him, with the title of 'special adviser', as an international summit sherpa and in the preparation of EU meetings. He was the President's personal emissary to foreign leaders, attending Mitterrand's meetings with them, as well as the Cabinet, post-Cabinet lunches, and Tuesday breakfasts with the PS leaders. A workaholic, Attali ranged widely. He saw memos to the President, prompted others, met large numbers of people, was never short of a suggestion.[23] Michel Charasse—the only member of Mitterrand's staff to have a flat in the Elysée for fourteen years—was used for advice on a variety of matters (especially constitutional ones) even after he became Budget Minister in 1988. He took the temperature of the socialist Assembly and Senate parliamentary groups and conveyed his assessment frequently to Mitterrand. His total discretion, devotion, and availability made him an invaluable troubleshooter.[24]

De Gaulle is reported as having said, 'The Elysée SG deals with France while the *cabinet* deals with the French'. The *directeur de cabinet* and *chef de cabinet* particularly look after the President's diary, his journeys, his speeches, the allocation of secret service funds, nominations, and links with the PS. Jean-Claude Colliard and Jean Glavany respectively held these offices for lengthy periods under Mitterrand. Colliard later became a member of the Constitutional Council (CC) and Glavany an Assembly deputy and Minister of Agriculture. Colliard was also involved in links with the prosecuting section of the judiciary. As we shall see, Colliard's successor, Gilles Ménage (a specialist in police matters from the prefectoral corps), dealt less with media matters than he had done and was involved in a disastrous

---

[23] Schifres and Sarrazin, pp. 128, 155–9; cf. Védrine, pp. 33–4 and interview. Attali selectively recorded much of what he witnessed at the Elysée from 1981 to 1991 in the volumes of his *Verbatim* which are informative if not always very reliable.   [24] Charasse, pp. 15, 18–19, 27–8, 119–24.

venture into the anti-terrorist unit, arising from his tendency to use the *cabinet* for covert operations that had little to do with core executive coordination. During the last two years of his failing health, Mitterrand leaned even more heavily on his personal staff to keep up appearances at a time when cohabitation had in any case deprived him of much of his power.

The functions of the other members of the presidential staff are divided between those who 'oversee' particular ministries and those with more transversal responsibilities. They have four main tasks. First, they keep a vigilant check on the activities of the ministries and on the reliability of their proposals for approval by the President, to whom they have to present succinct and firm recommendations. Memos from and to the ministries have to transit through the SGP and his deputy. Second, they exercise continuous pressure on the ministries to carry out presidential policy, acting in his name. Third, they evaluate the political implications and repercussions of the policies pursued. Fourth, they remain in touch with their opposite numbers at Matignon, with whom their potential and often actual rivalry can complicate rather than facilitate interministerial coordination. Appointments to senior posts are frequent sources of friction, with the *cabinets* of President, Prime Minister, and the relevant ministry each having their own candidates. The SGG helps to iron out these problems, notably in periods of cohabitation.

The President's staff input is greatest in the informal, wide-ranging ministerial 'seminars' which are held to discuss policy in a less day-to-day, responsive fashion, a function which passes to the Matignon staff in periods of cohabitation. Much of their routine activity, which regularly includes briefing the President on matters to be considered at Cabinet, involves visiting 'their' ministries, receiving visitors, and assessing the first-hand information collected, which is often unreliable. They can be contacted all day and every day through the confidential interministerial telephone system by the President, Prime Minister, leading ministers, and the SGP.[25] They receive no salary as presidential staff, which encourages the appointment of civil servants on detachment; otherwise they may be placed fictitiously on the payroll of a public enterprise, of which there are fewer as their privatization has proceeded.

COHABITENSION BETWEEN THE PRESIDENT AND PRIME MINISTER

The uneasy relationship between the dyarchs at the summit of French government has been graphically described as 'a submerged and tense tug-of-war between the two protagonists (and their respective supporters), with each needing yet resenting the other. Political circumstances combine with ideological and policy dissensions, as well as with personal ambitions and calculations, to make a blurred and shifting

[25] Védrine, pp. 37–9, 52–3. See A. de Romanet, *Le fonctionnement de l'institution présidentielle: la communication et les méthodes de travail à l'Elysée durant la Première année du septennant de M. Mitterrand* (Mémoire IEP de Paris, n.d.), pp. 32–54. More generally, see Anne Stevens, 'The President and his Staff', in Hayward (ed.), *De Gaulle to Mitterrand*, ch. 3 passim.

situation inevitably unstable'.[26] Before we consider some examples of this duo in action, to illustrate this general characterization it may be useful to indicate that whereas in the early years of the Fifth Republic Elysée seemed to overshadow Matignon, it has become increasingly clear that—especially in matters of core executive coordination—it is the Prime Minister and his staff who play the pivotal role, whether or not there is cohabitation. What analytic pathways can be cut through the forest of particular cases?

Guy Carcassonne has reversed the emphasis usually placed on the misleading notion of an exclusive presidential policy sector, consisting of foreign, defence, and post-colonial affairs, and the mass of mundane domestic political concerns of the Prime Minister and other ministers. He has argued that the Prime Minister has his own sphere of predominance, consisting principally of budgetary decisions and relations with parliament, where he has primacy although not exclusivity. Even in international affairs, the Prime Minister deals with foreign trade policy, notably the arms trade, while in EU policy the President deals principally with the exposed part of the iceberg, notably at summit meetings, rather than the mass of day-to-day matters whose importance is often underrated. Defence expenditure, controlled by Matignon, is a decisive constraint on presidential policy, which becomes especially evident in periods of cohabitation. As the Prime Minister, unlike the President, is accountable to the National Assembly and speaks there as well as in meetings of the parliamentary groups of the majority, he steers legislation with the assistance of the Minister for Relations with Parliament. While it is rather artificial to separate off what belongs to the President and to the Prime Minister, Carcassonne emphasizes (at the cost of exaggeration) that while 'the President always needs the Prime Minister, the opposite is not necessarily true'.[27]

Carcassonne recognizes that the dyarchs generally share power but he distinguishes three levels of cooperation, with the balance shifting increasingly from the Prime Minister to the President. First, on most matters, the President is content with summaries, although his staff receive detailed information. Second, on politically important or controversial issues, the President is fully informed and discusses the matter with the Prime Minister; they jointly weigh up the pros and cons before making a decision. Third, there are the matters to which the President personally attaches importance, whatever their intrinsic significance, such as Mitterrand's architectural *grands projets*, on which the Prime Minister usually deferred to him.[28] When the President gives the Prime Minister an instruction, it is very often made public but

---

[26] V. Wright, 'The President and Prime Minister: Subordination, Conflict, Symbiosis or Reciprocal Parasitism', in Hayward (ed.), *De Gaulle to Mitterrand*, p. 102 and ch. 4 passim. The term 'cohabitension' comes from ibid., p. 116.
[27] G. Carcassonne, 'Les rapports du président français et du premier ministre', *Revue Française d'Administration Publique*, 83 (July–September 1997), p. 399; cf. 406–9. This is a special issue on 'Administrer le Sommet de l'Exécutif'. See also G. Carcassonne, 'Le Premier Ministre et le domaine dit réservé', *Pouvoirs*, 83 (November 1997), pp. 65–74. Carcassonne was a member of Prime Minister Rocard's *cabinet* from 1988 to 1991.   [28] Carcassonne, 'Les rapports', pp. 400–1.

when he vetoes the Prime Minister's proposals, it is usually in private.[29] Since the President needs the Prime Minister to ensure that his decisions are implemented, the latter can block those with which he disagrees, at the risk of being sacked if he goes too far or does so too conspicuously.

The President and Prime Minister meet at least once a week in the presence of the SGP and the SGG, to settle finally any matters likely to come up at Cabinet. In periods of non-cohabitation, they usually meet tête-à-tête on Fridays for a more political discussion, although official ceremonies frequently provide the opportunity for confidential exchanges. Coordination may suffer as a result as their staffs usually only learn what has transpired if they fail to act on what has been informally decided. They also speak on the telephone (Chirac being much more addicted to this form of communication than Mitterrand) but as political scientists cannot tap the *interministériel*, there is nothing more to add on this score. The Prime Minister uses the SGG to submit Cabinet agenda proposals for presidential approval and modification each Monday but the most important contacts are between the SGP and the Prime Minister's *directeur de cabinet*, which usually takes place at Matignon.[30]

In a decisive confrontation, Mitterrand turned down the Prime Minister's advocacy of an austerity economic policy on taking office. Whereas Mauroy, on the advice of the Governor of the Bank of France and his *directeur de cabinet*, sought to stem the run on the franc, Mitterrand put political considerations first because he did not want to disappoint the voters too quickly.[31] A year later, in June 1982, the President sent a letter to Mauroy, largely drafted by SGP Bérégovoy, intended to prevent stabilization policy from inhibiting an expansionist public works investment programme.[32] This was the prelude to the 1982–83 struggle between Prime Minister Mauroy and Finance Minister Delors, supported by some of Mitterrand's own Elysée staff, to keep France within the European Monetary System (EMS), against those who advised the President that France should leave the EMS to retain its freedom of economic action by letting the franc float, thereby avoiding a third devaluation of the franc. It is worth dwelling on this episode, not merely because of its intrinsic importance but because it illustrates both the President's role as arbiter and the influences under which he exercises his power.

Both President Mitterrand and Prime Minister Mauroy were neither economically literate nor interested particularly in economic issues, so they were especially dependent on advice. Mauroy relied mainly on his own *cabinet*, while Mitterrand turned to a number of outsiders, whom Mauroy dubbed the *visiteurs du soir*. Nevertheless, the President read more than 700 memoranda on economic and monetary issues in the crucial period of March 1982–83—an average of fifteen each week. He relied on political instinct rather than economic reasoning, attaching most importance to the

[29] Ibid., p. 401. For an example of Mitterrand protesting in writing at not being consulted over legislation to reimburse abortion through social security, see Attali, *Verbatim*, i, pp. 274–5.

[30] Carcassonne, 'Les rapports', pp. 402–3. In February 2001, Chirac publicly postponed for a week Cabinet discussion of proposed Corsica reforms which was not challenged by the Jospin Government.

[31] Interview and Attali, *Verbatim*, ii, p. 581 quoting Mitterrand's retrospective confession of error in 1988.   [32] The letter is extensively quoted in Attali, *Verbatim*, i, pp. 387–8.

timing and language in which the decisions were taken and conveyed, although it was First Secretary Jospin who deliberately misdescribed the 1983 change of economic direction as a 'parenthesis'.[33]

From late August 1982, Mitterrand regularly met a group championing an alternative economic policy to the one favoured by his Prime Minister and Finance Minister. Bérégovoy (who had moved from SGP to Minister of Social Affairs at the end of June 1982) was a key figure, with Budget Minister Fabius and Jean Riboud, personal friend of the President and chairman of the prestigious merchant bank and industrial holding company Schlumberger, in the protectionist coalition. Attali ceased to be invited once it became clear that he sided with Mauroy and Delors, and by the beginning of October 1982, an anti-*visiteurs* group of Attali, Deputy SGP Christian Sautter, and two advisers on Mitterrand's staff was meeting daily at the Elysée and exchanging memos hostile to floating the franc outside the EMS, the rival policy—which they knew tempted Mitterrand.[34]

Mitterrand continued to hesitate between the alternative economic policies throughout the winter of 1982–83, torn between his wish to promote European integration and to expand the French economy. The contradictory economic advice he was receiving reinforced his predilection to take his decision on whether to float or devalue the franc on political grounds. By March 1983, Mitterrand was faced with a choice between agreeing with the German government on a devaluation as advocated by Delors, Mauroy, and most of his Elysée economic experts and a protectionist floating exchange-rate policy. He would have preferred to keep his Prime Minister if he was willing to carry out the alternative economic policy but Mauroy refused and offered his resignation. Finance Minister Delors also refused to replace Mauroy on such terms. The decisive moment came when Budget Minister Fabius consulted Michel Camdessus, director of the Treasury, who told him that French foreign exchange reserves would only last a fortnight if the franc was floated. This information led Fabius to change sides. Mitterrand now accepted devaluation combined with a face-saving mark revaluation, but wanted to replace Mauroy with Delors. However, the latter insisted that he combined the offices of Prime Minister and Finance Minister. Wanting Fabius as Finance Minister to counterbalance Delors, Mitterrand categorically refused, saying to Attali: 'I will not place myself in the hands of a single person. I shall keep Mauroy . . .'[35] The disabused verdict to Attali of the defeated Riboud was: 'An external adviser is powerless against a less competent person who is there every day.'[36] In the context of court politics, proximity to the prince is a potent source of influence but the prolonged struggle between and among insiders and outsiders suggests that the outcome, taken *in extremis*, was not a foregone conclusion.

---

[33] Favier and Martin-Roland, i, pp. 488–9; cf. 227, 412, 415–16, 418–21, 426–9, 437–43, 447, 461–2, 466–89, 502.

[34] Ibid., pp. 304, 321–2, 383, 452–3, 458, 469–72, 487–9, 503–4, 527, 532–3, 545–6, 552–6, 580.

[35] Ibid., p. 626; cf. 604–5, 609–12, 616–28. On Delors's repeated suggestions that Mauroy should be replaced as Prime Minister because of his lack of financial grip on the government, ibid., pp. 289, 332–8, 502, 585. On Fabius changing sides, see Fabius, pp. 74–5.   [36] Attali, *Verbatim*, i, p. 719.

When Fabius replaced Mauroy as Prime Minister in 1984, his relationship with Mitterrand was quite different from the start and closer to the letter of the Constitution. While Mauroy had little choice over his ministers, their selection was now joint. The Government's programme was also decided between them. To emphasize the Prime Minister's autonomy (because Fabius had earlier been Mitterrand's *directeur de cabinet*) Elysée staff were informed that all ministerial interventions should be referred to the Prime Minister. Fabius knew intuitively what Mitterrand would think on most issues, so it was less often necessary to coordinate than it had been in the case of Mauroy, who had relied upon conducting an 'uninterrupted conversation' with the President.[37] Fabius received advance approval by Mitterrand for the TV sound-bite in which he declared: 'Lui c'est lui, moi c'est moi'.[38] However, their relationship was not all plain sailing. For example, Fabius was forced to abandon budgetary cuts in the President's pet projects, such as the Opéra-Bastille and the Grande Arche de la Défense in 1984. Fabius seriously upset the President in 1985 by publicly dissociating himself in the National Assembly from the invitation to the Polish Prime Minister General Jaruzelski, who had imposed martial law. He was irritated at not having been consulted, the matter having instead been discussed with Foreign Minister Dumas. Even more serious was the 'state crime' perpetrated against the *Rainbow Warrior*, discussed in Chapter 4. Although Mitterrand left more decisions to Fabius, with some consequent change of the relative influence of the staffs of President and Prime Minister, when it came to deciding who should lead the PS campaign in the Assembly elections of 1986, Mitterrand decided against Fabius and in favour of Party Secretary Jospin who, for a period in 1985, were not on speaking terms.[39]

The first cohabitation between President Mitterrand and Prime Minister Chirac began with grim turf warfare to which the protagonists and their staffs adjusted. At the outset, Chirac sought in vain to secure Mitterrand's agreement to a formal contract laying down the rules of the cohabitation game and Balladur subsequently regretted that this attempt to tie the President's hands had not been made a precondition of taking office.[40] The first struggle was over the foreign and defence ministerial appointments, quickly followed by another over the government's right to issue ordinances, notably on privatisation, Mitterrand successfully calling Chirac's bluff over his threat of resignation. Mitterrand reassured Kissinger with the thought: 'They control everything except what is essential.'[41] What was 'essential' is revealed by his comment: 'The Prime Minister should understand that he has charge of the

---

[37] Favier and Martin-Roland, i, pp. 534–5, quoting an interview with Mauroy.

[38] Fabius, pp. 108; cf. 104–7, Favier and Martin-Roland, ii, pp. 216–18, and Schifres and Sarrazin, p. 164.

[39] Favier and Martin-Roland, ii, pp. 400–5, 444–56; Attali, *Verbatim*, i, Part II, pp. 1036–9, 1045, 1084, 1251, 1253, 1281, 1344, 1348–9, 1359, 1364, 1367. See also Fabius, pp. 139–41.

[40] Favier and Martin-Roland, ii, p. 581, quoting 1989 interviews with Mitterrand and Balladur. The authors comment on their conflictual coexistence: 'For two years, they spied, suspected and cursed each other ... owing to lack of rules and experience delimiting their respective territories' (ibid., p. 591).

[41] Attali, *Verbatim*, ii, p. 38; cf. 10–11, 13–25, 101–2, 152–7, 161–2. On the battle over the privatization ordinance, ibid., p. 51, 150–7, 166, and Favier and Martin-Roland, ii, pp. 631–43.

railways, I have charge of the armed forces.'[42] The squabble over Chirac's representation at the top table at summit meetings was another 'essential' policy sector in which the President successfully resisted an attempt by the Prime Minister to encroach on his prerogatives.[43] (We shall turn later to the way in which the Ministers of Defence and Foreign Affairs were involved in this tug of war.) Chirac's press officer, Denis Baudouin, blamed Chirac for the mutual aversion and distrust underlying their superficially polite formalities. 'Mitterrand did not forgive Chirac always lying to him and his encroachments on the president's foreign policy functions. I imagine that, knowing him as I do, Chirac always said yes to Mitterrand and did the opposite behind his back.'[44]

In 1988, Mitterrand appointed the presidential aspirant Michel Rocard as Prime Minister. He was in a doubly difficult position, as the head of a minority government and as a leader of a minority PS faction. Rocard failed to rid his government of the Mitterrand old guard, the President imposing many of the ministers on Rocard and refusing his plea to combine his post with that of Education Minister.[45] Rocard's 26 May 1988 circular to ministers on how they should carry out their duties failed to impose his authority because several of them considered that they could appeal over his head to the President. Their difficult coexistence, based upon mutual aversion between Rocard the reformist rationalist and Mitterrand the intuitive improviser, was eased by the good working relationship between SGP Bianco and Rocard's *directeur de cabinet*, Huchon.[46]

It has been observed that whereas the first Prime Minister of a President's team is usually an obvious choice in the wake of the election, the second is always a surprise because of the President's increased discretion. Of no one was this more true than the appointment of Edith Cresson in 1991.[47] Impatient after three years with what he regarded as Rocard's prudent inertia, Mitterrand hesitated between replacing him with Pierre Bérégovoy or Edith Cresson. She was preferred because he attributed to her the capacity to overcome the increasing public disenchantment with the PS. He did so against the advice of the Elysée staff and most of the PS leaders, who feared her abrasive capacity to make enemies. Mitterrand would not agree to her wish to exclude Bérégovoy and Dumas whom she saw as rivals from the government. Far from agreeing to the exclusion of the Finance Minister, he also blocked her wish to split the Finance Ministry, with a separate Ministry of the Economy, Industry, and Foreign Trade, reflecting her 'industrial' suspicions of Finance, whose senior officials damagingly returned the compliment. Instead Bérégovoy's functions were extended to all these activities, with four ministers attached to him in a super-Finance Ministry.[48] This was the prelude to a guerrilla war with Matignon that was prejudicial to intra-governmental coordination.

[42] Attali, *Verbatim*, ii, p. 288.   [43] Ibid., pp. 48, 63, 86, 106.

[44] Favier and Martin-Roland, ii, p. 769; cf. 766–8.

[45] Ibid., iii, p. 19. One of the ministers was his left-wing rival from former PSU days, Jean Poperen, who had nicknamed him 'Rocardestaing' (ibid., p. 41).   [46] Ibid., p. 49; cf. 576–9.

[47] Carcassonne, *La Constitution*, pp. 74–7.   [48] Favier and Martin-Roland, ii, pp. 19–20.

Cresson's isolation and resourcelessness were compounded by an improvised Matignon staff, with a weak *directeur de cabinet* and a trusted 'special adviser', to whom she accorded excessive influence and whose amateurish activism exacerbated her personally disruptive proclivities by frequently modifying her decisions. While some ministers concentrated on damage limitation, others did not bother to attend inter-ministerial committee meetings or left early. Védrine as SGP reported that 'The extent of chaos and violence was terrifying. Ministers and the line directors were exasperated by Matignon. They asked me to pass on their complaints to the President', including fears that their telephones were being tapped. He recalled that he had 'not spent a normal day during the Cresson Government' and that 'the extent of disorganisation had not been appreciated' by the press at the time. 'She detested me' to the point that from the start of 1992 he had almost no direct contact with her, Cresson having in vain sought to have him dismissed.[49] The Prime Minister's credibility was at such a low ebb that her authority could be ignored or challenged with impunity. Outsider assertiveness proved totally ineffective when confronted by the habitual politico-administrative superstructures. Her derisory vengeance was to transfer a major part of the training at the ENA from Paris to Strasbourg, which simply reinforced the conviction that she was an intrusive foreign body that had to be frozen out.

The 1991 preparation of the 1992 budget is an illustration of the general disarray and the particular problems between the Prime Minister and the Finance Minister in the context of keeping public expenditure growth down to the anticipated 3 per cent increase in inflation. While Cresson suspected that her budgetary advisers' first loyalty was to Bérégovoy, the spending ministers were in revolt over the cuts imposed on them in the 'ceiling letter' sent to them on 24 July. Unable to avoid increasing the deficit, they decided to abandon Mitterrand's commitment to a *ni, ni* policy of 'neither privatisation nor nationalisation' but Bérégovoy announced the end of the *ni, ni* formula before the Prime Minister could do so, ensuring that they remained at daggers drawn.[50] Mitterrand and Cresson also bypassed the Finance and Agriculture Ministers in November 1991 to appease farmer demonstrations by increasing expenditure.[51] The impression conveyed was of core executives at loggerheads, improvising piecemeal solutions to contain day-to-day pressures.

Cresson turned out to be an energetic but weak Prime Minister, despite Mitterrand's advice and help, which led a satirical TV programme to nickname her 'To heel', *A-ma-botte*. Budget Minister Charasse said that she 'sometimes gave the impression of governing against the whole world: the ministers, the administration, opinion, press, deputies, trade unions, PS etc. She imagined that she was surrounded by enemies', which she quickly was.[52] She compounded her difficulties with the PS by abandoning weekly meetings with its leaders, contenting herself with seeing First

---

[49] Ibid., p. 117 quoting interviews with Hubert Védrine; cf. 25–6, 116–18.   [50] Ibid., pp. 77–83.
[51] Ibid., pp. 97–100.
[52] Charasse, p. 208; cf. 205–11. More generally, see S. Ollitrault, 'Edith Cresson, the First Woman Prime Minister in France', paper to ECPR Workshop, Warwick, March 1998.

Secretary Mauroy and National Assembly President Fabius instead. Neither her past experience nor her personality had prepared her for the office of Prime Minister. Her worst ministerial battles were with Finance Minister Bérégovoy who succeeded her less than a year after she took office. He too was Prime Minister only briefly before the 1993 election swept the Left from power.

Chirac could not face another cohabitation with Mitterrand, so he supported Edouard Balladur's selection despite warnings that he was helping a future rival for the presidency. Not only did he believe that Balladur would not contest the 1995 presidential election; he expected, *sancta simplicitas*, that they would informally govern together, meanwhile. He should quickly have been disabused because he was not consulted about the formation of the Balladur Government. As we shall see, Balladur—a fellow Pompidolian—had been Chirac's second in command as Finance Minister from 1986 to 1988 but he was now preparing to become President. In comparison with their bitter fratricidal battle in 1994–95, his cohabitation with Mitterrand generally worked smoothly, despite their conflict over the Pasqua Law restricting the right of asylum (discussed in Chapter 8), which led to a constitutional reform. Védrine as SGP handled dealings with Balladur's *directeur de cabinet*, Nicholas Bazire, apart from foreign policy which was conducted with Foreign Minister Alain Juppé, who became Prime Minister following Chirac's victory in 1995. The coincidence of a hyper-interventionist President and Prime Minister with a large and mediocre government meant that from 1995 to 1997, when things went wrong, they shared the discredit.[53]

Chirac and Juppé operated as a diarchy even before the 1995 presidential election, Chirac having promised Juppé that he would be his Prime Minister, jointly with heading the RPR. Determined to avoid the habitual staff warfare, he actively promoted a paranoid bunker mentality by making Dominique de Villepin the SGP and supporting Maurice Gourdault-Montagne as Juppé's *directeur de cabinet*. This pair had been Juppé's head and deputy chief of staff when he was Balladur's Foreign Minister from 1993 to 1995 and it was from the Quai that they successfully organized Chirac's fratricidal anti-Balladur electoral campaign, with Villepin then and subsequently as the senior partner.[54] This double *entente* produced a hyper-centralized summit coordination. President Chirac telephoned Juppé about ten times a day and the Prime Minister consulted him before taking most decisions, so it is not surprising that groupthink prevailed. As Juppé became increasingly unpopular and his own parliamentary majority privately pressed for his resignation, Chirac remained totally committed to him, refusing periodic offers of resignation. Chirac said that he shuddered to think who he would have to call on as his replacement. Instead of the Prime Minister protecting the President, the roles were reversed, Chirac threatening—and eventually carrying out—a dissolution of a restive massively right-wing Assembly,

---

[53] Domenach and Szafran, *Le Roman*, pp. 25–9, 35–6, 246–7, 259–68, 300. See also Bazire, pp. 230–1. Ironically, in 1986 a reluctant Chirac was persuaded by Balladur to become Prime Minister precisely on the ground that it was the best stepping stone to the presidency in 1988, reasoning which also proved false in 1995. See Favier and Martin-Roland, ii, p. 460.   [54] Ottenheimer, p. 61; cf. 70–3.

which Juppé described as suffering from 'mad cow' disease. The disastrous results, leading first to Juppé's resignation and then Chirac's prolonged ordeal by cohabitation, was the consequence of a diarchy which concentrated power so incestuously, introspectively, and exclusively that it had lost touch with political reality. Ironically, when asked why he had not dissolved the Assembly in 1995 Chirac replied in a 14 July 1996 TV interview: 'One must have principles if one wishes to govern properly in a democracy. Dissolution was not provided to suit the President's convenience but to settle a political crisis.'[55] Less than a year later, on 21 April 1997, Chirac dissolved the Assembly in the absence of a political crisis, being forced to appoint as Prime Minister the man he had defeated in the presidential election two years previously.

After the prolonged Chirac–Juppé honeymoon, the Chirac–Jospin years were those of increasing cohabitension. Jospin was suspicious that, despite his superficial conviviality, Chirac was building up his public image as a sympathetic personality by contrast with the Prime Minister's stereotypical French Protestant intransigence. The President played on Jospin's irritation at the criticisms he meted out, hoping to provoke an overreaction. Expecting that they would face each other again in 2002, the sparring persisted as each in turn played to the public gallery, Jospin by his policies and Chirac by the symbolic gestures and demagogic pronouncements of a redoubtable electoral campaigner even if a poor executive. The evidence of Chirac's corrupt practices as Mayor of Paris in financing the Rassemblement Pour le République (RPR) that surfaced in the autumn of 2000 envenomed what was an institutionally confrontational relationship.

COMMITTEE POLITICS: THE PRIME MINISTER AND HIS STAFF

Although many have followed the first Prime Minister of the Fifth Republic, Michel Debré, in describing the President as its institutional 'keystone', Guy Carcassonne has suggested that this metaphor is misleading. While the President is at the hierarchical apex of the state system, he is a spire rather than a keystone[56] because it is the Prime Minister who alone has the capacity to exert control over the executive resources, a control that permits but does not ensure overall policy coordination. This is especially true of the diverse and complex domain of domestic policy. As French diplomatic and military power has dwindled, the presidential predominance in these matters has reduced his influence generally in the conduct of public policy. Although the autonomous role of the Prime Minister is maximized in periods of cohabitation, in terms of sustained and comprehensive steering of government, it is from Matignon that radiate the interministerial networks that articulate and animate its structures

---

[55] Quoted in Victor, p. 15; cf. 16–17. See also Domenach and Szafran's follow-up volume, *Le Miraculé. Le Roman d'un Président*, ii, 2000, pp. 29, 31, 39, 54, 62–73, 77.

[56] Carcassonne, *La Constitution*, p. 119. It was Benjamin Constant who first referred to the head of state as the keystone.

and enable it to carry out its functions. Most of the arbitration to resolve inter-ministerial conflicts should be the work of the Prime Minister and his staff. However, there is only a patchy relationship between what should be and what is.

Although Pierre Mauroy had never held ministerial office before becoming Prime Minister in 1981, President Mitterrand abandoned Giscard d'Estaing's practice of issuing general (as well as specific) public directives setting out the government's programme for the next six months. Having spent over twenty years in Opposition, almost all Mauroy's ministerial colleagues had never served in a government before either. Overambition led the inexperienced ministers to try to do too much too quickly, resulting in disorder. Clashes between the stronger personalities had to be resolved, especially when they were conducted in public. Having had to settle such a dispute over identity check procedures between the Ministers of the Interior and of Justice, Mauroy naïvely published an article, 'Governing Differently', in which he sought to rationalize the open ministerial discussion of differences prior to reaching a collective decision. Regarding this as an invitation to cacophony, Mitterrand was furious at the idea that ministers could engage in public debate. Jospin, PS First Secretary, and Pierre Joxe, leader of the PS Assembly Group, expressed their disagreement with Mauroy's standpoint.[57] Attali reports that by the end of 1982 Mauroy seemed to have lost control of his government. 'A great many ministers no longer obey his orders: either because they refuse to carry them out or because they do not even consult him in advance of their initiatives.'[58] In April 1984, Defence Minister Hernu said to Attali: 'I have long since ceased to telephone Mauroy but do so instead to his *directeur de cabinet*, Michel Delebarre; he is the real Prime Minister.'[59]

Fabius exercised a much firmer grip over his government than Mauroy. 'My prime concern is to be professional, less governmental 'happening', better coordination between ministers and clarification of our message to public opinion.'[60] The number of interministerial meetings was greatly reduced as were conflicts between ministers, who were now almost all Socialists. At 8 a.m. each morning, the Prime Minister and his *directeur de cabinet*, together with the Government Spokesman, the SGP, and a PS representative, spent half an hour concerting the declarations that ministers and PS leaders would be making, to give the impression of a united government. Controversy was to be avoided. Fabius, as we shall see, inaugurated in October 1984 a fifteen-minute TV 'fireside chat' (in the manner which Mendès France had borrowed in 1954 from Franklin Roosevelt) called *Parlons France*, as part of his concern to get through to public opinion at a time when an unpopular PS was facing the prospect of electoral defeat in 1986.[61]

---

[57] Pfister, pp. 193–7, and Attali, *Verbatim*, i, p. 311. See also Fabius, pp. 76–8, and Fournier, p. 275.

[58] Attali, *Verbatim*, i, p. 556. As Rocard's *directeur de cabinet* put it: 'the Prime Minister is the head of a team which should obey him and follow his initiatives' but they do so 'on two conditions. First, the Prime Minister must be intellectually respected by his ministers. Next, the impetus must come from him' (Huchon, p. 121). [59] Attali, *Verbatim*, i, p. 951.

[60] Favier and Martin-Roland, ii, p. 212. [61] Ibid., pp. 214–16.

We have already discussed the key role of *directeurs de cabinet* and their tendency to act as surrogates for their ministers, sometimes attending interministerial meetings in their stead when these are formally to confirm the preparatory work of officials, some of them going on to become ministers themselves. The Prime Minister's *cabinet* director's authority may be undermined by a special adviser, as was the case with Edith Cresson. While *cabinet* members can seldom act without consulting their *directeur de cabinet* and the budget adviser, 'some members of the Prime Minister's *cabinet* manage to elevate themselves into a pseudo-government, just as some *cabinet* members behave as if they themselves possess ministerial authority'.[62] The specialist members of the Prime Minister's staff frequently meet the *cabinet* director of 'their' ministry to exchange information and coordinate their activities. The Prime Minister's *cabinet* ranges from thirty to 100 in size, usually organized into five or so units dealing with the various aspects of its work. As with the presidency, the deputy director coordinates economic and financial affairs.

Monday meetings of all the *directeurs de cabinet*, chaired by that of the Prime Minister, facilitates the transmission and coordination of policy directives. Once they have received initial instructions from the Prime Minister or their minister via the director, the *cabinets* set to work in the interdepartmental meetings of officials which are convened by the SGG. At the end of the 1980s, up to twenty-three such meetings were held daily at Matignon under the chairmanship of a member of the Prime Minister's staff, by the director in the case of important ones. The ministerial *directeurs de cabinet* choose and brief their departmental representatives, usually the staff specialist, accompanied by one or more line division directors, who often resent being in a subordinate position as the staff member speaks on behalf of the minister. On important matters, the *cabinet* director may attend himself. In periods of non-cohabitation, the Elysée sends a usually silent observer. If he intervenes in a sense at variance with the Matignon representative, the matter is postponed for resolution between their superiors. The minutes are taken by an SGG member who communicates the decisions in what is known as a *bleu* because it is on blue paper.[63] To 'blue' a document means to give it the status of a formal decision to be implemented.

Prime Minister Balladur's *directeur de cabinet* from 1993 to 1995, Nicholas Bazire, had worked closely with him from 1988, so much so that their mutual understanding and trust were complete. Bazire was accustomed to say: 'Without bragging, I know instinctively, within a comma, what the "PM" will say on almost any occasion.'[64] Balladur only met his *cabinet* once at the start of his premiership, telling them that he wanted only short and infrequent memos via his *directeur de cabinet*, adding, 'If there are choices to be made, see Nicholas Bazire'.[65] Thereafter, the staff

---

[62] Schrameck, p. 58.

[63] Ibid., pp. 56–64. Robert Lion, Mauroy's first *directeur de cabinet*, writes that 'in autumn 1981 I forbade access to (interdepartmental meetings) by more than two ministerial representatives', a 'revolution' that drastically reduced their size (R. Lion, *L'Etat Passion*, Plon, 1992, p. 48). He described his conception of the *directeur de cabinet*'s role as 'above all steering files and orchestrating the work of government' (p. 11). [64] Brigouleix, p. 48.

[65] Ibid., p. 12, cf. pp. 12–13, 50–1.

only met briefly on Wednesdays to review the Prime Minister's activities in the coming week. Smaller meetings took place between members of the four units concerned with economic affairs, diplomacy, interior and security, and social affairs. A politically inexperienced Bazire mismanaged Balladur's amateurish 1995 presidential campaign in a way that reflected the failings of the *cabinet* he directed: 'obsessional secrecy, even within the *cabinet*, contempt for the press, inadequate practical organisation, an inability to take clearcut, simple, rapid decisions'.[66] The over-centralized neglect of committee politics was to be exacerbated during the centralized and personalized Juppé Governments of 1995 to 1997, with equally fatal consequences.

The two Juppé Governments of 1995–97 were weak, encouraging an overconfident Prime Minister to try to occupy all the front line himself. The President of the National Assembly, his RPR colleague and disappointed rival Philippe Séguin, accurately described the Juppé Government as 'the worst—post for post—of the Fifth Republic'.[67] Chirac had persuaded Juppé to include too many inexperienced women ministers in his first government but in addition there was a bitter early conflict with Finance Minister Madelin whom Chirac had insisted on appointing to this key position because of his early support in the dark days of 1994. Juppé's staff rubbished Madelin as an incompetent liberal ideologue, while he replied: 'I do not confuse social consensus with trade union consensus', which led Juppé to tolerate the privileges of public 'protected sector' employees at the expense of the 'exposed' market sector.[68] Having forced Madelin after three months to resign during budget discussions (replaced by the colourless Arthuis), Juppé decided to increase taxes to fill the larger deficit which had been concealed by the outgoing Balladur Government.[69] This dishonouring of Chirac's electoral commitment was followed by the October 1995 assertion of an European Monetary Union (EMU)-necessitated austerity policy. It showed that Juppé was in the driving seat, because while Chirac happily devoted his attention to international affairs, domestic policy constraints were imposed in the service of an EU policy that was more the Prime Minister's than the President's. However, when Juppé suggested bringing in the 'traitors' Balladur and Sarkozy to strengthen his failing government, Chirac vetoed them, putting personal vindictiveness before the need to reunify a fractured Right.[70]

On taking office, Lionel Jospin sent his ministers a circular setting out the criteria for matters on which he would act as final arbiter between them. He would not be concerned with 'secondary' differences between ministers but would take a hand if there were persisting divergences and in the preparation of important decisions. In practice, his style was to ensure that several ministers would be involved, so that he would be required to take the final decision. He was most frequently involved in settling familiar economic versus social priorities conflicts between his first Finance Minister, Dominique Strauss-Kahn, and Employment and Solidarity Minister,

---

[66] Brigouleix, p. 268; cf. 269–71. Brigouleix was the frustrated press adviser in the Balladur *cabinet*.
[67] Quoted in Domenach and Szafran, *Le Miraculé*, p. 35.   [68] Ottenheimer, p. 218; cf. 213–16.
[69] Domenach and Szafran, *Le Miraculé*, pp. 31–7, 54–62.   [70] Ibid., pp. 76–7.

Martine Aubry, both of whom he saw individually each week. The latter usually came out on top, notably in matters of health and social security contributions and on the reduction of working hours. Having been told to 'stop your childish disputes', they subsequently succeeded more often, for example, on the 1999 employment budget and on business taxation, in ironing out their differences bilaterally.[71]

Other interministerial conflicts were more public, for example, between Interior Minister Jean-Pierre Chevènement and both Environment Minister Dominique Voynet and Justice Minister Elisabeth Guigou. The Interior–Justice conflict was a classic one between the institutionalized forces of order and law but they took an ideological turn as the judiciary became more activist and refused to accept its traditionally more subordinate role. However, Prime Minister Jospin was able to present the image of a relatively harmonious 'plural Left' team, by contrast with the mutual detestation that had characterized the Juppé Government.[72]

THE FINANCE MINISTER AND THE FINANCE MINISTRY

The fact that virtually no aspect of public policy can be conducted without expenditure implications means that the ministers and senior officials of the Finance and Budget Ministries usually play a central role within the core executive through their sustained management of financial coordination. While the President and Prime Minister take major *ad hoc* decisions in line with their electoral programmes, these have most import at the beginning of their term of office. Thus, the decisions not to devalue until compelled to do so, and to reduce working hours to thirty-nine without a corresponding reduction in wages, were personally taken by Mitterrand, despite the strong reservations of his staff. Prime Minister Balladur was personally responsible for launching a major loan in 1993, the resumption of privatisation for which he had been responsible as Finance Minister in 1986–88, and the 'balladurette' encouragement to buy new cars. The fact that Prime Ministers have previously occupied relevant posts—Fabius and Chirac as Budget Ministers, Bérégovoy and Balladur as Finance Ministers—means that they have an understanding of the problems concerned.

Even when the budget is the responsibility of a junior minister or one directly under the authority of the Finance Minister, the person in charge exercises more influence in government than most ministers. Suggestions have been made periodically to attach the Budget Division to the Prime Minister but this threatens an over-concentration of power, although Raymond Barre exceptionally combined the offices of Prime Minister and Finance Minister from 1976 to 1978. Some Prime Ministers in periods of cohabitation have given their Finance Ministers wide powers—the case of Balladur in the Chirac Government from 1986 to 1988[73] and

[71] Reported in *Le Monde*, 2 June 1999, p. 9. On Martine Aubry's resignation in October 2000 preparatory to succeeding Mauroy as Mayor of Lille in 2001, *Le Monde* published a long profile of her by Isabelle Mandraud, 'Martine Aubry, en réserve de la gauche', 19 October 2000, pp. 16–17.

[72] See the comment of Bernadette Chirac (the President's wife) reported in *Le Monde*, 2 June 1999, p. 17.

[73] See Attali, *Verbatim*, ii, pp. 23, 34, 92, 248. Attali reports a senior minister in the Chirac Government complaining to him about the lack of coordination and the difficulty of contacting the

Strauss-Kahn in the Jospin Government from 1997 to 1999. Others have deliberately weakened their Finance Ministers by appointing a personally loyal Budget Minister, as Balladur did with Nicholas Sarkozy (1993–95) and Juppé with Alain Lamassoure (1995–97). This was also done by President Mitterrand in the case of Laurent Fabius in 1981, against the wishes of Delors.

Apart from exceptional cases, such as 1986–88, when Prime Minister Chirac delegated his arbiter powers in budgetary matters to Finance Minister Balladur, the Prime Minister retains an important role in overall budgetary decisions. He signs the 'framework letters' to spending ministers that are the basis for subsequent budget negotiations, after prior discussions with the Finance Minister about the short- and medium-term economic perspectives. Once the final budget allocations are made, the Prime Minister signs the 'ceiling letters' to which the ministries should conform. While in the 1960s the Planning Commissariat was a useful alternative source of economic advice to the Prime Minister, this subsequently ceased to be true, the Finance Ministry's Budget Division and its forecasting and statistical services providing the analyses on which the assessments are made. A strong Finance Minister, as we shall see, can minimize the Prime Minister's arbitral power, as Bérégovoy did during the premierships of Rocard and Cresson. However, can be they allied, as Mauroy and Delors were in 1982–83, when they eventually triumphed over Mitterrand's crucial hesitation between floating and devaluing the franc. The Governor of the Bank of France has been particularly involved when the franc is under threat but, with his increased independence and the move to a European Central Bank (ECB), his relationship with the Finance Ministry's Treasury Division has been drastically modified in his favour.

The overlapping preferences of a plurality of core executive actors mean that there is a built-in problem of securing unified control of economic and monetary policy. Since there are several claimants to taking an overall view, potential and actual tensions abound, of which one receives glimpses through manipulative press leaks. This is especially true when Finance Ministers aspire to become Prime Minister, because they are usually the key actors in conjunction with their staff advisers. Each can neutralize the other. Matignon can intervene for political reasons and Bercy can block decisions by circumscribing or not implementing them.[74]

From 1981 to 1984 President Mitterrand saw Finance Minister Delors on most Fridays, receiving frequent verbal and written complaints against the financial laxity of Prime Minister Mauroy, with periodic suggestions that he was unfit for the job. Sometimes Mitterrand refused to overrule his Prime Minister, as in the generous refinancing of the public sector in 1982 following the nationalization of firms in deficit, saying: 'This is a matter for the Government. The Elysée should not be involved.'[75] At others, such as the freeze on civil service salaries, he sided with his

Prime Minister by telephone or letter: 'if I write to him, my letter goes to an adviser who files it. All ministers except Balladur are treated in this way' (quoted ibid., p. 272).

[74] Interviews. See also Huchon, pp. 117–18.
[75] Quoted in Attali, *Verbatim*, i, p. 338; cf. 332–6, 727.

Finance Minister. Despite France facing a balance of payments crisis, Mitterrand was reluctant to adopt the austerity policy being pressed upon him in 1982–83 by Delors, backed by frequent threats of resignation that lost credibility when they were not carried out. (An underrated aspect of coordination is the frequent need to dissuade ministers from resigning because they have not got their way, have not been consulted or even informed about decisions affecting them, and so forth.) Neither Mauroy, nor—predictably—most of the spending ministries, supported Delors's tough line, increasing his sense of isolation. However, the 1983 move of Pascal Lamy (who played such an important part in Delors's EU Commission presidency as his *chef de cabinet*, 1985–94) from Delors's staff to Mauroy's, with responsibility for implementing the government's austerity programme, marked the belated recognition of the painful choices that had to be made, once the decision in favour of devaluation against flotation of the franc was taken.[76]

Bérégovoy, Delors's successor as Finance Minister in July 1984, abandoned his expansionist economic viewpoint for the monetarist departmental view by the end of the year. Attali ironically questions whether Bérégovoy's conquest by his officials should be regarded as the result of seduction or appropriation and quotes Mitterrand's comment on his copy of a December 1984 letter sent by the Finance Minister to the Prime Minister: 'I cannot believe that Pierre Bérégovoy wrote the letter he has signed.'[77] By February 1985, Bérégovoy criticizes the President's spendthrift proclivities in a letter to the Prime Minister, insisting that, to avoid a fourth devaluation, inflation should not exceed 3 per cent of GNP. Mitterrand's furious response was to annotate the letter: 'This is not a matter to be decided by the Finance Minister!'[78] Nevertheless, Bérégovoy was to go on, in Mitterrand's second term, to become the personification of the 'strong franc' policy both as Finance Minister and Prime Minister, as the logical consequences of the momentous 1983 choice in favour of European rigour over Socialist laxity imposed themselves on the President. His liberalization of the money markets and Stock Exchange ensured that he left an enduring mark on the French financial system.

The Treasury and Budget Divisions

The strength of the Finance Ministry has traditionally been based particularly on the Budget and Treasury Divisions. Their directors have usually exercised great influence, partly because of the influential inspectors of finance network to which they belong, members of which are to be found on most of the ministers' staffs. Two key personalities in the period we are examining were Jean-Claude Trichet and Daniel Bouton. Trichet served in the Treasury Division from 1981, with an interval as the director of

[76] Ibid., pp. 543, 575–6, 610–11. See also Favier and Martin-Roland, i, pp. 116, 404–6, 410–13, and C. Grant, *Delors. Inside the House that Jacques Built*, London, Brearly, 1994, pp. 50–2, 97.

[77] Attali, *Verbatim*, i, p. 1129; cf. 1094–5, 1127–8. See also P. Bauchard, *Deux ministres trop tranquilles*, Belfond, 1994, p. 39. Strauss-Kahn, who in 1997 became Finance Minister, recalls that in 1984 Bérégovoy said he knew nothing about finance and asked to be taught. 'He was first the pupil, then the spokesman, finally the exegetist of the Treasury view.' Quoted in I. Schemla, *Edith Cresson, la femme piégée*, Paris, Flammarion, 1993, p. 141. [78] Attali, *Verbatim*, i, p. 1117.

Finance Minister Balladur's *cabinet* (1986–87) before appointment as Governor of the Bank of France in 1993.[79] Bouton had served for fourteen years from 1977 in the Budget Division and in the *cabinet* of the Budget Minister in 1980–81. He was *directeur de cabinet* of Juppé as Budget Minister from 1986 to 1988, then director of the Budget Division from 1988 to 1991, before moving to the Société Générale, a major deposit bank, of which he became the head in 1997. Their careers and relationship exemplify how coordination can informally take place most effectively without recourse to meetings but such a degree of consensus is the exception rather than the rule, hence the need to rely, usually, upon more formal arrangements.

Especially for the two years from 1986 when Trichet and Bouton were respectively directors of the Balladur and Juppé *cabinets*, then as directors of the two key economic and monetary divisions, they applied by unspoken agreement an austerity, anti-inflationary policy in budgetary, social security, and wages policy, which continued as the 1990s orthodoxy. However in the early 1980s, when the political and the administrative members of the Finance core executive were out of step and coordination was difficult, once the political executive adopted the same priorities as their senior officials, a policy of 'competitive disinflation' was consistently pursued. Prime Minister Chirac having delegated the whole of economic policy to Balladur in 1986–88, the latter in turn delegated budgetary policy to Juppé, although proposals usually had to go through the Finance Minister to the Prime Minister. However, when VAT was lowered from 33 to 28 per cent in 1987, Bouton discussed the matter with Balladur but they decided not to inform Chirac's staff for fear of leaks leading to Stock Exchange speculation.[80] (The personal rivalry that then developed between Balladur and Juppé had serious political consequences in the 1993–95 government, when as Balladur's Foreign Affairs Minister Juppé was supporting Chirac for the presidency.)

The 1988–91 tensions between the Keynesian Prime Minister Rocard and the monetarist Finance Minister Bérégovoy, who met weekly, were exacerbated by the mutual detestation of their staffs; by the Finance Minister sometimes working with the President against the Prime Minister and by the Budget Division intransigently pressing for an end to the 'inflationary compromises' of the past. The main bone of contention was Rocard's promotion of the General Social Tax as the fairest way to stem the social security deficit, Mitterrand's staff helping to convince him not to support Bérégovoy's opposition. By 1991, Budget Minister Charasse commented, the Finance Minister 'was almost in a state of rebellion'.[81] This innovative tax, also opposed at the time by the Right, was subsequently increased under the Juppé Government.

When the Treasury and Budget Divisions are strong and their heads and the *directeurs de cabinet* of their ministers are agreed, coordination is straightforward.

---

[79] Bauchard, pp. 125, 150–1.

[80] Interviews. On Juppé's open dislike of Balladur's supervision, see Attali, *Verbatim*, ii, p. 182.

[81] Charasse, p. 151; cf. 148–54. See also Favier and Martin-Roland, iii, pp. 540–5, 556–63, and Huchon, pp. 114, 119.

However, from 1993 to 1997 weak Finance Ministers and a weakened Treasury (notably by the significant loss of monetary power to the Bank of France), combined with frequent intervention by the Prime Minister, made coordination more difficult. Juppé, as a former Budget Minister, chose to bypass the Finance Minister and work directly with the Budget Division, whose tough if narrow-minded, well-informed staff he admired. Finance Minister Bérégovoy rather than the Prime Minister had played the key role from 1988 to 1992, and he continued to do so when he became Prime Minister, a shift which continued under Balladur and then Juppé.

The traditional self-satisfaction of Treasury Division officials has taken severe blows since the 1990s, as the massive losses of certain state enterprises, such as the Crédit Lyonnais, mismanaged by a former Director of the Treasury Division, have revealed its inability to control state property, much less the private sector. It did not even know what it owned, as Finance Minister Arthuis discovered on taking office in 1995, much less the real costs of its services, so it could not compare the results achieved with its objectives. As General Rapporteur of the Senate Finance Committee, he had assumed that the Treasury's State Shareholdings Service des Participations, would be run like a holding company. When, as Finance Minister, he discovered this was not so and that the Treasury had neither the competent staff nor the capacity to discover if the state's properties were yielding profits or losses, he asked a private consultancy firm to undertake the task. What it found was that losses exceeded profits despite the fact that essential financial provision for pensions had not been made.[82] The June 1999 Arthuis-commissioned report on the state's patrimonial accounting system by a senior Finance official severely criticized its archaic and fragmented nature. Great losses ensued from the resulting neglect and from the unimaginative adherence to the annual nature of the budget, with observance of procedures being given priority over taking good decisions.[83] However, the Finance Ministry showed no sense of urgency in remedying the serious dysfunctions exposed.

The lack of effective parliamentary scrutiny, deliberately weakened under the Fifth Republic to liberate the executive from the paralysing effects of subjecting the bureaucracy to democratic control, has been costly. Rescuing the Crédit Lyonnais involved satisfying the European Competition Commissioner, Karel van Miert, who had to arbitrate Franco-French banking objections to refinancing a competitor, as well as protect the French taxpayer from the worst excesses of the Finance Ministry's pursuit of its priority: saving a leading French bank from bankruptcy. However, we must turn to the coordinating problems faced by the Treasury in the context of European monetary integration.

The Treasury and Economic and Monetary Union
French decision-making on the ECB was administratively dominated by the Finance Ministry and within it between the Treasury Division and the Bérégovoy staff. They worked with the Bank of France, the Foreign Office, and the Elysée, some fifteen

---

[82] J. Arthuis, *Dans les Coulisses de Bercy*, pp. 128, 132–4.
[83] *Le Monde*, 24 September 1999.

people in all. The private banking sector as such was excluded from the process. Mitterrand was not enthusiastic about an independent ECB or Bank of France but was content to leave it largely to Bérégovoy. The French central bank had a different conception of the need for an 'economic government' from the politicians. It was more concerned to restrain budgetary expenditure of the member states than to counterbalance concern with stability by the need to promote growth. It was, generally, more willing to leave matters to the market. Its main objective was to use the ECB to increase its own independence from the Treasury. Its head, Jacques de Larosière, a former director of the Treasury, was able to exercise informal coordination through its then director, Trichet. The Bank's membership of the Committee of Central Bank Governors, which prepared the draft ECB scheme, gave it a means of compensating its relative weakness within domestic decision-making. Finance Ministry and Bank of France officials served on the EC Monetary Committee's preparatory work from 1990 on the ECB.[84]

The Foreign Office took a broader, less specifically financial view of the ECB, linking the projects of EU monetary and political union. Its minister from 1988 to 1993, Roland Dumas—preoccupied with the preparation of the Maastricht IGC—left matters largely to a member of his *cabinet* and above all to Pierre de Boissieu, director of the Quai's Economic and Financial Affairs Division and to the Minister for European Affairs, Elisabeth Guigou. The latter not only had Mitterrand's confidence as a former member of his staff but had worked in the Treasury and as head of the SGCI (she combined this with being on Mitterrand's staff from 1986 to 1990), so she carried political as well as administrative weight in the discussions. The Foreign Office and European Affairs Minister's efforts to play a role of coordination were frustrated by the Finance Ministry's refusal to consult them in preparing the French draft Economic and Monetary Union (EMU) Treaty. Guigou and de Boissieu were only able to exert an influence at Elysée meetings, preparatory European Council meetings, and through Guigou's presence at the IGC on EMU. (She was the only European Affairs Minister to have this privilege.) The Quai successfully opposed the Finance Ministry's proposal that the ECB should not be included in the EC but be treated as a fourth intergovernmental 'pillar' of the EU. It also sought to make the European 'economic government' responsible to the European Council (in which it but not Finance was involved) rather than ECOFIN (where the reverse was true), which was the real ministerial monetary policy community.

It was the Treasury (especially its European Affairs office), and to a lesser extent the Forecasting Division of the Finance Ministry, that took the lead in preparing the French EMU proposals. Bérégovoy used consultation of the Forecasting Division as a check on the Treasury standpoint. As a politician, he was much more perturbed than the Treasury with excluding democratic control over the ECB, so he and his staff emphasized the need for a European 'economic government'. However, Bérégovoy's

---

[84] This and the next four paragraphs are mainly based on the doctoral thesis of Corinne Balleix-Banerjee, *La France et la Banque Centrale Européenne. Débats Politiques et Elaboration de la Décision*, Paris II, 1997, vol. I, ch. 3, pp. 309–82, itself based on extensive interviews with the leading participants.

representative in the EC negotiations, Treasury Director Trichet, was allowed to adopt a relatively conciliatory attitude towards German resistance against the idea of political intervention in the ECB's independence.

The then Prime Minister, Rocard, was largely excluded from the ECB discussions, the President relying only upon Bérégovoy and Dumas to share in what he regarded as his particular responsibility. Cresson, future European Commissioner, was also excluded from the ECB project. However, twice a month the President's European Affairs adviser called a coordination meeting of concerned ministries, including Matignon. In addition, the President held a few meetings with Bérégovoy, Dumas, and Guigou to finalize the French standpoint on the EC negotiations on the ECB, especially in January 1991. Mitterrand did a deal with Andreotti and Kohl in December 1991 to fix the final deadline for the single currency as 1999. In these ultimate discussions, the Finance Ministry usually prevailed over the Foreign Ministry, for example in making ECOFIN and not the European Council responsible in matters of 'economic government' and the establishment of the ECB, as well as allowing Finance Ministers to attend European Council meetings when EMU matters were discussed. On the stability pact, which the Finance Ministry did not favour, President Chirac and Prime Minister Juppé 'arbitrated' in favour of giving its enforcement to the Finance Ministry as a way of reassuring the Germans of France's intended monetary rectitude. Detailed matters were to be handled by the Monetary Committee, not the permanent representatives in Brussels as advocated by the Foreign Ministry. The final result of the ECB and EMU discussions in France was to shift the handling of European affairs from the Foreign to the Finance Ministry, the latter emerging as the disputed but effective lead ministry. Although the Elysée did intervene decisively from time to time, it was the Treasury Division of the Finance Ministry that prepared the way for its director, Trichet, to become the head of a more independent Bank of France and subsequently of the ECB. The Treasury did not so much coordinate policy as impose its views.

Dyson presents a more nuanced view of the insulated core executive negotiation of EMU in France as a contest for empowerment between the President, the Finance Ministry, and the Bank of France. While President Mitterrand imparted political legitimation and impetus to the process, he did not achieve control over it, despite the efforts of Foreign Minister Dumas and European Affairs Minister Guigou, who remained in overall charge of the Maastricht negotiations. The Treasury, accustomed to substantial latitude in EC matters, with the EC Monetary Committee enjoying freedom from coordination by the Brussels Committee of Permanent Representatives, was able to ensure that in the 1990–91 French Draft Treaty negotiations 'overall coordination remained with the Finance Ministry'.[85] It avoided the creation of an interdepartmental committee on EMU, such as existed in Germany, Italy, and the UK, which would have allowed Matignon to intervene. However, it failed to ensure

---

[85] K. Dyson and K. Featherstone, 'EMU and Presidential Leadership under François Mitterrand', in M. Maclean (ed.), *The Mitterrand Years. Legacy and Evaluation*, Basingstoke, Macmillan, 1998, p. 104; cf. 102–6.

that an effective countervailing economic policy coordination or 'economic government' was established that would give ECOFIN the capacity to curb the German-inspired propensity of the ECB to conduct an independent monetary policy. As a result, while monetary policy coordination would become supranational, economic policy coordination would remain largely national (notably fiscal and wage policy), with some efforts at intergovernmental coordination as envisaged in the 1987 proposal for a bilateral Franco-German Economic Council of Finance Ministers and Central Bank Governors meeting regularly. So, while the President had provided decisive political leadership and the Finance Ministry, through the Treasury, influenced the policy that followed, it was the Bank of France initially and the ECB eventually that were the EMU's main institutional beneficiaries of one-sided policy coordination.[86]

Budgetary Politics

Having considered an important policy in which the Treasury Division played a key role, let us now turn to the Budget Division and its minister. Frequently, quite junior line officials attend interdepartmental meetings in place of the staff officials because of the very large number of meetings that necessitate the presence of a Budget representative. Its critics describe the budget officials as arrogant and unintelligently negative, intellectually terrorizing the weaker spending ministries into submission. Suggestions to bring it under the Prime Minister's control, risk confusing the roles of containing public expenditure and choosing between expenditures, and would cut it off from the Treasury's macroeconomic and monetary policy role. Mitterrand did not want either too powerful a Prime Minister or Finance Minister. In 1981, he would not let Delors choose his own junior minister of Budget, imposing his own former *directeur de cabinet* Fabius, with the remit of preparing a Keynesian deficit budget to increase growth even at the cost of a devaluation. Poor relations between the *directeurs de cabinet* of the Prime Minister and Finance Minister in 1981–82 did not assist coordination. Delors's refusal to countersign the 1982 budget was a symbolic gesture, followed by his controversial calling for a 'pause' in costly reforms. Only when the key decisions to change direction in 1983 and the replacement of Fabius by Henri Emmanuelli as Budget Minister had been made did Delors seem to retrieve control over the budget.[87]

However, in September 1983 Mitterrand announced on TV that taxation would be reduced by 1 per cent without informing anyone. He tried presenting the Finance Ministry with a *fait accompli* via a letter to the Prime Minister a week later. In April 1984, he wrote again to Mauroy expressing impatience that the priority reduction in taxation was not envisaged in the 1985 budget but it remained a dead letter. In June the director of the Budget Division wrote to Attali showing that a reduction in the

---

[86] Dyson and Featherstone, pp. 109–10; cf. 97ff. See also more generally, K. Dyson, *Elusive Union: The Process of Economic and Monetary Union in Europe*, London, Longman, 1994, and Chapter 5 in this volume.

[87] Interview. See also Grant, p. 48 and ch. 4 passim; Attali, *Verbatim*, i, pp. 30, 100, 143–4, 247, 642; Favier and Martin-Roland, i, pp. 116, 404–6.

taxe professionelle would not be possible in 1985; it was abandoned and eventually the cut was only 0.3 per cent.[88] Despite the President's fiat, the problem was to persuade ministers to accept cuts in their estimates, leading to their lobbying the President by letter. The Culture Minister, Jack Lang, characteristically and grandiloquently appealed to 'the judgement of History and eternal France'.[89] He had more success than most in his frequent attempts to get the President to 'arbitrate' in his ministry's favour.

During the Chirac Government, Budget Minister Juppé and his *directeur de cabinet*, Bouton, had to go to Matignon two or three times each week to deal with budget allocations, so that the Prime Minister could 'arbitrate'. He seldom overruled them, knowing the difficulty of filling the financial gap that would arise. Their principal preoccupation was the perennially rising social security deficit (some 20 billion francs in 1987), leading to conflicts with Philippe Séguin, the combative minister concerned, who complained of being overruled by the tandem of Balladur and Juppé. After bemoaning that 'There is no pilot in the aircraft', he secured an increase in social security contributions to meet the deficit.[90]

The difficult relations between Séguin and Juppé in 1986–87 fostered their subsequent animosity and rivalry in the leadership struggle to control the RPR party, with Chirac favouring Juppé. When he became Prime Minister in 1995, Juppé worked with his Budget Minister, Lamassoure, bypassing the Finance Minister, just as Balladur had worked closely with Nicholas Sarkozy, who was almost a daily visitor to Matignon in his dual capacity as Budget Minister and Government Spokesman from 1993 to 1995. In a 1994 pre-electoral context, Sarkozy fudged the 1995 budget deficit to accommodate the concessions to various lobbies that Balladur had made. This is usually compensated by post-electoral austerity, which one may not have to impose if defeated. Since in the course of each year 'the government is entitled by decree massively to scrap more sums than those which were the subject of passionate debates in Parliament', so-called 'budgetary regulation' making a nonsense of parliamentary financial control, such collaboration between Prime Minister and Budget Minister enables them to modify past laborious compromises to meet present urgent priorities.[91]

An eminent member of the Court of Accounts has blamed the difficulty of reconciling government policies and their budgetary implementation on the fact that the former are usually fixed first and then fitted financially as best they may into the budget. This requires that compromises subsequently be made in the means to achieve the ends sought.[92] So despite the formal rigidity of budget procedures, flexibility is introduced in practice by freezing and then cancelling budgetary allocations. There has been an enduring contrast between the assertion of an ambitious

---

[88] Attali, *Verbatim*, i, pp. 992, 1244; cf. 762–3, 766–7, 852–3, 942–3, 963–4, 976, 987, 1035, 1056.

[89] Fabius, p. 68; cf. 66–72. See also Attali, *Verbatim*, i, pp. 893–4, 1049.

[90] Attali, *Verbatim*, ii, p. 400; cf. 404 and interview.

[91] Carcassonne, *La Constitution*, p. 201; cf. Bazire, p. 77. See also Bauchard, pp. 175–9, Domenach and Szafran, *Le Roman*, pp. 304–6 and interviews.

[92] Jacques Bonnet in ENA, *La Réforme de l'Etat*, op. cit. p. 79.

foreign policy and the long-term decline of the Foreign Ministry budget, which has struggled to retrieve a 1 per cent share.[93] This doubtless reflects the fact that French foreign policy is increasingly conducted by the President and his staff in matters of higher politics (with the Prime Minister in periods of cohabitation) and the Finance and other spending ministers in lower politics matters, a subject to which we shall return, as the Foreign Ministry seeks to preserve a coordinating role in a context of increasing dispersion.

Attempts to protect policy objectives from such depredations by medium-term contracts or programme laws have not been honoured in practice. The defence budget, which often involves very long-term investment commitments, operating within the framework of five-yearly programme laws, has been described as the 'adjustment variable of the general budget' over the last forty years. French defence cuts in the 1990s came later than in other countries but were especially brutal, underlining the fact that interministerial policy coordination had not made the hard choices that were later imposed financially. This represents a major distortion of the process, increasing rather than reducing uncertainty, in which 'budgetary law is in principle annual, infra-annual regulation is often budget reality and pluriannuality is the budgetary dream'.[94] The defence budget, by the sheer volume of military and civilian employment it involved (about 430,000 in 1990), coupled with another quarter of a million directly employed in the arms industry (particularly export-oriented advanced technology firms), has presented non-military problems when making cuts. French governments have presentationally reconciled rhetoric with reality by making ambitious medium-term spending commitments which were then dishonoured by annual clawbacks. They have also avoided the appearance of cuts by spreading spending over longer periods to the intense annoyance of the Defence Ministry. However, the preoccupation with maintaining a balance between expenditure on the army, navy, and air force has meant that the Chief of Staff—whose function it is to coordinate defence budgetary decisions—has failed to subordinate the preservation of inter-service parity to the need to reorient French defence, especially after the end of the Cold War. The mismatch between inordinate ambition and shrinking resources has not been faced by the core executives, President Mitterrand having preferred postponement and prudent compromise to painful choices.[95]

Despite the belated capacity in the 1990s to enforce draconian cuts in the case of defence, the continuing rigidities of budgetary expenditure frustrating redeployment are reflected in the decade from 1985; while the number of farmers had fallen by 35 per cent, the number of Agriculture Ministry officials had not changed; civil and

[93] M.-C. Kessler, *La Politique Etrangère de la France. Acteurs et Processus,* Presses de Sciences Po, 1999, pp. 178–84.

[94] Didier Casas in ENA, *La Réforme de l'Etat,* p. 77; cf. 88, 95. On defence, see particularly the remarks of Christian Schmidt and Jean Picq, ibid., pp. 151–3.

[95] Anand Menon, *The Ambivalent Ally. France, NATO and the Limits of Independence, 1981–97,* Macmillan, 1999, pp. 155–8, 160–8; cf. S. Cohen, *La Défaite des généraux, Le pouvoir politique et l'armée sous la Ve République,* Paris, Fayard, 1994, p. 67; cf. 192–3, 247.

penal court cases had increased by 235 per cent but the number of judges had only increased by 20 per cent.[96]

Before we turn in the next chapter to some selected spending ministries, it is worth taking a retrospective look at the role of the Budget Division as seen by Jean-Pierre Huchon, who spent ten years in it before becoming Prime Minister Rocard's *directeur de cabinet* from 1988 to 1991. He describes it as often 'irresistible and very powerful in interdepartmental discussions', its young officials—who seldom leave their offices—seeing themselves as abstemiously championing the 'public good' against spendthrift line directors representing sinful indulgence.[97] The latter were deliberately kept waiting before meetings, then sermonized on any new expenses, aimed at making them feel guilty and thereby containing public expenditure. Huchon describes how he tried to overcome their 'no complex' by organizing seminars, in the spirit of Rocardian consensus, to explain to ministers why and how their budgets were to be cut. Such a pedagogic approach cannot overcome the mutual suspicion that governs interdepartmental negotiations in general and budgetary negotiations in particular. The ensuing struggle between the short-term savers and medium-term spenders means that, especially in periods of slow growth in public revenue, the guardians of the public purse are not inclined to see *any* new expenditure as indispensable. As a former Planning Commissioner, Henri Guaino (1995–97) put it, 'As long as all problems are tackled from a budgetary viewpoint and it is given absolute priority . . . over everything else, it is clear that the very rules that govern the working of budgetary discussion and preparation prevent continuity in political and administrative behaviour.'[98] Having focused on the protagonists of institutionalized restraint, we shall turn to the would-be profligates in the next chapter. However, we must first deal with two other aspects of horizontal coordination: the Cabinet and communication.

THE CABINET

The French Cabinet is a much less significant political actor than in other democracies and so does not create a strong sense of collective responsibility for government action. Rather, it is an institution for recording decisions that have been made elsewhere by members of the core executive. They are taken at formal

[96] Martine Clément of the CNPF, ibid., p. 93, cf. 34.

[97] Huchon, pp. 125–7. For an excellent analysis, which despite its date of publication remains apposite, of the dealings between the Budget Division and spending ministries, see G. Lord, *The French Budgetary Process*, Berkeley, University of California Press, 1973, especially pp. 130–46, 197. See Elgie, pp. 14–15.

[98] ENA, *La Réforme de l'Etat*, report on a November 1997 conference, Cahier 3/March 1998, p. 25; cf. Huchon, pp. 122, 132–3. See also Lion, pp. 44–5, quoting the comments of the Budget Director from 1981 to 1986, Jean Choussat. Robert Elgie points out that immediately prior to the 1986–88 and 1993–95 cohabitations, Mitterrand appointed new Budget Directors with whom the Chirac and Balladur Governments had to cohabit (Unpublished paper on 'Budgetary Policy Making in France', 1996, p. 7).

interdepartmental or interministerial meetings, in informal negotiations between two or more senior officials or ministers, between the President and Prime Minister/ individual ministers, or personally by the President, the Prime Minister, or a particular minister. Matters are only allowed to come to Cabinet if the coordination processes have already been successfully completed, so no votes need to take place.

The fact that the weekly Cabinet meetings are usually brief (lasting seldom more than an hour) and boring—the President often dealing with his correspondence, or in Mitterrand's case annotating publishers' catalogues, and ministers passing notes to each other—is indicative that it is a required constitutional stage in the policy process, rubber-stamping important decisions with which those concerned are familiar. Sometimes there is an animated debate, such as the 23 July 1981 one on the return to resale price maintenance for books. Mitterrand was particularly keen on this, repeatedly prompting Culture Minister Jack Lang to act. Despite a majority of hostile views, conscious that price-cutting had been popular with most book purchasers, Mitterrand cleverly manoeuvred to carry the day, with the help of Defferre (whose wife was a novelist) and by asking Prime Minister Mauroy to decide. Despite his reticence, Mauroy out of loyalty to the President (whose favourite pastime was visiting bookshops and who feared for their survival) came down decisively in favour of resale price maintenance and the hostile majority acquiesced.[99] As in the matter of the architectural mega projects, Mitterrand was able to use his presidential position to indulge his personal preferences, thanks in this case to the support of the Prime Minister and the ardour of the lead minister. Neither of these policies, however significant they were symbolically, can be regarded as comparable substantively to decisions such as the pivotal 1983 imposition of economic austerity, which amounted to an acceptance of the priority of the liberal market economy imperatives over socialist redistribution and state-promoted industrial expansion, in which the Cabinet played an insignificant part.

While the Cabinet legitimizes the crucial preparatory discussions, it also provides a focus for them with a view to anticipating all the necessary legal and political problems that might subsequently arise. As such, it structures the preparatory timetable of government. Part A of its agenda—draft legislation and delegated legislation—is prepared months in advance, as is part C, consisting of ministerial statements that do not require immediate decision. Part B, prepared two or three weeks in advance, concerns nominations to some 500 important posts. The President calls on ministers to speak using the title of their office. There is usually little discussion of 'A' items but some ministers try and reverse defeats in interministerial discussions, record their dissent on specific points, or express dissatisfaction with their budget. There is no discussion of nominations and 'C' is dominated by the Foreign Minister's comments on world or EU events, comments by other ministers involved in EC meetings, and by the President giving policy directives. The Prime Minister usually sums up such desultory discussions as may occur, the President sometimes taking

---

[99] Favier and Martin-Roland, i, pp. 193–4; Attali, i, p. 95.

the opportunity during cohabitation to express his reservations. However, on foreign and defence policy matters, it is the President who sums up.[100]

Each Friday morning the SGG decides which items are administratively ready for the agenda of the next three Cabinet meetings. He then meets the Prime Minister's *directeur de cabinet* to decide what matters it would be politically desirable to postpone or accelerate. After approval by the Prime Minister on the same day, it goes to the Elysée for approval by the President and his staff on the following Monday. The President makes the final decision on the agenda, any changes being notified to the Prime Minister by the SGG or personally by telephone. The President then decides if any non-Cabinet ministers should attend. Agendas are not received by ministers until Tuesday evening. 'A' items emerge from interdepartmental discussions on pink paper: after Council of State amendments, the text is printed on green paper and the final government text is on blue paper. Only the staff of the President and Prime Minister see the pink and green versions but the blue text—after meetings chaired jointly by the SGG and a member of the Prime Minister's staff—goes to all ministers.[101]

That virtually everything is settled before the Cabinet meets is clear from the fact that a draft press communiqué is prepared in advance for publication, with any last-minute changes made immediately after the Cabinet meeting on Wednesday. The SGG prepares the rather austere draft on Tuesday afternoon to inform the ministries what requires action by them. Final adjustments are made over breakfast on Wednesday morning at a meeting with the spokesmen of the President and of the government by the SGP and his deputy, the SGG, and in Mitterrand's time by Attali and sometimes Charasse who could anticipate the President's probable viewpoint. Nevertheless, Mitterrand modified the style and content of the communiqué.

Before Cabinet, the Prime Minister and President have a preliminary discussion, of variable duration, on matters that are coming up. Cabinet seldom starts before 10 a.m. and not at 9.30 a.m. as scheduled, ministers informally chatting and sorting out mutual problems while they wait. From 1981 to 1995, Michel Charasse remained on hand (but not in the Cabinet room) to deal with frequently detailed questions requiring clarification during the Cabinet meeting, the SGP acting as an intermediary. Before each item on the agenda, Attali passed to the President memos prepared by the Elysée staff or his own on-the-spot comments when necessary. Minutes are taken by the SGG for the archives and are not approved by the participants. However, he also prepares a summary of decisions, including directives from the President and Prime Minister, which are not included in the press communiqué and must be approved by the President or his staff. Copies are kept at the Elysée and Matignon. The SGG then sends the legislation to parliament. After the necessary countersignatures are obtained, decrees and appointments are published in the *Journal Officiel*.[102]

[100] Fournier, pp. 57–9, 68–77, 226–9, 233–4.

[101] Ibid., pp. 229–30; Schifres and Sarrazin, pp. 183–5, 193–4; Pfister, pp. 73–8, 82–3.

[102] Fournier, pp. 231–6; Schifres and Sarrazin, pp. 185–7, 193–6; Attali, *Verbatim*, i, p. 399; cf. 34, 81. Attali's volumes give regular but tantalizing brief comments on the Cabinet meetings of the 1980s.

Apart from the Defence Council, the French President relies on *ad hoc* rather than permanent interministerial meetings, unlike countries which systematically use Cabinet Committees. However, in periods of cohabitation, Prime Ministers have revived the Fourth Republic practice of meetings of the Cabinet without the President. Such meetings did occasionally happen even in the non-cohabitation periods, although there was always a member of the Elysée staff taking notes. However, holding a 'Cabinet Council' is clearly intended to achieve government coordination in the absence of a hostile President, to avoid the embarrassment of ministers disagreeing in the face of the enemy. It shortens the duration of the Cabinet meeting and helps to ensure cohesion within a coalition government.[103] Chirac strongly discouraged debate among ministers in the President's presence, who send notes to each other. The shortest Cabinet meeting in 1986–88 lasted twelve minutes.[104] During the Chirac–Jospin cohabitation ten years later, the government ministers met without the President on one Thursday in two, where the real discussions could take place.

COORDINATION THROUGH COMMUNICATION

As there is no 'central actor' carrying out the communication function, the failure to personify control over the activities associated with it fragments the political message from the central actors. They do not speak with one voice. For government to engage in internally consistent activity, to ensure a coordinated presentation of its views outward and a regular and comprehensive flow of information inward, it has to pay close attention to its communications arrangements. We have already touched on the role of the SGG in verifying the legality and consistency of the many activities of government, counteracting the tendency of each ministry to go its own way. Here we shall consider certain aspects of the internal administrative coordination of communications before turning to its more political aspects, concentrating on how the core executive manages its outward and inward communications. For political coordination, the spokesmen of the President and the government occupy pivotal positions, although the *cabinets* of all the ministers have advisers specializing in fulfilling this function. In a context in which governments are expected to provide more information but have less control over the media, much more emphasis is being placed on manipulation because imposition is no longer an option.

In contrast with the British Central Office of Information or the German Bundespressamt, French ministries each organize their own public relations and communications and guard them jealously. The Prime Minister's Press Service did what it could to avoid the confusion that resulted from divergent interpretations on interministerial issues. Ministries often have a large public relations staff—notably Finance, Foreign Affairs, and Defence, with the latter alone having some 600 staff in

---

[103] Interviews and Favier and Martin-Roland, ii, pp. 770–3.
[104] Favier and Martin-Roland, ii, pp. 623–4; cf. 502.

1982. So large has communication bulked in ministerial priorities that 'ministers are concerned to communicate while acting and in some cases even to communicate before or even without acting.'[105] Some of the government's internal reports are published by *La Documentation Française* but most of the 3,000 produced annually— as estimated by the Commission for the Coordination of Administrative Documentation—are not. A sample of 116 reports from 1988 to 1993 show that only 13 per cent were instigated jointly by more than one ministry, 64 per cent by individual ministries, and 23 per cent by Matignon. The ministries that commissioned reports most frequently were Education and Social Affairs, Finance and Industry less often, and Interior, Defence, and Foreign Affairs least. The latter prefer to keep their investigations internal, officially for reasons of confidentiality. Two-thirds of those who write the reports are from the administration, 39 per cent from the *grands corps* and inspectorates.[106]

Most administrative reports are a response to a crisis, an attempt to assist in the preparations of decisions or to soften up public opinion for unpopular decisions to come. An example of crisis anticipation was the 1987 Long Commission (Long was a former SGG) on the naturalization of foreigners living in France. It both demonstrated the complexity of the problem as well as temporarily defused a highly controversial issue of political contention (discussed in Chapter 8). Since asking for a report is a matter of ministerial discretion, it is not necessary to inform the SGG or the Prime Minister, his colleagues, or officials of initiatives usually taken by the minister's *cabinet*. The resulting confusion has meant that on one occasion ten reports were prepared on the same subject over a six-year period . . . without their recommendations being followed by action. The lack of coordination owing to inadequate interministerial articulation led a 1993 Report to bewail the fact that 'the preparation of strategic decisions in a context of excessively numerous, unstable and fragmented government structures renders taking into account the interdependence between problems impossible'.[107] The multiplication of investigations was a perverse consequence of this incompatibility of compartmentalized structures and integrated functions.

The confusion created by the simultaneous announcement of too many electorally promised reforms, characteristic of the 1981 advent of the PS after over two decades in Opposition, was accompanied by the open expression of divergences that was mercilessly exploited by the media. In contrast with the Mauroy Government cacophony, Fabius managed things better from 1984 to 1986. 'The Prime Minister held a short communication meeting each morning with the Government Spokesman and one or two ministers concerned to review the situation and specify the messages to be diffused.'[108] It is above all necessary to be in frequent contact with most ministers—the Spokesman should ideally know all that is happening—to

---

[105] Schrameck, p. 75; cf. Fournier, pp. 269–70.

[106] 'Que fait-on des rapports administratifs?', ENA, *Le Travail Gouvernemental*, ii, 1996, pp. 582–7, 627–34.

[107] Ibid., p. 606; cf. 597–8, 609, quoting from the Blanc Report, *Pour un Etat stratège, garant de l'intérêt général*, Commissariat Général du Plan, 1993.   [108] Fournier, p. 277.

ensure that a consistent message is presented on behalf of the government. The Spokesman works with the Service d'Information et de Diffusion (SID) whose staff of 100 come under the Prime Minister. They are responsible for collecting press and opinion poll information for the government as well as coordinating government propaganda. The Prime Minister is too busy to coordinate communications himself, so someone he trusts—the Spokesman, his *directeur de cabinet*, or a specialist adviser—must be charged with this function. He must advocate the government's policies by: presenting a post-Cabinet account of the proceedings; holding regular press conferences; arranging interviews with the media. To this the Prime Minister or other ministers add press conferences and replies at parliamentary question time.[109] However, on 30 March 1998, Jospin abolished the post of Government Spokesman, declaring that each minister was responsible for his own communication while the Prime Minister spoke for the government as a whole.[110]

The Government Spokesman has competed with the President's Spokesman, especially during periods of cohabitation, when the President is the de facto leader of the Opposition to the government. Thus, Juppé in 1986–88 and Sarkozy in 1993–95 (both of whom had the advantage of also being in charge of the Budget) frequently asserted their Prime Minister's viewpoint as against that of the President. The latter's Spokesman is in daily contact with him, notably attending the meals which President Mitterrand had on Tuesday with party leaders, on Wednesday with ministers, and on Thursday with members of the PS Parliamentary Group. A few (five to eight) journalists were invited to breakfast—generally on Fridays—selected in relation to a theme or type of journalist, for an off-the-record discussion lasting an hour and a half. Once a week, the President's Spokesman spent an hour with him for a general review of the line the President wanted him to take. He saw the SGP daily and worked closely with the Press Service, which provided a daily press review for the President's staff. He authorized dealings between them and journalists.

During his first seven-year term, Mitterrand delivered 1,753 speeches and messages—far more than his predecessors—reflecting the important part public speaking plays in government.[111] The preparation for Mitterrand's TV interviews and press conferences was carefully coordinated. His staff provided memos, from which he made his own notes. This was followed by long talks with his close collaborators to refine and test his own ideas. After TV and radio broadcasts, a telephone poll was conducted to assess public reaction. The Spokesman accompanies the President on his provincial visits, briefing the press in advance. Balladur imitated this in 1994, as a way of conducting a surreptitious apolitical presidential campaign, but his inability to establish comfortable contact with the public and his press adviser's ignorance of his plans and decisions meant that it was much less effective than it could have been. Balladur preferred to rely upon the advice of a small circle of technocrats and

---

[109] Fournier, pp. 167, 270–2, 277–9. See also Pfister, pp. 224–6, 231, and A. Audier, *Le Porte-Parole du Gouvernement sous la Ve République*, Institut d'Etudes Politiques, Université d'Aix-Marseille, 1995–96, Mémoire.   [110] *Le Monde*, 1 April 1998.
[111] Favier and Martin-Roland, i, p. 543; cf. 544–7.

businessmen, supplemented by public opinion polls, owing to his contempt for politicians, for which he was to pay a heavy electoral price in 1995. The cunning of his Spokesman, Nicholas Sarkozy, could not compensate for his master's deficiencies. Brigouleix quotes a French diplomat as declaring that 'to be a spokesman is to know how to lie and to deny'—*mentir et démentir.*[112] Clearly, some spin doctors are better at this than others.

The annual ritual of a 14 July wide-ranging television interview with the President plays an important part in his public relations strategy. Chirac's daughter, Claude Chirac—his trusted adviser on communications—at first tried an American-style press conference but this was not capable of being controlled as desired and was abandoned after 1995. Thereafter, President Chirac reverted to the Mitterrand pattern of being interviewed by hand-picked journalists. So in 2000 Claude Chirac invited three TV journalists (from TF1, France 2, and France 3) for a discussion in advance of the themes to be raised in the broadcast, telling them the subjects on which the President would welcome the opportunity of speaking. The three journalists then held two meetings to coordinate their questions. When the President refused to reply—as he did when the fictional jobs and voters organized by the Paris Town Hall, which he had run as Mayor from 1977 to 1995, was raised—they did not insist on his doing so. As one of them said: 'It is not part of French culture to ask the same question five times. If the President will not reply, he will not reply.'[113]

The President is a good client for the leading polling firms as a source of information about public opinion on issues as well as his personal standing. The SID regularly tested opinion on the impact of government action, the SGP and leading members of the President's staff commenting on the questions suggested. Mitterrand's leading image-maker was Jacques Pilhan—the supposed author of the slogan '*la force tranquille*'—who advised the SGP and *directeur de cabinet*. That his advice was sometimes not followed is exemplified by two instances. When President Mitterrand envisaged replacing Rocard as Prime Minister in 1991, he had four names tested: Delors was way ahead of Bérégovoy and Charasse, with Cresson last. When Mitterrand dismissed Rocard, Pilhan, the SGP Bianco, and most members of his *cabinet* sought unsuccessfully to dissuade him from appointing Cresson—the shortest-lived and most unpopular Prime Minister of the Fifth Republic—who disdained opinion polls, to her cost.[114] Pilhan went on to work in a similar capacity for President Chirac, trying in vain to persuade him to replace Juppé—the second most unpopular Prime Minister—well before the disastrous 1997 dissolution of the National Assembly which led to his resignation.

The fragmented character of French government communications reflects the competition between a multiplicity of core executives: President, Prime Minister, ministers, ministerial staff, and directors of the line administration. Controlling the

---

[112] Brigouleix, p. 124; cf. 104–24, 232–44; Romanet, pp. 60–77; Bauchard, pp. 124, 137–8, 180, 206, 225; and Schifres and Sarrazin, pp. 233–7.

[113] *Le Monde*, 15 July 2000. When an examining magistrate asked him to testify in March 2001, he refused to do so.

[114] Favier and Martin-Roland, ii, pp. 561, 574–6; iv, pp. 148–9; cf. Schifres and Sarrazin, pp. 223–8.

'political fallout' by 'coordinating responses to emerging stories'[115] is a routine
necessity that can assume crisis proportions and is elsewhere accomplished by spin
doctors. Neither of the Spokesmen nor the SID has been capable of overcoming
these centrifugal forces and associated dissonances in the struggle with the media for
control of the public agenda. Particularly at times of crisis, for example the *Rainbow
Warrior* affair in 1985 (discussed in the next chapter), the usual mechanisms fail to
operate and the President, Prime Minister, and Defence Minister were in that case
exposed to probing by the media without protection from their communication
spin doctors.[116]

　　With Watergate as its model of investigative journalism, the exposure of the French
responsibility for the sinking of the *Rainbow Warrior*, leading to the resignation of
Defence Minister Hernu, and marking a watershed, with *Le Monde* henceforth
taking up the cudgels hitherto wielded only by the satirical weekly, *Le Canard
Enchaîné*. It could not be laughed off so easily. It had the advantage of inside
information on police matters from contacts in the Ministry of Interior—notably
with the *cabinets* of Public Security Minister Franceschi and Interior Minister Joxe—
and even the Elysée, as well as the police themselves. The hunt for those who were
leaking information, with dismissals of those regarded as too talkative, was especially
active in 1983.[117] Along with judicial activism which exposed corruption in high
places, the enthusiasm for investigative journalism—compensating for its past
subservience—contributed to discrediting the political class in general and many
members of the core executive in particular. It was ironically the left-wing press—
the *Canard*, *Monde*, and *Libération*—which led the investigative attack on their
political friends, owing to the coincidence of the Mitterrand presidency and new-
found newspaper 'impertinence'. Strenuous attempts are made to conceal or
selectively reveal some truths while others are publicized.

　　Prime Minister Fabius used the SID polls to ascertain the current preoccupations
of the public and successfully used them as the basis of his monthly *Parlons France*
TV programme, achieving a satisfaction rate of 70 to 75 per cent.[118] The SID, on
behalf of the Prime Minister and his *cabinet*, tries to achieve procedural coordination through its power to withhold six-monthly prior approval of the ministries'
communication proposals. Despite desperate efforts at self-promotion, most ministers leave behind them 'as little trace of their transitory presence as a commercial
traveller in a hotel room'[119] because, notwithstanding the persisting fissiparous
tendencies, the trend towards concentration of power creates an overriding capacity
to counteract them. The frequency with which ministers consider resignation
(which is seldom carried out) is an indication of the fact that they have often to

---

[115] G. Davis, *A Government of Routines*, p. 41; cf. 40–4.
[116] 'La Communication Gouvernementale', ENA, ii, pp. 898–910. The problem of coordinating
communication is illustrated by the fact that the French Defence Ministry alone issues over 400
publications. ENA, *La Réforme de l'Etat*, op. cit. p. 131.
[117] Ménage, pp. 507–2, 727–9, 741–7 and ch. 7 passim.
[118] Favier and Martin-Roland, ii, pp. 215–16.
[119] J. Rigaud, 'Pouvoir et non-pouvoir du ministre', *Pouvoirs*, 1986, no. 36, p. 11; cf. 7–14.

subordinate cherished personal projects to the requirements of collective government policy. The Prime Minister's *directeur de cabinet* usually comes closest to imposing an overall communications strategy, projecting a more or less spurious unity, but this is only one of his many preoccupations.[120]

Michel Bon has explained that when successively running the National Employment Agency and France Télécom, ministers were not interested, their *cabinet* only wanted to exercise control and no added value was offered to him, while the line officials were divided and those from the Budget Division were suspicious of any future commitments. 'All in all, the lack of interest, vision and continuity led me to build the strategy of the Employment Agency and then *France Télécom* without the state, without my "shareholder". So my experience is that of void: the state hands over strategic decisions to those who wish to take them. I wanted to take them and I took them... What was my legitimacy to do so? What will be the strategic coherence of the whole if each strategy can only be carried out by isolated individuals?'[121] Such pertinent questions expose a weakness in a system when both political and bureaucratic logics point to short-term improvisation and the lack of a strategy means that there is no stable point of reference for coordination efforts. The General Rapporteur of the Evaluation Scientific Council concluded from a survey of interministerial evaluations that imprecise and contradictory policy objectives and the discontinuity of public action meant that coherence was unattainable. He gave the example of employment policy which had 'changed doctrine each year for the last ten to fifteen years'.[122]

We must now turn from this survey of the problems posed by horizontal coordination to the vertical dimension of coordination, institutionally embodied in the spending ministries, whose compartmentalization places intimidating structural obstacles in the way of attempts at overall policy cohesion and consistency. Although differentiation and specialization through the division of labour have greatly increased the productive capacities of economic, administrative, and political organizations, without the countervailing force of coordination to correct the side-effects, they lead to counterproductive conflicts and transaction costs that neutralize their efficiency. However, deploying that countervailing coordination has proved very problematic in practice.

---

[120] ENA, ii, pp. 913–28, 936–8.

[121] Michel Bon speaking at an Ecole Nationale d'Administration conference in November 1999, *Les Cahiers de l'ENA*, No. 3, March 1998, 'La Réforme de l'Etat', p. 28; cf. 20–1, 23–4 for other contributions in the same sense.   [122] Ibid., p. 47.

4

Vertical Fragmentation: The Spending Ministries

Our starting point for an examination of the components of the policy mix that the core executive seek to shape into a coherent whole is a recognition of the multiplicity of autonomous yet interdependent actors that cluster around the spending ministerial structures. Their overlapping activities create externalities that necessitate coordination if uncooperative proclivities combined with conflicting preferences are not to lead to confusion, paralysis, or fiasco. Having considered the hierarchical and horizontal principles and practices calculated to avoid these outcomes, we now turn to the vertical dimension of the coordination process as it is encountered in some of the major spending ministries, postponing to Part II the transversal sectoral case studies that exemplify the complex problems encountered in starkly specific form. While a detailed comparison of the size and allocation of function amongst the French governments in the last two decades of the twentieth century would be instructive, we shall confine ourselves to a succinct contrast between the Rocard and Jospin Governments.

The relatively small size of the 1997 Jospin Government (twenty-six)—fourteen ministers, two ministers of state, and ten junior ministers—can be regarded as a deliberate reaction against the excessively large 1988 Rocard Government (forty-seven). As Rocard's *directeur de cabinet* wrote in retrospect, 'A superabundant government, with too many junior ministers, is a recipe for acquiring problems' of Matignon coordination, multiplied by 'obliging ministers and junior ministers to work together who were incapable of doing so, precisely because they did not belong to the same PS faction or because of their incompatible temperaments'.[1] The Jospin Government accorded four junior ministers to the Economy, Finance, and Industry Minister (dealing with the Budget, Trade, Foreign Trade, and Smaller Businesses); two each to Foreign Affairs (European Affairs and Overseas Cooperation) and Infrastructure (Housing and Tourism); one each to Defence, Education, Employment, and Interior. Despite its coalition character, the Jospin Government did not sacrifice efficiency to representation of countervailing Socialist Party (PS) factions in the Mitterrand manner. However, it was unable to avoid the habitual interdepartmental battles, starting with the initial *décrets d'attribution* of functions between them and subsequent turf wars, although fewer ministerial countersignatures had to be secured as the formal manifestation of co-responsibility for government decisions.

[1] Huchon, pp. 112–13.

FOREIGN AFFAIRS

The best guide to the core executive management of foreign affairs is provided by Hubert Védrine, who became Foreign Minister in the Jospin Government. From 1981 he worked closely with Mitterrand through both presidential terms: until 1986 as diplomatic adviser, from 1986 to 1991 as strategic affairs adviser, combined with presidential spokesman from 1988 to 1991, and finally as Secretary General of the Presidency (SGP), 1991–95. As Mitterrand was suspicious of the Quai, he deliberately chose Védrine partly because he was not a member of the diplomatic corps. However, it could not be said of him, as it was of some others, that when he took over the Quai in 1997, he was the minister of affairs foreign to him! Conscious of the ways in which a changing world had weakened France's capacity to protect its national independence and to influence international events, he, nevertheless, stressed the continuity that sought to sustain the national will to dominate events despite a prolonged crisis of self-doubt.

This central impulse to project itself as a great world power is expressed through a dispersed and complex process in which sectoral policies pursued by numerous actors must be coordinated by a strong decision-making core executive, dominated in France by the President. Even in periods of cohabitation, foreign affairs remain primarily a presidential preserve, although his staff work closely with the Quai as he does with the Foreign Minister, who consequently must be acceptable to him. While Mitterrand often confided a matter to more than one person to allow him to choose between them, he relied from 1982 to 1990 on Jacques Attali as his 'sherpa' in pre-negotiating frequent summit meetings. His diplomatic adviser drafted his speeches based on memoranda prepared by the Quai and synthesized the information sent by the Quai before each diplomatic visit to or by the President. Chirac simplified the arrangement, thanks partly to the fact that his SGP, Dominique de Villepin, was a diplomat. Chirac did not use personal emissaries, relying much more than Mitterrand on the telephone, each call being prepared in advance by his diplomatic staff, who inform the Prime Minister and Foreign Minister of their import.[2]

Due to the need for speed and security, foreign policy is the preserve of very few people. President Mitterrand's diplomatic adviser selected ten or so telegrams, out of the total of 200 to 250 received four times daily, for the President to annotate. He worked especially closely with the *directeur de cabinet* of the Foreign Minister to whom he would talk between ten and fifteen times each day. For his part, the Prime Minister's *directeur de cabinet* and staff frequently chair interdepartmental meetings involving major international concerns such as trade negotiations, arms sales, foreign loans, or terrorism. The Prime Minister personally chairs an interministerial committee coordinating the activities of the secret services. Given the frequency and unpredictability of crises, constant collaboration between the SGP and the President's diplomatic and economic staff on the one hand, and the Prime Minister's

---

[2] Kessler, pp. 32–6, 266.

cabinet on the other, is essential if overall coordination is to be achieved in foreign policy. Furthermore, each Prime Minister has been interested in particular bilateral relations: Mauroy in the post-1981 Polish crisis and in the Socialist International, Fabius with European Community Prime Ministers and anti-apartheid, Rocard in New Caledonia, Cresson in diplomatic support for French exports, Bérégovoy and Balladur in monetary relations with Germany and General Agreement on Tariffs and Trade (GATT). However, there is the example of Alain Juppé who, after being an influential Foreign Minister in the Balladur Government from 1993 to 1995, exercised little influence over foreign policy as Prime Minister from 1995 to 1997, when the end of cohabitension allowed President Chirac to exercise more exclusive control.[3] The ambassadors scattered around the world in some 150 embassies (second only to the USA) try to coordinate country by country what often is a microcosm of a sectorized French administration. In 1993, the Juppé reform of the Foreign Ministry created an interdepartmental committee, Comité Interministériel des Moyens de l'Etat à l'Etranger (CIMEE), chaired by its Secretary General to improve coordination in Paris, and annual meetings of all French ambassadors allows the far-flung network to meet the Minister and the President.[4]

In April 1993, the incoming Foreign Minister, Alain Juppé, asked Jean Picq to prepare the reform of the ministry to ensure better coordination and utilization of France's embassies abroad, the ministry having become rather demoralized during the preceding years when Dumas was Minister. A major innovation was CIMEE, which was required to coordinate external action, as well as rationalize and geographically redeploy the administrative resources available. (In the five years between 1993 and 1998, sixty-one posts were abolished and forty-five created, notably in Central and Eastern Europe, in the context of a declining budget.) Each ministry was asked in 1994 to prepare a development plan for its foreign activities. However, the principal organizational change was to reinforce the position of the Secretary General. Not merely was his role in linking Paris and the embassies and his function as the minister's representative in interministerial meetings reaffirmed; he chaired an increased number of intra-ministerial coordinating meetings. These were weekly meetings devoted to political affairs; fortnightly meetings with the heads of each of the major divisions and top line officials; and the regular preparation with all the division directors of his weekly meeting with the minister. As the Secretary General declared in 1997: 'the real problem of our foreign policy is to ensure its coherence and coordination abroad'.[5] An Assistant Secretary General for European and Economic Affairs was appointed to improve the Quai d'Orsay's capacity to play its role in European Community affairs. Nevertheless, these changes could not remedy the fact that the Foreign Ministry has irretrievably lost its semi-monopoly of external affairs.

[3] Kessler, 49.
[4] ENA, La Réforme de l'Etat, pp. 143, 156–9. See also Védrine, pp. 43–52; Schifres and Sarrazin, pp. 167–70.
[5] ENA, La Réforme de l'Etat, p. 159; cf. 156. See also Kessler, pp. 87, 104–7. More generally see 'Les affaires étrangères', special issue of *Revue française de l'administration publique*, No. 69, January–March 1994.

The President exercises a very personal role in foreign policy, often bypassing the Quai d'Orsay through direct dealings with other leaders, foreign ministers, or ambassadors. Furthermore, other bodies resist attempts to coordinate their foreign activities, particularly the Finance Ministry's Treasury and External Economic Relations Divisions or the Nuclear Energy Commissariat. The Elysée staff and such individuals as the President chooses to consult often act in centralized, secretive fashion, without the benefit of the detailed and comprehensive international views of the Quai d'Orsay and so cannot assess the full implications of actions taken. The result is often rapid but badly prepared instructions, poorly coordinated responses to crises, so that it could be claimed that French foreign policy was 'made in three admirably synchronized steps: it is prepared at the Quai d'Orsay, decided on at the Elysée and implemented nowhere'.[6]

The centralization of foreign policy decisions sometimes (e.g. during the Gulf War) works well in a crisis requiring decisive personal intervention but is far less well suited to the bulk of foreign affairs, in which not only the Quai d'Orsay but many other ministries are involved. 'There is a perverse paradox: on the one hand, the clear aggrandisement in the power of the president; on the other, the lack of the technical means to be fully effective for want of full knowledge. As a result, the head of state and his staff concentrate on those issues they consider the most urgent or most sensitive, leaving the administration without clear directives on many other matters and leaving ministers to act on their own. The political system leads to bottlenecks, with instructions badly prepared and actions badly coordinated.'[7]

During cohabitation, there is rivalry between President and Prime Minister to win credit for diplomatic successes, leading to a derisory competition for precedence and press coverage between them at international summit meetings. During the 1986–88 cohabitation, there was 'endemic mistrust' between Mitterrand and the Chirac Government, 'dissimulation and disparagement' envenoming the 'struggle for hegemony, interspersed with moments of agreement, even with real collaboration'.[8] Mitterrand largely kept control of Franco-German relations, while Chirac took over African as well as foreign economic and commercial relations. Other areas, such as major European Union (EU) matters and the Middle East, were managed jointly. However, in non-cohabitension periods, the duality of foreign policy leadership could be but was not always avoided by the Elysée working closely with the Quai d'Orsay. The second cohabitation led Mitterrand to side at weekly meetings with Foreign Minister Juppé against Prime Minister Balladur (notably on the Bosnian and Rwandan crises) in the pre-presidential election context in which Juppé was seeking to help Chirac against the Prime Minister. This enabled President Mitterrand to avoid the 1986–88 reduction in the flow of information deliberately engineered by Prime Minister Chirac.

---

[6] J. Hayward, *The One and Indivisible French Republic*, London, Weidenfeld and Nicolson, 1973, p. 228. See also S. Cohen, 'Decision-making in foreign policy' in F. de la Serre *et al.* (eds.), *French and British Foreign Policies in Transition: The Challenge of Adjustment*, Oxford, Berg, 1990, pp. 209–13.

[7] Samy Cohen, 'Decision-making in foreign policy', loc. cit. p. 213.   [8] Ibid., p. 215.

In the early 1980s, there was a regular Friday meeting of the SGP, Attali, Védrine, the Foreign Minister's *directeur de cabinet*, and the Secretary General of the Quai. In addition to this inner circle, there was an outer circle of interaction between national and international actors or with other national actors. Parliament plays a minor role but some Assembly Foreign Affairs Committee chairmen, such as ex-President Giscard from 1986 to 1989, have provided an input. In 1996, written parliamentary questions on foreign affairs numbered 1,285 (1,161 received replies), with fewer questions on humanitarian action (47) and European affairs (367).[9] Védrine singles out contacts with the heads of national champion firms, especially those selling arms, which 'live in symbiosis with the state. They have acquired an impressive capacity to dissuade it from taking decisions too opposed to their interests or even suggesting the right decision it should take'. Some behave like 'a sort of transnational sovereign state . . . dealing in all continents on equal terms with heads of state'.[10] The systematic corruption associated with arms deals in particular have, however, enjoyed less tolerance in the investigative 1990s than they received during the earlier prevalence of a conspiracy of silence. In particular, there was sometimes tension between the diplomats and the arms salesmen of the General Delegation for Armament.

Before the 1986 onset of cohabitation, Mitterrand and his Socialist Foreign Ministers Claude Cheysson and Roland Dumas had many occasions on their foreign journeys to concert their views, much more easily with the latter than with the former. Thereafter, this was much less straightforward. Whereas in 1981, Mitterrand could, without fear of contradiction, claim, 'foreign policy is mine. I define it and keep it [under my control]',[11] between 1986 and 1988 Chirac made determined efforts to take over as much control of foreign policy as he could, which meant that the weak compromise Foreign Minister, Jean-Bernard Raimond, was torn between them. Chirac's determination to occupy one of the three places at Group of Seven (G7) summits led to the exclusion of Finance Minister Balladur at a discussion of economic affairs and Foreign Minister Raimond from European Council meetings except when the President and Prime Minister were absent. Before the Tokyo G7 summit, Mitterrand made clear in a newspaper interview his relationship with the Prime Minister. 'Each of us has his role, which can be complementary but in the last resort, France must speak to the outside world with a single voice'—his.[12] Chirac's *cabinet* diplomatic unit of seven, which included Thibault de Silguy (EU matters) and Jean Picq (Defence), promoted a conflictual approach to institutional coexistence, despite Balladur's efforts to calm things down. The cat and mouse game between the President and Prime Minister included the denial of some diplomatic telegrams and

[9] Kessler, p. 55.

[10] Védrine, pp. 55–6. He mentions ELF–Aquitaine, Matra, Thomson, Aerospatiale, Générale des Eaux, Lyonnaise des Eaux, Renault, Peugeot, and the large banks.

[11] Favier and Martin-Roland, i, p. 69.

[12] Ibid., ii, p. 658; cf. 656–65 and J.-B. Raimond, *Le Quai d'Orsay à l'épreuve de la cohabitation*, Flammarion, 1989.

memoranda to the former, despite protests to the Foreign Minister.[13] In 1987, Mitterrand played a more active role in the GATT negotiations than he was to do in 1993. However, it was over European policy that Chirac's attempts at dealing directly with Chancellor Kohl threatened most confusion.

While the SGP, the diplomatic adviser, and European Affairs adviser on the President's staff play the most important preparatory role before bilateral and multilateral meetings dealing with the EU, the main quantitative burden falls on the General Secretariat of the Interministerial committee (SGCI) (discussed earlier) and the Quai's European Cooperation Division, the latter being controlled by the Foreign Ministry's Assistant Secretary General for European and Economic Affairs. The Quai is responsible for links with France's Permanent Representation in Brussels, headed by an ambassador. They are regularly consulted before and during the many specialized negotiating meetings attended by French officials from the Paris ministries. They prepare the French positions for some fifteen different EU Councils of Ministers and are involved in drawing up the conclusions. The Quai is the French lead ministry in matters covered by the EU's Common Foreign and Security Policy.[14] While the European Affairs Minister is usually formally subordinated to the Foreign Minister, some have exercised an independent role, especially when they enjoyed the confidence of the President.

The appointment of a member of Mitterrand's staff in 1986 concurrently as head of SGCI ensured that the President was kept fully informed of the day-to-day developments in middle-level EC matters. However, he relied principally on his informal links with the heads of the major EC states and the biannual European Councils to keep a grip on French policy. Only the President and Foreign Minister regularly attended the Council meetings, the European Affairs Minister occasionally replacing one or the other briefly. Their retinue of some thirty included officials representing Matignon, the Quai, and Bercy (the Director of the Treasury and International Economic Relations Divisions in particular), as well as from the SGCI and Permanent Representation in Brussels, who received debriefings at half-hourly intervals and could send a memo into the meeting if necessary. These officials had played their main role in advance interdepartmental preparations of the French position. At these European Council meetings, with their 'almost uninterrupted bartering, rough and often shabby negotiations ... François Mitterrand deployed all the facets of his talent: simultaneously far-seeing and tactical, accommodating or intransigent depending on circumstances or interlocutors, using both patience and surprise, clarity and ambiguity, drawing on his familiarity with history to convey the significance of long term objectives'; he took advantage of the fact that most things were negotiable because each state is in turn 'debtor, creditor, mediator, supplicant,

---

[13] J. Howorth, 'The President's Special Role in Foreign and Defence Policy' in Hayward (ed.), *De Gaulle to Mitterrand*, pp. 154–7; Favier and Martin-Roland, ii, pp. 594–7, 655–71, 674–81. Attali, *Verbatim*, ii, pp. 95, 261, 273, 295, 498. Chirac having pointedly sent him a copy of the Constitution, stressing article 20, Kohl reassured Mitterrand in May 1987: 'I know the Constitution; the most important meetings are those between the President and the Chancellor, especially between François Mitterrand and me!' (quoted ibid., p. 403).   [14] Kessler, pp. 196–8.

indifferent or the current (Council) President'.[15] These complicated manoeuvres were conducted away from the public eye and usually without consulting public opinion. Mitterrand belatedly acknowledged that the architects of European integration had acted as elitist enlightened despots, declaring: 'We are paying today for 40 years of silence on Europe. All the more reason for organising a referendum.'[16] When this was done in 1992 for the Maastricht Treaty, the President received a nasty shock from the narrow approval of his policy.

Dealing with the International Monetary Fund (IMF), the World Bank, and the G7 coordination of economic and monetary policies of the seven major advanced industrial states is primarily the concern of the Treasury Division of the Finance Ministry, which has traditionally taken the lead in resisting US hegemony. This has involved trying to make ECOFIN, the meetings of EU Finance Ministers (and since the creation of the Euro, the meetings of the Finance Ministers of the member countries), an increasingly powerful actor potentially capable of becoming an 'economic government'. In dealing with the World Trade Organization (WTO), it is the External Economic Relations Division of the Finance Ministry that takes the lead but it must coordinate its activities with the Quai and the ministries most directly affected under the aegis of the SGCI because of the involvement of the EC. Like the Treasury Division, it works for the Finance Minister but there is usually either a junior trade minister who has a say or foreign trade is combined with industry, which may either be an independent ministry or under the control of the Finance Minister. Despite its efforts to participate actively in these multilateral economic and financial matters, the Foreign Ministry is a 'spectator rather than an actor'.[17] Even in bilateral trade matters, the Foreign Ministry plays second fiddle to the External Economic Relations Division in the matter of promoting French exports, while the Treasury Division decides how much is spent. The Finance Minister—who has the final say on this expenditure—does not have the same priorities as the Foreign Minister on the countries that should be favoured, while the President will wish to sign contracts when on foreign visits (Mitterrand undertook 154 during his first term from 1981 to 1988), accompanied by a bevy of interested businessmen.[18]

The advent of the Socialists in 1981 led to symbolic changes in the names of some ministries. 'Foreign' became 'External' Affairs to reflect the fact that relations with other countries were an increasingly important part of the work of most ministries. The word 'Development' was added to 'Overseas Cooperation'—the intention being to indicate a more modern and less condescending approach in France's dealings with other countries and former colonies. However, there was a rapid reversion to the title of 'Foreign Ministry' and the Cooperation Ministry concerned principally with France's neo-colonial relations with African states did not fundamentally change them. The minister from 1981 to 1982, Jean-Pierre Cot, who sought to end the

---

[15] Védrine, pp. 393–4, 400; cf. 279–83, 300. Mitterrand's failures included his 1989 improvised proposal of European confederation.

[16] Ibid., p. 557. One of the few ministers supporting a referendum in 1992 was European Affairs Minister Guigou (ibid., pp. 554–5; cf. E. Guigou, *Pour les Européens*, Flammarion, 1994).

[17] Kessler, p. 274; cf. 267–73.   [18] Ibid., pp. 275–89; cf. Favier and Martin-Roland, i, pp. 556–7.

corrupt, clientelist relationships based upon highly personalized patrimonial ties between French and African Presidents, mediated by the special adviser for African Affairs, and substitute an emphasis on human rights and the encouragement of democratization, gradually discovered he was being bypassed. Under de Gaulle and his successor, the Presidents of France's former African colonies had become accustomed to depend on the French government financially, militarily, and for a host of personal favours. Concerned to retain their fragile hold on power, they desperately clutched the leading strings to the Elysée which was happy to buy back much of the substance of its former imperial status by supporting corrupt dictatorships. Once he realized that Mitterrand had reverted to past malpractices, Cot—who had also lost the support of Prime Minister Mauroy by dealing directly with Foreign Minister Cheysson and Finance Minister Delors—resigned in frustration.[19]

Weakly institutionalized because of the nature of the newly 'independent' former colonies, Franco-African links were based upon occult networks coordinated from the Elysée because 'Africa' was part of the President's 'reserved sector'. In place of Jacques Foccart—who operated under de Gaulle and later Chirac—Mitterrand relied upon a Third Republic-style Freemason network, linking his friend Guy Penne with African leaders, supplemented by his journalist son Jean-Christophe Mitterrand, who was quickly nicknamed 'Papamadit' (Daddy told me).[20] This highly personalized form of coordination not only meant that French management of neo-colonial relations was conducted on the African rather than European model; it lent itself to a state corruption which, it is estimated, accounted for at least 40 per cent of the French aid provided. While educational and military cooperation in kind rather than in cash ensured that some aid did materialize, there was little effective control over the bilateral programmes involved and these declined in the 1980s and 1990s. Frequently, official reports denounced the poor medium-term coordination between the Ministries of Finance, Foreign Affairs, and Overseas Cooperation with the French Development Fund.[21] However, little changed.

This continuity with pre-independence malpractices has been challenged in the context of French unwillingness to continue to carry the financial burdens in a region where the costs of influence increasingly far exceed the benefits of perpetuating post-imperial pretence. Already under the second cohabitation, the staffs of the President and Prime Minister Balladur had prepared the halving of the value of the French African franc. The Overseas Cooperation budget having regularly declined since 1992, in February 1998 the Jospin Government merged 'Overseas Cooperation' with the Foreign Ministry, a junior minister being attached to the latter. An Interministerial Committee for International Cooperation and Development coordinates

---

[19] Favier and Martin-Roland, i, pp. 326–33, 338–9.

[20] Schifres and Sarrazin, pp. 170–1; cf. J.-F. Médard, 'France-Afrique: des affaires de famille' in D. della Porta and Y. Mény (eds.), *Démocratie et corruption en Europe*, La Découverte, 1995, pp. 29–41. On the earlier role of Foccart, see S. Cohen, *Les Conseillers du Président. De Charles de Gaulle à Valéry Giscard d'Estaing*, PUF, 1980, ch. 8. Foccart resumed his position during the 1986–88 Chirac Government.

[21] Kessler, p. 340; cf. 306–44, 352–3.

the work of nine or more ministries, under the joint aegis of the Finance and Foreign Affairs Ministries.[22]

A good example of the resistance to coordination is the innovation by President Mitterrand to promote the 'North–South' emphasis he wished to give to French foreign policy on taking office. An Interministerial Delegation for Cooperation and Development was created by a decree of 31 December 1981, but quickly encountered opposition to being coordinated from both Finance Minister Delors and Foreign Minister Cheysson. The result was that this body only met once and then disappeared, testimony to the veto power of these ministers.[23] By the late 1990s, the Secretary General of the Foreign Ministry could claim that closer concertation existed with the Finance Ministry in matters concerning development aid, without having recourse to a formal coordinating body.[24] However, there are continuing problems, for example, in the embassies, where the financial counsellor often reports direct to the Treasury Division and the commercial counsellor to the Foreign Economic Relations Division of the Finance Ministry, making it difficult for the ambassador to play his formal role of overall coordinator. Most ministries make their own foreign contacts directly, rendering general oversight a forlorn pursuit.

A particular type of crisis intervention in which France took the initiative resulted in the resolution adopted by the United Nations in December 1988, on assistance to endangered populations. Credit for this must be given to Dr Bernard Kouchner, who had founded Médecins sans Frontières in 1971, following his dissatisfaction with the role of the Red Cross in the Biafran war to secede from Nigeria. In 1985, the Ministries of Cooperation and of Foreign Affairs established a joint urgent humanitarian intervention unit to assist financially and work with NGOs who carried out operations on the spot. In 1987, during the period of cohabitation, Kouchner persuaded President Mitterrand and Prime Minister Chirac that they should support the 'right of humanitarian intervention' which led to the 1988 UN resolution, subsequently used to help the Kurds, Bosnians, Somalians, and Kosovars in the 1990s. In 1988, Kouchner became a junior minister of humanitarian action in the Rocard Government, taking this responsibility with him when he became Health Minister in the Bérégovoy Government (1992–93). Ten years later he gave up office as Junior Health Minister in the Jospin Government to take charge of the UN operation in Kosovo. He had in 1989 persuaded Foreign Minister Dumas to establish posts of humanitarian attachés in French embassies as part of the campaign to recognize a right to intervene in the affairs of sovereign states for humanitarian purposes. To counteract the dispersion of efforts by the many NGOs involved, a Liaison Committee of International Solidarity Organizations was established in 1991, but it has proved ineffective in coordinating their activities.[25]

Crisis decision-making can place coordination between the President and Prime Minister under intolerable strain, especially in periods of cohabitation in the

---

[22] Kessler, pp. 356–62. On the working of the African franc area, see J. Hayward, *The One and Indivisible French Republic*, p. 250; cf. 251–2 on Franco-African 'cooperation'.
[23] Kessler, p. 103.   [24] Bertrand Dufourcq in ENA, La Réforme de l'Etat, p. 159.
[25] Kessler, pp. 441–51.

approach to a presidential election in which both are to be candidates. This occurred in 1987–88 over the issues of the French hostages in Lebanon and New Caledonia. While the French hostages in New Caledonia were freed violently, with the reluctant support of President Mitterrand for a decision by Prime Minister Chirac, the hostages in Lebanon were exchanged against an Iranian organizer of terrorism, Wahid Gordji. The confrontation with Iran involved a major conflict not only between Mitterrand and Chirac but also between the Foreign Minister, Raimond, and the Interior Ministers, Pasqua and Pandraud (the latter responsible for police matters). The contentious issue was whether Franco-Iranian diplomatic relations should be broken off, with the embassies in Paris and Teheran being surrounded. Chirac and Pasqua favoured a diplomatic break while Raimond advised against it. Mitterrand only supported a diplomatic break if violence was used against French diplomatic personnel. The President was not kept informed of the secret negotiations that led to the eventual partial exchange of French hostages for Gordji and the understanding that diplomatic relations would subsequently be restored. This resulted in a spectacular clash in the TV debate with Chirac before the second ballot of the 1988 presidential election, with reciprocal accusations of lying about this affair. The first institutional coexistence thus ended in bitter recrimination between the contenders for the position of President, without the deliberate timing of the resolution of the two crises apparently shifting votes in favour of the Prime Minister.[26]

The 1993–95 second cohabitation worked much more smoothly, partly because there were few points on which Mitterrand and Balladur disagreed. They were at one over Algeria and Rwanda but not always on Bosnia. This, together with the President's prolonged and debilitating illness, allowed the Prime Minister to encroach discreetly on the President's sphere without ostentatiously appearing to do so. Increasingly, Mitterrand asked Balladur to replace him for periods while he rested during European and North Atlantic Treaty Organization (NATO) Council meetings and at Franco-African summits. More rivalry occurred with Balladur's Foreign Minister, Juppé, as we have mentioned. Nevertheless, they worked together closely and successfully on the difficult GATT negotiations of 1993, ably assisted by Balladur's EU adviser and head of the SGCI, de Silguy. For the French EU Presidency of January–June 1995, de Silguy established an interdepartmental working party at Matignon to manage French government communications, Juppé insisting that the Quai should be closely involved.[27] Monthly meetings between Balladur and Delors ensured that the French Prime Minister and EU President kept in step. The early Chirac–Jospin competitive cohabitation from 1997 did not extend to foreign and EU policy, which was not a significant source of discord, allowing it to sound as though France spoke with one voice.

Despite the advent of a supposedly 'Gaullist' President in 1995 in the person of Jacques Chirac, France has had to accommodate itself to the fact that since the

---

[26] Favier and Martin-Roland, ii, pp. 813–26 and 921–7 on New Caledonia and 838–51, 913–14, and 918–20 on Iran crises.

[27] Brigouleix, pp. 135–8, 168–76. On Mitterrand–Juppé complicity see Domenach and Szafran, *Le Roman*, p. 111.

collapse of the Soviet Union, there is no counterweight to US hegemony in world politics. After the 1991 Gulf War, NATO has confirmed its place as the only truly operational multilateral military organization and the 1999 war in the Balkans with Yugoslavia led France—with reservations—once again to accept a subsidiary role in an Alliance strategy. Shortly before taking office as Foreign Minister in the Jospin Government, Hubert Védrine accepted in testimony to the Assembly Foreign Affairs Committee that France could no longer pursue a 'relatively autonomous role' and was 'potentially threatened by world development'.[28] Foreign policy became increasingly interdependent on EU policy, France seeking to compensate for its incapacity to act alone by associating its EU 'partners' with its objectives without compromising them in the process. Chirac, Jospin, and Védrine have struggled to find a way of reinforcing the European pillar of NATO as a way of reconciling Mitterrand's earlier efforts to create a European defence independent of NATO with the increasing de facto dependence on NATO.

Finally, a consensual part of French foreign policy—cultural diplomacy in general and *francophonie* in particular—has been a traditional, integral, and distinctive feature of the national approach to foreign affairs. This branch of diplomacy is systematically organized by the Cultural, Scientific, and Technical Division of the Foreign Ministry, using its network (1996 figures) of 300 *lycées*, 132 cultural centres and institutes, 1,060 Alliances Françaises, and 200 archaeological excavation *missions*. In each foreign country, their activities are supposed to be coordinated by the cultural counsellor in the embassy but the diversity of activities and actors makes this very difficult.[29] Most of these activities have been bilateral but their linguistic basis was given a multilateral impetus by the 1960s French politico-cultural revival in Quebec. In 1970, an Agency for Cultural and Technical Cooperation was established in Paris and although some thirty states were initially members, most of the cost was financed by France and Canada. By 1997, *francophonie* had attracted fifty states, although only in thirty did French have the status of official language. This was of great value to successive French government strategies of perpetuating the official status of their language in most international organizations.[30]

Summit meetings of francophone leaders have taken place since 1986. In 1988, at the Francophonia summit at Dakar, Mitterrand announced as a *fait accompli* (which the French parliament subsequently honoured) a reduction in the debt of the thirty-five poorest and most indebted countries.[31] Between summits, activities have since 1991 been coordinated by a Permanent Francophonia Council and in 1997, it acquired a Secretary General, former UN Secretary General Boutros-Ghali, 'imposed' by President Chirac. In 1986, Chirac had been the first Prime Minister to appoint a minister responsible for francophone affairs, a practice that was subsequently perpetuated until 1998, usually at junior minister level. This caused coordination problems because many 'francophone' activities were the responsibility of either the Foreign Ministry or the Cooperation Ministry, until they were amalgamated in 1998.

---

[28] *Politique etrangère de la France*, May–June 1997, p. 219, quoted in Kessler, p. 154.
[29] Kessler, p. 379; cf. 369–71, 387–8.   [30] Ibid., pp. 411–19.   [31] Ibid., p. 65.

However, the fact that 'Francophonia is an institutionalised ideology',[32] symbolizing a nationalist belief in the superiority of French culture despite the threat from 'Anglo-Saxon' English, ensures its defence by both politico-administrative and literary-artistic elites, even if this increasingly resembles a rearguard action.

Although we shall consider in the next chapter the diminished role of the Quai in EU affairs—apart from retaining control of the Foreign and Security second 'pillar', a separation which itself raises serious problems of coordination—the attempt to counteract this trend particularly motivated the radical reorganization of the ministry in 1993, by Alain Juppé. Whereas in other EU countries the Foreign Ministry has retained a pivotal role in interministerial coordination for Community purposes, rivalry between French ministries—notably resistance by the Finance Ministry—has frustrated this in France. The result, as we shall see, is that the President, the Prime Minister (to whom the SGCI is subordinate), and the European Affairs Minister are all also involved in trying to coordinate EU policy, with the Finance Ministry seeking to lead in the first 'pillar' and the Interior Ministry in the third 'pillar'. The increasing specialization and internalization of EU affairs means that a ministry dedicated to international—particularly bilateral—diplomatic relations between states, is incapable of effectively implementing its general claim to being the EU lead ministry. The reduction in status of the Quai has resulted in a prolonged identity crisis.[33]

DEFENCE, NUCLEAR TESTS, AND THE *RAINBOW WARRIOR* CRISIS

Due to the need to sustain a contradictory equilibrium between the assertion of an independent foreign and defence policy on the one hand and the increasing need to work with European and NATO allies on the other, Mitterrand was particularly concerned to monopolize personal control of defence strategy. The Prime Minister, Defence Minister, or the military establishment were confined to a subordinate position with the aim of ensuring that 'everything that does not come from the Elysée is blocked by the Elysée'.[34] However, the reality is much more complex than such a presidential monocracy might suggest. This is partly because the small Elysée civil and military staff cannot provide the strategic military-diplomatic-industrial guidelines for a medium- and long-term policy, Mitterrand refusing to confine his advice to one source. He preferred to take full advantage of the diversity within the defence policy community, utilizing its fragmentation to preserve a large measure of personal domination.

The President's key defence adviser is the head of his personal general staff, which is often a stepping stone to the post of Chief of the General Staff. For example, the President cannot simply press the button of the French nuclear deterrent without the involvement of the head of his personal general staff in carrying out the necessary

---

[32] Kessler, p. 436; cf. 424, 437. More generally, see M. Tétu, *La francophonie. Histoire, problématique, perspectives*, Hachette, 1988.　　　　　　　　[33] ENA, *Le Travail Gouvernemental*, ii, p. 769; cf. 752.

[34] This is a quotation from a former Defence Secretariat (SGDN) official in S. Cohen, *La défaite des généraux. Le pouvoir politique et l'armée sous la Ve République*, Fayard, 1994, p. 88; cf. 89–92.

procedures. Relations with the Defence Minister during cohabitation can be diffi-cult. In 1986–88 the President successfully fought a running battle with Defence Minister Giraud, notably over mobile, land-based, tactical nuclear missiles, the Prime Minister rallying to the President to preserve an appearance of consensus. At times of crisis during the second cohabitation of 1993, the President called weekly meetings at the Elysée of the Prime Minister, other concerned ministers, the Chief of the General Staff, his personal chief of staff, and the SGP. Use of France's nuclear deterrent is the President's sole responsibility, although the bunker under the Elysée from which it is controlled is linked to the Defence Ministry and Matignon. Overall, 'Defence policy is the result of a mixture of consensus choices and presidential diktats. In the first case, experts play quite a large part in the detailed refinement of the choices. In the second, powerless and bewildered, they carry out decisions whose logic often escapes them.'[35]

The French concern to have its own independent nuclear deterrent led to two major crises involving core executive coordination, one in 1985 and the other in 1993. The *Rainbow Warrior* fiasco exposed an over-extended and ambiguous chain of command in matters of external security that resulted in poor coordination with disastrous consequences. Ironically the General Direction of External Security (DGSE) had in 1966 been placed under the Defence Ministry to ensure better discipline following the Ben Barka scandal. However, it weakened political supervision, which under Mitterrand was in any case divided between the head of his military staff, General Saulnier and François de Grossouvre in his civil *cabinet*.[36] The sabotage of the Greenpeace *Rainbow Warrior* in Auckland harbour, which was seeking to disrupt France's nuclear tests in the Pacific, amounted to a 'state crime' which led to the per-petration of 'state lies' in the subsequent cover-up. It began with the President's unspecific authorization of Admiral Lacoste, head of the secret service DGSE, to prevent the disruption. Defence Minister Charles Hernu was directly involved in the decision, although neither he nor Lacoste would at the time admit it, even under intense pressure from Prime Minister Fabius. They used the argument of *raison d'état* to justify denying first French involvement in the sinking of the spoiler ship (exacerbated by the death of a photographer crew member) and then their personal responsibility for giving the orders. Lacoste insisted that he was not accountable to the Prime Minister but directly to the President as head of the armed forces. While at an April 1985 Matignon meeting of the Military Nuclear Committee, at which Fabius and Hernu were present, a note was presented on the plan to 'anticipate' the ecologist disruption, it was part of a substantial dossier which the Prime Minister did not read. The head of the President's military staff authorized the expenditure of 1.5 million francs for the operation, in the belief that Lacoste had discussed the matter with Mitterrand, saying, 'As for me, I did not speak to François Mitterrand, as it was a routine matter'.[37]

---

[35] Cohen, *La défaite des généraux*, pp. 32–33; cf. 24–5, 56–7, 66–7, 135, 260–1. See also Schifres and Sarrazin, p. 174; Favier and Martin-Roland, i, p. 55 and ii, pp. 781–813.   [36] Ménage, pp. 446–8.
[37] Favier and Martin-Roland, ii, p. 415; cf. 408–14.

However, the 'routine matter' of preventative action assumed crisis proportions even before the media revealed details of French involvement in August 1995. Informed by Interior Minister Joxe of the veracity of the press reports, the President summoned Fabius and Hernu to a meeting on 15 July to find out the truth, only to be told by the Defence Minister that he did not know who had decided on the sabotage operation. Called to a meeting by Fabius (at which Joxe, SGP Bianco, and the Prime Minister's *directeur de cabinet*, Schweitzer, were present), Hernu's reaction was, 'It is none of his business'. Although conceding that the DGSE was involved, Hernu denied he had ordered the sabotage. Fabius expressed his scepticism, saying that he would not be party to a cover-up.[38] To avoid the crisis gathering force, Fabius was advised to accept collective responsibility for the decision and shelter under an appeal to 'defence secrecy'. With two weeklies about to reveal French involvement in the sabotage, Fabius agreed to concoct an exchange of letters with Mitterrand insisting on a rigorous enquiry into the affair, to be conducted rapidly, but it was a whitewash.[39]

The view from inside the Elysée is provided by Gilles Ménage. He sent a memo to Mitterrand on 5 August 1985 warning him that the government had lost control of the affair, with differences (notably between Hernu and Fabius) threatening to confuse the reaction to the revelations. This made it 'urgent that very close, day to day coordination should henceforth take place between the various ministers concerned'.[40] However, the obstinate denials of Hernu and dissimulations of the DGSE were counterbalanced by Fabius's assertion that 'the guilty would be punished without conveying the impression that he was actively seeking the guilty'.[41] He was clearly handicapped by Mitterrand's lack of will to extract the truth which would require the resignations of Lacoste and probably of Hernu. While Hernu lied to the Prime Minister and President, neither of them saw fit to speak directly to Admiral Lacoste and nor did Fabius himself threaten the resignation that might have precipitated a denouement.[42]

While Fabius continued to press Hernu to admit his responsibility, Mitterrand agreed—against his Prime Minister's advice—to help out his old friend by sending a directive to the armed forces 'reiterating' his order to prevent by force, if necessary, intrusion into French nuclear activities in the Pacific. This could be interpreted as an *ex post facto* justification of the sinking.[43] The culmination of the crisis was finally precipitated by *Le Monde* (17 September)'s detailed revelations of who had carried out the sabotage, leading Fabius to demand of Hernu that the three senior officers concerned should state in writing whether they had advance information or given instructions to carry out the sabotage of the *Rainbow Warrior*. Admiral Lacoste thrice refused to reply, preferring to take the consequences of disobeying the Prime Minister. President Mitterrand agreed, after heated discussions with the Prime

---

[38] Favier and Martin-Roland, ii, p. 418; cf. Ménage, pp. 511, 517–21.

[39] Attali, *Verbatim*, i, p. 1274; cf. Favier and Martin-Roland, ii, pp. 422–5.

[40] Ménage, p. 549; cf. 456.   [41] Ibid., p. 493; cf. 517–22.

[42] Ibid., pp. 524–6; cf. 498, 502, 529.

[43] Attali, *Verbatim*, i, pp. 1276–7; cf. Favier and Martin-Roland, ii, pp. 422–3.

Minister, that Fabius should dismiss Lacoste and Hernu's resignation quickly followed on 20 September. On 25 September, speaking on TV, Fabius belatedly admitted that the DGSE had carried out the sabotage, acting on orders, implying without specifying that Lacoste and Hernu had given them, because they refused to confess.[44] In retrospect, French public opinion was not scandalized by the sabotage, merely annoyed that its perpetrators had been caught after the act, due to their amateurish incompetence.

In time of war, the Chief of the General Staff and the Chief of the President's General Staff play roles that dwarf those of the Prime Minister and Minister of Defence because they are directly answerable to the President. The 1991 Gulf War exemplifies this situation. From mid-January 1991, when the Allies launched their offensive against Iraq, there were meetings of the Defence Council every evening. After a report from the Chief of the General Staff, there were reports from the Defence, Foreign Affairs, and Interior Ministers and sometimes from the Prime Minister. As well as chairing the meeting and settling disagreements, the President informed those present of his direct dealings with foreign leaders. Others who attended the Council were the heads of the three armed services and three members of President's staff: the SGP, his adviser on strategic affairs (Védrine), and Admiral Lanxade, the Chief of his General Staff. It was the latter who acted as the President's spokesman to the media, a role that would normally have been performed by the Defence Minister.[45] This was due to Mitterrand's distrust of Chevènement, known to oppose the war, which was a contributory factor to his resignation.

NATO's air war against Yugoslavia over Kosovo in 1999 resulted in a close strategic collaboration between the President, Prime Minister, Foreign Minister, and Defence Minister and their staffs, despite the fact that it took place during a period of cohabitation. Chirac and Jospin were agreed on both French participation and the need to create a somewhat illusory counterweight to American domination of the military operations. They shared in the conduct of crisis diplomacy, involving not merely frequent contacts by telephone between them for mutual information about their conversations with foreign leaders but similar exchanges between members of their staffs. Twice daily, there were meetings of the head of the President's personal general staff, the Chief of the General Staff, and the defence and diplomatic advisers of the Prime Minister to discuss the progress of military operations. Following these meetings, the Prime Minister received twice daily 'synthesis notes' from his defence and diplomatic *cabinet*. In this context of co-decision, President Chirac did not exploit the potential embarrassment of a Prime Minister whose government included members known to have strong reservations about the French involvement, such as Interior Minister Chevènement and the Communist ministers. This crisis was very much an inner core executive preserve, with the politico-administrative-military superstructure coordinating their activities smoothly.

[44] Attali, *Verbatim*, i, pp. 1283–6, 1289, 1291; cf. Favier and Martin-Roland, ii, pp. 425–40 and Ménage, pp. 521–6, 535, 565.

[45] Kessler, pp. 166–9. See also 'La France en guerre', *Pouvoirs*, No. 58, 1991.

Védrine played an important role in Mitterrand's moratorium on French nuclear tests in the Pacific. In January 1992, the President had approved the programme for later that year but following the Environment Minister's warning that it would be embarrassing if the tests were held before the Rio World Environment Summit of June, the President's military adviser suggested a postponement until the end of that month. Védrine as SGP added a note questioning the need—in the geopolitical and financial context—for such tests, which Mitterrand laconically annotated: 'Yes, quite so'.[46] Faced by a threat of renewed opposition by Greenpeace, Mitterrand decided to suspend nuclear tests. The Chief of Defence Staff Lanxade sent a message to the armed forces making clear the bitterness of their senior officers at not having been consulted, which Mitterrand had avoided doing because it would have allowed the defence lobby to mobilize opposition.[47] Although the President had not expected other nuclear powers to follow the French example, President George Bush suspended US tests in October 1992, which his successor Bill Clinton perpetuated in July 1993.

Under pressure from Chirac and his parliamentary majority, Prime Minister Balladur and Defence Minister Léotard reopened the nuclear tests issue but Mitterrand, using the American and Russian suspension of tests and moves towards partial nuclear disarmament, refused a unilateral resumption, preferring to rely on simulation. Chirac advised Balladur to order the army to carry out the tests, saying they would obey him rather than the President. Balladur sent for Chief of Defence Staff Lanxade and asked point blank: 'Who would you obey?' The unhesitating reply was: 'The President of the Republic'.[48] The only fundamental conflict during the second cohabitation was thus resolved in the President's favour. As President, Chirac in 1995 resumed nuclear tests as a symbolic reassertion of French willingness to act alone.

While the Foreign Office has remained committed to a Gaullist conception of the links between defence and foreign policy, the Defence Ministry and the military have been much more willing to contemplate increased integration into NATO. However, until the 1995 presidential advent of Chirac, such divergences were concealed by the rhetorical reassertion by the President and ministers of a consensus that was intended to maximize political support for an over-extended military stance, whose cost was becoming increasingly difficult to sustain and to justify. Interministerial divergence over French military collaboration with NATO sometimes led to direct confrontation. The Defence Ministry was inclined to negotiate numerous piecemeal agreements with NATO, encouraged by Charles Hernu in the early 1980s, whereas the Foreign Ministry reiterated the Gaullist refusal to accept a *rapprochement*. The 1991 Gulf War having exposed European dependence upon a US-dominated NATO, France was being impelled to accept the logic of military reintegration but this led to disagreements requiring presidential arbitrament. At the end of 1991 Defence Minister Joxe advocated greater participation in NATO, only to be flatly contradicted by Foreign Minister Dumas the next day, asserting that France had no intention of

[46] Favier and Martin-Roland, iv, p. 270.   [47] Ibid., iv, p. 279; cf. 453.
[48] Ibid., iv, p. 459; cf. 454–8.

doing so.[49] Dumas was closer to Mitterrand's standpoint on this issue, reflecting a priority for geopolitical over strictly military factors.

After effectively playing the role of 'head of the armed forces' during the Gulf War, supported by the institutionalized coordination between Elysée, Matignon, the Quai, and the Defence Ministry established well in advance by the head of the President's military staff, Admiral Lanxade, Mitterrand operated less effectively at the start of the French military intervention in Yugoslavia. This led to contradictory statements by, amongst others, Foreign Minister Dumas and Prime Minister Bérégovoy. To put a stop to such discord, President Mitterrand chaired weekly meetings at the Elysée of the Prime Minister, other ministers concerned, his chief of military staff, and the Chief of Staff, with the Government General Secretariat (SGG) present. During the second cohabitation, preceded by meetings at the Quai and Matignon, they played a major role in coordinating crisis management by the President and government. The Bosnian and Kosovo interventions reinforced the lesson of the Gulf War: without US involvement through NATO, even the most independent minded of European nations could not act effectively. On this, Mitterrand, Balladur, and Juppé, Chirac, Jospin, and Védrine, reluctantly agreed.

Chirac subsequently abandoned the hallowed conscript-based conventional army, unsuited for modern warfare, whilst temporarily reversing the Mitterrand moratorium on nuclear tests to preserve the illusion of Gaullist continuity. He left it to Foreign Minister Hervé de Charette to announce France's rejoining the military committee of NATO in December 1995, while postponing a decision to rejoin its integrated military structures pending agreement on co-decision. The Jospin Government, with Védrine as Foreign Minister and Communist participation, stayed much closer to the Mitterrand orthodoxy. While it accepted the abandonment of conscription, which had long since ceased to fulfil its traditional role of creating a civic consciousness, vestigially preserved in the five-day *rendez vous citoyen*, it halted any further reintegration with NATO.[50]

Defence Ministers have been both forced to resign (Hernu, in 1985, over the sinking of the *Rainbow Warrior*) and chosen to resign over policy differences (Chevènement over the Gulf War, in 1991) but apart from the 1986–88 cohabitation, which was characterized by running skirmishes with André Giraud and Chirac, they have concentrated upon dealing with the 'military–industrial complex'. The Prime Minister chairs the Arms Export Council, which includes the Defence, Finance, and Foreign Ministers as well as the head of the President's military *cabinet*, who refers matters to the President when he judges necessary, as he also does on technology transfer. The General Delegation for Armament has usually been given a free hand to play the roles of both client and supplier, promoter of national champion firms, and exporter. The only Defence Minister who attempted to get a grip on it was Pierre Joxe through the ministry's administrative secretary general.[51]

[49] Menon, p. 154. See also Cohen, *La défaite des généraux*, pp. 134–5.
[50] This paragraph is based on A. Menon, *The Ambivalent Ally*, op. cit.
[51] Cohen, *La défaite des généraux*, pp. 241–3. See also E. A. Kolodziej, *Making and Marketing Arms: The French Experience and the Implications for the International System*, Princeton, Princeton University

Chirac deserves the credit for dispelling the illusory Gaullist consensus in French defence policy. Bipartisan support in the Mitterrand years had strengthened the President's freedom of action but under the impact of defence cuts the support dissipated. As the credibility of France's independent stance diminished, the case for sinking differences also weakened. The patriotic posturing and gesture politics in the service of national standing could no longer suppress debate over the shibboleths, especially after the collapse of the Soviet regime. Chirac's Defence Minister, Charles Millon, put the matter bluntly in 1996: 'For more than a decade, the wish to conserve the "consensus" on defence has served as an alibi for the maintenance of the status quo. France, however, can no longer afford to put off decisions that everyone has known for a long time to be inevitable. There can be no sacred cows in defence any more than in anything else.'[52]

The medium-term military programmes are prepared principally by the Defence Ministry, in conjunction with the Finance and Foreign Affairs Ministries. However, these were always more or less drastically modified subsequently. Defence Council meetings, chaired by the President, are prepared by the *directeurs de cabinet* of the Prime Minister, and of the Finance, Foreign, and Interior Ministries. It is at these meetings that adjustments in the military budget—prepared in advance between the Defence and Prime Ministers—are formalized. Defence expenditure has been regularly used to adjust the balance of government expenditure, often in the course of the year and in the 1990s the cuts became significant. In 1995–96 Prime Minister Juppé's attempts further to reduce military expenditure were prevented by Defence Minister Millon getting President Chirac's support. In 1997, Prime Minister Jospin, with the support of his Defence Minister Alain Richard, was able to introduce these cuts in the 1997–2002 medium-term military programme. The SGDN is the Defence Council's secretariat and should, but does not, play a similar coordinating role as the SGCI does in EU policy. As such, while it is involved in arms sales, intelligence, counter-terrorism and the 'proliferation of sensitive technologies', it has not—despite its 1995 reorganization—succeeded in coordinating the military, diplomatic, industrial, and budgetary aspects of defence policy. Crisis Defence Councils can be summoned within hours, involving the chiefs of staff of the armed forces as well as the Foreign and Defence Ministers, the head of the President's military *cabinet* and the SGP.[53]

Press, 1987, pp. 268, 275–82, 287. On the *Rainbow Warrior* sinking in 1985 and Defence Minister Hernu's reluctant resignation, see Favier and Martin-Roland, ii, pp. 404–40. On the struggle between Mitterrand, Chirac, and Giraud, see Howorth, pp. 158–60 for a summary and synthesis; while for more episodic comment, see Attali, *Verbatim*, ii, especially pp. 124–5, 149, 230–2, 238–9, 241–5, 284, 316, 382–3, 398, 408–9, 414–5, 484, 491–3, 500. Mitterrand asserted to Defence Minister Giraud, while visiting a military base on 18 August 1987: 'The President of the Republic does what he wishes, where and when he wants' (Cohendet, p. 229).

[52] Charles Millon in *Le Monde*, 30 June 1996, quoted in Menon, p. 192 and ch. 7 passim. See also J. Isnard, 'Une armée Française "otanisée"', *Le Monde*, 3 July 1988.

[53] Joxe, p. 113 and interview. See also Schifres and Sarrazin, pp. 179–82 and Ottenheimer, p. 314. Elgie points out that 'in 1986 the only budget to be decided at the Elysée was that of the Defence Ministry' (Unpublished paper, p. 13).

An example of how an institution—conscription—with its legitimacy rooted in the French Revolution's 'nations in arms' and having developed an important nineteenth-century role of socializing and integrating provincial and predominantly peasant Frenchmen, came to be abandoned under the pressure of changing circumstances is worth brief consideration. President Mitterrand's 105th proposal in 1981 had been to reduce the period of national military service from a year to six months. There was no clear defence requirement for a large conscript army but it quickly transpired that, as well as leading to greater unemployment at a time when this was increasing, costs would rise by a shift to professional armed forces. The proposal was quickly abandoned on the initiative of Defence Minister Hernu but Socialist opinion was placated through a number of measures including recognition of non-military service by conscientious objectors as a respectable form of national service.[54] However, the 1983 establishment of a Rapid Action Force in an EU context prepared the way for a decisive shift towards fully professional armed forces, which was made by President Chirac (shortcircuiting Defence Minister Millon) with the minimum of fuss, in acknowledgement of the anticipated military requirements of the twenty-first century.

INTERIOR, POLICE, AND PRESIDENT

The historic Interior Ministry, from which so many of the specialized spending ministries were hived off in the nineteenth and twentieth centuries, continues to have a broad competence. This is reflected in the territorial role of the prefects, who seek to coordinate at the local and regional levels the activities of the field services of the spending ministries. As an extension of its traditional law and order responsibilities, the Ministry of the Interior was drawn into international affairs with the growth of terrorism and into European cooperation in police matters. It became a contender for the lead role in matters of immigration policy, while the problems posed by Corsican nationalism challenged the conception of a unitary and indivisible Republic of which Interior Ministers were usually prime protagonists.

Mitterrand's first Interior Minister, Gaston Defferre, paid far more attention to his decentralization reforms than to the police and immigration matters that subsequently bulked much larger in the ministry's activities. All Interior Ministers have also struggled ineffectively with the Corsican problem, which involves problems of terrorism and crime as well as issues over the unity of the Republic. Differences with Prime Minister Jospin were to lead to Interior Minister Chevènement's resignation in 2000 over the issue of greater autonomy for Corsica as a way of ending nationalist violence. In 1999, Prefect Bernard Bonnet, sent to Corsica to replace his murdered predecessor, was arrested for seeking to enforce the law by illegal methods. The problem of how to create the conditions for the rule of law in an endemically lawless context was compounded by a coordination problem, with rival police forces being responsible to the Interior Ministry or, in the case of gendarmes, to the Defence

---

[54] Favier and Martin-Roland, i, p. 391.

Ministry. In a memo to the Prime Minister before the surreptitious incendiary act, Bonnet declared: 'If a minimum of coordination had existed between the investigating magistrates on the one hand and the various police and gendarmery services on the other, inquiries (into the assassination of his predecessor) could have proceeded in a less compartmentalised fashion. This lack of coordination is astounding...'[55]

Corsica is an extreme case of such problems but the attempts to bypass an ineffectually coordinated police by recourse to special anti-terrorist units had already led to disastrous results when used by President Mitterrand in the 1980s. The 'anti-terrorist unit' headed at Defence Minister Hernu's suggestion by gendarme Major Prouteau (later promoted to Prefect!) was to 'distinguish' itself by several exploits. These included arresting in 1982 so-called Vincennes Irish terrorists (having been deliberately misled by the police) and illegal telephone tapping for the President from 1982 to 1986, which led in 1994, when the evidence was discovered, to the indictment of Prouteau and Mitterrand's former *directeur de cabinet*, Gilles Ménage.[56]

Defferre left law and order largely to his junior minister Franceschi, but their relations were so bad that the coordination between police forces suffered. Defferre's successor from 1984 to 1986, Pierre Joxe, rationalized his refusal to be coordinated by claiming that 'the President of the Republic and the Prime Minister do not wish to be bothered with difficult decisions: the minister has to sort things out himself'.[57] Rocard's *directeur de cabinet* says that the intimidating Joxe (Interior Minister again from 1988 to 1991) was second only to Foreign Minister Dumas in refusing systematically to recognize the Prime Minister's authority, taking advantage of their longstanding personal relations with the President. Huchon was forced to obtain from other sources certain memos on police matters that Joxe had not transmitted. After a year, Joxe agreed to have fortnightly meetings with the Prime Minister to discuss security matters and prefectoral appointments, to avoid Rocard being bypassed.[58] Joxe also objected to the Elysée anti-terrorist group's activities, insisting that they not interfere with his police, so he was willing to take on the President if necessary.[59]

Police forces—a perennial problem for French governments—on whom reliance has all too readily led to cynical tolerance of abuse of extensive prerogative police powers, had been used and misused for the partisan and even personal convenience of ministers long before Mitterrand's advent. However, this was an area of state activity where an initial wish by Gaston Defferre and his staff to break with past

---

[55] See the text in *Le Monde*, 28 May 1999, p. 8.

[56] Favier and Martin-Roland, iv, pp. 568–70; cf. i, pp. 515–16, 548–51.

[57] Huchon, pp. 114–16. Cresson also refused to report to Rocard, going direct to Mitterrand (ibid., p. 117). The Pasqua–Pandraud team at Interior in 1986–88 was more united than Defferre–Franceschi, having adjoining offices and a common press office which also controlled the internal circulation of information (Favier and Martin-Roland, ii, p. 703). Pandraud denied some police information to the presidency (ibid. pp. 707–8). [58] Joxe, pp. 203, 206–10.

[59] P. Weil, *La France et ses étrangers*, 1991, 1995 edition, Gallimard, pp. 217–18, 222–4. For details on the various ministries involved in immigration policy, see Appendix 2, pp. 536–41.

malpractices failed badly.[60] Terrorist acts in 1982 led Mitterrand on 17 August 1982 to call a meeting of those responsible for anti-terrorist intelligence and police work. He decided that they were lacking in both competence and the determination to deal with their task and had most of them removed. He announced on TV that day two decisions that were to have disastrous consequences, reflecting the danger of personal fiat leading to precipitate action to impress the public. They were the appointment of Christian Prouteau to head a unit to coordinate anti-terrorism based in the Elysée and of Joseph Franceschi as junior minister for public security, attached to the Interior Minister. Furthermore, Mitterrand made clear that he sought 'an active loyalty, especially someone attached to me personally because ministers change but I stay put. That is why I want personally to choose the prefect of police.'[61] When he did so in 1993, the name was not stated on the decree of appointment until the Cabinet met and it is not clear when either the Prime Minister or the Interior Minister were informed of the President's arbitrary exercise of his discretionary power.[62] Mitterrand's insistence on *personal* loyalty to him was also reflected in the activities of the Elysée anti-terrorist unit. After the 1983 revelation (with photos) by an extreme right-wing weekly, *Minute,* of the weekends regularly spent with his illegitimate daughter and her mother at Souzy-la-Briche, this unit was used to defend the President's privacy from intrusion, a source of damaging functional confusion.[63]

First, let us consider the more classical and predictable confusion caused by the appointment of a minister in charge of public security. Defferre had proposed Frédéric Thiriez, the person in charge of police matters in his *cabinet,* as the new minister but the President instead chose a Mitterrand loyalist, Franceschi. Defferre riposted by imposing Thiriez as *directeur de cabinet* on Franceschi, ensuring that there would be conflict between them, particularly as Defferre now concerned himself more actively with police matters. The rivalry between their *cabinets* exacerbated the disorder caused by a duality of ministerial responsibility, requiring Mitterrand and his staff to intervene. Although Franceschi managed to replace Thiriez, the jealous preservation of 'turf' by senior versus junior minister persisted in police matters, where unexpected events especially required rapid reaction incompatible with such dissension. Mitterrand was reluctant to sacrifice one or both ministers to whom he was close, so it was not until the reshuffle in July 1984 that the problem was resolved by the appointment as Interior Minister of Pierre Joxe with undivided authority.[64]

Second, Mitterrand's adviser on police matters, Gilles Ménage, has testified to the simplifying effects of the change on coordination. 'The arrival of Pierre Joxe led to an essential and decisive innovation: henceforth there was a boss Place Beauvau. Consequently, the Elysée did not have to deal with numerous matters which were not its responsibility and had unnecessarily been coming to it for decision or arbitration.'[65] Joxe made clear that he would deal directly with the President only on important matters and on all others with the SGP and Ménage. Joxe tried in vain to

[60] Ménage, pp. 55–61, 77. On the French police forces, see J. Hayward, *Governing France,* pp. 149–55.
[61] Ménage, p. 66; cf. 63–4, 178.　　　[62] Ibid., p. 80.　　　[63] Ibid., p. 96; cf. 266, 297–8.
[64] Ibid., pp. 69–71, 79, 89, 92–3, 97–8, 125.　　　[65] Ibid., p. 123.

persuade Mitterrand to let him take full responsibility both for anti-terrorism and the protection of his personal privacy out of the hands of the Elysée unit, which however survived until 1988.[66] He had more success with his police modernization plan, whose cost brought him into conflict with Finance Minister Bérégovoy. Joxe made effective use of his good relations with the *Le Monde* investigative journalist Edwy Plenel to activate police, trade union, and public pressure to overcome Finance's opposition.[67] The tapping of this journalist's telephone was one of the Elysée anti-terrorist unit's exploits, to which we now turn.

Ménage was not involved in the creation of this ill-fated unit and he made it his first business on becoming Mitterrand's *directeur de cabinet* in 1988 to abolish it. The lack of security coordination was the reason—if not the justification—for setting it up. 'In France, until 1983, the President of the Republic's security was organised not separately but under the authority and responsibility of the ministers concerned, in a particularly complex and compartmentalised sharing of duties.'[68] In addition, Mitterrand's suspicion of the right-wing political sympathies of many in the police forces, and his low opinion of their competence, combined to lead him to turn to Christian Prouteau, the head of the special gendarmerie unit *Groupe d'Intervention de la Gendarmerie Nationale* (GIGN), with the encouragement of Defence Minister Hernu (son of a gendarme and in charge of the gendarmerie).[69]

The confusion of roles of this Elysée unit, initially intended to protect the President but quickly extended to cover anti-terrorism in the wake of the frequent outrages, notably the 9 August 1982 anti-semitic explosion in the Rue des Rosiers, was initiated by Prouteau himself. In a note to the President on 13 August 1982, he asked to be placed in charge of a secret Elysée unit because 'the centralisation in a single unit of a mission actually shared by at least four "rival" services will alone be effective'.[70] Mitterrand's public adoption of this proposal, with a 'coordination, information and action mission' in conjunction with Defferre and Franceschi, was initially welcomed as a sign that terrorism was being taken so seriously that it was being made part of the President's 'reserved domain'.[71] Two coordinating mechanisms were established in the Ministry of the Interior. Every morning an Anti-Terrorist Liaison Bureau met under the chairmanship of Franceschi's *directeur de cabinet*, Thiriez, to overcome compartmentalization. It published a daily bulletin. Once or twice weekly and when circumstances required, a meeting jointly chaired by Defferre and Franceschi brought together the heads of police from the central administration and the prefect of police with the *directeurs de cabinet* of the Prime Minister and External Relations Minister, the special adviser of the Defence Minister, and Ménage on behalf of the Elysée. These informal interministerial meetings for sharing information prepared the way for Joxe's formal Interministerial Anti-Terrorist Committee.[72]

---

[66] Ménage, pp. 124–5, 297–8, 310.
[67] Ibid., pp. 149–51; cf. 799, 803. See also P. Joxe, *A propos de la France*, 1995, p. 211.
[68] Ménage, p. 169; cf. 167, 171.   [69] Ibid., pp. 174–7.   [70] Ibid., p. 180; cf. 178–81.
[71] Ibid., pp. 182–6; cf. L. Greilsamer, 'Le gardien du président', *Le Monde*, 28 August 1982.
[72] Ménage, pp. 187–8.

The Elysée unit was to reveal the dangers of Mitterrand's preferred mode of decision-making, relying on 'direct and exclusive' personal accountability to him, based on 'a series of vertical and parallel links, as watertight as possible'.[73] Nothing could be more anti-coordination in its procedures, preventing team work, accentuated in this case because of Prouteau needing to know in detail about Mitterrand's private life to protect his security. He enjoyed almost complete autonomy, reporting only to the President, to the great irritation of the police and the Ministry of the Interior.[74] The confusion of the President's personal security with the anti-terrorist requirements of national security was a striking example of the 'court politics' that has been—along with hierarchical politics and committee politics—such a distinctive feature of the Fifth Republic.[75]

The scope for the abuse of personal power that the Fifth Republic allowed the President and his chosen acolytes is exemplified by the recourse to telephone tapping, not merely for the respectable needs of fighting crime, but for partisan and arbitrary purposes. Ironically, Mitterrand was one of the politicians whose telephone had been 'bugged' in the past and he had repeatedly condemned it[76] but he now had unscrupulous recourse to it. The Elysée unit nevertheless survived until 1988, Mitterrand wishing to preserve it during the two cohabitension years until the next presidential election, after which it was wound up.[77]

Mitterrand assumed office in 1981 committed to giving new rights to immigrants, of which the right to vote in local elections was to be the most difficult to enact, while the reduction in illegal immigration proved to be the most difficult to enforce. Periodically, previous illegal immigrants—the *sans papiers*—were accorded 'exceptional regularization' in the hope that the slate could be wiped clean. Some 130,000 people benefited from the gesture in 1981, providing grist to the National Front propaganda mill. As for voting in local elections, we shall see in Chapter 8 that it was not Mitterrand's intention that it should be rapidly implemented and Prime Minister Mauroy recalled that 'In 1981 it was not a matter of urgency and afterwards it would have been a provocation'.[78] From 1982, faced by a public opinion that was responding with increased favour to anti-immigrant sentiments, under the influence of the Socialist leaders—especially the mayors of large towns, like Mauroy (Lille) and Defferre (Marseille), in direct contact with the problem—the immigration policy emphasis changed from generosity to harshness, although, compared to Germany, France never succeeded in expelling more than a tiny fraction of the illegal immigrants.[79]

Many ministries are involved in dealing with immigration policy—notably Foreign Affairs and Justice—but the Interior Ministry has tended to play a lead role in its more repressive aspects. A separate junior minister to deal with immigrants

---

[73] Ménage, p. 189.   [74] Ibid., pp. 190–6.   [75] See above (p. 3).

[76] Hayward, *Governing France*, p. 152; cf. 151–3.

[77] Ménage, pp. 233–4, 245, 263, 319–23. On the 'Vincennes Irish' affair, see ibid., pp. 576–82, 596–620, 638–41, 697–705. On the bizarre Hallier saga, see ibid., pp. 276–96, 762.

[78] Quoted in Favier and Martin-Roland, i, p. 171; cf. 169–70.   [79] Ibid., pp. 172–4.

was attached to the Minister for National Solidarity (Social Affairs) in 1981, motivated specifically by the lack of coordination, as well as for symbolic reasons. However, he quickly came into conflict with the Interior Ministry over the expulsion of illegal immigrants, part of a continuing guerrilla warfare that was won by Interior.[80] The abolition of the post of junior minister for immigration by the Chirac Government allowed the new Minister of the Interior, Charles Pasqua, to adopt a hard line, reversing in 1986 the more permissive Socialist legislation of 1981 and 1984. This was symbolized by the priority given to repression in the competitive political context with a revitalized National Front. The return of the Left in 1988 led Mitterrand to press Prime Minister Rocard and Interior Minister Joxe to abrogate the 1986 Pasqua Law's strengthening of anti-immigration police powers. Reluctance on their part, despite pressure from the Foreign Affairs and Justice Ministers, ensured that there were minimal differences between the 1989 Joxe Law and the 1986 Pasqua Law.[81]

The resuscitation of the post of a junior immigration minister in the Cresson and Bérégovoy Governments changed little and the victory of the Right in 1993 led to the return of Pasqua as Minister of the Interior and renewed repressive legislation, exacerbated by his successor Jean-Louis Debré from 1995 to 1997. After the Constitutional Council (CC) (presided over by Mitterrand's former Justice Minister Badinter) struck out key articles in the 1993 Pasqua Immigration Law, Mitterrand secured a concession on the right of asylum from Balladur in the subsequent referendum, the matter being negotiated between Bazire, Balladur's *directeur de cabinet*, and Michel Charasse. The victory of the Left in 1997 resulted in further legislation with nationality matters being confided to Justice Minister Guigou and immigration to Interior Minister Chevènement, the ensuing coordination problems being discussed in Chapter 8.

JUSTICE AND JUDICIAL INDEPENDENCE

In the 1981 Mauroy Government, Robert Badinter as Justice Minister was very much Mitterrand's choice. Having discussed his plans in advance, he enjoyed Mitterrand's support (except in his efforts to increase his ministry's budget) until he left the ministry to become president of the CC in 1986. He had an impressive ministerial record of achievement: abolition of the death penalty (France was the last European democracy to abandon the death penalty, which continued to enjoy majority public support), of the State Security Court, and of the crime of homosexuality, as well as according the right of appeal to the European Court of Human Rights. By accepting the European Convention of Human Rights protocol on the death penalty, he made this decision virtually irreversible, despite the persistent hostility of majority opinion. By contrast, a disastrous appointment in the Rocard Government was Pierre Arpaillange, whose distinguished legal career had not prepared him to act decisively

---

[80] Weil, pp. 294–5, 303–5 and Favier and Martin-Roland, ii, pp. 287–90.
[81] Charasse, pp. 247–8.

as Minister of Justice. Rocard's *directeur de cabinet* was forced to deal with him each week because the Prime Minister, having failed to have him dismissed, refused to see him.[82]

Access to the President's archives has revealed that, far from abandoning the previous habit of presidential intervention both in politically sensitive judicial appointments and in particular court cases by instruction to the state prosecutors, Mitterrand indulged his personal and political preferences without inhibition. In 1981, a confidential note from the SGP identified four appointments that were 'levers of power', so it was desirable that suitable changes should rapidly be made. They were: the director of criminal affairs, the director of judicial services, the Paris Prosecutor General, and the Secretary General of the Superior Council of the Magistrature. These changes were expeditiously made. Appointments to this Council in the President's gift were decided on grounds of 'personal familiarity and political proximity' to Mitterrand or a member of his staff. Interventions in court proceedings ranged from civil to criminal cases, not merely those concerning politicians but even mundane matters such as driving and hunting permits! Such intervention might be prompted by a newspaper article or at the request of an individual or an association. It might merely amount to asking for information but could involve giving an order, conveyed in a euphemistic formula. For example, Mitterrand asked for sanctions to be imposed upon two judges who had virulently given vent to anti-immigrant sentiments. He was told by the Justice Minister that he could not interfere in freedom of expression in court proceedings but that such conduct would be borne in mind in future promotion decisions.[83]

When the Jospin Government took office in 1997, concerned to avoid the mistakes of the Mitterrand era, it proceeded to carry out its electoral promise to end such abuses of power. Justice Minister Elisabeth Guigou declared that no interventions in particular cases would be made and prosecutors have since confirmed that they have no longer received any, even by telephone. This practice had frequently involved delaying or dropping a case. Thus, her PS predecessor, Henri Nallet, admitted that in 1989, when the Urba corrupt PS party funding affair surfaced, he had slowed down the judicial process until amnesty legislation had been passed by the Rocard Government. Her right-wing predecessor, Pierre Méhaignerie, in 1994 delayed the prosecution of his ministerial colleague Gérard Longuet, to allow him time quietly to resign first. Many other examples could be given to show why—under the pretext of avoiding a 'Judges' Republic'—it required Prime Minister Jospin's full weight behind his Justice Minister to beat off resistance to the legislation reforming the relationship between prosecuting judges and governments. Both the Ministers for the Civil Service and the Interior were particularly hostile to this major step in shifting France from *raison d'état* to an *état de droit*, as were many members of parliament,

[82] Huchon, p. 115 and Favier and Martin-Roland, ii, pp. 318, 521. On Badinter, see Favier and Martin-Roland, i, Part II, ch. 6.

[83] Paper presented by Alain Bancaud to the 14–16 January 1999 colloquium of the Institut François Mitterrand, *Changer la Vie. Les Années Mitterrand, 1981–1984*, reported in *Le Monde*, 23 June 1999, p. 9.

especially after the 1999 resignation of Finance Minister Strauss-Kahn. However, the concurrent reform of the Superior Council of the Magistrature leaves the appointment of state prosecutors to the Minister of Justice.[84] The constitutional amendments incorporating this reform and that of the prosecuting service relationship with the Justice Ministry were postponed by President Chirac until the bill strengthening the presumption of innocence was passed, it being freely asserted that this was due to his wish to benefit from its safeguards personally in relation to Paris Town Hall corrupt practices when he was Mayor.

EDUCATION MINISTER, PRIME MINISTER, AND PRESIDENT: THE 1984 CRISIS

Education in France has an explosive quality that defies attempts at core executive coordination. It has been marked by periodic presidential crisis interventions, either to defuse unrest or to encourage it. Mitterrand, generalizing from the attempts to implement his electoral commitment to create a unified education service, declared that 'in France problems are only resolved as a result of crises. Until one has reached maximum tension in the trial of strength, nothing happens, nothing is resolved'.[85] The 1984 Savary Education Bill's attempt to integrate private schools into the state system, despite heroic efforts at compromise to placate now the Church lobby, now the secularist lobby, led to the President—after personally redrafting it—deciding to withdraw the bill. This followed massive public demonstrations (culminating in Paris with 1.3 million people), the resignation of the Education Minister who had been disavowed, and the resignation of an exhausted Mauroy as Prime Minister, who had identified himself with Savary. How did this fiasco come about, with the Prime Minister siding with his Education Minister, who had been disavowed by the President?

In 1981, the Mauroy Government would have been in a strong position to enact the ninetieth of Mitterrand's 110 electoral 'Propositions for France', the creation of a 'great unified and secular public service of national education', before the opponents could mobilize effectively. However, Mitterrand had committed himself in a letter to a weighty Catholic lobby, the National Union of Parents of Private Schoolchildren (UNAPEL), that this integration would only be brought about as 'the result of a negotiation and not of a unilateral decision...I intend to convince and not compel'.[86] Minister of Education Alain Savary, in his retrospective account, wrote: 'For over three years, until the 12 July 1984, when I decided to resign from the Government, I continuously referred to this letter as my source of inspiration, especially as I never had any subsequent guidance that was as coherent and

---

[84] See the report in *Le Monde*, 23 June 1999, p. 8.

[85] Favier and Martin-Roland, ii, pp. 184–5.

[86] Ibid., p. 122. For a blow-by-blow account, on which this discussion draws heavily, see Favier and Martin-Roland, ii, pp. 119–73, 184–94 and Attali, *Verbatim*, i, pp. 912, 962, 965–9, 1012–17.

comprehensive, so I decided to consider its contents as directives.'[87] This initial policy choice, to seek consensus on an issue that involved the confrontation of the histori- cally institutionalized protagonists of the Church, supported by the Right and the secularizers, championed by the Left, could be considered with hindsight as doomed to failure. However, compromise appeared possible at certain moments between 1981 and 1984, only to be frustrated by the reciprocal intransigence of the prota- gonists and the decisive reluctance of President Mitterrand to enforce integration.

What is not in doubt is that Savary and his adviser-negotiator Jean Gasol acted throughout in good faith in the prolonged process of concertation with both sides. For most of the pre-1984 period, when matters came to a head, the President and Prime Minister were content to leave this delicate exercise in reconciliation to the Education Minister, who in turn relied principally upon Gasol, a committed Christian as well as a Socialist. However, each side—the teachers' unions in state schools (FEN and SNI) and the National Committee for Secular Action (CNAL) versus the National Committee of Catholic Education (CNEC) and the UNAPEL—used the time afforded by Mitterrand's initial commitment to mobilize their supporters for a trial of strength. After 100,000 came out for the Church Schools in Paris in April 1982, the secularists brought out 200,000 for the centenary of the Ferry school legislation at the Bourget. However, at the latter meeting, Savary's speech, which attempted to equate secularization with tolerance and pluralism, was greeted with catcalls, reflecting a sense that 'their Government' was abandoning its commitment to a unified state system of education.[88]

Before preparing legislation, Savary took the precaution of showing President Mitterrand three alternative memoranda prepared by Gasol setting out the guide- lines, prior to adoption by the Cabinet on 4 August 1992 of the one he preferred. Mitterrand deleted the two that represented the strongest and intermediate affir- mations of the unified state system, so that by the summer of 1982 that commitment had clearly been abandoned.[89] The attempt to secure a compromise was pursued by a series of official and secret bilateral discussions with the disappointed secularists and the Catholic lobby, which was increasingly optimistic about diluting the proposed reform. This was reflected in the poor turnout at secularist demonstrations and increasingly enthusiastic mass meetings of the Catholic lobby. At the 21 December 1983 Cabinet meeting at which Savary presented his proposed legislation, Mitterrand rounded on the minister for having adopted the strategy he had forced upon him. He now described the problem as insoluble and declared that the government had been guilty of excessive optimism from the start.[90] This volte-face amounts to being wise after the event.

Mitterrand now decided to become much more directly involved, having lost confidence in the Education Minister's capacity to reach a settlement. While keeping the legislative option open by devoting several Saturday mornings to redrafting the

---

[87] Favier and Martin-Roland, p. 122, quoting A. Savary, *En toute liberté*, Hachette, 1985.
[88] Favier and Martin-Roland, pp. 127–9.   [89] Ibid., pp. 129–30.
[90] Attali, *Verbatim*, i, p. 845; cf. Favier and Martin-Roland, pp. 136–8.

Savary Bill, the President was seeking a way out. With the Catholic capacity to mobilize showing its growing strength—80,000 demonstrators in Bordeaux in January 1984, about 150,000 in Lyon, 300,000 in Lille, and 400,000 in Rennes in February, 800,000 at Versailles in March—Mitterrand and his staff prepared the ground for a final retreat. While Mitterrand asked Charasse to work on a diversionary proposal to submit the issue to a referendum, which would first require an amendment of article 11 of the Constitution, he also secured the support of PS First Secretary Jospin for a tactical withdrawal to overcome unrest of the secularists.[91]

However, to confuse problems of coordination further, apart from the President negotiating separately from the Education Minister, Prime Minister Mauroy also decided to take the matter personally in hand. Savary, under pressure from the Assembly Socialists—themselves pressured by the secularist FEN and in the knowledge that party membership cards were being torn up and sent to Mitterrand—appealed to Mauroy to reject amendments that would destroy the fragile balance of his bill. However, the Prime Minister decided in May to give way to his parliamentary party pressure because he feared he would lose their support for the Bill. He sought to secure Mitterrand's support for his decision, only to be told: 'the Prime Minister must do as he wishes and accept responsibility'.[92] The Catholic leaders decided that, the compromise having been abandoned, they would call a massive public demonstration in Paris for their supporters on 24 June 1984; 1.3 million people attended, the largest turnout since the Liberation.

A few days before, an opinion poll had indicated that 44 per cent thought the Savary Bill threatened the very existence of private education, 35 per cent disagreed, and 21 per cent did not express an opinion. Emboldened by the poll and the demonstration, the Right called for a referendum on the Savary Bill, which played into Mitterrand's hands. Having judged that the crisis had reached 'maximum tension', he now returned to his idea of proposing a referendum to amend article 11 of the Constitution—which he expected would not materialize—preparatory to not calling the referendum proposed by the Right which he knew he would lose. This would provide the smokescreen behind which he would abandon the Savary Bill. He decided this after securing the support of PS First Secretary Jospin and the constitutional advice of Charasse. Prime Minister Mauroy was faced with a *fait accompli*, being informed on 12 July 1984, the day Mitterrand spoke to the nation on TV, after a Cabinet meeting at which the matter was not discussed! In retrospect, Mitterrand said that he realized that his decision to abandon the Savary Bill would not only lead to the Education Minister's resignation but probably also that of the Prime Minister.[93]

The surprise created by Mitterrand's announcement of a 'referendum on the referendum' achieved its intention of switching press and public attention away from the education policy fiasco. Savary's resignation was quickly followed by that

---

[91] Favier and Martin-Roland, pp. 139–45.   [92] Ibid., p. 157; cf. 145ff.
[93] See the interview of Mitterrand reported ibid., pp. 184–5; cf. 177–86. See also Attali, *Verbatim*, i, pp. 1013–14 which describes the post-Cabinet meeting 'surrealist' lunch of PS leaders at which Mauroy alone was in favour of continuing with the Savary Bill.

of Mauroy, against Mitterrand's wish that 'He should manage this crisis to the end'.[94] The smokescreen referendum proposal duly dissipated but meanwhile the French people were becoming accustomed to a young, new Prime Minister, Laurent Fabius. The integration of the dualist French education system had been postponed indefinitely and everyone could return to the status quo. Mitterrand subsequently supported direct action by university students against the Chirac Government in 1986 (leading to the resignation of the Higher Education Minister) and the mass *lycée* movement demonstrations in 1990. The latter forced Prime Minister Rocard to deal with a 4.5 million franc budget deficit arising from the increased education expenditure the President had promised without consulting either him or Education Minister Jospin. The *directeur de cabinet* of the Prime Minister commented that Mitterrand had stabbed Rocard in the back.[95] He survived this indignity longer than Savary and Mauroy did in 1984!

INADEQUATE HEALTH POLICY COORDINATION AND THE CONTAMINATED BLOOD CRISIS

Despite the massive importance in financial and human terms of public expenditure on health, the Health Minister has always been low in the pecking order, annually attracting those at the bottom of the ENA competition for senior administrative posts. Another indicator of its low standing is that in 1986, when Chirac was forming his government, he overlooked the need to appoint a Health Minister, an omission that was only repaired several days later.[96]

In a very critical report on the reform of health administration to an ENA colloquium in 1997, it was suggested that to overcome its compartmentalization and lack of coherence, it would be necessary to appoint a secretary general to improve coordination in three ways: first, to provide coordination between the ministry's divisions and the actors in the health system; second, to avoid short-term concerns preventing strategic attention to long-term issues; third, to improve links with other ministries.[97]

The contaminated blood crisis was to highlight all these inadequacies, as well as pinpointing the difficulty of personalizing responsibility for dispersed policy decisions that go badly wrong in a political system with a weak commitment to collective responsibility. The phrase that this scandal contributed to the anthology of memorable political sayings was the statement in November 1991 by Social Affairs Minister Georgina Dufoix that she was politically 'responsible but not guilty' penally. In the

---

[94] Attali, *Verbatim*, i, p. 1017; cf. 115–16 and Favier and Martin-Roland, pp. 190–3.
[95] Favier and Martin-Roland, ii, p. 538; cf. 532–7 and Huchon, p. 117.
[96] R. Bacqué and M. Van Renterghem, 'La Santé Paralysé', *Le Monde*, 10 March 1999, p. 15.
[97] ENA, *La Réforme de l'Etat*, pp. 170–2. The resignation of the Director General of Health in May 1999, criticizing the internal organization of the Ministry of Health for its inability to programme and coordinate its priorities, is indicative that these weaknesses continued to the end of the century. See *Le Monde*, 20 May 1999.

1999 trial of three ministers concerned, only Health Minister Edmond Hervé was found guilty but he was not punished. The scandal led to a major setback in the political career of Laurent Fabius, Prime Minister when the lethal blood transfusions took place.

The 1980s contaminated blood transfusions, which in France infected four times the number of people as in Italy, five times the number in Spain, six times that of Germany, and thirteen times that of the UK, was a sinister example of French exceptionalism at work, as a source not of national pride but of self-inflicted shame. It was a by-product of the Aids epidemic and was particularly poignant because the people that suffered especially were haemophiliacs. In health matters of life and death, such as Britain was to experience in the 'mad cow' affair, public opinion sought the guilty. In France, the contaminated blood scandal was exploited politically by the Right in the run-up to the 1993 general election. A Former Premier, Chirac, argued that it was 'materially impossible for a Prime Minister to know about all that is dealt with in the ministries. His *cabinet* should theoretically know everything, but in practice it does not either, and any doubt should lead to a presumption of innocence.'[98] However, in the face of hostile public opinion in search of scapegoats, Fabius asked the National Assembly 'to accuse me of acts which I have not committed', and it duly included him with the two ministers more directly concerned.[99]

A Court of Justice of the Republic having been established in July 1993 to try ministers penally for acts committed while in office, the twelve members of parliament and three judges constituting the Court tried Fabius, Dufoix, and Hervé in February and March 1999. One of the themes that quickly emerged was the one referred to by Chirac—the reliance of all ministers and not just the Prime Minister on their *cabinets*, particularly their *directeur de cabinet*. Another was the extent to which the Junior Health Minister, Hervé, apart from financial matters, had de facto autonomy from the Social Affairs Minister, Dufoix. Yet another was the fact that information was so filtered before reaching the Prime Minister that he was not aware of the health problems that would emerge. As the Advocate General declared: 'The ministers' fundamental fault is that they have allowed a barrier to be built between them and their entourage which acts like an impermeable membrane so that technical information was not transmitted from the *cabinets*.'[100] So 'technical' matters such as the use of prisoners as blood donors (a major source of contamination) and the type of Aids test used (American Abbot or French Pasteur) only belatedly reached ministers. In fact, as soon as he was informed, Fabius acted quickly in the matter of compulsory testing of blood donors. The prosecution asked that the ministers be declared not guilty, as they might be politically, but were not penally, responsible for the actions and inactions of their subordinates.[101]

---

[98] Favier and Martin-Roland, iv, p. 357; cf. 110, 347–54.   [99] Ibid., p. 360; cf. 355–9.

[100] *Le Monde*, 18 February 1999, p. 9. The very full Court Reports of *Le Monde* from 9 February to 11 March 1999 can be consulted with advantage.

[101] Ibid., 25 February 1999 for Fabius's declaration to the court and 26 February 1999 for the statement of the prosecution case reflecting the charges. See also 10 March 1999 report on the court's decision.

A collective series of mistakes of the medical profession and the politico-administrative superstructure could not be satisfactorily resolved other than by holding ministers politically responsible but not penally guilty...as Georgina Dufoix had said in 1991, provoking public outcry. In the event, voting along partisan lines, the Court of Justice condemned Health Minister Hervé for negligence but dispensed with imposing any penalty. The Prime Minister and Social Affairs Ministers were judged not to have delayed vital decisions and in the former case to have actually speeded them up once he was properly informed. Those deemed culpable were a junior minister and others lower down who had not enabled their superiors to coordinate and decide in full knowledge of the facts then available. The limits of control from above were thereby demonstrated, with those 'in charge' at the mercy of those who served them. The magistrate investigating the non-ministerial actors decided in 1999, after six years' investigation, that thirty people should be charged with offences connected with 'involuntary homicide'. These included Louis Schweitzer (then *directeur de cabinet* of Fabius) head of Renault, Fabius's scientific adviser, the *directeur de cabinet* of Dufoix and the most directly involved member of Hervé's *cabinet*. From a core executive standpoint, it is of interest that, in marked contrast with the attempt to integrate the dualist French schools system, the President of the Republic was at no point involved in this crisis. This was not the case, to put it mildly, in the next example we shall examine.

STATE CULTURE AND THE PRESIDENT'S ARCHITECTURAL PROJECTS

The French Fifth Republic established a Ministry of Cultural Affairs in 1959, which by 1989 had—in celebration of the French Revolution—expanded into a Ministry of Culture, Communication, the Bicentenary, and Major Public Works. Whereas de Gaulle had been content to leave cultural matters to his renowned minister André Malraux, Mitterrand—a self-conscious 'cultural Head of State'—was accused of promoting through his minister Jack Lang a modernizing and missionary secular cult united to a frivolous mass consumption society. Champions of an elite culture, allergic to the imitation of American methods for the extensive cultivation of the provincial French desert, vociferously attacked the interventionist zeal with which state-subsidized mass culture was propagated with the support of incentives broadcast by committed politico-administrative missionaries. As Marc Fumaroli vitriolically put it, 'This Culture was invented by an oligarchy suffering from a complex consisting of a little mythomania, plenty of megalomania, even more paranoia and very little real culture'.[102] This uninhibitedly assertive populist approach, of which Lang was the official exponent for the decade from 1981 (apart from the 1986 to 1988 interlude), proved popular, ensuring that President Mitterrand's capacity to

---

[102] M. Fumaroli, *L'Etat Culturel. Essai sur une religion moderne*, Editions de Fallois, 1992, p. 393; cf. 179–83, 217, 234, 250–3.

indulge his more traditional architectural proclivities could benefit from broad-based public support.[103] However, it was part of a pre-1981 Socialist programme to establish 'a powerful, properly funded central-government department to coordinate all types of cultural action'. As early as 1974, Mitterrand had declared that devoting 1 per cent of the budget to culture was 'an indispensable minimum'.[104]

Mitterrand restored Culture's separate ministerial status in 1981 but frustrated the desire for a more coordinated policy of 'state-initiated spontaneity' by separating it from Communication, as well as establishing a Ministry of Free Time! Given the PS expansive—almost all-inclusive—conception of culture, Mitterrand had not given his minister Jack Lang 'a ministry broad enough to carry out such a hegemonic enterprise'.[105] Although his rather exhibitionist personal style led to the ministry being identified with the minister, Lang deserves the credit for ensuring that culture was accorded political priority even in the hard economic times of the 1980s, enabling him finally to carry out Mitterrand's 1974 promise, renewed by him in 1981, of increasing the Culture budget to 1 per cent of the total.[106] Despite the urge to redefine as well as reassert a cultural priority, the first Bill introduced by Lang in 1981 was to reverse the 1979 decision to end resale price maintenance for books[107]—to protect the smaller bookshops beloved of President Mitterrand—while the last of Mitterrand's monolithic architectural projects was the library that was to acquire his name. So books had pride of place from beginning to end.

While President Mitterrand's preoccupation with monumental architecture as the distinguished feature *par excellence* of France's contribution to civilization might seem to be a personal obsession, it conforms to the pattern we would expect from a historical institutionalist conception of French political culture. Forerunners such as Louis XIV, Napoleon, and Louis Napoleon indicate that the Republic's monarch was following in the footsteps of kings and emperors, with Pompidou and Giscard more modestly seeking to leave a prestigious, permanent visible mark on the capital, a modesty dictated primarily by their shorter period in office. The term *grands projets* draws our attention to the regal preoccupation with grandeur, flamboyantly symbolizing the head of state's ambition to demonstrate for all to see his prowess as 'the nation's most successful political architect'.[108] The prime concern was to identify presidential with national prestige in the country's capital, Paris, which was given priority over the interests of the Parisians out of a desire to assert the exemplary character of French cultural achievements.

Jack Lang had difficulty in asserting Culture's role as lead ministry. The President ensured that he kept control in his own hands (his *domaine réservé*) by entrusting the

---

[103] David Looseley, *The Politics of Fun. Cultural Policy and Debate in Contemporary France*, Oxford, Berg, 1995, p. 58; cf. 56–63.

[104] Ibid., p. 58, quoting 'Un Entretien avec M. F. Mitterrand' in *Le Monde*, 2 May 1974.

[105] Ibid., pp. 122 and 84; cf. 82–3, 114–20.   [106] Ibid., pp. 176–9; cf. 233.

[107] Ibid., pp. 97–9. The spectacular budget doubling secured by Lang in 1981 enabled him to increase spending on municipal libraries twelvefold (ibid., pp. 80–1).

[108] Sue Collard, 'Mission impossible: les chantiers du Président', *French Cultural Studies*, II, 1992, p. 128; cf. 130–1.

planning of his architectural projects to an *ad hoc Mission de Coordination des Grandes Opérations d'Architecture et d'Urbanisme*. Besides Culture, four other ministries were involved—Education, Finance, Foreign Affairs, and Research— hence the particular need for coordination, but the President continued to exercise oversight through an informal group of four, linked to him by his Deputy SGP.[109]

The *Mission*'s explicit tasks were not merely to keep the projects on timetable and within cost limits but to prepare for the annual budgetary allocation discussions, ensure the overall coherence of the programmes, and coordinate information as well as public relations. Its implicit function was to bypass the bureaucratic procedures and political difficulties that had blocked or slowed down previous major schemes and would be an even greater threat to such a complex of ambitious projects. Since difficulties were expected from the Paris Town Hall, controlled by the President's main opponent Jacques Chirac, the Coordinator Yves Dauge's title was changed by decree to President of the slightly renamed *Mission Interministérielle Relative à la Coordination des Grandes Opérations d'Architecture et d'Urbanisme* by a formal Cabinet decision, which could not subsequently be reversed without Mitterrand's approval. Dauge regretted that his *Mission* could not be attached to the Elysée and would be interministerial, involving the Ministries of Budget, Culture, Education, External Relations, Finance, Research and Technology, and Town Planning. Culture (i.e. Lang) strongly opposed the reinforced *Mission*, believing that his ministry should control the *grands projets*. However, Mitterrand ensured that he could rely on oversight by a deputy director and another member of his staff to expedite his favourite schemes.[110] Despite Chirac's hostility to the expenditure involved, the President's projects were slowed down and modified but not fundamentally frustrated and the *Mission* avoided abolition. Lost time was made up after Mitterrand's re-election in 1988, with a junior minister, Emile Biasini, in charge of his projects. Formally attached to the Culture Ministry at the insistence of Jack Lang, Biasini's offices were in the same building as the *Mission*, physically detached from the Culture and Town Planning Ministries, both working in fact for the President.[111]

The President's willingness to spend public money ostentatiously was nowhere better revealed than in his architectural-cum-cultural projects, aided by Minister of Culture Jack Lang, who was able to double official cultural expenditure in real terms. In May 1981, Mitterrand proclaimed: 'I propose that the French join with me in inventing a culture, an art of living, in brief a French model of civilisation.'[112] Concerned to leave enduring monuments to his presidency and to promote the international prestige of Paris, Mitterrand chaired an interministerial committee which made a selection from among numerous proposals and decided where they would be located. He announced in March 1982 eight major projects in Paris, which included the future Opera-Bastille and the expansion of the Louvre museum by dislodging the Finance Ministry, following discussions with the Paris municipality, controlled by his political rival Chirac. Mitterrand forced through his ambitious

---

[109] Sue Collard, pp. 114–16.   [110] Presidential archive.
[111] Collard, pp. 118–19.   [112] Quoted in Favier and Martin-Roland, i, p. 192; cf. 193–51, 562–8.

plans despite the escalating costs that prompted resistance from successive Prime Ministers and Finance Ministers. He claimed that he had to fight off repeated attempts to reduce expenditure on the Louvre project every few months.[113] Thus, in a memo of 27 May 1982, Budget Minister Fabius suggested slowing down some projects, as proposed in a working party report, shifting others to the Culture budget and appointing a clear *grands projets* lead ministry. Mitterrand asked a member of his staff to make Fabius 'understand the importance I attach to these projects'.[114] Again, in a letter to Prime Minister Mauroy in February 1984, Mitterrand asserted: 'All confusion must be avoided with the budget, the *grands travaux* are neither a mere appendix or makeweight to the budget.'[115] Despite repeated Court of Accounts attempts to pierce the veil of creative accounting, the leading investigator of the presidential projects confessed failure to achieve transparency in the expenditure involved. 'There is at least one thing that we do know about the presidential projects: that we know nothing.'[116]

The most extraordinary episode and the one dearest to his heart was Mitterrand's hastening the transfer of the Finance Ministry to an unfinished Bercy site in December 1985 to present the incoming Chirac Government with a *fait accompli*. Despite Chirac's reassurances to the President, Finance Minister Balladur refused to move from the Louvre, which would displace his ministry from proximity to the Elysée and Matignon. At great expense (estimated at 70 million francs) he restored the demolished offices (described as a piece of 'state vandalism') quite apart from the additional cost of delaying the museum's extension. Culture Minister François Léotard sided with the President to preserve this and other projects, but yielded to the alliance of Balladur and Chirac. In 1988, with Lang back as Culture Minister, the Finance Ministry offices were redemolished and new projects—the future Mitterrand National Library and the Grand Arch at la Défense—were launched. Although they were slowed down in 1986–88, Mitterrand's architectural '*grands projets* stand among the purest expressions of sovereign presidential power in the Fifth Republic'.[117] The President was able to organize privileged coordination arrangements for his pet projects and largely preserve them from the vicissitudes of financial cuts and from prime ministerial coordination.

---

[113] Favier and Martin-Roland, i, p. 566; cf. 562–9. When at his first press conference, on 24 September 1981, Mitterrand announced the transfer of the Finance Ministry from the Louvre, Delors's exasperated comment was: 'With what will we finance it? It is not provided for in the Budget!' (quoted by Attali, *Verbatim*, i, p. 143). [114] Presidential archive.

[115] Ibid.

[116] F. Chaslin, Director of the *Institut Français d'Architecture* and author of *Les Paris de François Mitterrand*, Gallimard, 1985, quoted by Collard, pp. 125–6 from 'Bercy: un ministère pré-visible', *Le Nouvel Observateur*, 29 May 1987.

[117] M. Harrison, 'The President, Cultural Projects and Broadcasting Policy' in Hayward (ed.), *De Gaulle to Mitterrand*, p. 206; cf. 190–206. On the running fight over the Louvre, see Favier and Martin-Roland, ii, 775–81 and Attali, *Verbatim*, i, p. 1366 and *Verbatim*, ii, pp. 42, 123, 349, 352, 387. See also E. Cahm, 'Mitterrand's *Grands Projets*: Monuments to a Man or Monuments to an Age?' in M. Maclean (ed.), *The Mitterrand Years. Legacy and Evaluation*, op. cit. pp. 263–7, Loosely, ch. 7, and C. Bergeron 'Où en sont les grands chantiers de Paris?', *Le Point*, No. 753, 23 February 1987.

Having surveyed the complexities of core executive coordination historically and normatively, politically and administratively, horizontally and vertically, we turn in Part II to four case studies of sectoral coordination. This will enable us to delve in greater depth into the different types of coordination problems characteristic of European Union policy and budget policy, of privatisation and immigration policies. We shall more systematically consider in each sector how coordination has been undertaken in routine and non-routine cases, in those which are politicized and those that remain depoliticized, bearing in mind that particular issues frequently move between these analytic categories.

What we shall be particularly looking for in the case studies will be the coordination problems raised by a number of interrelated factors that have both increased and complicated them. Have greater national, transnational, and international interdependencies made new and intricate demands for French coordinators by changing their policy agenda? Has there been a substantial Europeanization of French actors, structures, arenas, and policy pressures? Has there been a weakening of the French state-centred approach to public policy, with the decline of traditional sectoral networks and the acquisition of insider status by new actors and networks? Has there been a weakening of traditional props of governance, owing to a discrediting of the legitimacy and authority of state, partisan, and organized interest elites? Have new decision processes, related to increased sectoralization and fragmentation of the central state apparatus, frustrated French efforts to achieve cohesion through coordination? Have the various attempts to reduce the coordination burden been successful in France during the 1980s and 1990s? Only when we have undertaken our case study investigations will we be in a position to formulate general conclusions on the subject of central coordination based upon our specific findings.

PART II

SECTORAL POLICY COORDINATION: FOUR CASE STUDIES

5

European Union Coordination and the Core Executive

European Community policy began as foreign economic affairs but increasingly penetrated into almost every part of domestic affairs, so that it has posed problems of predominance especially between the President and Prime Minister, the Foreign Minister and the Finance Minister. The need to adopt a clear and consistent posture in negotiations at Brussels and other European Union (EU) fora has been a stronger driving force promoting coordination than in other public policies but, although the institutionalized arrangements for such coordination have been impressive, they have encountered serious problems. While the General Secretariat of the Inter-ministerial Committee for European Economic Cooperation (SGCI) is intended to be the pivot of the coordination process, intervention by the President, rivalry with the Prime Minister—especially in periods of cohabitension—rivalry between the Foreign Ministry and the sectoral ministries, especially the Finance Ministry, as well as the informal bilateral relations between ministry officials and the Commission, all contribute towards a disruption of the smooth working of a centralized coordination process.

Prime Minister Rocard's circular of 22 September 1988 (reiterating earlier and later injunctions) stressed that with government action increasingly decided within the European Community, ministers should remember that 'The views which French representatives express on behalf of the Government are defined interministerially by the SGCI under the authority of the Prime Minister. In the case of an unresolved dispute between two members of the Government, it is the task of the SGCI to inform me of the difficulties. However, I wish to intervene only in exceptional circumstances.'[1] In a 21 March 1994 circular Prime Minister Balladur reaffirmed Rocard's injunction. 'The French standpoint must be presented with clarity and the greatest possible coherence in all EU venues. Furthermore, administrative activity must take full account of the European dimension . . . The unity of the positions taken by French representatives is a precondition of the efficacy of our action. Every minister or French delegate speaking in the context of EU institutions is making commitments on behalf of France.'[2] It went on virtually to repeat the passage of the Rocard circular

---

[1] Quoted in Alain Guyomarch, 'The European Effect: Imposing French Policy Coordination', *Staatswissenschaften und Staatspraxis*, 1993/3, p. 463.

[2] The text of *Circulaire du 21 mars relative aux relations entre les administrations françaises et les institutions de l'Union Européenne* is included in ENA, *Le Travail Gouvernemental*, ii, pp. 800–1.

quoted and asked the head of SGCI and the French Permanent Representative in Brussels to inform Balladur of any difficulties encountered in applying the circular. How far have such pious hopes been fulfilled in practice?

It has been argued that 'the coordination of French inputs into the EU policy-making system is far more effective than that in many other areas of domestic public policy-making' which are characterized by 'poor coordination'.[3] Furthermore, the need to present an agreed French standpoint on matters that are at the intersection of domestic and foreign policy has facilitated 'cooperation and coordination between domestic policy-making institutions'.[4] Postponing such comparative judgements until after we have considered specific cases, we may take a preliminary view that, while the well-established and institutionalized system of routine coordination achieved by the SGCI works well, it works for the Prime Minister and not for the President, who frequently takes uncoordinated initiatives on 'history-making', high policy issues. Nor has the rivalry for the role of lead ministry between Finance and Foreign Affairs—which prompted the creation of the 'interministerial' SGCI in 1948—been overcome in EU affairs. Both need to be intimately involved in the process of exerting informal influence, combining classical diplomatic negotiation and technical commercial negotiation. More generally, the sectorized and 'poly-centric' nature of EU structures means that 'Governmental coordination must find a balance between the national interest and the sectoral interests of ministries', bearing in mind the 'complex bureaucratic networks' within and between ministries.[5]

COORDINATING WITHIN THE EU QUAGMIRE

Whether it aims at ambitious, purposive overall steering or the minimal avoidance of particular mishaps, success in EU negotiations depends in part on a country's capacity to coordinate across the extended and multi-level policy chain in an active and reactive continuous policy-making process. Operating in a highly unstable policy environment, the 'ricochet effect between national and EU levels is constant'.[6] Ten distinctive features of the way EU institutions work have posed severe

---

[3] Guyomarch, 'The European Effect', p. 455.

[4] Ibid., p. 458. See also Dietrich Rometsch and Wolfgang Wessels (eds.), *The European Union and member states. Towards institutional fusion?* Manchester University Press, 1996, pp. 332–3.

[5] ENA, 'Le Travail Gouvernemental et l'Europe' in *Le Travail Gouvernemental*, p. 745; cf. 743.

[6] Vincent Wright, 'The National Coordination of European Policy-making. Negotiating the Quagmire' in Jeremy Richardson (ed.), *European Union. Power and Policy-making*, Routledge, 1996, p. 149. The discussion of the context of EU core executive coordination is summarized here from chapter 8 of this book. On poor internal EU coordination in the Council of Ministers and its Secretariat, 'the European Council can resolve only a limited number of cross-sectoral issues and then only under intense political pressures', see Fiona Hayes-Renshaw and Helen Wallace, *The Council of Ministers*, Macmillan, 1997, p. 286. As this applies in a particular instance, see Stephen Woolcock and Michael Hodges, 'EU policy in the Uruguay Round' in Helen and William Wallace (eds.), *Policy-Making in the European Union*, OUP, 1996, pp. 313–23.

coordination problems to core executives.

1. The structural ambivalence of EU decision-making extends from its variable constitutional status and its confusion of powers to the persistent interaction between national officials, Commission officials, and political executives, leading to a blurring of responsibilities.
2. Successive and impending enlargements modify the parameters of the coordination processes.
3. The expansion in the scope, diversity, and political saliency of the EU agenda has increased the unpredictability and complexity of coordination.
4. EU Commission proposals are often drastically modified by complex consultative processes and interstate diplomatic deals, especially between France and Germany.
5. Brussels is an organizational maze of committees taking a mass of micro-level decisions in conjunction with overlapping bargaining networks in relation to which the influence of Commissioners waxes and wanes.
6. The multiplicity, complexity, and fluidity of decision-making procedures necessitate different coordinating styles and mechanisms, as well as result in different outcomes.
7. EU alliance-building is much more difficult and time-consuming. Coalitions are unstable because of the effects of multiple bilateralism, with cleavages often being cross-cutting and intra-national.
8. The unofficial party and sectoral networks that help to bolster official coordination within states are weaker in the EU, where transnational networks are more significant.
9. Administrative mismatch between the lead national ministries responsible for particular policy issues complicates coordination of policy preparation and implementation because of differing administrative cultures and priorities.
10. The consensual type of coordinating skill required in the EU conflicts with the confrontational and impositional skills that generally prevail in French politico-administrative decision-making.

If one takes for granted that the capacity to anticipate and shape the EU policy agenda are essential objectives of national coordination arrangements, three kinds of congruence determine a country's ability to do so, other than its political clout, derived from its size and alliance-building skill.

1. Constitutional congruence of EU principles and aspirations, with France being out of sympathy with the liberalizing logic of the open common market, has created increasing problems notably on competition issues.
2. The need for policy congruence with both the *acquis communautaire* and prevailing climate of opinion has meant, for example, that France has had increasing difficulty in preserving the advantages of the Common Agricultural Policy.

3. As pointed out in 10 above, the lack of administrative congruence between the confrontational French decision-making style and the predominantly consensual EU style is counterproductive, notably in matters of industrial policy.

ROUTINE COORDINATION

The hub of EU interministerial communication and coordination is located in the SGCI, which is the arena in which day-to-day coordination procedures are organized, meetings held, and information circulated. Precisely because de Gaulle and his successors feared that the national interest would not be properly defended if French ministers and officials colluded piecemeal with their EU counterparts, the SGCI was regarded as a watchdog centrally supervising—insofar as it could—the complex process of intercommunication within the French administration and with Brussels. Thus, the SGCI is in almost daily contact with the French Permanent Representation in Brussels through a video conferencing link, the formalized process of interministerial coordination in Paris issuing instructions from the SGCI to the Permanent Representation.

That the SGCI does not confine itself to routine activities (which in any case may unpredictably become controversial ones) is evident from the fact that, as early as the Pompidou premiership, a future President of the EC Commission, François-Xavier Ortoli combined from 1962 to 1966 the headship of SGCI with membership of Pompidou's *cabinet*, before directing the latter and later serving him at the Elysée from 1973 to 1974. When Raymond Barre was Prime Minister (1977–81) both heads of the SGCI were also his *cabinet* advisers, which greatly increased its authority. After being initially downgraded in 1981 by being attached to the Minister of European Affairs during the Mauroy Government, it returned to the Prime Minister in 1984.[7] A combination of a weak European Affairs Minister and the high politics confrontations from May 1982 to May 1983 about whether EU integration should be given priority over 'socialism in one country' protectionism meant that there was great politico-administrative confusion and frequent interministerial coordination meetings, with the Prime Minister called upon to arbitrate. On the big economic decisions, it was the President's Elysée staff, supporting the Mauroy–Delors alliance, which carried the day.[8] From 1984, when Mitterrand took a more direct interest in EC affairs, SGCI coordination had to attempt procedurally to routinize the personal initiatives of the President.

In November 1985, in anticipation of the post-electoral likelihood of the Socialists losing the premiership in 1986, Mitterrand appointed his European Affairs adviser, Elisabeth Guigou, as SGCI head, in the hope that this would ensure his oversight of EC coordination. However, Prime Minister Chirac bypassed her, holding numerous informal interministerial meetings to deal with non-routine matters. She was left with the 90 per cent administrative coordination,[9] while the 10 per cent higher profile

---

[7] Christian Lequesne, *Paris–Bruxelles. Comment se fait la politique européenne de la France.* Presses de la Fondation Nationale des Sciences Politiqués, 1993, pp. 65, 99–104; cf. *Le Travail Gouvernemental*, p. 752.

[8] Lequesne, pp. 136–43.1   [9] Ibid., pp. 157–8.

matters were dealt with by future head of SGCI and then EU Commissioner Yves Thibault de Silguy, whose role we shall discuss later, particularly in relation to the 1986–88 and 1993–95 cohabitension periods. Guigou subsequently became Minister delegate for European Affairs in 1990 and Justice Minister in the 1997 Jospin Government.

The politico-administrative nature of the post of Secretary General of the SGCI has been particularly evident since April 1993 when Prime Minister Balladur appointed Thibault de Silguy as its head jointly with the role of his European Affairs *cabinet* adviser, a practice that has persisted since then, allowing linkage between administrative and political coordination. The Secretary General chairs the Wednesday morning meetings that coordinate the supervision of matters under discussion in Brussels and conflicts that need to be resolved by political 'arbitration'. The Secretary General's 'high politics' preoccupations mean that the supervision of the work of about 160 staff organized into sectors, each of which deals with several policy areas and ministries, falls on the shoulders of his two Deputy Secretaries General. They check and modify the results of interministerial coordination, involving on average about eight meetings each working day. However, much coordination is done informally by telephone and fax and this applies to bilateral coordination between ministries as well as to the SGCI's multilateral coordination activities. (Unfortunately for the researcher, these activities leave few traces.) When disagreements have not been resolved, they send an 'arbitration note' to the Prime Minister's *cabinet* prior to a meeting in Matignon.

Since 1981, the two SGCI deputies have, significantly, come from the Finance and Foreign Affairs Ministries. Like the sector heads, they are always from the *grands corps*, in their case from the Finance Inspectorate and diplomatic service.[10] Trans-national coordination through 'Bilateral meetings between ministers and their foreign equivalents can have an important impact on Community business. In some cases, especially given the fact that ministers do not always see fit to consult the SGCI on the positions of other ministries first, the outcomes of such bilateral meetings are seen to conflict with French positions in EC or to raise doubts on the part of other ministries. When this occurs, the Deputy Secretary General initiates a process of *ex post facto* coordination, writing to the *cabinet* director of the ministry concerned. Matignon is informed and whole process of interministerial meetings can be started. Ministerial involvement in fact can be seen as undermining co-ordination.'[11]

The SGCI organises the interministerial meetings to co-ordinate France's position from the moment when a Commission proposal is discussed in the working groups of the Council of Ministers. One week prior to the Council of Ministers meeting, a meeting is held at the SGCI under the chairmanship of a Deputy Secretary General with representatives from the relevant

[10] Ibid., pp. 102–7. For an update by Lequesne on the SGCI, see his 'Union européenne et coordination gouvernemental: *quid novi* en France' in F. d'Arcy and L. Rouban (eds.), *De la Ve République à l'Europe*, Paris, Presses de Sciences Po, 1996, ch. 13.

[11] This is a slightly amended quotation from a draft working paper by Anand Menon, a more elaborate and updated version of which was published in H. Kassim *et al.* (eds.), *The National Coordination of EU Policy. The Domestic Level*, OUP, 2000, ch. 3. More generally, see the Introduction and the Conclusion to this volume.

ministries. Foreign Affairs and Finances are always present. On average, such meetings are attended by four or five ministries. When a final position is adopted, diplomatic telegrams are sent by the SGCI to the Permanent Representation in Brussels and to all French ambassadors in EU member states. One telegram is devoted to each subject on the agenda, along with one which is an overall *note de synthèse*. The telegrams not only point out the French position on the issues involved but also indicate likely supporters amongst other countries.[12]

The Foreign Ministry has managed, as we shall see, partially to exclude political cooperation from the SGCI's overall coordination, emphasizing the intergovernmental character of foreign and security, 'second pillar' EU affairs. Although the Maastricht Treaty gave the EU the right to 'coordinate defence activity within West European Union', it was only after the 1997 Amsterdam IGC that Javier Solana, previously NATO Secretary General, was appointed in 1999 to manage the common foreign and security policy as a High Representative heading a coordinating unit within the EU General Secretariat. However, in 'third pillar' affairs, the 1993 appointment of a 'coordinator' for the matters involving the 'coordinating ministries' of Interior (dealing with crime and immigration) and Justice, shows that, in other intergovernmental affairs 'requiring a strong arbitration capacity', the SGCI has acquired an oversight role. The person in charge has not been entitled Deputy Secretary General out of deference to the susceptibilities of the ministries coordinated, notably the 'lead' ministry, Interior.[13]

With a view to keeping the SGCI small, as much coordination as possible is delegated to the lead ministries. This began in the 1970s with Agriculture, owing to the volume and specialized character of the matters covered by the Common Agricultural Policy (CAP). The ministry's International Relations Section (particularly its EU, EU Foreign Relations, and European Legal Affairs bureaux) is responsible for arriving at a standpoint that can be put each Monday and Tuesday when the Special Committee on Agriculture meets in Brussels to prepare the ground for the Council of Ministers of Agriculture. If an agreed position cannot be reached by the line staff, the Minister's *cabinet* will make a decision, political rather than strictly agricultural factors now receiving priority. Due to the financial implications of the CAP and the aggressive pressure of the French farm lobby, a strongly nationalist line is pursued, especially when the Prime Minister or President is someone, like Chirac, with strong electoral and visceral ties to the farm community. This nationalism spills over periodically into bitterly disputed international trade negotiations, notably the General Agreement on Tariffs and Trade (GATT) Uruguay Round discussions, when the Agriculture–President alliance in 1991–92 to block agreement was followed in 1993 by a Prime Minister-dominated coordination of French policy based on SGCI-organized interministerial coordination. Despite attempts to allow the lead ministry to handle the humdrum bulk of agricultural affairs, crises arise that require 'heroic' action. We shall later consider the French response to the 'Mad Cow' emergency that precipitated just such a crisis.

---

[12] See footnote 11.
[13] ENA, *Le Travail Gouvernemental*, p. 750; cf. Appendix 2, p. 794. On France and the Common Foreign and Security Policy, see Alain Guyomarch *et al.*, *France in the European Union*, Macmillan, 1998, ch. 4.

Before discussing intra-ministerial coordination more generally, criticism of the highly regarded SGCI should be mentioned when compared to German and Italian arrangements (where negotiators often do not have instructions) but with lessons to learn from the UK. The 1,100 meetings held annually at the SGCI often result in the formalized juxtaposition of the standpoints of the various ministries, which the negotiators find difficult to reconcile and unify. Centralized coordination is overwhelmed by the sheer volume and complexity of the cases to be discussed, leading to an overloaded SGCI concentrating on virtually non-stop daily concertation at the expense of advance preparation and strategic guidance. Much of the blame falls on the lead ministries, which fail to resolve conflicts, leaving this task to the SGCI or even Matignon, leading the Prime Minister's EU adviser to ask the Secretary General of Government (SGG) to arrange an 'arbitration' meeting that does not start from where the SGCI process ended but reopens the whole issue anew. So it has been suggested that the SGCI should always clearly designate the lead ministry to deal with each proposal from the EU Commission and maintain closer links with France's Permanent Representative in Brussels and its EU member state embassies on the model of the British Cabinet Office European Secretariat.[14] A more radical proposal is the amalgamation of the SGCI and the SGG on the ground that EU coordination and intra-French coordination have become increasingly inseparable. They already work together a great deal. However, both the need to preserve the efficiency of small outfits and because they work to different timetables—the SGG controls French practices while the SGCI has to respond to Brussels initiatives over which it has no control—mean that a merger between them will only be a long-term prospect.[15]

Moving from the arena to the actors, interministerial conflicts predictably and usually oppose Finance to the spending ministries. Finance has a special incentive in the SGCI coordinating as early and as effectively as possible, because the spending ministries seek to conceal their proposals with spending implications. In Finance, even more than in most ministries, coordination is dealt with at levels below what would usually be regarded as that of the core executive. Like Agriculture, Finance does not have a separate horizontal EU division or sub-division—since 1990 the usual practice—which can be marginalized, but European bureaux within each of its vertical divisions. However, Finance's own European bureaux in each division have to try to resolve internal differences and although the Minister's *cabinet* may ultimately do so, the fact that at least two and sometimes eight of the eleven divisions are present at SGCI meetings means that, apart from always seeking to save money, disagreements between them may emerge. When EU budget questions are discussed (see later) Finance is clearly the lead ministry. Despite their widespread impact, in Economic and Monetary Union matters Finance is not coordinated by the SGCI, the Treasury Division Director communicating the government's instructions to the European Monetary Union (EMU) monetary committee. The French draft of EMU was prepared in the Treasury by a team headed by its Director, Jean-Claude Trichet.

---

[14] ENA, *Le Travail Gouvernemental*, pp. 763–4, 777–8.
[15] Ibid., p. 782; cf. 749–50. More generally on the SGCI, Guyomarch *et al.*, pp. 54–60.

As we shall see later, the partial privatisation of France Télécom in 1997 helped the French Government meet the public sector deficit criterion for Euroland candidates. So it is important to consider the impact of the European Monetary System (EMS) constraint on French financial management.

Although President Mitterrand had, in proposal 20 of his 1981 programme, stated that 'The franc will be protected from speculation', he refused to emulate de Gaulle in 1958 and Pompidou in 1969 (who blamed their rapid devaluations on their predecessors). This meant that he was forced to do so five months later on 4 October 1981. Devaluation of a substantially overvalued franc was long overdue and was disguised by a realignment with the mark, a process that was repeated on 12 June 1982. Finance Minister Delors secured German agreement to revalue the mark by promising a contractionary budget and macroeconomic policy that was only approved by the French Cabinet *after the commitment had irretrievably been made*. The 21 March 1983 currency realignment required further tightening of fiscal and monetary policy as a condition of German agreement but the decisive change of direction had been made, replacing a policy of competitive devaluation by one of competitive disinflation. Thereafter, a 'strong franc' policy was pursued, helped in the late 1980s and early 1990s by a 'concerted and coordinated defence mounted by the French and German governments and central banks',[16] which allowed France to avoid the devaluation that Britain and Italy suffered in 1992.

As Prime Minister, Balladur—who had in 1987 started the supranational move towards EMU that was incorporated into the 1992 Maastricht European Union Treaty—nevertheless was able to reduce the German constraint on French monetary policy by securing in August 1993 a widening of the permitted currency fluctuations from 2.25 to 15 per cent.[17] Thus, Delors as Finance Minister in 1982–83 and Balladur in 1987 as Finance Minister and as Prime Minister in 1993 (but directly handling monetary policy instead of the weak Finance Minister Alphandéry) used their dealings with the German government to enforce a policy that was dictated by European considerations that were outside the national coordination procedures. The key trio in 1985–92 were Delors–Kohl–Mitterrand. Finally, the monthly meetings of the Council of Finance Ministers (ECOFIN) mean that the coordination of economic and monetary policies may become a step towards the French aspiration to a European 'economic government'.

The great rivals for the role of lead ministry on EU affairs have been the Finance and Foreign Affairs Ministries, with the latter having the advantage of a more comprehensive remit as well as its specific functions in relation to the European Foreign and Security Policy. The Foreign Ministry has a predominant role in staffing the French Permanent Representation in Brussels (and therefore the Committee of Permanent Representation or COREPER) which is headed by an ambassador, assisted by a career diplomat. (Finance officials are also well represented, followed by

[16] David R. Cameron, 'From Barre to Balladur: Economic Policy in the Era of the EMS' in Flynn (ed.), *Remaking the Hexagon*, Westview Press, Boulder, 1995, p. 139; cf. 128–38.

[17] Ibid., p. 142; cf. 140–1 and Cameron, 'National Interest, the Dilemmas of European Integration and Malaise' in Keeler and Schain (eds.), *Chirac's Challenge*, pp. 340–1, 362.

those from the Agriculture and Industry Ministries). The Foreign Ministry, as the external representative of French sovereignty, enjoyed pride of place. Nevertheless, until its 1993 reorganization, the Foreign Ministry had not adapted its own structure to fulfil a lead role in European affairs. This was due to the increasing extension and specialization of European policies and their interdependence with domestic policies. Furthermore, the role played by the President, the Prime Minister, and their staffs, as well as the establishment of a junior minister for European Affairs, have detracted from the Foreign Ministry's pretensions.

The 1993 reorganization of the Foreign Affairs Ministry by Alain Juppé was aimed particularly at giving it the capacity to play a more effective role in EU policies. There has been a switch from treating 'Europe' as a subordinate part of a predominantly geographical structure to placing it alongside political and security affairs, and juridical affairs under one of the three deputy secretaries general. EU affairs are handled by all three functional parts of the Quai as well as European and Economic Affairs (especially the European Cooperation Division many of whose officials have previously worked in Brussels), Foreign and Security policy is dealt with by Political and Security Affairs, while the many legal problems posed by EU affairs are the responsibility of Juridical Affairs. However, the latter's advice often conflicts with that of the legal section of the SGCI, leaving it to Matignon to decide, acting on the advice of the SGG! Such problems are not helped by the Quai's Juridical Affairs being responsible for presenting France's case to the European Court of Justice while the SGCI's legal section does the preliminary administrative coordination. The post-1993 functional structure alongside the traditional divisions was intended to improve the Foreign Ministry's intra-ministerial coordination to reverse its decline in interministerial influence,[18] but tensions remain, notably between the political-security and economic-European parts of the Quai d'Orsay.

In 1981, the innovation of appointing a European Affairs Minister—the first of seven during Mitterrand's two terms compared to four Foreign Ministers—was, as we saw earlier, a weak junior minister attached to the Foreign Office. André Chandernagor's nominal control of the SGCI was a cause of poor coordination, as was his exclusion from European Council meetings. His successor, Roland Dumas, was given full ministerial status from 1983 to 1984 and used by the President to make informal contacts in support of an active European policy during France's EC presidency in the first half of 1984, prior to replacing Cheysson as External Affairs Minister at the end of the year.[19] Thereafter, except for Edith Cresson (1988–90) and Michel Barnier (1995–97), the post was held by a junior minister attached to the Foreign Minister but the role played has fluctuated a great deal whatever the formal status, tending to be stronger when either the Prime Minister or Foreign Minister is weak.

In 1986, Prime Minister Chirac at first dispensed with the post but was prevailed upon by Foreign Minister Raimond to appoint Bernard Bosson as a delegate minister

---

[18] Bertrand Dufourcq (Secretary General of the Foreign Affairs Ministry), 'La réforme du quai d'Orsay', *Revue Francaise d'Administration Publique*, No. 77, January–March 1996, pp. 27–8.

[19] Lequesne, *Paris–Bruxelles*, pp. 61–6, 137.

to him in August 1986. An ardent European integrationist, Bosson worked with President Mitterrand to expand EC expenditure as requested by Delors (President of the EC Commission) against the wishes of Chirac and Finance Minister Balladur.[20] Much to his annoyance, the Foreign Minister was excluded from European Council meetings on the grounds that Chirac insisted on occupying the only place other than that of the President, a by-product of the cohabitension then existing.

Cresson's 1988–90 tenure of the European Affairs portfolio was marked by a high degree of autonomy from Foreign Minister Dumas, symbolized physically by not being located in the Quai d'Orsay. Her role was to prepare the completion of the internal market and the correlative adaptation of the French economy, which she set about vigorously. This brought her into frequent collision with other ministries (especially Finance Minister Bérégovoy and Industry Minister Strauss-Kahn), notably through her 1988 initiative establishing Study and Mobilization Groups (GEMs) of civil servants, local councillors, and business interests dealing with matters within their competence. Angry at not being supported by Prime Minister Rocard in her wish to adopt an aggressively protectionist response to Japanese car imports, she resigned in October 1990, to replace Rocard in May 1991. During her brief tenure as Prime Minister, she tried to promote her GEMs, only to discover that their infringement of the lead responsibilities of ministries condemned them to ineffectiveness.[21] Her controversial years as an EU Commissioner, importing questionable French patronage practices to Brussels, was a major factor in the collective resignation of the EU Commission in March 1999.

Cresson's successor from 1990 to 1993, Elisabeth Guigou, had formerly run the SGCI and was given a wider remit, covering all European policy, not just the EC, although she concentrated on the preparation and defence of the Maastricht Treaty. Prime Minister Cresson was excluded from this delicate set of negotiations, necessitating close contact with Chancellor Kohl. They were politically controlled by the President, Foreign Minister Dumas, Finance Minister Bérégovoy, and Guigou, with the aid of two key officials: Pierre de Boissieu of the Quai, who is credited with inventing the three pillar structure, and Jean-Claude Trichet of the Treasury for the EMU.[22] (We shall return to this matter in relation to the 1991 Intergovernmental Conference (IGC).) Of Guigou, as of Dumas, Cresson, Bosson, and Barnier, it can be said that the significant European Affairs Ministers were those who worked with the President rather than the Foreign Minister. This caused jealousy and resentment in that quarter, even though the European Minister's staff have been dominated by diplomats, who have usually worked in the French Permanent Representation in Brussels, trying to coordinate what are essentially sectoral activities.

Apart from periods of cohabitation, and aside from routine matters settled by SGCI, the Prime Minister has usually played second fiddle to the President, who has preferred to work through the Foreign and European ministers and rely more

---

[20] Ibid., pp. 68–9.
[21] Ibid., pp. 70–4, 170–1; cf. ENA, *Le Travail Gouvernemental*, p. 762.
[22] Lequesne, *Paris–Bruxelles*, pp. 74–7, 179.

particularly upon his own Elysée staff, when he did not engage in personal shuttle diplomacy (e.g. he met Kohl and Thatcher each month during the 1984 French EC presidency). We have seen that the 1986–88 period witnessed a 'no holds barred' tussle between Mitterrand and Chirac, in which their personal staffs sought informally to keep open lines of communication, although attempts were made to deny the President vital information and officials loyal to him were bypassed. Pierre de Boissieu, then head of the Foreign Ministry Economic Cooperation sub-department, provided the informal and neutral meeting place at which presidential–prime ministerial disputes could be amicably ironed out.[23] The later cohabitations of 1993–95 and since 1997 have not required recourse to such improvised coordination because the European views of the two heads of the executive were closer. However, this example shows that while *cabinets* are often blamed for exacerbating conflicts between their political masters, they can also counteract the dissensions between them, thereby preventing the policy paralysis or confusion that might otherwise ensue.

During the second cohabitation, the key role in linking EU and international trade policy of Prime Minister Balladur is illustrated in the 1993 GATT Uruguay Round negotiations. Douglas Webber's searching analysis of this revealing confrontation shows that 'Of the ministries involved in policy-making on GATT issues, the Foreign Office was most favourable to a settlement and the Agricultural Ministry most hostile with the Economics and Finance Ministry oscillating between the two, but leaning increasingly in favour of the former', with Balladur in favour 'but "not at any price"'.[24] Having worked out the French position, he successfully persuaded Chancellor Kohl that his government would fall if it accepted the initial Blair House agreement with the USA, a prospect that Kohl did not welcome because of Chirac's then anti-GATT position. As the way the German government voted on the EU Council of Ministers would be decisive, great efforts were made to coordinate a Franco-German position between officials and ministers—notably the French Foreign Minister Juppé. The result was that the French government proffered 'semantic concessions in exchange for securing the support of first Germany and then the other member states' to what 'was in reality less a "Franco-German" text than a French one approved by the German delegation'.[25] Webber concludes that 'the French Government was extremely skilful and effective in deploying and making credible its threat to veto a final GATT agreement', ensuring that virtually 'every bilateral Franco-German agreement seems to have been transposed into an EU decision'.[26]

The decisive role that joint pre-negotiation by France and Germany had generally played, illustrated by this example, makes it important to see how this bilateral

---

[23] Guyomarch *et al.*, pp. 52–3. In the 1993–95 cohabitation, Prime Minister Balladur revived a monthly interministerial meeting devoted to European affairs.

[24] Douglas Webber, 'High midnight in Brussels: An Analysis of the September 1993 Council Meeting on the GATT Uruguay Round', *Journal of European Public Policy*, 5(4), December 1998, 582; cf. Edouard Balladur, *Deux ans à Matignon*, Paris, Plon, 1995, pp. 139–40, 145.

[25] Webber, 'High midnight', p. 588; cf. 586–7. Juppé claimed that 'We got exactly what we wanted' (*Agra Europe*, English edn. 1561 of 24 September 1993, quoted by Webber).   [26] Ibid., pp. 589–90.

cross-national coordination relates to overall core executive coordination. Webber's considered assessment is that 'In general, the intensity of Franco-German coordination appears to vary along two dimensions, depending upon the salience of the issue in the one or other or both states and the identity of the issue-area or participating ministries. The more politically explosive or sensitive the issue to one or other or both the governments, the greater is, of course, their propensity to seek the other's aid to try to manage it. Equally, the heads of government [as well as the French President] and their offices and foreign ministries practise closer coordination than do the respective sectoral ministries, while, among the sectoral ministries, coordination, other things being equal, is more intensive between those in charge of domains where the EU has stronger and long-established competences than between those responsible for issue-areas where the EU competences are weaker and younger.'[27] However, outside periods of cohabitation, it is the President rather than the Prime Minister that exercises—through his staff—the overall coordination of French relations with Germany that, despite its ups and downs, has hitherto always been the bedrock of France's EU strategy and tactics.

Since the President and his staff are not involved in the mass of routine coordination channelled through the SGCI, when they choose to intervene difficulties may arise. There are the high politics EU matters which the Elysée always deals with directly: institutional reforms that are the subject of IGCs (discussed later), enlargement of EU membership, or crisis resolution, which do not pose significant coordination problems. The President 'sets and changes the rules at will' but he decides institutional issues 'often by imposition rather than by arbitration or coordination'.[28] Preparation of European Council and Group of Seven (G7) leading industrial countries meetings are also clearly the responsibility of the Elysée staff. During the French EU presidencies, the SGCI prepares the ground by coordinating proposals coming from the French ministries but it is the President's staff that selects in the light of his priorities, leaving the SGCI with the task of providing the administrative backup.[29] Mitterrand intervened directly in certain matters, such as the 1985 creation (following the French presidency in 1984) of Eureka, the European Research Coordination Agency, which was devised by French experts. He was particularly active during the 1989 French EU presidency and in the Maastricht negotiations of 1991–92, culminating in his decision to hold a referendum to ratify the Treaty which proved a 'damned close run thing'.[30]

The post-1995 Chirac view of EU policy was shaped by the President's reliance upon a team of advisers he had inherited from his Prime Minister, Juppé, when he was at the Foreign Ministry. The new SGP, Dominique de Villepin, and the two specifically

[27] Ibid., p. 591. See also Douglas Webber, *The Franco-German Relationship in the European Union*, Routledge, 1999.

[28] Guyomarch, p. 472; cf. 473 and Guyomarch *et al.*, pp. 47–8.

[29] Lequesne, Paris–Bruxelles, p. 116.

[30] Ibid., pp. 150–1 and ENA, *Le Travail Gouvernemental*, Paris–Bruxelles, p. 760. See also Jean Petot, 'L'Europe, la France et son Président', *La Revue du Droit Public*, March–April 1993, especially pp. 374–95 on the 1992 referendum.

European Affairs Elysée advisers were all imbued with a pro-integrationist approach that shifted Chirac from his equivocal position, torn between his party's divisions over EU policy and the pressures to pursue previous policies with which Juppé had been actively associated in the 1993–95 Balladur Government. This entourage ensured close coordination between Prime Minister and President, with Foreign Minister Hervé de Charette playing a subdued role. We have elsewhere seen that the policy adopted, notably towards EMU, led to an unpopular budgetary strategy that contributed to electoral defeat in 1997 and Juppé's resignation. The subsequent period of cohabitation between Chirac and Jospin followed until 2000 the pacific pattern of 1993–95 rather than belligerent one of 1986–88, with EU policy being a matter of core executive consensus and smooth summit coordination.

To sum up French general EU coordination practices, prior to considering our case studies, their salient features are a combination of lower-level formalized centralization that can be frustrated by presidential intervention with sectorally dependent policies of a highly technical (e.g. environment) or politicized (e.g. industrial competition) kind. The tendency to see things in a top-down way means that the French often try to coordinate at too high a level, which is not necessarily the pertinent level in the Brussels Commission. The SGCI is developing its coordination of the activities of officials in each ministry responsible for dealing with the European Parliament as the latter has become more active. Unlike Britain, France places a top priority on avoiding isolation in the Council of Ministers and on seeking to initiate rather than react to EU policies, which mean that negotiating discretion must sometimes take precedence over coordination.

EUROPEAN ECONOMIC AND MONETARY UNION

In their superbly researched study of the complex and prolonged negotiations leading to the Maastricht Treaty adoption of EMU, Kenneth Dyson and Kevin Featherstone show that they were confined to 'a small, intimate and isolated set of actors in the "core executive" ... insulated from public pressure and demands for public accountability ... only a tiny group of politicians and officials were active players'.[31] The competition for core executive control in France was between President and Prime Minister; between the Prime Minister and other ministers, notably the Finance and Foreign Ministers and their *cabinets*; between senior line officials in these two ministries. Delors and his *cabinet* (especially Pascal Lamy) and some members of DG2 of the EC Commission, sought to prevent the process becoming exclusively intergovernmental, while facilitating the crucial collaboration between Chancellor Kohl and President Mitterrand by close coordination with Bonn and Paris.

---

[31] K. Dyson and K. Featherstone, *The Road to Maastricht. Negotiating Economic and Monetary Union*, OUP, Oxford, 1999, pp. 13–14. This case study relies very heavily on this detailed account to identify the French role.

Post-1981, French EMU strategy continued along the liberal conservative lines laid down by Giscard and Barre. Mitterrand (who was more interested in political union than monetary union) concentrated on the essential points of principle, for example central bank independence, and tactics, for example sustaining Franco-German consensus and leadership, while leaving the technicalities to the officials and ministers. 'Mitterrand's governing style was designed to exploit the expertise of technocrats while minimizing their power' by suspicious scrutiny of their proposals whose significance he did not always comprehend.[32] He was especially mistrustful of the 'intellectual terrorism' of the Financial Inspectors of the Treasury and the Bank of France.[33] Mitterrand concentrated on statesmanlike dealing with other EC leaders, particularly during the French presidency in 1984 and 1989, holding some thirty bilateral meetings with his counterparts in the first half of 1984.[34]

On EMU, Mitterrand relied particularly on two people: Roland Dumas and Elisabeth Guigou. Dumas had been a close political associate of Mitterrand's since the 1950s. From December 1984 to April 1986 and again from May 1988 to March 1993, Dumas was simultaneously his Foreign Minister, 'most intimate diplomatic adviser and his closest confidant. He enjoyed a uniquely privileged dialogue with the President as the most trusted of Mitterrand loyalists.'[35] Dumas had previously been appointed Minister for European Affairs to help Mitterrand play an active role during the 1984 French EC presidency. He produced a memo on 1 June 1984 proposing a coordinated monetary policy, medium-term economic programming, and fiscal harmonization, as steps towards a European currency.[36] Dumas worked closely with Guigou, then on the Elysée staff, continuing to do so after she combined that post with heading the SGCI in November 1985. During the 1986–88 cohabitation, she worked amicably with Chirac's EC adviser de Silguy because their masters were agreed on EMU, while Dumas worked with German Foreign Minister Genscher to sustain EMU momentum. From 1988, Dumas and Guigou kept the Foreign Ministry and Elysée in close harmony. Guigou played the key coordinating role with Delors (in whose *cabinet* she had briefly served when he was Finance Minister) who chaired the Committee on Monetary Union in 1989, filtering progress reports on its thinking into 'her bi-weekly meetings in the Elysée with relevant EC cabinet members from the Foreign and Finance Ministries and from the Prime Minister's and the President's Office. In these meetings the priority issues . . . were identified and strategy for coordination between the current Spanish and impending French EC Presidencies was considered.'[37] However, when she became European Affairs Minister in October 1990, she was rather sidelined by Dumas, who worked directly with the President and Finance Minister. So, transition to a formally higher status led to a loss

---

[32] Dyson and Featherstone, p. 133; cf. 97–9, 124–5.   [33] Ibid., p. 173; cf. 122, 125.
[34] Ibid., p. 152.
[35] Ibid., p. 173. Dumas was later appointed President of the Constitutional Council, a position from which he was forced to resign, when he was judicially investigated for financial irregularities when Foreign Minister.   [36] Ibid., pp. 152–4.
[37] Ibid., pp. 187–8; cf. 157–8, 191.

of her influence in the processes of core executive coordination, as well as weakening the President's grip on the EMU policy process.[38]

Mitterrand used Dumas and Guigou as vital counterweights to both the Finance Ministry, the President fearing that its minister Bérégovoy had been 'captured', and the banker-dominated Delors Committee which favoured a Bundesbank-style independent European Central Bank (ECB). The Finance Ministry's Treasury Division, having lost much of its power through the deregulation of financial markets and privatisation, saw the EMU proposals as threatening a loss of its monetary policy powers. The Governor of the Bank of France, de Larosière, had secured President Mitterrand's support for an independent ECB at a private meeting on 1 December 1988. So, when Finance Minister Bérégovoy and Treasury Director Trichet reproached him in April 1989 for signing 'too Germanic' a Delors Report, he could reply that he had Mitterrand's support for an independent ECB as a concession to secure German agreement.[39] German reunification at the end of 1989 convinced Bérégovoy that he had to accept ECB independence as the price of binding it into the EC, but he called on Trichet and the Treasury to devise a mechanism for the political coordination of EC economic policy to counterbalance the future ECB's monetary power—what later ambitiously came to be called an 'economic government'. Concerned above all to secure Finance Ministry control over the EMU negotiations, 'Bérégovoy had to make himself irreplaceable to Mitterrand by becoming the symbol of the strength of the French franc'.[40]

While the Foreign and Finance Ministries formally had joint responsibility for EMU, Dumas and Bérégovoy settled 'a division of labour between themselves and their officials. Guigou and de Boissieu (of the Foreign Ministry) would concern themselves with the legal, institutional and broader strategic aspects of EMU for European policy. But otherwise the Finance Ministry was to be in the driving seat on EMU.'[41] Mitterrand exercised an informal and bilateral coordinating role, receiving written reports and seeing Dumas, Bérégovoy, and Guigou at least weekly to confirm agreements that had usually already been made between them. Prime Minister Cresson, like her predecessor Rocard, was largely left out of these discussions, Bérégovoy in particular regarding her as unfit for a job for which he was better equipped and in which he would succeed her. Trichet headed the Finance Ministry EMU negotiating team, holding frequent bilateral meetings with de Boissieu but without having to report to an interministerial coordinating group.

The Finance Ministry used preparation of 'the French Draft Treaty on EMU as a means of gaining control of the process of coordination and conflict resolution in Paris'.[42] Its cherished notion of an EMU 'economic government', to give countervailing power to Council of Finance Ministers (ECOFIN) over the ECB, was central to its strategy, endorsed by the Cabinet on 5 December 1990. However, the term was abandoned at the instance of the Foreign Ministry, which feared that the German

---

[38] Dyson and Featherstone, p. 217. Guigou became Minister of Justice in the 1997 Jospin Government.   [39] Ibid., pp. 181–6.
[40] Ibid., p. 210; cf. 191–4.   [41] Ibid., p. 218; cf. 212–13.   [42] Ibid., p. 221; cf. 220, 247.

government would suspect that the intention was to curb ECB independence. The Finance Ministry worked intensively on the draft EMU treaty, followed by inter-ministerial negotiations with de Boissieu and Guigou, the Prime Minister's Office, and the Bank of France, conducted mainly by Treasury Director Trichet. The final draft that emerged from this 'complex and intensive iterative process centred on the Finance Ministry' was approved in January 1991 at a meeting chaired by Mitterrand.[43]

The French core executive having got their act together, it remained above all to secure the agreement of the German government. In this they were assisted both by Delors's good standing with Chancellor Kohl, allowing him to sustain the momentum behind the Franco-German negotiations. His efforts were structurally sustained by the institutionalized links between the two countries: central banks, finance ministries, foreign ministries, and above all Mitterrand–Kohl summits. From 'April to November 1991, French and German IGC negotiations held six top secret bilaterals on EMU, designed to narrow the differences and thereby speed progress in the larger negotiation'.[44] Skill in coordinating their strategies ensured the successful outcome of the EMU venture, which was a highly politicized and non-routine core executive exercise in historic decision-making.

The run-up to the establishment of the Euro currency led to increased tension between the Treasury and the independent Bank of France, Trichet having moved as head of the one to the other in 1993. He defended the same 'sound money' policies but this led him to criticize French monetary and economic policies that caused altercations with Chirac as presidential candidate and the Juppé Government. However, lacking the public support and legitimacy of the Bundesbank, the Bank of France had to be more circumspect but Trichet was looking to succeed Duisenberg as head of the ECB, so he had a vested interest in promoting banking independence. The Treasury continued to press the case for an 'economic government' under Jospin (the priority given to growth and employment being stressed by Jospin's *cabinet* economic adviser and head of the Economic Analysis Council set up by Jospin) but only succeeded in the establishment of a weak coordinating Euro-Council, deflated into a Euro-Group to stress that all its decisions would need to be confirmed by ECOFIN. Like the Cologne Macro-Economic Dialogue, these were symbolic gestures to allow the Jospin Government to claim that the Euro-Group was moving to close economic and monetary coordination. The 1999 creation of a Planning Commis-sariat working group, to propose ways of increasing macroeconomic policy coordination as part of the Quermonne Report on the reform of European insti-tutions, was similarly motivated by the desire to sustain pressure to achieve the aims of a Euro economic government.[45] One may be sceptical about such aspirations, as

---

[43] Dyson and Featherstone, p. 225; cf. 219–27, 254.

[44] Ibid., p. 758; cf. 692–4, 743, 747, 757, 780–1. See more generally K. Dyson, 'EMU, Political Discourse and the Fifth French Republic: Historical Institutionalism, Path Dependency and "Craftsmen" of Discourse', *Modern and Contemporary France*, 7(2), 1999, 179–96.

[45] This paragraph is based on a draft paper (September 2000) by David Howarth, 'The French State in the Euro Zone' to be published in K. Dyson (ed.), *European States and the Euro: Playing the Semi-Sovereignty Game*, OUP, Oxford, 2001. On Muet and the Economic Analysis Council, see Victor,

one can of cosmetic changes, such as adding 'Growth' to the title of the EMU Stability Pact, with no sanctions to enforce the positive coordination presupposed alongside the negative coordination equipped with them.

The persistent drumbeat demand by the Jospin Government for macroeconomic policy coordination begs both the political and management questions of its feasibility in a monetary union without full political union. The 1999 report of the Boyer Group on the 'Coordination of Macro-economic policies in Europe' for the Planning Commissariat was the most thorough investigation of discretionary coordination between a multiplicity of autonomous but interdependent actors, notably in the interaction between budgetary, monetary, and incomes policies. Without such coordination by the Euro-Council, there would be conflicts between the European Central Bank (with a majority of governors of national banks) on the one hand and governments, firms, and public opinions on the other, leading to a confused policy-mix. While budgetary coordination of nationally diverse processes would be helped by four-year programming, there was the likelihood that competitive devaluation would be replaced by fiscal competition. The early experience with the Euro has confirmed fears that the European Central Bank, owing to its lack of democratic legitimacy, would become the scapegoat for the currency's weakness which, thus far, has not been a Bundesbank writ European, borrowing the former's credibility. The Boyer Report favoured a strategy of 'apprenticeship and pragmatism', with the Stability and Growth Pact's provisions leading to an increasing coordination of macroeconomic policies.[46] The as yet unanswered question is whether the integrationist logic of this French lead will be followed in the coming years by its hitherto reluctant partners.

THE EU BUDGET

It may seem paradoxical to treat the core executive coordination of EU budget matters as a case of routine and non-politicized decision-making, when the running sore of the British budget contribution threatened to paralyse the Council of Ministers in the early 1980s. It was to Mitterrand's credit, as President of the Community in the first half of 1984, that he successfully resolved the issue by putting together a package deal at the Fontainebleau European Council of June 1984. Much of the detailed preparatory work was done by the Foreign Ministers, with an important role being played by discussions between the French and British Foreign Minister. However, the decisive duo were Mitterrand and Kohl, who deliberately

Le Matignon de Jospin, pp. 429–32. The Quermonne Project has been translated. See National Planning Office, *The European Union in pursuit of legitimate and effective institutions,* Commissariat général du Plan, Paris, November 1999. It argues that 'the European institutions' capacity to coordinate and arbitrate across-the-board must be enhanced' (p. 33) whereas the Amsterdam Treaty reinforced sectorization (p. 34).

[46] Commissariat général du Plan, *Le gouvernement économique de la zone euro,* Rapport Boyer, La Documentation Française, May 1999, pp. 111, 139–40; cf. 12, 23, 35, 44–55, 80, 86–7, 93.

leaked to the British a plan to manage EC affairs between the remaining nine member states if Margaret Thatcher continued her blocking tactics.[47] The German government, which as the principal EC paymaster would have to foot the bill, sided with the French and together they called Thatcher's bluff. The financial compromise achieved on the British rebate ensured that the process of European integration could be relaunched when Delors took over as President of the EC Commission. This example of heroic crisis coordination has more in common with the IGC case study that follows and is untypical of the relatively routine and non-politicized processes on which we shall first focus, although the ease with which winners and losers can be calculated in budgetary matters ensures that they are seldom entirely humdrum.

The EU budget, at a little over 1 per cent of Community GNP, is also small relative to national budgets because the EU relies primarily on negative integration through regulation rather than expenditure.[48] Positive integration through the Common Agricultural Policy (CAP) and structural funds is exceptional. Having on several occasions rejected the EU budget, the European Parliament concentrates on promoting spending on regional, transport, social, and education policies, which brings it into conflict with the Council of Ministers, rather than monitoring how EU funds are spent, which is left to the Commission. In 1988, the Commission established an Anti-Fraud Coordination Unit but it proved inadequate to its task because national governments showed less interest in those defrauding the EU budget than in repressing fraud against their own budgets.[49]

However, in the wake of the adoption of the Single European Act (1985), it was necessary to deal with the EC's increasing financial crisis. The first 'Delors package'—described as 'the most underdiscussed major event in Europe's post-1985 renewal'—combined 'a five year commitment to a greatly enlarged Community budget', with the implementation of the single market, controlling agricultural expenditure and avoiding annual intergovernmental wrangles over finance.[50] The coordination and doubling of three separate structural funds with the work of the European Investment Bank was combined with medium-term planning, such as Delors had practised in the French Planning Commissariat in the 1960s, to substitute communitarian resource redistribution to reduce regional and other disparities for national 'just return' which had prevailed hitherto. Ironically, this French-inspired proposal by the Commission President and his team was resisted by Prime Minister Chirac, (who in 1999 was characteristically to declare 'We are all peasants') but Delors was

---

[47] Favier and Martin-Roland, ii, p. 249; cf. 244–55. See also on the Fontainebleau Summit, Desmond Dinan, *Ever Closer Union? An Introduction to the European Community*, Macmillan, 1994, pp. 113–15 and John Newhouse, 'One Against Nine', *The New Yorker*, 22 October 1984, pp. 64–92.

[48] Brigid Laffan and Michael Shackleton, 'The Budget' in Helen Wallace and William Wallace (eds.), *Policy-Making in the European Union*, pp. 72–9.

[49] Ibid., pp. 89–90. See the critique of EU budgetary procedure by Alain Lamassoure, *Rapport d'information au nom de la délégation du Sénat pour les Communautés européennes sur la procédure budgétaire communautaire*, Appendix to Senate proceedings of 12 June 1991. No. 377, p. 75.

[50] George Ross, *Jacques Delors and European Integration*, Polity Press, Oxford, 1995, p. 40.

able to win through, thanks to the decisive support of Chancellor Kohl as Germany would carry the bulk of the increased budgetary burden.[51]

The French Socialist governments in 1991–93 were also reluctant to accept the second 'Delors package', which linked CAP reform with the GATT Uruguay Round negotiations, Delors this time using the Maastricht Treaty as the lever for pushing through further budgetary expansion. Delors added his advocacy to that of Prime Minister Cresson to persuade Mitterrand to accept CAP reform, helped by the specialist advice of the Elysée and Matignon staff. Fear of the farm lobby proved correct, the Opposition nearly securing a vote of censure against the Bérégovoy Government (three votes short) on 1 June 1992.[52] Mitterrand threatened to boycott the extraordinary October 1992 Birmingham European Council if the EU made more agricultural concessions to secure a GATT deal but Delors helped avoid France becoming too isolated.[53] Nevertheless, France now became a significant net contributor to the EU budget.

As EU budgets were so heavily dependent upon the cost of the CAP, agriculture ministers were actively involved in these negotiations but they acted to placate the irate farm lobbies rather than as coordinators. High profile coordination mainly fell on the Prime Minister and Finance Minister but when it comes to more routine matters, these can be left to less conspicuous sectoral core executives, although this results in inadequate coordination between the various EU policies. Much of the coordination that occurs actually takes place between the Commission and national administrations, or between representatives of national administrations in Brussels. The initial drafting of the budget is a task that falls to the Commission, following consultation with such officials.

Through the various phases of the budgetary process, it is the Bureau G3 located in the Budget Division within the Finance Ministry that plays the leading role in the coordination process.[54] A Foreign Ministry official deals with the budget, in order specifically to attempt to maintain consistency between this strand of policy and the overall thrust of French EC policy. In this sense the Foreign Ministry, and particularly the Minister for Foreign Affairs, plays a watchdog and firefighting role aimed at warning of contradictions between the French position in the various sectoral councils. However, on matters of detail, the Quai d'Orsay routinely defers to the Finance Ministry. Real challenges to the position of the Finance Ministry occur, if at all, at the political level.

The EC budgetary process shows the strength of horizontal but also the relative unpredictability of vertical coordination mechanisms. At the technical level, interministerial coordination is carried out via the SGCI system. Discussions regarding France's position on the Commission's draft budget, prior to formal negotiations commencing within the Council of Ministers, take place in an interministerial meeting organized by, and held in, the SGCI. All ministries with an interest in the

---

[51] Ibid., p. 42; cf. 41.   [52] Favier and Martin-Roland, iv, pp. 285–9.
[53] Ross, pp. 110–14, 197–200, 211–12. See also Laffan and Shackleton, pp. 79–85.
[54] The rest of this section is largely based on a working draft by Anand Menon.

budget are invited to attend this meeting. During these interministerial discussions, the Finance Ministry plays the lead role. Along with officials from the Foreign Ministry, Finance Ministry officials are present throughout the two-day discussions, whilst officials from spending ministries attend only those parts of the proceedings directly related to them. Finance also enjoys structural power over budgetary matters as Budget Division circulates the paperwork and hence controls the flow of information. This stands in marked contrast to discussions in the SGCI over routine sectoral business, where the ministry most directly involved can enjoy an information advantage over the Finance Ministry.

Most issues related to the EC budget are successfully resolved within the SGCI. One weakness of the system stems from the relative lack of contact between the heads of the SGCI's fifteen sectors, which impedes the formulation of effective cross-sectoral bargaining packages. The diffuse nature of the budgetary meetings merely serves to underline such problems, with only the Finance Ministry being in a position to achieve this. One of the reasons for the relative efficacy of the administrative coordination system is the relatively low importance accorded in France to the EC budget. Adjustments to the EC budgets are often used (by the Finance Ministry in particular) as a way of modifying spending without causing the uproar that changes to national budget provoke. As one SGCI official with experience of dealing with the budget put it, it 'is easier to cut the EC budget than the budget of individual ministries'.[55] This trend may be coming to an end. As the profile of the EC increases, and national budgets contract, spending ministries are becoming increasingly interested in the EC as a potential revenue source.

The EC budget usually falls into the category of non-politicized issues, the resolution to interministerial disputes being normally found between specialists. On occasion, however, the issue becomes politicized, which can occur in two ways. Either an official dissatisfied with the settlement agreed at official level coordination can appeal to the *cabinet* of his minister to intervene or political initiatives concerning the budget can effectively shape the nature of interministerial coordination. Thus, in 1996, France proposed a substantial cut in agricultural spending, a decision taken at *cabinet* level. In 1997, disagreement over funding led to the need for political intervention. In 1998, the EC budget became politicized and was discussed at the ministerial level, as it involved a political proposal to aim for a 0 per cent increase. Debates were particularly fierce between Finance and Agriculture, which had to bear the brunt of the drastic reduction of EC export subsidies and structural supports.

The context within which the budget is discussed clearly helps to determine the effectiveness of coordination. Whilst appeals to the political level can result in spending ministries sometimes achieving more funding than desired by Bercy, the fact that EMU is the object of a broad political consensus in France makes it easier for Finance to get its own way. In the 1990s context of convergence-inspired fiscal stringency, Bercy enjoyed political support for frugality in addition to its structural power over the budgetary process. The quinquennial review of the EC budget is

---

[55] Interview.

clearly an issue which is politicized from the start. For the review following the post 1993–99 settlement, a reflection group was set up under the authority of the Prime Minister's Office. Whilst, again, the SGCI was used as a source of specialist information, the problems of coordination created by this budgetary package was resolved only by ministers themselves and ultimately the Prime Minister.

Finally, various aspects of the EU policy process not directly related to the budget itself have budgetary implications. Spending ministries can lobby hard on those funding issues relevant to them during IGCs. Finance too protects its budgetary interests during such negotiations. Thus, during the Amsterdam IGC, Bercy supported the notion of a re-weighting of votes within the Council of Ministers in the hope that this would reinforce the position of the net contributor states, and hence the probability of reduction in EC budgetary spending. In order to reinforce its stance, the Finance Ministry maintains links with finance ministries in partner states, especially in the capitals of other net contributor states, representing a measure of functional financial policy community coordination cross-cutting national coordination on budgetary issues.

INTERGOVERNMENTAL CONFERENCES AND EU COORDINATION

Intergovernmental Conferences are quintessentially the kind of historic 'grand bargain' that are beloved of intergovernmental analysts of European integration because by the time the defining moment of decision has been reached it has become an intergovernmental matter.[56] However, if the preliminary work done, notably by the President of the EC Commission and his *cabinet* for the 1985 and one of the two 1991 IGCs, is given its due attention, it is clear that although the voices may be ministerial, the hymn sheets have largely been prepared by another core executive, that of the EC. Delors's institutional concern was to increase the Commission's capacity to promote further integration so as to make it irreversible. The organizational capacity to formulate and enforce comprehensive rules to coordinate the multiplicity of interactions that were corollaries of increasing integration could not be satisfactorily provided by member state intergovernmentalism. This was to be amply demonstrated by the contrast between the 1991 IGCs on Economic and Monetary Union and Political Union. The former exemplified the Delors Commission's ability 'energetically to push the member states beyond where they would have gone on their own', based upon a polished 1989 Delors EMU Report that was 'simultaneously market-reinforcing and "state-building"'.[57] The Political Union IGC was much more

---

[56] Alec Stone Sweet and Wayne Sandholtz in Sandholtz and Sweet (eds.), *European Integration and Supranational Governance*, OUP, 1998, pp. 11–12. For an extended defence of the intergovernmentalist and economic determinist interpretation of the making of the Single European Act and the Maastricht Treaty, see Andrew Moravcsik, *The Choice for Europe. Social Purpose and State Power from Messina to Maastricht*, Ithaca, Cornell University Press, 1998, chs. 5 and 6.

[57] Ross, pp. 144, 82; cf. 232–3, 240. For a discussion of the leadership role of Delors in the gestation of the Single European Act and as Chairman of the Central Bankers Committee for the Study of Economic

unprepared and intergovernmental, the Commission having had the issue sprung on it at short notice. The result was 'a nervous review of kilograms of paper coming from everywhere about virtually everything . . . the member states emptied their filing cabinets, not always to the point of the central issues'.[58]

For the 1991 IGCs, Delors ambitiously used Commission-prepared papers to link the completion of the single market with the reform of decision procedures and successfully placed the Commission at the centre of policy-making. Delors proposed in January 1990 that the political and institutional implications of EMU required an IGC and at the April 1990 Dublin European Council this suggestion was endorsed jointly by Kohl and Mitterrand. One of the objectives set was to achieve 'the unity and coherence of the Community across economic, monetary and political areas'.[59] At a preparatory Elysée interministerial council on 27 November 1991, European Affairs Minister Guigou suggested that to ensure commitment to the creation of a single currency, a firm deadline should be fixed for the final stage of its adoption. This idea commended itself to the President, who preferred to keep it up his sleeve for the European Council summit, whilst informing the Foreign and Finance Ministers of his tactics. He secured Kohl's last minute support for his proposal that the final date should be 1 January 1999, knowing that the Chancellor could constitutionally take this decision without seeking the approval of his Cabinet.[60] Had Mitterrand not pulled off this manoeuvre, it is doubtful whether the severe economic preparation measures to meet the convergence criteria would have been pursued with the necessary resolution.

In the run-up to the Maastricht IGC, Mitterrand was engaged in a flurry of bilateral meetings (as were the other leaders) and received an average eight memoranda daily from his staff, the ministries, and embassies.[61] On matters pertaining to the IGC, the President comes to the fore as the ultimate decision-maker and, if need be, coordinator.[62] Since so much of the work for IGCs is carried out either personally by the President, or within his own staff, there is often no real need for coordination. Indeed, even on this matter of the highest political salience, it is striking to note that the French Cabinet never discussed the 1997 Amsterdam IGC during the negotiation phase.

However, the President and his staff do engage in coordination, much of it informal, if only with the Prime Minister and the Foreign Ministry. During the Maastricht European Union Treaty (EUT) negotiations, only a small number of

and Monetary Union, see Ken Endo, *The Presidency of the European Commission under Jacques Delors. The Politics of Shared Leadership*, Macmillan, 1999, chs. 7 and 8.

[58] Ross, p. 91. On the 1991 IGC on Political Union, see Endo, ch. 9.

[59] Ibid., p. 89; cf. 31–3 and ch. 3 passim. The 'Single European Act' was so called because it modified all preceding EC Treaties in one text, representing a legislative act of coordination.

[60] Favier and Martin-Roland, iv, pp. 222, 228. Moravcsik (p. 443, note 129) claims that 'the German government, as opposed to the Bundesbank, had long favored setting a date'.

[61] Favier and Martin-Roland, iv, pp. 219–23.

[62] The rest of this section is largely based on a working draft by Anand Menon which formed part of his contribution to Kassim *et al.* (ed.), *The National Coordination of EU Policy. The Domestic Level*, pp. 93–6.

actors were involved. At the political level, these were Mitterrand himself, Dumas (Foreign Minister), Bérégovoy (Minister of Finance), and Guigou (Minister for European Affairs). At the administrative level, certain senior officials participated: Pierre de Boissieu (personal representative of Dumas during the negotiations), Jean-Claude Trichet, Treasury Director and personal representative of Bérégovoy for IGC–EMU matters. In addition, the Director and two other members of Mitterrand's *cabinet*, one member each of Dumas's and Guigou's *cabinet*, the Secretary General of the SGCI, and the French Permanent Representative in Brussels participated. The restricted number of actors involved limited the inputs of certain ministries. Even on defence questions, which were prominent on the agenda of the EUT, the Ministry of Defence played no role in the process, often being ignored in favour of defence specialists in the Quai d'Orsay, which may explain why the defence clauses proved unworkable.

During the Maastricht II IGC in preparation of the Amsterdam Treaty, many aspects of the French position were again drawn up in the Foreign Ministry. During the work of the reflection group, the Elysée was only minimally involved, though President Chirac was kept informed of progress. The Minister for European Affairs represented France during these preliminary negotiations. Once the President intervened more directly but Chirac's position paper of December 1995 was drafted by the *cabinet* of the Minister of European Affairs and involved careful consultation of a personal, informal kind, between him and the Foreign Minister, Matignon, and Elysée. The system of coordination involved frequent informal consultations between the highly limited number of actors involved in the process. The Matignon, Elysée, and Quai d'Orsay kept in regular contact by telephone about matters related to the IGC. When the SCGI protested that the effects of these discussions on various ministries were being neglected, it was told that it had no part in presidential initiatives.[63] So much for the requirements of horizontal coordination!

A striking feature of the Maastricht II IGC was the degree to which those directly involved represented a set of individuals with substantial experience of European affairs and who had worked together in the past either in the SGCI, the Quai, or the Permanent Representation in Brussels. One reason why the French negotiating stance remained as consistent as it did even after the 1997 election of the Jospin Government was that the new Prime Minister's adviser on European questions was a member of this tightly knit group. Indeed, the Socialists had maintained informal contact with those in the administration working on European affairs prior to the election. The Socialists' last-minute attempt to counterbalance the power of the ECB by an imprecise proposal for an EU 'economic government' failed, as had a similar pre-Maastricht attempt by Delors. 'We've lost the game on economic policy. Policy coordination, such as it will be, will be intergovernmental' was how Delors's EMU adviser expressed it.[64]

Once the actual 1997 IGC negotiations started, regular meetings were co-chaired by Foreign and European Affairs Ministers. In addition, ministries were invited to

---

[63] Interviews.   [64] François Lamoureux quoted in Ross, p. 156.

meetings at *cabinet* or ministerial level, to discuss French proposals prior to the meetings of negotiators, but these tended to be largely 'rubber-stamping affairs',[65] rather than an arena for real policy formulation, held simply as a way of informing ministers about initiatives that were planned. Nevertheless, this in itself marks an increase in coordination activity from what was the case under Mitterrand when there was virtually no involvement of sectoral ministries even though highly technical matters were at stake. A Deputy Secretary General of the SGCI attended, together with the Foreign and European Affairs Ministers, the Prime Minister's EU adviser, and on occasion his presidential counterpart. Until March 1996, the SGCI played virtually no part in the coordination of policy for the Amsterdam IGC. Its role was limited to being asked by Matignon or sectoral ministries to carry out studies on various aspects of European policy related to the IGC.

Problems of vertical coordination between the administrative and political levels become apparent in attempts to separate institutional questions and policy questions. The SGCI repeatedly complained that institutional questions such as Qualified Majority Voting had huge policy implications and therefore should not be treated independently of interministerial coordination mechanisms. The system of keeping the SGCI out of the process also came under pressure as the agenda of the IGC shifted. The French initially wanted to limit the agenda of the conference to purely institutional questions. However, pressure from the other states led to increasing incorporation of discussions on policy areas such as social policy and environmental questions. From March 1996, the SGCI hosted regular meetings—sometimes two per week—of ministry officials to discuss IGC-related issues. As evidence of the rivalry that can exist for prominence in coordinating policy, the Foreign Ministry at first adopted an empty chair policy at these meetings, considering that the SGCI had no standing as far as 'real policy' was concerned.[66] One of the striking features of the IGC was thus the lack of coordination between the organs of administrative coordination and political initiatives. Although the nature of issues sometimes discussed at IGCs can require detailed, technical cross-sectoral knowledge of the kind that the SGCI can supply, the latter enjoys no formalized role as a strategic thinker in the context of IGCs. As a consequence, political initiatives can on occasion be nonsensical.

The 1997 IGC also shed light on the problems that can arise as a result of personal difficulties within the core executive. European Affairs Minister Barnier and de Charette as Foreign Minister competed openly for influence during the IGC negotiations, souring relations to the point where even the two *cabinets* failed to communicate satisfactorily. Barnier enjoyed close relations with the President, which gave him the ability to compete with his ministerial senior. The initiatives of the two were on occasion contradictory. The situation was further complicated not only by the tendency of the Elysée to launch unilateral initiatives without prior consultation, but also by the decision to remove the head of the European Affairs section of the Foreign Ministry, only months prior to the Amsterdam summit. As a

[65] Interview.   [66] Interviews.

result of such difficulties, French negotiating strategy for the Amsterdam IGC suffered from inconsistencies due to ineffective coordination, derived more fundamentally from the fact that France is the 'prisoner of an extraordinary contradiction: we want a strong Europe, like the Germans, but weak institutions, like the British'.[67]

THE PROLONGED BSE CRISIS

Although France was not the origin of the escalation of what had previously been a primarily scientific and technical matter for specialists into a non-routine and political attempt at a coordinated response by core executives, it provides yet another insight into state–EU relations in a matter on which the Community has prime responsibilities. It shows that governments like France and particularly Germany were able to take unilateral emergency action under article 30 of the Rome Treaty despite the normal EU decision procedures, even though President Chirac sought to avoid diplomatic difficulties with Britain until the full seriousness of the crisis and the public and parliamentary outcry, suspicious since the contaminated blood fiasco (see above) of both political and scientific reassurances, forced him belatedly to support a ban on British beef. It also shows that in a political crisis, the Finance Ministry is forced onto the defensive, reluctantly compelled to meet the costs involved, while the Prime Minister regains control as domestic concerns come to predominate over relations with EU partners. Although the crisis continued to the end of the century, threatening to lead to a bitter trade war between Britain and France when the latter unsuccessfully pitted its own 'scientific' advice against that of the EU, we shall focus on its Spring 1996 inception. What the 1996 and 1999 paroxysms both demonstrate is the tension facing core executives between EU pressures and internal French pressures, reflecting the fact that 'European affairs, which are no longer foreign affairs, yet are still not only domestic affairs'.[68]

French core executive coordination during the Bovine Spongiform Encephalopathy (BSE) crisis demonstrates both its strengths and weaknesses.[69] While the Prime Minister sought to impose tightly controlled coherence, there were also politically damaging episodes of incoherence. The Prime Minister's Office and most government ministers focused principally upon domestic concerns, while the President and his staff, the Foreign and European Affairs Ministers, also focused upon diplomatic objectives which were not consistent with domestic preoccupations. Coordination in the public presentation of government objectives at the two levels was inadequately managed largely because the President and his staff engaged in diplomatic activities

---

[67] Jean-Louis Bourlanges, French MEP, in *Le Figaro*, 26 June 1995.

[68] Robert Pandraud at hearings of the National Assembly EU Committee, published in Nicole Catala and Nicole Ameline, *Quelles Réformes pour l'Europe de Demain?* Rapport d'information 1939, 8 February 1995, p. 135.

[69] This case study is derived mainly from a paper by David Howarth which has been substantially shortened, based on press reports and interviews undertaken by him as a Research Officer for the Governing from the Centre ESRC project.

outside the framework of coordination imposed by the Prime Minister's Office. So, in spite of the attempt at very tightly controlled coordination, given the extreme sensitivity of the issue, there was significant fragmentation.

Furthermore, Agriculture was clearly the lead ministry on an issue where the Ministry of Health might be expected to play an equally important role (as it did in Germany). However, the much stronger position of Agriculture in Brussels (with Agriculture Councils of Ministers meeting monthly and Health Councils only twice annually) gave the Agriculture Minister a decisive advantage.[70] Furthermore, whereas a powerful Social Affairs and Health Minister had been able in 1994 to impose upon reluctant Agriculture and Foreign Affairs Ministers a pro-ban policy on British beef products, a weak Junior Health Minister in 1996 only played an insignificant role. By 1999, the belated recognition of the need to put consumer protection before producer interests led the British government to transfer responsibility for food safety from the Agriculture to the Health Ministry.

The period from 20 March (when a British minister officially admitted the health dangers from BSE, after which consumption of beef plummeted) to the end of July 1996 is the most revealing. It was then that the Prime Minister's adviser on agriculture imposed tightly controlled coordination, that divergence in the public presentation of government priorities created political difficulties for the government, and that the Prime Minister personally intervened to reimpose consistency upon the ministers involved. The principal source of difficulties was the opposition of Agriculture officials to the President's diplomatic wish to appease British demands by lifting the embargo on three beef-derived products. The Minister of Agriculture was required to defend Chirac's standpoint at the 6 and 7 May Council of Agricultural Ministers and thereafter. Shortly after the meeting, the minister commented to the French press that the European partners 'should avoid diplomatic gestures on the issue as this would lead to a total rejection by consumers' shortly after having encouraged just such diplomatic gestures.[71] On 15 May, during his state visit to London, President Chirac claimed that the British met the conditions imposed by the European Commission to permit lifting the embargo, even though the European expert veterinary committee had previously decided that this was definitely not the case. Faced by considerable pressure from consumer and farming groups, the Minister of Agriculture claimed that the government had no intention of lifting the embargo on these three products and members of his *cabinet* let it be known to the press that the minister would not make any diplomatic gestures in the coming Council of Agricultural Ministers meetings.[72]

---

[70] G. P. E. Walzenbach, 'Convergent Coordination Patterns in the French and German Core Executive: the case of the BSE Crisis' in *West European Politics*, XXII, 3 July 1999, p. 70; cf. 82, which incorporates work on France by Dr Howarth.   [71] *Le Monde*, 9–10 May 1996.

[72] Ibid., 2–3 June 1996; cf. 28 April 1996 and 16 May 1996. As of March 1996, 4 per cent of French beef consumption was British in origin. On 6 June 1996, the leading French consumers' organization, *Union Fédérale des Consommateurs—Que Choisir* launched a boycott of all beef-derived British food and in a *Le Monde* article President Chirac backtracked, declaring after all that British measures were inadequate to justify lifting the embargo on the three derived products.

Some government statements were clearly aimed at different audiences, one British, the other domestic, which led to the public perception of contradiction. The European Commission's decision to lift the embargo if Britain met certain conditions was hailed by the French government as an important step in resolving the dispute with Britain. At the same time, ministerial officials were clearly unenthusiastic and the French Director General for Health pointed out to the press that the British had made no progress whatsoever in meeting the conditions, that the embargo would remain until all the conditions had been met, and that the European expert veterinary committee had refused to support the decision as it lacked sufficient scientific information.[73] The result was considerable confusion as to official government policy, Chirac subsequently keeping his diplomatic gestures out of the public glare. His public statements focused upon the need to defend public health and assist French livestock owners.

The press leak of advice from the Dormont interministerial expert committee (set up on 17 April 1966 to lend scientific credibility to public policy), which was submitted to the Prime Minister's Office on 9 May and not disclosed to the public for a month despite claims that policy-making would closely follow scientific recommendations and would be as transparent as possible, caused embarrassment. It recommended that the government not lift the embargo on any British beef products, given the unknown nature of the link between BSE and Creutzfeldt–Jakob Disease (CJD) and the inadequate British controls. A copy was sent to the newspaper *Le Monde*, which claimed that the government sought to conceal the scientific facts in order to have sufficient room to manoeuvre to reach a diplomatic settlement with the British.[74] The resulting political difficulties encouraged the Prime Minister personally to coordinate the government's rapid response to the subsequent opinions of the interministerial expert committee, aligning government policy with the committee's opinions.

The Ministry of Agriculture and, to a far lesser extent the Ministry of Health, as the most technically competent ministries and the most involved in the details of policy-making, regularly informed other ministries of their actions and likely policy developments. Interdepartmental consultation took place, although it was limited, given the domination of agricultural interests in the process. This consisted principally of Ministry of Agriculture officials asking Budget officials how to secure special national agricultural funds in addition to those provided by the EC.[75] Arbitration was necessary only on certain disagreements between Agriculture and Budget officials. Within the policy-making framework established by the core executive, there remained some room to manoeuvre for ministerial actors. The Budget Division was therefore able to affect the supply of funds especially on the less sensitive elements of the agricultural problems created by the crisis, but its ability to do was always subject

---

[73] Ibid., 6 and 7 June 1996.

[74] Ibid., 9–10 June 1996. The Dormont Committee was the joint creation of the Agricultural, Health, and Research Ministers, each of whom appointed eight members to it.

[75] Interview. In the allocation of EU and national financial compensation to farmers, the Budget officials' role was secondary to the Production and Exchange Division of the Agriculture Ministry.

to decision in the Prime Minister's Office and by the Prime Minister himself, who imposed financial flexibility on the Budget officials.

Prior to 20 March 1996, coordination of policy implementation was left almost entirely to SGCI advisers and the civil servants of concerned ministries. Matignon and Elysée advisers intervened principally to consider the diplomatic consequences of actions, in terms of the risk for French cattle-owners and public health. Responsibility for arbitration was often given to the Director of the Prime Minister's staff. After 20 March, the Prime Minister's adviser on agriculture kept close surveillance over ministerial action on the issue and constantly monitored and advised the Ministry of Agriculture on appropriate policy responses. The issue had become both a European crisis and a domestic one and, as such, necessitated cautious and controlled policy-making. Multilateral formal coordination took place frequently. Policy-making on the issue suffered from over-coordination, with even relatively unimportant details rising to Matignon.[76] In such a politically sensitive context, centralized control becomes increasingly necessary in order to avoid political scandals, especially in the context of a government and administration prone to fragmentation. Although for political, jurisdictional, and organizational reasons, the Minister of Agriculture became the government spokesman on virtually all elements of the crisis, no policy was presented prior to its confirmation with Matignon. The Prime Minister himself took charge of coordination only when the perceived incoherence in government policy statements and public controversy over government priorities threatened serious political damage for the government. He thus became actively involved in coordination when it was a matter of restoring public confidence in government policy-making on the issue and when government needed clear direction.

The BSE crisis provides an example of the extent to which the SGCI is marginalized in the context of highly politicized European issues or on issues which transcend the technical capacity of French civil servants. SGCI meetings took place weekly but their purpose was principally to inform ministerial officials of any developments at the European level, transferring information from officials in the French Permanent Representation. The SGCI was not the principal arena for coordination on European policy for two main reasons. First, the French position on the embargo was established by the Minister of Agriculture with the support of the Prime Minister prior to the Europe-wide embargo, not in reaction to it. The details of the French embargo were thus organized via interministerial meetings organized by the SGG and chaired by the Prime Minister's adviser on agriculture. Subsequent unilateral French decisions—inspired by the 'precautionary principle'—were made on the basis of the opinions of the national interministerial expert committee. Second, French officials participated in negotiations to resolve the European crisis in several fora: within the Committee of Permanent Representation (COREPER) (between agriculture advisers and more senior officials); in contacts between the

---

[76] Interviews. At the height of the crisis—May and June 1996—up to three meetings were organized at Matignon each week on BSE problems.

presidential envoy and ministerial officials in the other European member states; in meetings between European ministries of agriculture; the President's personal contacts with other heads of government and ministers; and meetings between visiting European ministers (notably the British) and French ministers. The SGCI played no role in these negotiations.

The contrast in perception between the lead and other ministries in their attitude towards formal interdepartmental meetings is striking.[77] While the Agriculture Ministry's officials thought their function was to clarify and slightly modify but primarily to confirm what had been decided by informal bilateral coordination, the latter stressed the tentative nature of the preliminary discussions. The predominance of agricultural concerns was reflected in the larger number of Agriculture Ministry officials who attended, frequently including the Minister's *cabinet* Director, the only person of this seniority to do so. Informal, bilateral coordination between the Prime Minister's adviser on agriculture and the Minister of Agriculture and his two technical advisers was the most important in terms of crisis decision-making. This normally consisted of the Minister's advisers contacting the Prime Minister's adviser in order to discuss and confirm a particular policy. Multilateral formal meetings were chaired by the Prime Minister's technical adviser on agriculture.

The purpose of Matignon-led coordination was to ensure that the non-Agriculture officials on whom policy was imposed believed that their views had nevertheless been considered if not incorporated. The Prime Minister's Office and the Agriculture Ministry worked in a mutually dependent fashion. The latter's officials provided all the necessary information to the Prime Minister's adviser, who kept the complaints of Budget officials in check, ensured compliance by other ministries, and legitimized decisions mainly shaped by Agriculture officials. The process was assisted by the fact that all the core executives shared four objectives: preventing the spread of BSE in France; encouraging the consumption of French-produced beef; convincing the public that all the necessary measures to ensure public health had been taken; avoiding political damage to the government.[78]

Placating the British government was not one of the French core executive's agreed objectives, even though that government's systematic obstruction of other EU policies resulted in a compromise agreement on a framework for the eventual lifting of the EU ban on British beef at the Florence European Council on 21–22 June 1996. President Chirac persuaded the Council to increase the Commission's recommended compensation for cattle destruction and a few days later EU agriculture ministers shared out this allocation, with France securing a quarter of the total (increased in October 1996) and the right to provide an equal amount from national funds. So the immediate crisis was temporarily contained but subsequent events were to show that it had not been resolved. The consumer panic following the rise in French BSE cases in the autumn of 2000 led to distasteful rivalry between President and Prime Minister in their response to the crisis. Meanwhile, French beef exports suffered the boycott from other EU countries which the French government had earlier imposed

[77] Interviews.   [78] Interviews.

on British beef exports, resulting in the Commission taking it to the European Court of Justice.

TRAVERSING THE EU QUAGMIRE

What conclusions emerge from a comparison of our four cases of EU coordination: EMU, the budget, the IGCs, and the BSE crisis? The central core executive coordination capability for routine and non-political affairs—the bulk of EU activity—can be competently handled at the SGCI in Paris and the Permanent Representation in Brussels. However, the aim of centralized coordination threatens to be frustrated by the overwhelming volume and complexity of matters dealt with. The resulting overloading has led to concentration on day-to-day tactical concertation at the expense of advance preparation and strategic guidance.[79] Furthermore, as we saw in connection with the EU budget, the SGCI has internal problems of coordination, reproducing the sectoral specialization which it is intended to overcome in the endeavour to ensure that all ministries concerned get a look in. The powerful Finance Ministry generally combines spending ministry coordination with the imposition of its views on others—notably its Foreign and European Affairs rivals for overall coordination—although once the issue becomes non-routine and politicized, as in the case of BSE, it loses this capacity, and a spending ministry, like Agriculture, takes over in tandem with Matignon. (The expensive CAP occupies an intermediate position, with CAP and EC budget matters becoming part of the high profile first 'Delors package'.) When Finance is itself the lead ministry in high profile Economic and Monetary Union matters, it escapes SGCI coordination, as does the Foreign Ministry in European Foreign and Security Policy. However, both are subject to the more or less improvised personal interventions of the President, who regards all EU matters as ultimately and often actually his preserve at the decisive phase of any political important issue.

While the IGCs represent a high point of sustained presidential intervention, presidential watchdogs are always on the lookout for matters susceptible of attracting his attention, even when foreign or French actors do not require it. Painfully achieved sectoral consensus may have to be sacrificed in the light of more general policy priorities, of which the Prime Minister or President will be the ultimate judge. The Foreign and European Ministers and key members of their staffs will also have an input into these wider considerations, especially during the preparation of IGCs, although they have had a more occasional and marginal role in the other three cases.

Informal and hierarchical strategic coordination displaces rather than supplements the formal and horizontal administrative coordination exemplified by the activities of the SGCI, although we have mentioned the linkage between its Secretary General and the Prime Minister's *cabinet*. The consequent centralization of interministerial coordination has sometimes resulted in the neglect of important factors owing to

---

[79] See the criticisms in ENA, *Le Travail Gouvernemental*, pp. 760–4.

ignorance due to the lack of indispensable information. The pressures exerted by forces outside the core executive—notably public confidence in scientific opinion in the case of the BSE crisis—complicate coordination problems within France, bilaterally with the UK or Germany, and within the EU. As usual, conflicts between ministers and their staffs—between Foreign and European Affairs, Finance and spending ministers, lead ministries wishing to go their own way—result in failures of coordination and inconsistencies in action. However, the additional complications and tensions entailed by the multi-government and sectorized EU dimension compound the coordination problems encountered in the budget, immigration, and privatisation examples investigated. This has led to additional efforts to achieve cohesion and consistency, faced by the perils posed by operating in the European quagmire.

The failure of the Amsterdam Treaty to deal with EU institutional reform prompted French attempts to move on from ideas of 'economic government' to a reformed EU form of 'two-headed government' based upon the Commission and Council of Ministers, both symmetrically and structurally organized around about fifteen bodies, coordinated by a General Affairs Council usually consisting of European Affairs ministers reporting to their prime ministers.[80] This is not the appropriate place to examine the imaginative proposals of the Quermonne Report on the reform of EU institutions but they demonstrate that France is actively considering how to cope not merely with the prospect of EU enlargement but with the inadequacies of the present procedures and their unsuitability to future needs. The coordination problems posed by piecemeal and pragmatic cooperation prompted President Chirac to press for a European constitution, without going as far as a full-blooded European federalism.[81]

---

[80] National Planning Office, *The European Union*, pp. 48–9; cf. 42–3.

[81] See, for example, A. Cole and H. Drake, 'The Europeanization of French Policy: Continuity, Change and Adaptation', *Journal of European Public Policy*, March 2000, 7(1), 38–9; cf. 26–43. See also *Le Monde*, 30 August 2000.

6

Budget Coordination and the Core Executive

'All the ministries have at least one important function in common: they must prepare their annual budgets.'[1] While this truism suggests a very dispersed and fragmented budgetary process, coordination proceeding by stages within spending ministerial bureaux, through their budget bureau and the minister's *cabinet* budget specialist, and then the minister in person, much of the work at this level is dominated by past commitments and is of a largely routine character. Although heroic attempts such as 'zero budgeting' have been made to overcome this inertial effect and reopen the compromise results of past adversarial encounters between spenders and the guardians of public finance, they have been quickly followed by a return to the humdrum, well-tried incremental adjustments at the margin.

However, the predictable negotiation of the annual budget round is punctuated by major and minor crises that exert an impact upon the process. They may originate from outside the country, due to a balance of payments crisis or the decisions of international or EU institutions, or from domestic events such as a strike or an election. In both cases, the financial consequences may need to be contained by changes in both macroeconomic policy and by modifying budgetary policy priorities. At these times, the Budget Division of the Finance Ministry at the coordinating centre comes particularly into its own but the President and Prime Minister, and their financial specialists will act as arbiters, rather than leaving the Finance Minister and his staff not only to take the lead but the final decisions. Then the top of the core executive hierarchy will not merely deal with the unresolved residue of conflicts between Finance and the spending ministries. The inner core executive will have to improvise choices that decisively deviate from the path of inertia.

The budgetary constitutional and financial procedures were decisively revised in 1958–59 to change from a traditionally parliamentary-centred process to one dominated throughout by bureaucratic and political core executives. While the Finance Bill is an apparently simple summary of the government's financial and general economic commitments, it includes a large number of appendices setting out the detailed government expenditure programmes, as well as the main economic assumptions underlying them. While it was intended to replace a ministry-focused

---

[1] G. Lord, *The French Budgetary Process*, Berkeley, University of California Press, 1973, p. 45. This excellent study was based upon a 1969 D.Phil thesis for the University of Oxford.

presentation of public expenditure with a broader and more integrated approach, the budget has continued to be primarily a piecemeal collection of particular ministry estimates. There was no attempt to include the roughly two-thirds of total public expenditure by local authority, public enterprises, and on social security in the budget, the Finance Ministry preferring to control these without being subjected to parliamentary scrutiny. As a result, the budget is far from being a comprehensive instrument of financial coordination and control. Increasing use of the cosmetic device of 'debudgetization' to ease conjunctural constraints in the context of European Monetary Union (EMU) criteria and domestic pressures makes the norm of the 'balanced budget' a somewhat meaningless exercise in reassuring rhetoric.[2]

Considered as an annual routine exercise, budget preparation is an incremental process concentrating upon modest adjustments to the previous year's spending bureaucratically coordinated by the budget bureau within each spending ministry, acting as the intermediary with the Budget Division of the Finance Ministry. The bureau head, usually a civil administrator, not a member of the *grands corps*, helps to prepare the minister's two- to three-page brief for presentations at interministerial budgetary negotiations. Administrative coordination is complicated by the fact that the line divisions jealously guard their budgetary responsibilities, frequently having their own budget bureau. Furthermore, there is usually a Financial Affairs and General Administration division which seeks to coordinate the preliminary work of the other division budget bureaux. However, the minister prefers to rely upon his personal staff, especially his *directeur de cabinet* and budgetary adviser, to formulate a strategy, settle disputes, and impose overall political coordination. 'Generally, the minister does not intervene personally in the discussion between his departmental officials and those of the Ministry of Finances [*sic*], but, because of the importance of budgetary matters, he may ask to be kept informed of what goes on, and in some cases he may have a word with the director of the budget division in the Ministry of Finance. When the discussions between his ministry and the budget division are completed, the minister is sent a memorandum on the points of agreement and disagreement.'[3]

Control over the budget is crucial both to the spending minister's ability to coordinate his ministry's activities and the capacity to demonstrate to his officials, clientele, parliament, and the electorate that he is a success. Although he may try to influence the outcome of unresolved disputes with the Budget Division by negotiations between his staff and that of the Prime Minister, this usually fails because the Prime Minister's staff find the Finance Ministry's arguments more convincing and the Prime Minister often consults the Finance Minister before making his decision.[4] The bottom line for the spending minister is to secure renewal of the previous year's expenditure, even when it has not been fully expended. Obtaining at least an average share of any extra spending is then sought, even though this allocation will have usually been settled between President, Prime Minister, and Finance Minister.[5]

[2] Ibid., pp. 16–18, 20–4, 191.   [3] Ibid., p. 51; cf. 29, 45–53, 130–4, 142–3.
[4] Ibid., pp. 154–7, 164–6.   [5] Ibid., pp. 135–40.

Ultimately the spending minister may threaten to resign if his pleas are rejected, thereby injecting an element of political crisis into what may otherwise be a rather technical discussion.

FIXING OVERALL BUDGETARY PRIORITIES: A CASCADE OF COORDINATIONS[6]

1. Actors and Annual Timetable

Within each spending ministry the budgetary process is fragmented between a proliferation of coordinating bodies. Each ministerial division is responsible for establishing its own preliminary budgetary proposal. This will be prepared in January and February on the basis of ongoing commitments, such as roll-over spending obligations (e.g. contracts exceeding one year), as well as demands for new funding. The draft budget for each division will be prepared with the participation of each sub-division which receives propositions for new spending from each of the different services for which it has responsibility. At this stage the budget bureau in each division has an important role to play. It will draft the division's budget on the basis of its own calculations and the figures from the different sub-divisions. By the end of February it will have drawn up a *dossier d'arbitrage* for the director who will decide the division's own budgetary priorities and then defend those priorities in the arbitration meetings with the other departmental directors in the presence of a ministerial *cabinet* member and, if necessary, the minister personally.

Within each department, therefore, there are three levels of budgetary responsibilities. *Services* will be in competition within each other, which places the deputy director in the first strategically important position of arbitration. Sub-divisions will also be in competition within each other, which places the director in the second strategically important position of arbitration. Finally, divisions will be in competition within each other, which places the minister and *cabinet* members in the third strategically important position of arbitration. Responsibility for coordinating the process on the administrative side will lie first and foremost with the various budget bureaux and more generally and formally with the ministerial Financial Affairs and General Administration Divisions (DAFAG). Responsibility for coordinating the process on the political side will lie with the ministerial budgetary adviser in the *cabinet*.

Within the Budget Division, the process is no less fragmented. With regard to tax commitments and proposals the main role will be played by the Service de la Législation Fiscale (SLF). With regard to the identification of macroeconomic trends, the main role will be played by the Forecasting Division in consultation with other organizations such as the Statistical Service, Institut National de la Statistique et des Etudes (INSEE). In spending matters the many bureaux within the Budget

---

[6] This section is a heavily edited version of a November 1997 working paper for the research project prepared by Dr Robert Elgie but incorporates material from the chapter on Budgetary Policy in his *The Role of the Prime Minister, 1981–91*, Basingstoke, Macmillan, 1993 and Supplementary Research.

Division are each responsible for identifying the budgetary demands of the departmental sectors which they shadow. By mid-February each bureau prepares a forecast detailing the likely contents of each sector's budget, presenting 'reasoned justifications for each of the proposals: renewal of past expenditures, economies, new spending envisaged and accepted, measures that one expects the minister to request but which it is proposed not to accept'.[7] It is discussed between representatives of the bureau and the deputy director with responsibility for that bureau before being passed on to the first sub-division which coordinates the information received from all parts of the Budget Division. On the basis of this information, senior officials in the Budget Division engage in two internal and unofficial exercises, the *budget de reconduction*, calculating the budget for the year *n* simply on the basis of the Finance Act for the year *n* − 1 plus projected figures for inflation, growth, and so on, and the *budget tendanciel*, calculating the budget for the year *n* on the basis of the *budget de reconduction* plus a notional amount for so-called 'unavoidable new measures'.

For much of the January to February period, then, budgetary policy-making is a strictly internal process within both the spending ministries and the Budget Division. Towards the end of this period, there are the first routinized set of informal contacts between them. Members of the various bureaux within the Budget Division will be in touch with deputy directors and budget bureau members in the ministries to share information about the assumptions being made on both sides. This allows officials in the Budget Division to establish realistic budgetary predictions and officials in the ministries to identify the issues which are likely to be problematic later.

By early March the second stage of the budgetary process is ready to begin. The Budget Director presents the Budget Minister with a formal document outlining the proposed rate of increase in expenditure, budget priorities chosen, tax proposals, economies, and anticipated budget deficit.[8] The minister's *cabinet* will already be aware of most of the issues at stake. He does not simply describe the budgetary situation but also proposes key reforms which the minister may wish to adopt. It is then the responsibility of the Budget Minister and *cabinet*, to present a similar document to the Prime Minister, who will then consult with the Finance Minister and, with the exception of periods of cohabitation, the President too. (Prior to 1996, parliament was not associated with this phase of the process.) The result is that by mid-April the main political decisions regarding the budget have been taken. Before this time, political representatives may signal their priorities formally or informally, publicly or privately, to budgetary officials. However, it is only at this stage that the general involvement of political actors begins.

The final step in fixing overall budgetary priorities usually takes place in mid- to late April. The Prime Minister calls a meeting at which all ministers are presented with the government's budgetary priorities (the level of the budget deficit and the level of increase or decrease in government spending and taxation) and the opportunity for

---

[7] *Le budget de l'Etat. De la préparation à l'exécution*, Paris, Les Editions de Bercy, 1995, p. 37.
[8] Ibid., p. 39.

debate scarcely changes the main thrust of the measures which have been proposed. Following this meeting, the Prime Minister formally issues the 'framework letter' which outlines to all ministers the choices which have been collectively agreed. While the details of some of the government's priorities may be revisited as a result of the formal spending arbitrations in June–July and fiscal arbitrations in August, for the most part the framework letter contains the definitive set of figures which will form the basis of the budget for the year *n*. The 1996 process contained an important innovation whereby, rather than all ministers receiving a fairly general framework letter, each minister received a very detailed 'preparatory directive'. This delayed the public announcement of the government's budgetary figures and permitted changes at a later stage in the process than was usually the case, as well as procedurally shifting control from the spending ministries to the Budget Division.

2. General Budgetary Constraints

Budgetary policy-making is subject to three constraints: a considerable degree of incrementalism, especial susceptibility to exogenous factors, and the customary political constraints.

First, there is a massive inertia to the expenditure side of the budgetary equation. It has been estimated by a former director that about 94 per cent of total spending commitments can be classed as continuing items carried on quasi-automatically from one year to the next.[9] These items are collectively known as *services votés*. They consist mainly of debt interest charges, departmental wages, pensions, material costs, and authorized capital expenditure. Governments have twice tried to change the principle of continuity which underpins the *service votés*. In the late 1960s there was an attempt to rationalize budgetary policy-making procedures and in the mid-1980s there was an attempt to introduce zero-base budgeting. Both innovations were short-lived and there continues to be an overwhelming automaticity to spending items. To ease budgetary pressures, defence contracts have increasingly been spread over a number of years and the lifetime of the government's contracts exceeding one year has generally been extended in the attempt to reduce their annual cost. The government's room for manoeuvre, then, is severely limited by the recurring nature of spending commitments.

Second, the degree of manoeuvrability is further shaped by a multiplicity of exogenous factors. For example, they include the level of the dollar which influences the cost of private sector imports and exports and, hence, the level of government revenue via taxable private sector profits. They also include the level of interest rates (set, since January 1994, by an independent Bank of France usually following a lead from the Bundesbank and, since 1999, by the European Central Bank (ECB)) which affects the cost of servicing the national debt. They include the state of the international financial markets which changes the general environment in which interest

---

[9] Michel Prada, 'La préparation du budget vue par la direction du budget', in *Le Budget de l'Etat*, Paris, Economica, 1988, p. 28. The official estimate of unallocated expenditure was 12 per cent in 1998 (Ministère de l'Economie, *Politique Economique*, 1998) but this is not a realistic measure of actual budgetary discretion.

rates are set. They further include the level of household saving, which also impacts on the cost of debt-financing. They include the cost of EU contributions and the financial constraints set out in the Maastricht Treaty. Finally, they include the general impact of macroeconomic conditions generally which determine, for example, taxation receipts as a function of the level of consumer spending and employment, as well as expenditure obligations as a function of inflation and the increasing cost of pensions and public sector wages.

Third, in addition to ongoing budgetary items and exogenous factors, the budgetary equation is also influenced by political constraints. Newly elected governments come to office with commitments, at least some of which they usually try to uphold. So, for example, spending in the education and culture policy sectors was prioritized after the 1988 presidential election. In addition, budgetary policy-making can be shaped at any time by premeditated or off-the-cuff pronouncements from senior political figures. For example, on 15 September 1983, President Mitterrand announced on TV that the overall level of taxation would be reduced by 1 percentage point in the following year's budget and that at the same time the budget deficit would not be allowed to exceed 3 per cent of GNP.[10] This measure was announced without the Prime Minister's or Finance Minister's consent and yet it considerably altered the course of budgetary negotiations as Mitterrand's senior advisers worked to ensure that the President's decisions were followed. Let us now consider five specific budgets for the years 1983, 1985, 1987, 1990, and 1997, each of which is distinctively instructive.

1983: Panic Budgeting

The elaboration of the 1983 budget in 1982 was characterized by a sense of core executive panic at the escalating deficit, in a context of worsening balance of payments and unemployment. Budget Minister Fabius persuaded the President on 8 March that the deficit should be confined to 3 per cent of GDP and, in the face of speculation against the franc, the decision was announced after the Cabinet meeting on 10 March 1982.[11] It was quickly followed by a letter from Prime Minister Mauroy asking all ministers for economies in proposed expenditure. Fabius's verdict on this exercise (which as we shall see was repeated by Mauroy in December 1983 with ineffective results) was blunt. 'Five ministries have not proposed any economies. The others have restricted their suggestions generally to derisory amounts. Only the Ministries of Labour and Finance have treated the exercise seriously.'[12] Future Industry Minister Fabius wanted to cut back industrial subsidies, which had multiplied anarchically, with each sponsor ministry supporting its own protégés. A memorandum declared that 'interministerial coordination procedures have increased but are aimed at

---

[10] Elgie, *The Role of the Prime Minister in France*, p. 76. On the protests in May–June 1983 of various spending ministers at cuts imposed and pleas to the Prime Minister to reverse them, see the Mauroy Archive at Lille Town Hall on the Budget.   [11] Attali, *Verbatim*, i, pp. 273, 276.

[12] Mitterrand Archive.

particular clientèles and are subject to conflicts of influence, so that they have increased rather than reduced confusion'.[13] However, industrial subsidies were frozen at 1982 levels, not reduced.

In the context of recapitalizing the newly nationalized industries—many of which were in deficit—the Finance and Industry Ministers had written a joint letter on 4 May 1982 to the President proposing increased funding. This prompted a protest next day from Fabius, who claimed that Delors was reversing the position agreed previously under Prime Minister Mauroy's arbitration. Delors had, in the wake of the October 1981 devaluation, called for a 'pause' in public expenditure but Fabius had nevertheless proceeded substantially to increase both spending and the budget deficit, which led to a further attack in the currency markets and the June 1982 devaluation. The open squabbling between Finance Minister and Budget Minister is put into perspective by a note from Fabius to Mitterrand of 28 April 1982 on increased investment in which he described the debudgetization of 5 billion francs for the public sector as an 'accounting artifice'. He went on to add that 'In general, the budgetary economies are fictional', and that if money was not taken from banks to pay for the investment, it would mean either increased taxation or an increased budget deficit.[14]

The Budget Directeur sought to inject a greater sense of urgency in memos to the President's economic adviser, declaring with exasperation in June 1982 at the time of the second of three devaluations: 'How many devaluations will be necessary before it is realised that general government expenditure—especially increasing numbers of civil servants—reduces French competitiveness?'[15] The advice to the Prime Minister from Hervé Hannoun (a future Deputy Governor of the Bank of France) and Daniel Lebègue (a future Director of the Treasury) of his *cabinet* was usually to stick to the Budget Ministry's proposals in the 'arbitrations' they were called upon to make. Negative comments on particular cases included 'exorbitant request to be rejected' and 'waste regularly denounced by the Court of Accounts'. Supporting increased funds for iron-miners is explained by 'decision of the President on a visit to Lorraine'.[16] A 20 May 1982 Hannoun–Lebègue note for the Prime Minister explained that the unprecedented 31 billion franc programme of economies meant mastering current but sparing investment expenditure, while spreading out the cost of some presidential and governmental commitments beyond 1983. Within an overall 125 billion budget deficit (3 per cent of GDP), the Prime Minister's margin of discretion amounted to 4 or 5 billion francs for which they suggested thirteen 'inflexions'.[17] The encounter at the beginning of June 1982 between Mauroy and Mitterrand to settle budgetary matters was prepared by a meeting at which Budget Minister Fabius but not Finance Minister Delors was present!

[13] Mitterrand Archive.

[14] Ibid. For a discussion of the 1981–82 budget context of the Delors–Fabius conflict, see David R. Cameron, 'From Barre to Balladur: Economic Policy in the Era of the EMS' in Gregory Flynn (ed.), *Remaking the Hexagon. The New France in the New Europe*, Boulder, Westview Press, pp. 130–1.

[15] Mitterrand Archive, memo dated 17 June 1982; cf. 28 May 1982.   [16] Mitterrand Archive.

[17] Ibid.

The Culture budget deserves particular attention because of Lang's determination to buck the constraints imposed on other ministers. On 19 May 1982, a Hannoun–Lebègue note to the Prime Minister pointed out that despite Lang's appeal to President Mitterrand's 24 September 1981 press conference commitment to increase the Culture budget to 1 per cent, this would be incompatible with the President's injunction to keep the budget deficit to 3 per cent. They recalled that the 1982 Culture budget had already been doubled from 2.9 to 5.9 billion and recommended an increase to 7 and not 10 billion francs as requested by Lang. The larger sum would be provocative to other ministers, who had been told that increasing employment was the only priority, as well as threatening the credibility of the rigorous policy on which the President had insisted. The President's budget adviser took the same line, suggesting resistance to Lang's pleas, who wrote to Mitterrand: 'I once again need your help ... I beg you to intervene ... It is a matter of hours as the ceiling letters are decided this morning.'[18] Despite his special pleading, the Culture budget's 13 per cent increase from 0.78 to 0.83 of the whole was a 'relative pause'.[19]

1985: Budgeting by Presidential Fait Accompli Fiat

The explanation of why the 1985 budget procedure dramatically reversed the normal relationship of settling public expenditure before the revenue decisions requires us to return to Mitterrand's 1981 presidential campaign commitments, whose implications were worked out in 1983–84. It also means that we have to consider the government's income as well as its expenditure decisions, which we will not do in relation to other budgets. As early as April 1982, the Deputy Secretary General of the Presidency (SGP) sent a memo to Mitterrand pointing out the 'latent contradiction' between his pledges both to increase public expenditure and to restrain mandatory tax deductions (including local authority and social security impositions) called *prélèvements obligatoires*. Since increasing the budget deficit was unacceptable and increased growth problematic, the only recourse was achieving 'tax' reduction (which will henceforth be used to cover all mandatory deductions) by reducing expenditure. This would require detailed investigation implying 'issuing a firm directive in this sense to the ministries concerned'.[20]

It was more than a year later, on 15 September 1983, that Mitterrand struck with the announcement that 'taxes' would be reduced by 1 per cent in the 1985 budget. Attali commented: 'Everyone will think that this measure was carefully prepared in secret at the Elysée. Not at all; it was improvised on the spot. Now the Government will be forced to implement it. The President regards this surprise tactic as the only way to achieve results; without a *fait accompli* nothing important is ever decided.'[21] It was up to the Elysée staff to deal with the fallout of Mitterrand's bombshell. Some 80 billion francs would need to be 'found'. How was this to be achieved?

---

[18] Mitterrand Archive.
[19] Ibid. Charasse wrote to SGP Bérégovoy on 27 May 1982: 'Jack Lang has enough funds which he is not spending sufficiently quickly' (ibid). [20] Mitterrand Archive.
[21] Attali, *Verbatim*, i, Part 2, pp. 762–3. See also Favier and Martin-Roland, ii, pp. 229–30.

On 21 September 1983, Deputy SGP Christian Sautter, who in the late 1990s would become Budget Minister (1997–99) and Finance Minister (1999–2000), wrote to SGP Bianco and Attali suggesting abandoning the classic procedure of a letter from the President to the Prime Minister. Having discussed the matter with three other members of the Elysée staff, he proposed 'a procedure driven by the Elysée: launched by a meeting in the President's office with M. Mauroy, M. Delors and M. Bérégovoy (Social Affairs Minister), followed by monthly meetings . . . the SGP ensuring that matters progressed between meetings'.[22] The next day Bianco and Attali wrote to Mitterrand supporting this centralized coordination, adding that 'one of your collaborators should be specially designated to follow this up'. Suggesting a simultaneous reduction of public expenditure, debudgetization of social expenditure, and tax reduction, they stressed that 'Only a very determined approach will be successful, if the Minister of Finance and Social Affairs are totally mobilised from October'.[23] Bianco followed this up with a letter to Delors and Bérégovoy on 5 October 1983 on the need to propose ways of reducing 'taxes' by 1 per cent in 1985.

Papers on ways of attaining this objective were summarized on 21 October 1983 by Sautter, following a meeting with the *directeurs de cabinet* of the Finance, Social Affairs, Industry, Housing, and Interior Ministries. Commenting on this note to Mitterrand, Attali declared rather melodramatically on 7 November: 'To achieve this, it will be necessary to win a *great battle* with the Administration between January and April. Your government will have to act like a real commando, with an iron hand. It will be necessary to settle revenue before expenditure and not the opposite which is the usual practice . . . '[24]

However, Sautter's suggestion of centralizing coordination was not adopted. For the President (read Elysée staff) to appear to displace Matignon would weaken the Prime Minister's authority with the ministers, who had to conduct the technically complex work. While it would be very imprudent to abandon the normal and tested way of preparing such matters, the President's economic adviser warned: 'If Jacques Delors does not receive an order from the President, his officials will treat this cuts exercise with contempt. As it is technically very awkward, the active cooperation of (Finance) officials is indispensable.'[25] He recommended that the Prime Minister should write to ministers, explicitly backed by the President in Cabinet.

At a meeting with Delors a few days later Mitterrand, briefed by a memo from Sautter, stressed that the Finance Minister should make the 'tax' reduction exercise a personal priority. To fulfil his commitment, the Finance Minister would have to reverse the budgetary timetable and take revenue decisions before preparing the consequential expenditure economies. In a 20 December 1983 memo to the President, Sautter wrote that the meeting with Delors had injected a 'belated sense of urgency' into the Finance Ministry, and set out a new 1985 budget timetable from December 1983 to September 1984. A covering note by Attali commented: 'This procedure constitutes a real administrative revolution. It is possible and necessary to succeed.'[26]

---

[22] Mitterrand Archive.   [23] Ibid.   [24] Ibid.   [25] Ibid.   [26] Ibid.

However, the 'economies' letter sent by Prime Minister Mauroy to all spending ministers on 28 December 1983 produced a poor response. Finance and Budget Ministers complained and there was no reply from the Culture and Ex-Servicemen's Ministries. Social Affairs said it would offer cuts but had not done so. Four others—Communication, Defence, Justice, and Vocational Training—said the exercise was impracticable. Commerce and Industry proposed redeploying, not reducing, spending. Five offered derisory cuts: Education, Environment, Regional Planning, Tourism, Youth and Sport. The only ministries to treat the exercise seriously were Agriculture, Cooperation, Finance, Housing, Interior, Transport, and Maritime Affairs. Clearly, voluntary cuts would not suffice, as they had not in 1982.

At the 18 January 1984 Cabinet meeting, the Prime Minister explained that the end of February Cabinet would fix the fiscal guidelines and that only then would public expenditure allocation be decided. Spending would have to fit the revenue constraints imposed by the 3 per cent limit on the budget deficit. Each minister would be personally accountable to the President and Prime Minister for their contribution to the reduction of 'taxes' in 1985. The next day, President Mitterrand wrote to all ministers formally underlining the Cabinet decision reversing the customary budget procedure.

The context in 1984 was one in which the austerity policies of the 1983 and 1984 budgets had caused a recession that further increased the deficit owing to a fall in revenue. 'In contrast to its anomalous role in 1981 when it had to recommend additional spending plans to a government which did not possess sufficient ideas about how to spend public money, in 1984 the *direction du Budget* had to draw up a long list of spending cuts. As a result, the role of the Prime Minister and Finance Minister was reduced. They became more reliant than usual on the administrators of the Budget Division.'[27] Preliminary work by the Budget Division led not merely to the proposed minimization of new spending but a 1 per cent cut in the personnel of all ministries. This was adopted by Delors and Mauroy, combined with an overall 2 per cent cut in spending, with the intention of shocking their colleagues into accepting the draconian framework letters sent to ministers at the end of March 1984. Certain ministries were exempted, the President insisting on Defence, Research, and Culture being treated as expenditure priorities. Fear of unrest in Education and Agriculture meant that these were also spared, as was Justice because of badly overcrowded prisons.

The replacement of Mauroy as Prime Minister by Fabius and Delors by Bérégovoy in July 1984 resulted in much better politico-administrative coordination between those concerned. Fabius had from 1981 to 1983 been Budget Minister and many members of the staffs of the Prime Minister and Finance Minister were mutually familiar members of the Finance Inspectorate network which eased the task of preparing difficult decisions.[28]

Before the 1985 budget was settled, meetings took place in early March 1984 at which it was worked out. These notably involved the Prime Minister, Finance,

[27] Elgie, p. 75.   [28] Ibid., p. 80; cf. 79.

Budget, and Social Affairs Ministers meeting the President and then the Prime Minister meeting these ministers and staff from his *cabinet* and that of the President to decide details of the 45 billion francs of economies which were presented by Mauroy to Mitterrand on 14 March 1984. Counter-proposals from Social Affairs Minister Bérégovoy and Budget Minister Emmanuelli having been rejected, the remaining symbolic issue was whether the unpopular business *taxe professionnelle* should be abolished—Mitterrand had called it an 'idiotic tax'—or merely reduced, which was Delors's position, acting on the advice of the Budget Division and his *cabinet*. The battle was finally settled in Delors's favour, thanks to the inability of the Prime Minister's specialist to 'outsmart the *direction du Budget*'.[29] This was decided at the end of June, shortly before the resignation of the Mauroy Government. Fabius only made marginal, politically inspired modifications, reducing the budgets of the ministries formerly headed by Communists (for example, Transport), whom Mauroy had wanted to retain in his government. The President largely got his way, not only on public expenditure but also on taxation.

1987: Preparing the First Cohabitation Budget

The incoming Chirac Government, notably Finance Minister Balladur and Budget Minister Juppé, decided that the best way of expediting their economic programme, such as abolishing the wealth tax, promised in the 1986 election campaign, was to give priority quickly to adopting a supplementary mini-budget. Once this was done, the framework letter went out at the end of May. It increased the mini-budget cut of 10 billion francs to 40 billion. The President had no influence on the process, his staff merely being kept informed of developments by the *directeurs de cabinet* of Balladur (Trichet) and Juppé (Bouton). Curiously, this lack of influence was also largely true of the Prime Minister, who delegated his budgetary responsibilities to the Finance and Budget Ministers. Even Chirac's economic and budgetary advisers were described as 'more spectators than actors'.[30] The heroic attempt at imposing zero budgeting, which Bouton persuaded Juppé to adopt, was patchy in its results. At the extremes, Léotard at the Culture Ministry simply refused to cooperate, while Madelin at Industry for ideological reasons proposed cutting the level of subsidies to ailing firms more heavily, which was gratefully accepted.

Budget Minister Juppé was allowed to settle as many disputes as possible, negotiating with each spending minister, with his *directeur de cabinet* Bouton, the President's budget adviser, and two of the Finance Minister's advisers present. In the event, about half the disputes were resolved in this way. Of the remainder, Balladur had to settle cases where the spending ministers refused to accept the cuts requested, for example Telecommunications, Transport, and Employment, or because some ministers had to be handled diplomatically for political reasons, for example Pasqua at Interior. Chirac decided from the start that he would deal with agriculture and overseas territories, out of personal interest and because they were politically

---

[29] Elgie, pp. 76–7.   [30] Ibid., p. 83; cf. 81–2.

sensitive. He was forced to 'arbitrate' in the conflict between Balladur and Léotard over the Finance Minister's wish to halt the Bastille Opera, one of Mitterrand's architectural–cultural projects. Léotard, leader of the Republican Party, threatened to resign over the issue and Chirac (also Mayor of Paris) largely backed him. More generally, Balladur and Juppé decided to give tax reduction precedence over reducing the budget deficit and received the support of the trio of economic liberal ministers, Léotard, Longuet, and Madelin, who met to concert their tactics.[31]

1990: The Minority Rocard Government's Budget

After Mitterrand's re-election as President in 1988, Prime Minister Rocard was rapidly plunged into the wearing piecemeal process of budgetary negotiations as we saw in Chapter 2. To avoid repeating this in 1989, he adopted a procedural innovation promoted by the Budget Division that brought forward the constraints on ministerial expenditure estimates by telescoping the framework letter and ceiling letter stages of the budget process. Following lengthy discussions of the options in March and early April 1989 by the President, Prime Minister, and Finance Minister, a meeting of all ministers on 13 April discussed the government's budgetary strategy. Finance Minister Bérégovoy's proposed reduction of the budget deficit by 10 billion francs to 90 billion francs was accepted. The following day, the framework letter sent to ministers was specific and not general. It set the spending limit for each department. While the Prime Minister's detailed involvement in budget negotiations was reduced as a result, his overall control, exercised jointly with the Finance Minister, was increased.[32] As we shall see, this lesson was not lost on Juppé when he became Prime Minister.

The Finance Ministry having estimated that GDP would increase by 5 per cent in 1990, it decided that within an overall 5 per cent growth in public expenditure, increases for some ministries would have to be compensated by decreases for others. In preliminary discussions between the staffs of the Prime Minister and Finance Minister, three categories of spending departments were distinguished. First, the Education, Research, and Cooperation ministries were given priority as promised by Mitterrand in the 1988 presidential election. The only margin of discretion exercised by Rocard was how much more than 5 per cent they should receive, exercised in conjunction with the presidential staff, with Finance pressing for moderation. A second group of ministries, such as Interior, Justice, and Telecommunications, only received increases of 3 per cent, in line with estimated inflation, while most of the rest—the third category—received no increase at all. The Prime Minister played a more central role in deciding which ministries went into the inflation-protected and actually decreased expenditure categories, although he did so in coordination with Finance and the presidency. Despite resistance by Finance Minister Bérégovoy and Budget Minister Charasse, Mitterrand secured increases for the Culture Ministry (in answer

---

[31] Elgie, pp. 85–8.   [32] Ibid., p. 90.

to the usual pleas from Jack Lang) and Housing (in favour of low rented accommodation), the latter receiving an extra 2.3 billion francs.[33]

The Defence Ministry's budget was treated as a special case because the timing coincided with the 1990–93 medium-term military programme's preparation. Thus, the short-term allocation had to be coordinated with defence strategy and the end of the Cold War, as well as other longer term objectives, such as the planned quinquennial 24 billion franc increase in education expenditure. Bérégovoy saw this context as an opportunity for reducing the defence budget by 70 billion francs from its projected increase to 470 billion francs five years later. Defence Minister Chevènement fought to protect his major project while accepting a 30 billion franc cut in personnel costs. In what was a reserved presidential matter, Rocard postponed the decision to a Defence Council at the presidency. Faced with Bérégovoy's warning that the budget's balance would be upset if the full cut was not made and Chevènement's threat of resignation, Mitterrand's compromise was a cut of 45 billion francs. As the Finance Ministry had engaged in its customary deliberate underestimation of total public expenditure, no dramatic consequences occurred.[34]

1997: The Budgetary Road to Electoral Defeat

The 1997 Finance Bill was prepared under particularly difficult conditions. The first constraint under which the Juppé Government had to operate concerned the criteria set out in the Maastricht Treaty in the run-up to joining the club of Euro countries. The obligation to reduce the budget deficit to 3 per cent by 1997 had weighed heavily on the shoulders of policy-makers since 1994. However, the budgetary process in 1996 was particularly affected by this requirement, both because the budget deficit was still high and the deadline was imminent and because in October 1995 President Chirac had ended many months of ambiguity by announcing that he was fully committed to the conditions laid out in the Maastricht Treaty. Chirac's unequivocal pronouncement was primarily made to reassure the international money markets but also in the hope that it would provoke a fall in the level of interest rates.[35] It ended the carefully cultivated ambiguity about the newly elected President's commitment to EMU which had been lingering since his election in May 1995. Thereafter, Chirac, Prime Minister Juppé, and Bank of France Governor Trichet insisted that the budget deficit had to be cut annually by 1 per cent, Trichet acquiring the nickname '5, 4, 3'.[36]

Chirac's declaration decisively predetermined the 1997 Finance Bill, obliging decision-makers to adopt the Maastricht budget deficit criterion as the baseline for the 1996 budgetary negotiations. Indeed, in early May 1996, Chirac reinforced this point, stating that 'Maastricht and its criteria . . . are our inspiration' as he publicly emphasized the need for his ministers to make spending cuts.[37] The result was that

---

[33] Elgie, pp. 91–3.   [34] Ibid., pp. 93–4.

[35] See Robert Elgie and Helen Thompson, *The Politics of Central Banks*, London, Routledge, 1998, ch. 6.

[36] Personal interview and J. Arthuis, *Dans les coulisses de Bercy. Le cinquième pouvoir*, Albin Michel, 1998, p. 212.   [37] Interview in *Le Monde*, 7 May 1996, p. 15.

from January 1996, Budget Division officials sought to obtain a net reduction in government expenditure of nearly 40 billion francs. In the context of the largely irremovable mass represented by the *services votés*, attainment of this objective inspired the procedural reforms that were characteristic of the 1996 budgetary negotiations.

The second constraint that the government faced concerned the unfavourable macroeconomic environment within which the budget was prepared. On 25 March 1996, Finance Minister Jean Arthuis presented a report which painted a bleak picture of the economic situation. Based on calculations from the government's various statistical offices, the Minister announced that the economy would grow by only 1.3 per cent rather than 2.8 per cent as previously announced. He estimated that the increase in consumer spending would be only 0.8 per cent down from 2.9 per cent in 1995 and that the annual level of inflation would be around 2 per cent. The low level of consumer expenditure would reduce the level of value added tax (VAT) receipts in the 1996 budget. Similarly, the fact that the government had frozen 20 billion francs of public spending in January meant it was even more difficult to find ways to reduce spending by the extra 40 million francs needed to meet the Maastricht criteria. Both of these considerations weakened the government's ability to meet its budgetary objectives.

Another factor which shaped the priorities of the 1996 budgetary process concerned the government's desire to reduce taxation. When it came to power in May 1995, the Juppé Government was faced with an extremely difficult budgetary situation. Balladur had underestimated the 1995 budget deficit at 275 billion francs but it was in fact 400 billion, so Juppé could not honour Chirac's pre-electoral promises and had to raise taxes in a supplementary budget in the summer of that year.[38] This increase was unpopular and ran counter to the popular expectations that had been created during Chirac's presidential campaign. As a result of this increase, the overall level of taxation in the economy stood at 44.7 per cent in 1996 and was predicted to rise to over 45 per cent in 1997. The national debt as a share of GDP was rising rapidly from 39 per cent in 1992 and would reach 58 per cent by the end of 1997, just short of the Maastricht 60 per cent limit. All this presented the government with an awkward problem. It wanted to reduce taxation, yet any reduction would necessitate an even greater level of spending cuts, given the absolute commitment to reduce the level of the budget deficit to 3 per cent. Faced with this situation, the government tried to square the circle.

In the draft budget presented to the Budget Minister and Prime Minister in early April 1996, there was no provision for tax reductions. During the first set of political discussions, however, the need for tax cuts was consistently raised. By the end of the month the Prime Minister and others were starting to hint that there might be tax cuts in the 1997 Finance Bill but were unwilling either to make any detailed commitments or, indeed, to promise any cuts. No figure for the level of tax cuts was indicated in the governmental budgetary meeting on 2 May. Nevertheless, official sources began to say that cuts were going to be made. On 7 May the President gave the

---

[38] Ottenheimer, pp. 124–34, 236.

first firm commitment stating that there would be 20 billion francs in tax cuts, although the Finance Minister refused to confirm the exact amount.[39] By this time, it was apparent that such was approximately the level of tax cuts which would be made.

The government was faced with a fixed figure for its budget deficit, an unfavourable macroeconomic situation, spending commitments which were difficult to cut back, and the urge to reduce taxes. In order to make the budgetary arithmetic add up, four particular strategies were followed. The first strategy was to reinforce the Rocard procedure for fixing spending commitments and to replace the framework letter by the more detailed and definitive preparatory directive, which meant that it became easier to prevent an increase in spending commitments in the period from April to July. The second strategy was to delay the formal announcement of the government's priorities. So, the document which the Prime Minister prepared in advance of the parliamentary discussion of the budget in mid-April contained no details about overall levels of spending, taxation, and the deficit. Similarly, these details were not released at the 2 May government meeting. In part, this delay was simply a reflection of the government's difficulties. In part, though, it was also a deliberate attempt to force ministers to make unpalatable spending cuts. There was no baseline by which ministers could judge the increase (or more often than not decrease) in their departmental budget against those in other budgets. In short, the Prime Minister engaged in a secretive process of divide and rule. Third, the President publicly insisted that ministers had to make 'draconian' spending cuts.[40] He also repeatedly did so in Cabinet. This increased the Prime Minister's authority in the arbitration process and made it easier for him to insist on the need to cut expenditure. Finally, the government engaged in creative accounting.

Despite the procedural reforms, the process of divide and rule, and the President's pronouncements, the expenditure side of the budgetary equation remained stubbornly high. Therefore, in order to meet the Maastricht deficit criterion and to reduce taxes in the context of rigid spending commitments, it was finally agreed to increase the budget deficit to 283.7 billion but to offset this figure with an exceptional revenue item of 37.5 billion from the accounts of France Télécom. This decision was finally taken on 24–25 August at an informal meeting between the President and Prime Minister, together with the main fiscal decisions, and was publicly announced to the Cabinet on 18 September.

On expenditure, Chirac only intervened in the case of Defence, all other appeals to overrule the Prime Minister being rejected. He had deliberately decided—as in 1986–88—to play a non-interventionist role, having only one personal adviser to keep an eye on all aspects of economic affairs. This is not so surprising, because Chirac as Mayor of Paris had entrusted its dubious finances to Juppé with the status of one of his deputies. Juppé was personally selected as his successor as President of the Rassemblement Pour le République (RPR) when Chirac was elected President in 1995 and appointed Juppé as Prime Minister.

---

[39] Interview in *Le Monde*, 15 May 1996; cf. Juppé interview in *Le Point*, No. 1232, 27 April 1996 and Arthuis, pp. 135–9, 186–98, 205–6.   [40] See *Le Monde*, 28–29 April 1996, p. 6.

One of the factors that led President Chirac in 1997 to take the disastrous step of dissolving the National Assembly, in which he had a large majority of supporters, was the fear of the electoral consequences if he delayed allowing the voters to express their resentment at the broken promises of 1995 in a worsening economic context. Chirac had been panicked by the Finance Ministry's habitual precautions of underestimated revenue and overestimating expenditure, when a politician of his experience should have known better. Ironically, the economy rapidly recovered in 1998 and it was Prime Minister Jospin and his Finance Minister who reaped the budgetary benefits and popularity, following the Left's victory in 1997.

Both houses of parliament had an opportunity to discuss the draft budget in May. The senators argued that the seriousness of the situation was being deliberately overestimated, so that ministers would accept large spending cuts to make room for a modest income tax reduction.[41] However, only slight changes were made.

The budgetary process is characterized both by its inherently adversarial, zero-sum character and by the need to conform strictly to a precise timetable, within an apparently routine procedural framework. Since parliament is more electorally preoccupied with and sometimes influential in taxation matters (which we have chosen not to study in detail here), rather than the expenditure side of the budget, there is a danger that its role will be underestimated. As Guy Lord put it, 'Without Parlement [*sic*], the budget would be different, and the spending ministries, particularly those with electorally important clientèle, would be in a much weaker position vis à vis the budget division when they fought for their estimates.'[42] The core executives find it tiresome that they have to run their carefully crafted budget past the parliamentary gauntlet. The Finance Ministry's time-honoured technique is to set aside a tiny fraction of public expenditure to make concessions aimed to forestall trouble in parliament. Spending ministries and parliamentarians compete—and sometimes collaborate—to secure a share of this money. Particularly when the government lacks a secure majority in the Assembly, more substantial concessions can be secured despite recourse to the procedural constraints of the package vote and confidence vote.[43] The humiliating Fourth Republic practice of stopping the clock on 31 December and voting a twelfth of the previous year's budget until the new budget was finally approved has not had to be invoked in the Fifth Republic. The fact that parliament's financial experts and chairmen of the Finance Committees of Assembly and Senate are frequently former Finance Ministry officials or ministers facilitates relations and a wise Finance Minister will cultivate ties with the chairmen and rapporteurs of these committees.[44] This proved especially necessary during the 1988–93 period of minority Socialist-led governments.

The Finance Ministry has in recent years strengthened its capacity to coordinate others by the *directeur de cabinet* of the Budget Minister being also deputy director of

---

[41] See the report in *Les Echos*, 22 May 1996, p. 4.   [42] Lord, p. 152.

[43] See above, p. 40, reference to Huber, *Rationalizing Parliament*, for a detailed discussion of the role of budget parliamentary debates in 1988–89 during the minority Rocard Government.

[44] Lord, pp. 153–4, 169–72; cf. 111–14.

the Finance Minister's *cabinet* and the institution of a Secretary General in 2000. However, the Finance Ministry's power has often been exaggerated. A former Finance Minister and future President, Giscard d'Estaing, declared in 1966: 'I do not approve of this tendency to consider the Ministry of Finances as a second French government, a conception sometimes shared by the budget division.'[45] At best the Finance Minister, backed by the Budget Division, exercises 'a veto power rather than a power to initiate, or, even to coordinate policy'.[46] At worst, 'in budgetary matters the Minister of Finances is often in the position of one who has to pay for decisions made or agreements reached outside his sphere of direct influence'.[47] Core executive coordination turns out on close inspection to be a much more complex matter than commonplace superficial generalizations suggest, in budgetary as in other matters.

ULTRA-CENTRALIZED COORDINATION: THE 1995 JUPPÉ PLAN TO CONTROL THE SOCIAL SECURITY DEFICIT[48]

If fixing the overall budget priorities has provided an example of how a politicized and routine policy process gave rise to contrasting ways of dealing with coordination problems by the core executive, the attempt at reforming the French social security system in 1995–96 exemplifies how a politicized and non-routine predicament was handled at core executive level under prime ministerial leadership. The social security budget has periodically caused French governments severe financial headaches because of the size of the sums involved, the symbolic importance of the issues at stake, and the resistance of vested interests to any restriction to their 'rights' or increase in their contributions. It has been accurately advanced that in France 'The process of social policy formulation is statist in style, corporatist in form and pluralist in practice. State officials in Paris tend to act as if social policy is their prerogative and can be formulated in private and announced according to administrative convenience.' They find, 'however, that the actual policy process is a loosely coordinated, highly pluralistic and intensely conflictual struggle among a host of interest groups organized around particular programmes and benefit schemes'.[49] The 1995 Juppé Plan was an intransigent assertion of that state prerogative by formulating it secretively and springing it on the veto groups that had in the past succeeded in blocking ambitious attempts at reform.

The Socialist governments after 1981 had sought to conciliate the veto groups by restoring election to the administrative councils of the social security funds (such as the National Sickness Insurance Fund), increasing minimum pensions by approximately a quarter and—most damaging in the long term—reducing the age of

---

[45] Lord, p. 159, quoting *Le Monde*, 15 November 1966.   [46] Lord, p. 67.   [47] Ibid., p. 190.
[48] This case study is based upon research conducted by Dr David Howarth, a research officer on the Hayward–Wright project.
[49] Gary P. Freeman, 'Financial crisis and policy continuity in the Welfare State' in P. Hall *et al.* (eds.), *Developments in French Politics*, Basingstoke, Macmillan, 1994 edn., p. 190.

retirement from 65 to 60. Their initial spendthrift approach was most forthrightly expressed by the first Solidarity Minister, Nicole Questiaux, who declared that she was not the 'accounts minister'. She was determined to stick to Mitterrand's uncosted electoral commitments even when economic constraint precluded continuing to do so. A victim of Finance Minister Delors's 'pause', she resentfully said of the Social Affairs Ministry: 'Not one of its acts can be undertaken without Finance and its countersignature. Finance administration has always dominated social administration.'[50] She resigned when she did not receive the support of Prime Minister Mauroy and President Mitterrand against Delors. She was replaced in 1982 by Pierre Bérégovoy who—anticipating his future role as Finance Minister, identified with the strong franc—pointedly indicated that 'he knew how to count' when it came to social security deficits. This change marked something of the same turning point in welfare state matters that the Socialists faced in economic policy in 1982–83. It was quickly followed in 1983 by the establishment of a comprehensive budget for hospitals, which would have to manage 'within predetermined constraints, rather than pass on the costs of providing services on to the health funds or the state'.[51] More resolute action was required than temporarily freezing medical fees and pharmaceutical prices but was not taken, as contaminated blood and other problems came to the fore.

By the 1990s the deficit was escalating dramatically and reached 67 billion francs in 1995 (40 billion for health alone). About a quarter of the social security budget was accounted for by generous pensions, another quarter by procreation-encouraging family allowances, but the cost of health provision was the largest problem. Consumption of medicines had increased by 60 per cent since 1970, with doctors—in league with the chemists—reluctant to prescribe cheaper generic medicines instead of patented brands and over-prescribing record quantities of tranquillizers. Earlier attempts at curbing the social security deficit in the 1970s and 1980s had been defeated by the doctors and the trade union protagonists of the work-related insurance funds which they jointly controlled with employers. In the context of the post-Maastricht need to reduce the budget deficit, it would be necessary to curb the financial drain caused by pensions, family allowances, and hospital costs, as well as asserting state control over the semi-autonomous funds that managed reimbursements of health expenditures in a country whose citizens are renowned for their hypochondria.[52]

Prime Minister Juppé, with President Chirac's support, decided to take radical social security reform out of the hands of the ministers whose remit it might have been presumed to be, and to assume personal charge, operating through a member of his staff at Matignon. This centralization of decision-making was to symbolize a change in the determination with which deficit reduction would be pursued,

---

[50] Quoted from an interview reported by Pierre Chabal in his unpublished doctoral thesis, *Des conditions de l'efficacité ministérielle dans le changement des politiques publiques*, III, Appendix, p. 983; cf. 982 and I, pp. 181–3, 295–6, University of Grenoble, 1999.   [51] Ibid., p. 195; cf. 194.

[52] See J. Ardagh, *France in the New Century. Portrait of a Changing Society*, London, Viking, 1999, pp. 151–3.

particularly as it involved an abandonment of Chirac's electoral emphasis on reducing social exclusion in favour of economic austerity as required by European Economic and Monetary Union.

To achieve this objective, there was no single lead department such as had existed in the preceding Balladur Government in the shape of a Social Affairs Ministry, headed by a powerful minister, Simone Veil. To reward those who had helped him win the presidency, Chirac appointed four ministers to do what one had done previously. In addition to Jacques Barrot in charge of Labour, Social Dialogue, and Participation, there were three RPR loyalists in charge of Health, Solidarity between the Generations, and Social Exclusion. They were all excluded from the formulation of the Juppé Plan, in part because Health Minister Hubert—who should have been most directly concerned—lacked ministerial experience and, as a doctor, was inclined to side with the lobbies in favour of more resources rather than champion introducing economies. As a result, they and their personal staffs and the senior officials in their ministries were confined to engaging in discussion of the technical details of the reform and softening up the 'social partners' at regional public consultative meetings, but not sharing in policy preparation.

The central role in the formulation of the Juppé Plan was played by Antoine Durrlemann. As head of social affairs for over a decade at the Paris Town Hall, with Chirac as Mayor and Juppé as his close associate, Durrlemann was entrusted by both of them with steering the flagship of Juppé's first year as Prime Minister. To keep a firm grip on the proceedings and to avoid leaks of the sensitive matters to be discussed, preparatory work was conducted secretively in two informal settings, linked by Durrlemann who organized and chaired the meetings at Matignon. Commencing less than a month after the presidential election, from June 1995 the more important of the two working parties met informally on Saturday mornings, without minutes being taken. A small group of social security experts prepared the Juppé Plan, relying on previous reports, notably that in 1994 of Robert Briet, who attended these meetings, being appointed in 1995 Director of Social Security in the Health Ministry to implement the reform. It was Durrlemann's decision, with Juppé's support, that this reform be kept separate from the Finance Act to give it freestanding prominence, against the prudent advice of Juppé's budget adviser, who warned of the public backlash that duly followed.

A second group of senior officials (most of whom were unaware of the existence of the first working party and were only informed of the Juppé Plan's contents a few days before it was publicly announced) were involved in exploring the financial, political, and practical implications of the alternatives considered. Under Durrlemann's chairmanship, they included: Juppé's budget adviser, Chirac's social affairs adviser, the Finance Minister's social adviser, the *directeurs de cabinet* of the Health and Solidarity ministers, and the Budget Division bureau head for social expenditure. They particularly focused on the financial sanctions that might be imposed upon over-prescribing doctors, as well as on family allowances.

What is clear is that both the Budget Division of the Finance Ministry and the Social Security Division of the Health Ministry were deliberately marginalized by

Juppé. Apart from Juppé's distrust of ephemeral Finance Minister Madelin, it can be argued that because the need to reduce the deficit was the starting point of the reform, the Budget Division's prime concern was accepted and it did not need to take part in discussing how the balanced social security budget was to be achieved. The Social Security Division (which was in any case suspect because of its officials' socialist sympathies) could not make up for the weakness of the Health Minister and her personal staff, who made no general reform proposals. However, once Briet became head of the division, his expertise and sympathetic grasp of the reform's political dimension, as well as his close contact with Durrlemann, allowed it to play a more effective part in implementation.

The more formal stage of the Juppé Plan's introduction followed between December 1995 and April 1996, preceded by a Cabinet reshuffle in November. The experienced Barrot took over the responsibilities of the Health and Solidarity Ministers, subsumed in a Labour and Social Affairs Ministry that became the lead ministry on social security reform as part of a public relations exercise to downplay its financial emphasis. This was especially necessary in face of the three-week national strike in November–December 1995, following Juppe's announcement of his reform plans, although it was simultaneous changes to railway-worker pensions rights that proved especially provocative. Fixing the annual ceiling on social security spending was nominally transferred to parliament but in fact to the government, while the cost of funding was partly shifted to the CSG tax instituted by Rocard against the bitter opposition of Juppé and others on the Right. Hospitals were forced to make staffing and other economies, while doctors were to be penalized if they exceeded the expenditure totals fixed. (The latter reform was declared illegal by the Council of State in 1998.) The Government General Secretariat (SGG) prepared the four ordinances and constitutional changes required, with Durrlemann chairing the meetings and the Social Security Division under Briet drafting the details. The Budget and Finance Ministers and the Budget Division were reduced to a secondary role.

The Juppé Plan, which largely became law in April 1996, had—against bitter opposition—managed to introduce bold changes in health care, marking a departure from the sub-optimal, incrementalist inertia induced by institutional structures that had existed for half a century.[53] Apart from dropping the hot potato of pension reform (which the Jospin Government after 1997 handled with circumspection), the 1996 reforms largely survived the social unrest of 1995–96 and the resignation in 1997 of the Juppé Government. The social security deficit fell from 67 billion francs in 1995 to 35 billion in 1997, and 13 billion in 1998, assisted in 1998 by a fall in unemployment.[54] By the time Martine Aubry resigned as Employment and Solidarity Minister in October 2000, the social security budget was in surplus.

[53] David Wilsford, 'Reforming French Health Care Policy', in J. Keeler and M. Schain (eds.), *Chirac's Challenge. Liberalization, Europeanization and Malaise in France*, New York, St. Martin's Press, 1996, p. 254 and pp. 243–4 on the path dependence of French health policy. On Juppé's mishandling of the November–December public sector strikes and demonstrations see G. Ottenheimer, *Le Fiasco*, pp. 215, 257–71. [54] Wilsford, pp. 153–6.

The 1995–96 Juppé Social Security Reform demonstrates that in a highly politicized, non-routine policy issue, high-handed circumvention of the formal coordination processes, excluding the ministers formally responsible, can overcome the paralysis that had afflicted a costly subject for years. To break the hold of the health policy community veto groups, a secretively prepared assertion of state power could be successfully sprung on the entrenched interests from within the core executive, bypassing and then replacing the political and administrative actors who were the agents of inertia. Juppé paid for this as well as other uninhibited prime ministerial assertions of power when the electors ejected him from office in 1997.

THE EU AND THE SPLIT-LEVEL HYBRIDIZATION OF THE FRENCH BUDGETARY PROCESS

Catherine Albert-Roulhac deserves the credit for emphasizing that French and EU budgetary processes have become so closely entangled that this has necessitated the reorganization of French budgetary procedures. She usefully distinguishes the internal changes required by compliance with the Maastricht Treaty from the hybridization effects of a budgetary process simultaneously involving EU and French procedures, institutions, and actors.[55] Let us take these in turn, starting with compliance.

The Maastricht Treaty guidelines set out in article 104 led to the revision of French budgetary procedures which not only ended the dependence of the Bank of France on the Finance Ministry, notably by denying the latter overdraft facilities and privileged access to credit. It led to the adoption of the October 1994 Quinquennial Law on Controlling Public Deficits, linking the annual budget with 'rolling' targets for the main budgetary aggregates, particularly the reduction of the budget deficit. As Prime Minister Balladur pointed out, this reduction 'is a priority objective, as much to respect our commitments made in the Treaty on European Union as to loosen the constraint of increasing interest payable on public debt due to accumulated deficits'.[56] This EU constraint was used first by the Budget Division and later by the Prime Minister to reduce departmental bids for increased expenditure. A paradoxical consequence was the reinforcement of stringent annual control over departmental expenditure despite the quinquennial forward looks that might have afforded greater flexibility. The priority of reducing the public deficit was followed through under the Jospin Government, when economic growth generated unexpectedly large revenues, allowing substantial cuts in the budget deficit.

In addition to these formal domestic targets and sanctions, there is the more informal promotion of voluntary budgetary coordination through the EU Economic and Financial Committee (ex-Committee for Economic Policy) which reports annually on the national budgetary estimates for the following year. However, its impact is limited by what the French and other governments find acceptable. This underlines the need to go beyond the negative enforcement of convergence criteria

---

[55] C. Albert-Roulhac, 'The Influence of EU Membership on Methods and Processes of Budgeting in Britain and France, 1970–1995', *Governance*, 11(2), April 1998.   [56] *Le Monde*, 27 April 1994.

to the complex, positive interaction between national core executives and their officials, and those of the EU, who overlap and duplicate their activities. It is here that a significant institutional shift in budgeting has been taking place, especially in the 1990s, with the increasing interdependence of EU and French government expenditure.

The split-level hybridization of budgeting has a differential impact on those ministries, such as Agriculture and to a lesser extent Transport, which have higher expectations of financial returns, compared to those such as Health or Culture which have not experienced significant expenditure integration. Even when large sums are not involved, 'Actors expect from the EU budget the financial flexibility at the margin that national governments cannot offer them and the political impetus for taking policy decisions.'[57] A more general consequence arises from the fact that 'National budgetary choices take into account the EU budget to complement, reinforce or correct its effects', which Prime Minister Balladur explicitly emphasized in his 1994 guidance to ministers making budgetary bids.[58] As the process involves national officials simultaneously in both EU and French budgeting, the need and capacity to coordinate both levels exists but there are practical difficulties in achieving it.

French ministries are officially precluded from having direct links with the EU Commission, which has the policy initiative, although informal influence can be attempted at the various stages—interministerial bargaining, working group, or European Council—at which expenditure decisions take place. The Finance Ministry has lost the capacity to control the detailed departmental EU negotiations because it is absent from them. However, an unwritten rule, the so-called 'constancy principle', allows it to retrieve some general control by requiring that specific French domestic expenditures decrease to counterbalance EU increases.[59] So, the national and EU budgeting are in fact parts of a single process, although the failure to acknowledge this contributes to the lack of transparency and accountability in budgeting, as well as imposing a severe burden of both vertical and horizontal coordination.

REASSERTING PARLIAMENTARY FINANCIAL CONTROL

In 2001, a momentous reform of budgetary procedure was adopted that will take years to implement. Let us first consider the context in which it came about. Ironically, the unexpected increased revenues arising from the rapid economic growth of the 1998–2000 years led to controversy over how the windfall should be spent, which led to the April 2000 resignation of Finance Minister Sautter. Unaccustomed to dealing with affluence rather than austerity, the Finance Ministry was accused of concealing the increased revenues to build up a large treasure chest for the 2002 legislative and presidential elections. The argument over how much should be set aside to reduce public debt (as required by the EMU Growth and Stability Pact), in tax reductions, or to meet the impending pensions burden was resolved by Finance Minister Fabius

---

[57] Albert-Roulhac, p. 220.   [58] Ibid.   [59] Ibid., p. 223, 228 note 12.

in 2000 by allocating some of the windfall to each of these. The attempt to curb overmanning in the civil service by starting with non-replacement of tax staff in Finance was abandoned after Sautter's replacement by Fabius, a surrender to public sector resistance that would be quickly followed by a surrender to direct action on fuel prices in the private sector.

An investigation by the Senate Finance Committee, which led to an October 2000 Report entitled 'To End Budgetary Mendacity', revealed that as early as 13 July 1999 the Budget Director had alerted the Finance and Budget Ministers that the deficit would be 210.7 billion francs, not 236.5 billion. This information leaked to President Chirac, who on 14 July accused the Finance Minister of hiding a surplus—in fact a smaller deficit. The Senate report showed that the Budget Division in a memo dated 25 October 1999 had lied to parliament in estimating the budget deficit as 228.7 billion francs, while next day in an internal memo it estimated the deficit at 211.2 billion! By the end of the process, the official deficit was fixed at 234.1 billion francs but in practice turned out to be 206 billion.[60] This episode strengthened parliamentary determination to modify the 1959 ordinance that set budgetary procedures which ensured an executive dominance that had been demonstrated as leading to a manipulative abuse of powers.

Laurent Fabius had, as President of the National Assembly, expressed his support for making the budgetary process simpler and more transparent, so that when he became Finance Minister, he was well positioned to favour reform despite the resistance of his own officials. His successor as Assembly President set up a committee to prepare the reform of the fundamental 1959 ordinance and the Assembly's Budget Committee *rapporteur* drew up detailed proposals. In doing so, he had the help of former senior officials who were working in the private sector and of the Court of Accounts, prompted by former minister Pierre Joxe, who was then its president. An organic law was carried with cross-party support by both Assembly and Senate, being validated by the Constitutional Council (CC) in July 2001. What were its main features?

It sought not only to improve parliamentary financial control but to loosen the grip of the Budget officials over their spending ministry colleagues, thereby facilitating a drastic change in the way the French state has operated. By shifting from input to output budgeting, 850 expenditure headings will in 2006 be reduced to some 150–200 programmes, that may cut across the expenditures of particular ministries. Within these programmes, which can be pluriannual, it will be possible to vary current and investment spending but there will be an upper limit on expenditure on personnel. Each programme will have to specify precise objectives and performance indicators, allowing parliament to check each year on whether they are being applied as previously approved. Furthermore, if the government decides to increase, reduce, or redeploy expenditure between programmes, it will first have to consult the relevant parliamentary commissions. The Jospin Government had already taken steps to stop the past practice of unilateral, arbitrary freezing, and reduction of budget allocations to ensure that the approved priorities were respected.[61]

[60] *Le Monde*, 7 October 2000.   [61] Schrameck, *Matignon Rive Gauche*, 46.

While it is too early to judge whether this reform will amount to what the Budget Minister Florence Parly called 'a real cultural revolution . . . in the Budget Division and the other ministries'[62] or what Jospin's *directeur de cabinet* called 'certainly the most important reform of the state undertaken since 1945',[63] parliamentary oversight and transversal coordination can be expected to improve. Meanwhile, the Assembly—in discussing the 2002 budget—sought to control escalating Elysée expenditure, as well as including in the estimates for each ministry the remuneration of *cabinet* members, both of which had hitherto escaped all supervision. This suggests that forty years after the imposition of executive financial supremacy, parliamentary reassertion of its democratic function will curb some of the arrogant authoritarianism of Finance Ministry officials, all too convinced that they know best.

[62] *Le Monde*, 28 July 2001, 8.   [63] Schrameck, *Matignon Rive Gauche*, 139.

7

Tactical Privatisation: Changing the Mix in a Mixed Economy

A widespread but oversimplified conception of state–market relations in France is to see them as state-centred and *dirigiste*. However, while '*in comparative terms*, extensive *dirigisme* was a distinctive feature of the French system', outside the Communist countries '*dirigisme* was probably always more powerful as a rhetorical mobilising device and as a pervasive myth... than as a strategy or coherent set of matching policies. In truth, the French model marked a messy reality in which public and private intertwined, in which private interests were often more powerful than public actors, in which the latter were fragmented and divided', but 'the very "incoherences" of the idealised model facilitated the transition of the 1980s', which is the subject of this chapter.[1] Since it touched on state–market relations at the sensitive point of ownership, privatisation raised especially controversial coordination issues in France.

Although privatisation in France was initially in part a 1986–87 reaction to the extensive nationalization programme of the Mauroy Government in 1981–82, it was partly an emulation of an international trend towards economic liberalization that had been spearheaded by Thatcherite Britain. More generally and fundamentally, it was a response to changes in the international economy that ended the postwar 'Thirty Glorious Years' and a reflection of public disenchantment with the failures of government to preserve the prosperity associated with full employment and high rates of economic growth. It was also a by-product of an increasing inability to assert a national set of preferences that were incompatible with external pressures, increasingly internalized through the requirement to conform to European Union (EU) norms and directives. The attempt to protect French decision-makers and citizens by recourse to increased public ownership, in the hope that it would permit greater public control, having rapidly proved a failure, the Mitterrand presidency witnessed a reversal of this defensive strategy, despite rhetorical smokescreens to conceal successive improvisations that marked the retreat.

Notwithstanding the two waves of nationalization in the immediate aftermath of the Second World War and at the start of the Mitterrand presidency, the public sector was always much smaller than the French private sector, being concentrated in the banking, insurance, energy, and transport sectors in the 1940s and then in the banking and industrial sectors in the 1980s. Over and above the hybrid or mixed

---

[1] V. Wright, 'Introduction: la fin du dirigisme?', special issue of *Modern and Contemporary France*, V(2), May 1997, pp. 151–2.

public/private firms that were set up after the First World War and subsequently extended, for example ELF and Total,[2] the French economy was therefore a dual one, with the state-owned sector regarded as the senior partner. Attempts to theorize the government's leadership role in coordinating their activities were made by the economic planners who gravitated towards Jean Monnet and the Finance Ministry officials looking to François Bloch-Laîné for administrative guidance. The concepts on which they focused successively were 'concerted economy' and 'contractual economy'. Although it was Monnet's successor as Planning Commissioner, Etienne Hirsch, who coined the first term,[3] it was Bloch-Laîné who gave this ambiguous appellation its clearest exposition.

Bloch-Laîné, as head of the Finance Ministry's Treasury Division from 1947 to 1952 and then Director General of the *Caisse des Dépots et Consignations* from 1952 to 1967, was in a position 'to break down the futile doctrinal opposition between liberalism and *dirigisme*, reconciling in a realistic way the freedom of firms and the new rôle of the state'.[4] The term 'concerted economy' had been mentioned in the First Monnet Plan and Bloch-Laîné's description of the collusive coordination between public officials and private or public businessmen reflected the national planning process of the postwar-years. 'It is a regime in which the representatives of the state or its subordinate bodies and those of business (whether public or private) meet to exchange information, compare their forecasts and together either take decisions or present advice to the government. It is a regime in which the major investment, production and exchange decisions do not wholly depend either on the heads of firms or of government bodies alone but are based upon continuous collaboration, so that the public and private sectors do not correspond to two sets of separate, autonomous, unconnected acts.'[5] While this ambitious objective of comprehensive public–private consensus was not achieved in practice, nevertheless the adversarial approach was generally avoided and unilateral state domination reduced, so that the claims made on behalf of a concerted political economy attained a sectorally variable measure of plausibility.

As comprehensive national planning retreated from the late 1960s, particularly after the Oil Shock of 1973, a more piecemeal semi-contractual approach came to the fore. A multitude of contracts were negotiated by French governments, which 'extended the techniques of *concertation* and contractual agreements, used first in their dealings with the state's private "partners", to their dealings with public enterprise and local authorities'.[6] What Hayward in 1986 dubbed 'Recentralizing Decentralization or Coordination by Contract' reflected the attempt by the centre to

[2] P. Marchat, *L'Economie Mixte*, PUF, 1971.

[3] J. Monnet, *Memoirs*, 1976, Collins, 1978, p. 258 and Hirsch's testimony in F. Fourquet, *Les Comptes de la Puissance. Histoire de la Comptabilité Nationale et du Plan*, Encres/Recherches, 1980, p. 56.

[4] F. Bloch-Laîné, *A la Recherche d'une Economie Concertée*, Editions de l'Epargne, 1964, p. 18. See also his *Profession: Fonctionnaire*, Editions du Seuil, 1976, chs. 4 and 5.

[5] Bloch-Laîné, *A la Recherche*, pp. 5–6.

[6] J. Hayward, *The State and the Market Economy: Industrial Patriotism and Economic Intervention in France*, Harvester/Wheatsheaf, Brighton, p. 162.

counteract the potential for fragmentation that the move to increase the autonomy of the local authorities and state firms involved by substituting 'low-constraint contract for high-constraint law'.[7] The proliferation of contracts—a contractualized *dirigisme*—multiplied interministerial conflict as the Finance Ministry sought to curb the inflationary public expenditure consequences of advocacy by the sponsor ministries (Interior for the localities and Industry for the public enterprises) with the *Caisse des Dépôts* providing a source of extra-budgetary funds.[8] Recourse to retrieving a measure of central coordinating capacity through the *Caisse des Dépôts* was pursued after 1982 by Robert Lion (who had been Prime Minister Mauroy's first *directeur de cabinet*), which was injudiciously extended to supporting an attempt at renationalizing a privatised bank, the Société Générale, to be discussed later.

The French state, more particularly the *Caisse des Dépôts*, owned minority shareholdings averaging all told about 8 per cent in the industrial concerns nationalized in February 1982, thanks to its banks and insurance companies.[9] This was simply one manifestation of the interlocking directorate that managed both large private and public firms between which the politico-economic elites circulated, after graduating from the *grandes écoles* that staff the senior civil service and are the incubators of leading politicians and more especially ministers and ministerial staffs. It also explains why little changed in 1982. The private national champions were transmuted into nationalized champions, operating in a similar fashion, with similar managers, and liable to similar mismanagement, as Crédit Lyonnais was to show spectacularly in the early 1990s. This weakened the case for nationalization, which was also undermined by both budgetary and public opinion considerations. Public borrowing had been dramatically increased to recapitalize many of the firms in deficit which were nationalized, whereas privatisation offered the tempting prospect of reducing the public sector borrowing requirement. Furthermore, the main attractions to the public in 1980 of nationalization (as measured by opinion poll) were expectations that it would—like the civil service—provide a large number of stable jobs (64 per cent) and the best possible service to the consumers (56 per cent).[10] However, the need to restore the newly nationalized firms' finances required job cuts, while consumers came to regard competition (too readily equated with privatisation) as a better incentive to serving consumers than monopoly public services. So the Hirschman pendulum, from periods of an expanding to a contracting public sector,[11] was about to swing in favour of market privatisation in France, as it was doing elsewhere.

[7] Ibid., pp. 162, 168. More generally, see J.-P. Gaudin, *Gouverner par Contrat. L'Action publique en question*, Paris, Presses de Sciences Po, 1999, especially pp. 32–4, 126–8.

[8] D. Ashford, *British Dogmatism and French Pragmatism*, Allen & Unwin, 1982, pp. 337–8. On the close relationship between the Finance Ministry's Treasury Division and the Caisse des Dépôts, see Bloch-Lainé, *Profession*, pp. 128–43.

[9] A. G. Delion and M. Durupty, *Les Nationalisations 1982*, Paris, Economica, 1982, pp. 42, 45, 48–9, 52–9, 70, 72, 119. See also Hayward, *The State and the Market Economy*, pp. 226–7.

[10] March–April 1980 SOFRES poll reported in *Le Monde, Dossiers et Documents*, supplement October 1980, p. 23.

[11] A. Hirschman, *Shifting Involvements: Private Interest and Public Policy*, Blackwell, Oxford, 1982.

PRIVATISATION: RESPONDING TO
CONVERGENT PRESSURES

As Wright has pointed out, 'France had a long history of "back-door" privatization', which in conjunction with surreptitious nationalization was euphemistically described as 'respiration' by a mixed economy. 'What is unique about the 1980s and the early 1990s is that the sporadic and limited phenomenon of the 1960s has become widespread and frequent, almost routine.'[12] He detected five factors that created a favourable intellectual and economic environment for this paradigm shift away from a statist mixed economy towards a market-centred international economy.

First, having come belatedly to Keynesianism, the French Socialists lost faith in the ability of macroeconomic intervention to deal with the problems of stagflation and escalating public indebtedness. Second, technologically induced industrial innovation was 'transforming single-product monoliths into complex multi-product enter-prises' and 'erstwhile "strategic industries" into industrial dinosaurs'.[13] Losing their status as natural monopolies, many nationalized firms had become costly political embarrassments. Third, internationalization of both product markets and financial markets, by takeover, merger, and joint venture, were detaching former national champions from their country identities and substituting profit for patriotism as the prime motivator of management. 'Economies of scale are no longer national in character.'[14] Monetary convergence, competition policy, and public procurement policy inhibit *dirigiste* governments supporting their national champions, and so fourth, an increasingly liberalized and integrated EU restricted the state's ability to subsidize its firms and frustrate the intrusions of foreign ownership, substituting interventions from Brussels in favour of market competition for Parisian pro-tectionism. Fifth, the apparent success of the British model of privatisation—from which the French learnt through consultants—inspired the liberal rhetoric and implementation methods (such as selling in instalments and reserving shares for employees or the public at below-market prices) rather than the *dirigiste* form the privatised firms were to take.[15]

Privatisation is an umbrella term covering a bewildering variety of activities that seek to reduce and reshape the role of the state in favour of market mechanisms. What have been the motives behind this change in the institutional arrangements from public to private provision? Identifying these is obscured by the fact that in the pioneer privatiser, Thatcherite Britain, 'the rationale for the programme was invented after the event', having in a characteristically empirical British way learnt

---

[12] V. Wright, 'Industrial Privatization in Western Europe: Pressures, Problems and Paradoxes' in V. Wright (ed.), *Privatization in Western Europe. Pressures, Problems and Paradoxes*, Pinter, London, 1994, p. 1.   [13] Ibid., p. 3.
[14] V. Wright, 'The Industrial Privatisation Programmes of Britain and France. The Impact of Political and Institutional Factors' in P. Jones (ed.), *Party, Parliament and Personality. Essays presented to Hugh Berrington*, Routledge, 1995, p. 101.
[15] Ibid., p. 5. See also N. Zahariadis, *Markets, States and Public Policy. Privatization in Britain and France*, University of Michigan Press, Ann Arbor, 1995, pp. 170, 220 (footnote 25).

by doing.[16] Nevertheless, in his search for the motives inspiring the protagonists of privatisation, Wright starts with the neo-liberal ideological one.

First, anti-state sentiment, more deep-seated in Britain and more superficial in France, was coupled by political calculation with a populist capitalism, to which Left Gaullist advocacy of profit-sharing participation by workers to promote cross-class solidarity offered a comparable way of luring mass support to the Conservative 'property-owning democracy' rhetoric. This materialist incentive took the practical form of encouraging the public generally and employees to buy and hold privatised shares, in the hope that it would promote individualism at the expense of the collectivism underpinning nationalization.

Second, the economic motivation combined an ambitious general policy of changing the rules of the economic game with a more specific switch of power from budget-maximizing bureaucrats and vote-maximizing politicians to profit-seeking entrepreneurs, to achieve greater competitive efficiency. Not market failures but government failures were the justification for the switch from public to private provision. However, private firms are not intrinsically more efficient if they do not operate in a competitive environment[17] and many of the firms that were reprivatised in France had become profitable during their period in public ownership.

Third, the managerial motivation has a dual appeal to both ministers and the managers themselves. Privatisation 'enables ministers to extricate themselves from time-consuming and debilitating relationships with the public sector', in which they are 'captured' and interfere too little or interfere excessively and in detail.[18] To secure greater autonomy, the French public sector managers became active proponents of privatisation, pressing the Finance Ministry to sell their firms rapidly. They would no longer have to pursue ambiguous and inconsistent goals, while the ministers would not need to try to coordinate public enterprises.[19] The failure of parliament to protect the public by enforcing ministerial responsibility for the lapses of public firms would cease to be a problem.

Fourth, the most obvious motivation has been the political opportunism of right-wing parties to attract voters and weaken the public sector whose employees have been disproportionate supporters of the Left. If a larger number of people became shareholders than were trade unionists, parties of the Right could expand their support base. We shall return to this agenda-setting political motivation shortly.

Fifth, financial motivations have been predictably conspicuous in banking circles, including the Central Bank, the Stock Exchange, in the Finance Ministry, and generally in private industry. The need to promote the Paris Stock Exchange has been part of the French government's urge to promote its place in the world's capital markets. Privatisation would reduce the need for bailing out loss-making public

[16] D. Heald, 'The United Kingdom: Privatisation and its Political Context', *West European Politics*, 11(4), October 1988, p. 43; cf. 37.

[17] J. Kay, C. Mayer, and D. Thompson (eds.), *Privatization and Regulation*, Clarendon Press, Oxford, 1986.   [18] Wright, 'Industrial Privatization', p. 16; cf. 17, 27–8.

[19] G. Majone, 'Paradoxes of Privatization and Deregulation', *Journal of European Public Policy*, I(1), June 1994, p. 60.

firms and give private firms quicker and more direct access to international capital markets.

Sixth, the need to reduce budget deficits and the increasing burden of public debt explains why senior Finance Ministry officials were among the most ardent and influential advocates of privatisation. From 0.18 per cent in 1980, the French central government budget deficit increased rapidly to 5.4 per cent in 1981 and 7.4 per cent in 1982, before being stabilized at 7.5 per cent in 1986[20] when the Chirac Government took office, committed to privatisation and personal and corporate tax cuts. This deficit was high by French standards, an example of path dependency in policy perception. The French 1986 Privatisation Act allowed the proceeds to be used only for disindebtment and for recapitalizing the remaining public sector firms, the Chirac Government using 72 per cent of the sales for the former and 28 per cent for the latter purpose.[21]

Is it possible to reduce these six motivation clusters to two: a primarily pragmatic and tactical privatisation characteristic of France, by contrast with a predominantly ideological and systemic privatisation characteristic of Britain? Although an interesting tripartite distinction has been proposed between bureaucratic-inspired pragmatic privatisation, party and interest-group driven, opportunistic tactical privatisation, and ideologically motivated systemic privatisation aimed at a fundamental redistribution of power and control amounting to an 'institutional shift', its authors admit its limitations. They concede that motivations and key actors may change over time and their typology 'tends to understate the complexity of the phenomenon under review. Policies often have multiple authors who have different agendas, so specific privatization initiatives rarely constitute pure examples of one type or another.'[22] Although there is perhaps a stronger case for a dichotomy between the first two motivations—the ideological and economic—and the other four, which are more pragmatic and tactical, it also simplistically polarizes diversity into duality. The motivating will cannot be divorced in practice from the contextual constraints, so that 'ideology by itself cannot determine policy choice; some dose of pragmatism, in this case budgetary considerations, is an essential element in the policy-making process . . . Pragmatism and ideology are therefore not mutually exclusive, but complementary factors' in the matter of privatisation.[23] As we shall see in the French case, the liberal ideological veneer did not conceal the predominantly pragmatic and tactical preoccupations.

However, before we turn to how the successive French programmes were coordinated, we need to consider the constitutional, institutional, and political constraints on the privatisation process. First, the conception of what constitutes the inalienable sphere of state activity and the constitutional protection provided for state-owned monopolies restrain radical schemes. We shall see that the form and content of French privatisation were affected by both its nationalistic industrial

---

[20] Zahariadis, *Markets*, pp. 136–7.   [21] Wright, 'Industrial Privatization', p. 32.
[22] H. Feigenbaum, J. Henig, and C. Hamnett, *Shrinking the State. The Political Underpinnings of Privatization*, Cambridge University Press, Cambridge, 1999, p. 43; cf. 36–54.
[23] Zahariadis, *Markets*, p. 177; cf. 176.

culture and constitutional norms. Second, the structure and durability of executive power may favour or hamper the process. The French programmes were hampered by the political defeat of the Right in 1988 and 1997—in marked contrast with the continuous eighteen-year duration of Conservative government in Britain. However, like Britain, France had 'the ability to reduce the number of actors involved in the privatization programme at the executive level and to ensure that those actors are enthusiastic pro-privatizers'.[24] Third, the constraints of coalition government and the internal party politics of the coalition partners lead to tensions between minimalists and maximalists. Thus, the more ideologically liberal UDF junior partner wanted to go further in a Thatcherite direction than the Rassemblement Pour le République (RPR) senior partner,[25] steered by the expeditious but prudent Balladur as Finance Minister from 1986 to 1988 and Prime Minister from 1993 to 1995, whose standpoint prevailed. Fourth, the wide political ramifications of public sector firms may give privatisers pause. Aerospace and oil have clear defence and political significance, with the oil national champion ELF's intimate involvement in France's post-colonial African policy being a complicating factor. Fifth, whereas British privatisation rode roughshod over trade union hostility, in France—where unions in the private sector were weak or non-existent—resistance in the unionized public sector monopolies such as Renault and Air France delayed their privatisation. Although public opinion swung into support for privatisation, it had little influence on the process.

CORE EXECUTIVE COORDINATION OF FRENCH PRIVATISATION

In France, as throughout Western Europe, core executives are intimately involved in the initiation, agenda-setting and formalization and, even in some respects, the implementation and monitoring stages of privatisation. They are required to take six decisions.

1. Choosing the enterprise to be privatised (priority-setting) and its place in the sequence of privatisation.
2. Preparing the enterprise for privatisation (personnel statutes, recapitalization).
3. Choosing the method of privatisation (flotation on stock exchange or off-market sale; total, majority, or minority sale; sale to another firm, to managers, or to employees).
4. Fixing the initial structure of shareholding (ceiling on foreign or individual stakes; proportion of shares for institutional investors, employees, and public; composition of core shareholdings and the conditions imposed on them; golden share and its terms).
5. Selecting the date for privatisation, advised by financial market consultants.

---

[24] Wright, 'Industrial Privatization', p. 25; cf. 24.   [25] Zahariadis, *Markets*, pp. 129–30.

6. Deciding on the price, which after 1993 was left to the Privatisation Commission.

Four features of privatisation coordination set it somewhat apart from other case studies. First, immigration and budget-making, for example, are generally routinized, with sporadic non-routine issues that need to be addressed. Policy changes take place, but within reasonably predictable parameters: path dependencies are discernible as are the principal agents of coordination, guided by embedded cognitive maps. They are, with the EU, also increasingly heavily institutionalized and bureaucratized, and structured by identifiable actors and core networks. Privatisation, on the other hand, relatively new on the policy agenda, is a process involving a series of discrete measures, with no set timetable, no path dependency which lowers coordination costs, and little institutionalization. The sporadic nature of privatisation, as well as its varied character, has an important consequence: there are no stable networks which are an important coordinating instrument in some other policy areas, although Balladur deliberately tried to constitute them. To add to the unstable character of the policy-making arena, *some* privatisations—notably those involving prior recapitalization of enterprises or those which pose competition policy issues—bring European Union (EU) officials (particularly from DG4) into the process, a feature it shares with our EU study.

Second, in the privatisation process, *all* governments are extremely dependent on outside expertise (merchant banks, stock exchange dealers, advertising agencies, global coordinators), with France benefitting from British experience.

Third, the privatisation process is peculiarly vulnerable to outside pressures, notably the state of the financial markets. The market crash in October 1987 had a disastrous impact in France, where Suez lost 17 per cent of its value overnight, whilst the privatisation of the Union des Assurances de Paris (a public company which had become a major shareholder in several recently privatised companies) was suspended, and had to wait for the re-election of the Right in 1993 in order to proceed. Several privatisations have been delayed as the result of adverse market conditions, or become more ambitious (the 1997 Jospin Government's partial privatisation of France Télécom) as markets suddenly become bullish.

Fourth, the success of major flotations critically hinges on the cooperation of private and often foreign actors (notably American institutional investors). Privatisation involves not only supply but also demand, and judging that demand is not always easy. Thus, underwriters for the sale of Pechiney, the leading French aluminium and packaging company, were so uncertain of the public response that the flotation was nearly cancelled before it went ahead in December 1995.

DISTINCTIVE FEATURES OF THE FRENCH PROGRAMMES

The French programmes have had six distinctive features. In the first place, they have taken two diametrically opposed forms: 'back-door', defensive, limited, discreet, guilt-ridden—the policy of successive Socialist administrations—and highly publicized, offensive, and radical. They constitute the third most radical in Western Europe after those of the UK and Germany (following the East German sales), with some $40 billion of sales between 1986 and 1997. The radical character of the programmes may be seen most sharply in the speed with which parts of them were carried out. Between October 1986 and October 1987, no fewer than thirteen major enterprises, worth 120 billion francs, were sold—to the surprise of many investors, who were anxious about the Stock Exchange's capacity to absorb so much so quickly. Even during the Socialist governments of 1981–86 and 1988–93, receipts from various forms of limited privatisation (sale of a minority of shares or of subsidiaries, the introduction of outside capital, often without voting rights) were not negligible, with the 1997 partial privatisation of France Télécom alone raising some 40 billion badly needed francs for a government struggling to meet the Maastricht criteria. The programmes have embraced insurance, banking, industry, and the media, and over time became more radical in scope, since the 1993 Balladur Government's programme included 'strategic' industries such as Aerospatiale and Thomson, and national flag carriers such as Renault and Air France—companies which were excluded from the Chirac Government's list of 1986. Even the unthinkable was achieved, with the change of status and partial privatisation of France Télécom. Only the great public utilities of EDF, GDF, and SNCF have so far escaped the eye of the privatisers, although measures (often under pressure from Europe) have been taken to encourage competition and to change their corporate structures and tariff arrangements in order to facilitate future privatisation.

The second distinctive feature of the French programmes have been the scale and politically driven pace of its implementation. Between October 1986 and October 1987 and after May 1993 the French disposed of all but a handful of the firms destined for privatisation. Only the constitutionally protected or the politically delicate (Air France and Aerospatiale), the legally complicated (France Télécom), and the financially insolvent (GAN and Crédit Lyonnais) had to wait the advent of the Jospin Government in 1997. The botched privatisation of the CIC bank and of Thomson—both in autumn 1996—initially involved delay, and were resumed after the election of the Jospin Government, which quickly consented to a sale of a minority holding of both France Télécom and Crédit Lyonnais, and the sale of GAN. Also, in spite of the sacking of the head of Air France, whose impatience for privatisation was public knowledge, the transfer of the country's flag carrier to the private sector is a matter of time. Finally, *all* the remaining public enterprises have been endowed with a private sector logic: politically motivated deficits and heavy cross-subsidization are frowned upon.

Third, the first two batches of privatisations—those of the Chirac and Juppé premierships—were covered by general enabling laws (2 and 6 August 1986, and 19 July 1993) which listed the firms to be privatised within the lifetime of the legislature. This is in sharp contrast with the *ad hoc* programmes elsewhere and the Jospin Government's substantial but incremental privatisations. The French privatisation process *automatically* ensures a role for parliament and for the Council of State, which has to be consulted on all government bills, and provides for a potential role for the Constitutional Council (CC) in the event of any bill being tested for its constitutionality. The first privatisation programme of Chirac was subjected to sustained guerrilla tactics in the National Assembly (over 400 amendments were proposed), leading to some changes in the bill. The 1993 programme ran into a barrage of parliamentary opposition (Socialist and Communist deputies and senators tabled over 3,500 amendments), and an extraordinary session of parliament was needed to push through the required legislation. However, the main lines of the Bill were never in any serious danger. Nevertheless, in 1986 and 1993, parliament was able to coax out of a reluctant government concessions relating to the golden share, the ceiling on foreign stakes, and the role of the Privatisation Commission. It also successfully insisted that the government present an annual report to parliament on the implementation of the programmes.

The existence of an independent Privatisation Commission represents the fourth distinctive feature of the French process. This body was initially created by Prime Minister Chirac in 1986 but was disbanded in 1988 when the Left regained power. It was reshaped by Prime Minister Balladur (Law of 19 July 1993) who, sensitive to some of the criticisms levelled against the privatisations carried out when he had been Finance Minister in the Chirac Government, expanded its functions and powers. An independent agency, composed of eight members (appointed for five years by decree), its principal tasks are to determine the value of any enterprise proposed for privatisation and to examine the procedures involved in any off-market sale. Critically, it also gives binding judgements on the choice of the new shareholders. Initially, it was criticized as a cipher, simply nodding through government privatisation proposals. However, in February 1996, the Commission turned down the proposed sale of Radio Monte Carlo, and in October 1996, the Commission also prevented the privatisation of CIC, the state-owned banking network. In the following month, it made an even more spectacular judgement, when it rejected the financial terms proposed by the French government for the sale of Thomson, the defence and domestic electronics group. The proposed sale had to be cancelled, to the joy of the Opposition, the dismay of the Right, and the disgust of the potential purchaser.

Fifth, unlike the British privatisations, many of those in France have been strategically linked by the government to objectives beyond mere revenue-raising: these range from the enlargement of the capital base of the Paris Stock Exchange to the restructuring of a particular sector of French industry. This latter ambition has been the source of great complications for some of the privatisations (notably those of Aerospatiale and of Thomson) and widens the arena of actors. The wish to make the Stock Exchange rather than the Finance Ministry 'the symbolic and true heart of the world of business'[26] was somewhat less problematic.

Finally, the French privatisation programmes have had implicit political objectives, even if they were quickly divested of their ideological motivation. The resort to *noyaux durs*—selected core shareholders in a particular privatised enterprise whose

---

[26] M. Bauer, 'The Politics of State-Directed Privatisation: The Case of France, 1986–88', *West European Politics*, 11(4), October 1988, p. 49.

task is to provide stability and protection against unwelcome market takeovers—and their composition (friends of the RPR) have added a controversial pragmatic and tactical political dimension to the programmes.

THE WHO AND HOW OF PRIVATISATION COORDINATION

We need to answer four questions. First, who have been the key actors involved in the privatisation process? Second, what has dictated the constellation of actors within the core executive and their respective roles in the process? Third, what has determined the role and influence of the actors within the core executive? Fourth, what have been the types and styles of coordination employed?

Who are the Key Actors in the Privatisation Process?

The supply side of privatisation involves the presidency, Matignon, the Finance Ministry (under its ever-changing nomenclature which in 1986 included Privatisation), the Industry Ministry, the relevant sponsoring ministry (which usually harbours a privatisation unit), the holding group, enterprise, or company involved. On the demand side, there are the investors (core shareholders or other institutional investors, the managers and workforce, and even the public in the case of major flotations).

Yet there are other important actors who belong neither to the demand nor the supply side, but who play essential roles as facilitators (finance advisers, underwriters, and advertising agencies), or as guardians of constitutional, legal, or financial propriety: the CC, COB (Stock Exchange Commission), the Council of State, and the Privatisation Commission. The Council of State and more particularly the CC introduced amendments to the two major programmes, but, more importantly, they also defined a number of general principles for guiding specific privatisations. The CC imposed several amendments on the 1986 bill, including one that led to the creation of a panel of independent experts—the Privatisation Commission—charged with assessing the value of any company due for privatisation, and fixing a minimum price for the shares at the point of flotation. The reticence of the Council of State when consulted about the proposed change in the corporate status of France Télécom constituted a considerable and irritating delay in preparing the company for privatisation. Any change in the legal status of the personnel of a public company prior to privatisation would necessarily bring into play the Civil Service Ministry. In some cases (those involving the wiping out of the debt, or the recapitalizing of a public firm prior to privatisation—Air France, Crédit Lyonnais, GAN, Thomson spring to mind—or potential competition issues after privatisation) the European Commission (notably DG4) has become a major player. Indeed, the Commission has, in some cases, pressed for promises of privatisation before consenting to the requested subsidies. When this occurs, new domestic actors have to be mobilized—the Quai d'Orsay, the General Secretariat of the Interministerial Committee (SGCI)—as well as the French representation in Brussels. Relations between the Commission and successive French governments were notoriously tense but eased when Strauss-Kahn was Finance Minister from 1997 to 1999. In short, whilst a stable core of critical actors may be identified for all privatisations, each one has mobilized different constellations of actors.

What has Dictated the Constellation of Actors within the Core Executive and their Respective Role in the Process?

If we focus on the actual rather than the formal functions of the various actors, the first—and most important—factor has been *the size, sector, significance, and method of the privatisation involved.* An off-market sale of a small subsidiary to another French company would involve the officials of the group and the firm, and those of the sponsoring ministry and of the Treasury. The blessing of the Prime Minister's *cabinet* might be sought. A similar constellation of actors would arise in the event of the sale of a further minority stake in a company. For a major sale (stock market flotation or one involving a 'strategic industry') the range of core executive actors would widen to include Matignon.

The role of the Elysée has depended on the prevailing political circumstances. Mitterrand tolerated and even encouraged the surreptitious privatisations carried out by Socialist governments between 1981 and 1986, publicly criticized the Right's programmes of 1986 and 1993 but was quickly sidelined by Chirac and Juppé, and gave his blessings to the partial privatisations implemented by Rocard and by Bérégovoy between 1988 and 1993. President Chirac was kept closely informed of privatisation developments by members of his staff, but was directly and personally involved in two proposed sales—those of Aerospatiale and Thomson in 1996. It was the President who, acting on wildly inaccurate information fed by highly suspect sources, decided between the two contenders wishing to buy the group.

The second major factor which has determined the constellation of core executive actors involved, as well as their respective roles, is no less obvious than the previous one: *the degree of politicization.* This politicization may be an internal phenomenon (the choice of core shareholders) or, more generally, imposed from the outside by the trade unions (Air France, Thomson), by opposition parties (Pechiney, Thomson), by group chairmen (GAN for CIC and Framatome), or by cross-party locally elected officials (CIC). As general rules, the more politically controversial the privatisation the higher up the core executive hierarchy it is likely to ascend, while the weaker the core executive the more politicized privatisation is likely to become, yet another stick with which to beat a vulnerable government. In that sense, the privatisation fiascos of 1996 (three had to be scrapped) must be seen as part of a wider political process, while the uncontroversial success of the early Jospin Government privatisations was assisted by its high standing.

A third factor which shapes the inner configuration of core executive actors is *the degree of policy linkage.* As already noted, French governments have sometimes been reluctant merely to privatise. They have also linked privatisations to other questions, such as the foreign investment strategy of the government and industrial restructuring (in defence, electronics, and telecommunications, most notably), even if the grandiose ambitions to 'transform French capitalism' through privatisations were discreetly dropped in the 1990s. On occasions, therefore, governments had upped the stakes by widening them, thus triggering the need for presidential or prime ministerial intervention.

More importantly, this latter point may be tapping a fourth significant factor which shapes the internal core executive configuration—*the sectoral context within which a particular privatisation takes place.* The paranoia which explains some of the misjudgements surrounding the Thomson privatisation fiasco of 1996 can be explained largely by the profound ambivalence and inconsistency of French governments when confronted with changes in the international market, especially in the defence industry. More specifically, in the months preceding the proposed privatisation of Thomson the Juppé Government was explicitly seeking increased foreign investment. Hence the ready acceptance of the proposed takeover of the domestic side of Thomson electronics by Daewoo Corporation from South Korea for a symbolic 1 franc of what later turned out to be profitable (valued at 100 billion francs in September 2000), while Daewoo was, in 2000, forced into bankruptcy. It was uneasy at the unravelling of several core shareholdings which had been designed to protect French privatised firms. Heightened sensitivities of an industrial or sectoral nature and policy ambivalence may dictate the intervention of either the President or the Prime Minister, or both, which disrupts what others have sought to coordinate.

Fifth, some privatisations (GAN, Crédit Lyonnais), which have an *EU policy dimension,* are inevitably pushed up the political hierarchy and involve a wider range of actors, as we have seen earlier.

Finally, account must be taken of *the internal dynamics of the government* in order to explain the configuration of core executive actors involved as well as their respective roles. This may best be illustrated by contrasting the experience of 1986–88 with that of 1993–96. There is no doubt that the privatisation programme of the first period was assiduously directed by Edouard Balladur, whose full title was Minister of the Economy, of Finance, and of Privatisation. Balladur had a personal interest in the programme, and enjoyed the full backing of Prime Minister Chirac. Balladur also had banking and financial expertise, and personal links with the financial community. The virtually exclusive role of Finance Minister is underlined in his *Je crois en l'homme plus qu'en l'Etat,* an informative, if self-justificatory epistle.

It is the minister who decides, with the Prime Minister's agreement, in what order the firms should be privatised, he who chooses the merchant bank who advise the government and who, as Finance Minister, having at his disposition the Treasury Division, knows the exact situation of these firms. He it is who, in the end, fixes the sale price, after receiving the Privatisation Commission's advice, he who decides the composition of the core shareholders' group, who fixes the percentage allocated to institutional investors and to the public, who defines the ways in which shares are allocated after the public subscription, who decides the preferential sale terms to the firm's employees. So many discussions rendered unnecessary—and so much time saved![27]

Why bother with coordination when one can impose one's own views?

Balladur declared that he wished to avoid the 'interminable arbitrations' by the Prime Minister.[28] He preferred to work with his personal staff and line officials. Aided initially by a privatisation junior minister (Camille Cabana, who had been responsible in Chirac's Paris team for the privatisation of some municipal services, but he rapidly had him transferred to Administrative Reform[29]) and a special privatisation unit within the Treasury Division of the Finance Ministry, Balladur was also able to mobilize the unofficial network forged by *pantouflage* amongst members of the Finance Inspectorate and which linked the worlds of high politics, high administration, high finance, and industry. During the 1986–88 period, the role of the Industry Ministry and the respective sponsoring ministries was reduced to a largely consultative one. The concentration of decision-making authority with respect to privatisation was also a feature of the Bérégovoy tenancy of the Finance Ministry and of Matignon. (He was, as we shall see, also deeply and compromisingly implicated in attempts to restructure the core shareholdings of two enterprises which had been privatised under Balladur that ended in fiasco.) When Balladur became Prime Minister in 1993, he showed a keen and persistent interest in the renewed privatisation programme. However, he delegated the implementation of the major privatisations to the Finance Ministry which maintained close communication with state-owned group chairmen, banks, and the Stock Exchange.

The Juppé premiership heralded an important change in the role of the actors within the core executive. The Prime Minister was generally incapable of delegating authority even over trivial matters. His intervention in any new major policy was immediate, detailed—and deeply resented. Privatisation was no exception. Although officially in the hands of the Finance Minister, Juppé constantly interfered in the programme. This situation was tolerated by a weak Finance Minister, who was by training an accountant, more interested in the finer points of banking regulation than in the politically charged privatisation programme.[30] In the absence of an authoritative lead coordinator, squabbles broke out between contending corps (Aerospatiale) and bureaucracies (Thomson), and between the government and the chairmen of some enterprises designated for privatisation. In the CIC case, the government took the unprecedented step of sacking (he refused to resign under pressure) the chairman of GAN, CIC's parent company.

In short, during the privatisation process, coordination has been either centralized or fragmented, depending on the size, sector, industrial significance, and method of privatisation, its political dimension, its linkage with other policies, and especially in internal dynamics of the government.

---

[27] E. Balladur, *Je crois en l'homme plus qu'en l'Etat*, Paris, Flammarion, 1987, p. 96.

[28] Ibid., p. 81.   [29] Favier and Martin-Roland, ii, pp. 643–4.

[30] There is, significantly, almost nothing about privatisation in J. Arthuis's *Dans les coulisses de Bercy. Le cinquième pouvoir*, covering his 1995–97 tenure of the Finance Ministry.

What Have Been the Types and Styles of Coordination Employed?

In the French privatisation process we may discern at least four different types of coordination at work, the first two being activist, the others reactivist. First, there is *coordination as steering*: establishing the general parameters within which privatisation has had to be implemented, and guiding a desired set of objectives through the initiation, agenda-setting, and formalization stages of the process. Second, there is *coordination as direction*: unilaterally choosing specific firms for privatisation or selecting a particular firm as the purchaser. Moving to the responsive types of coordination, there is, third, *coordination as arbitration*: mediating the multiple and often conflicting political pressures in a particular privatisation. Finally, there is *coordination as a fire-fighting exercise*: a reactive set of tactics designed to pick up the pieces and minimize the political fallout.

In terms of coordination *style*, contrasts may again be discerned, ranging from the ostentatiously impositional and autocratic style of Juppé, through the circumspectly forceful style of Balladur, to the persuasively bargained style of Strauss-Kahn. Here, personal resources and personality traits are unavoidably important explanatory variables, precluding facile generalizations.

Nevertheless, some general structural characterizations can be mentioned. The French system appears to be well equipped to achieve effective core executive coordination. It has a majoritarian system with a relatively high degree of governmental cohesion, high quality administrative staffing in the Elysée, Matignon, and the Finance Ministry, strong hierarchical structures of decision-making, a quality of technical expertise throughout the administration which has no equivalent in Western Europe, horizontal channels of political-administrative coordination provided by membership of a *grand école* or a *grand corps*, plentiful links to the private, industrial, and financial sectors ensured by *pantouflage*. The privatisation process illustrates all the strengths of the system and most privatisations have been achieved with a minimum of fuss.

However, the process also reveals the ten functional conditions which are required to achieve successful coordination by a use of incentives, manipulation, and exclusion in the service of 'heroic' decision-making:[31]

(1) a clear programme unencumbered by either complicated constitutional, legal, financial obstacles, or political or policy spill-over effects;

(2) a united government with political authority, with ministers not specifically involved in a particular privatisation having no say;

(3) a majority party or government party coalition which was largely in favour of the programme, able to overcome the sustained guerrilla tactics of hundreds (1986) or thousands (1993) of Assembly amendments;

(4) an identifiable and authoritative lead coordinator capable of marshalling and mobilizing the required information and expertise;

---

[31] For a more extended and somewhat different set of heroic preconditions, see Wright, 'Industrial Privatisation', pp. 106–10.

(5) clear vertical and horizontal lines of coordinating competences;

(6) a bargained style to promote consensus, to mediate compromise (which requires a free flow of information), and to minimize bureaucratic in-fighting;

(7) securing the support of the state-owned management;

(8) political sensitivity and skills in dealing with managerial or trade union hostility. Employee opposition was bought off by the attractive offer of shares at below market price. In October 1993, a nine-day strike brought air traffic to a standstill, forcing the Balladur Government into humiliating retreat on Air France privatisation and the resignation of its chairman;

(9) careful negotiating, when needed, to gain the assent of the EU authorities in Brussels;

(10) a capacity to develop a legitimizing discourse for the programme to be regarded as both desirable and inevitable, identified with efficiency, competitive entrepreneurship, and a property-owning democracy.

If any one of these functional conditions is absent then coordination becomes highly problematic. Indeed, the 1996 Thomson affair fully revealed one of the fatal defects of the French system: when the principal elements of the core executive (President, Prime Minister, and Finance Minister) are at odds, the entire system falters. To consider how the internal dynamics of the coordination process within the core executive worked, we turn to our first case study: the politicized and non-routine successive privatisation programmes from 1986, although by the time of the Jospin Government privatisations, the process had become largely depoliticized and almost routine.

THE PRIVATISATION PROGRAMMES: FROM POLITICAL INNOVATION TO DEPOLITICIZED ROUTINE

Although we shall concentrate upon the four programmes, 1986–88, 1988–93 (sub-divided in 1991), 1993–97 (sub-divided in 1995), and since 1997, it is first necessary to point out that despite the 1981 presidential fiat in favour of 100 per cent nationalization, the process of moving away from this dogmatic position began as early as 1983. In the prevailing context of budget austerity, the need to recapitalize many of the firms nationalized led Finance Minister Delors to have a law adopted in January 1983 allowing them to turn for funds to the private sector through the issue of non-voting 'participation shares' and 'investment certificates' which respectively secured 25 and 24 billion francs. This shamefaced recourse to mixed economy financing was accompanied by the illegal privatisation of numerous subsidiaries, the Mauroy Government having prepared legislation to authorize this in 1982 but recoiled from proceeding with it out of fear of the way its PS deputies would react. Ironically, these illegalities were retrospectively validated by the Chirac Government.[32]

---

[32] M. Durupty, *Les Privatisations en France*, La Documentation Française, Notes et Etudes Documentaires, No. 4857, 1988, p. 28; cf. 24–9. See also Bauer, pp. 50–1.

On 17 January 1986, the RPR and Union pour la Démocratie Française (UDF) presented their 'Platform for Governing Together' in anticipation of their March electoral victory. The thirteenth of their twenty fundamental commitments stated: 'Return to private initiative, as in all western democracies, the competitive sector enterprises, in particular denationalise in the lifetime of the legislature all the banks and insurance companies, the information sector and the firms nationalised in 1982'.[33] Three of the four policy sectors we have chosen for investigation raised issues that divided the Right and Left. The restriction of immigration and reducing the national debt burden on the budget deficit were important issues but the latter was linked with privatisation. National debt having escalated from 15.5 per cent in 1981 to 23.8 per cent of GDP in 1986, the sale of state assets could help reverse this worrying rise. (In the event, 55 per cent of the 85 billion francs raised in 1986–88 was used to reduce national debt.[34]) Privatisation was undoubtedly the electoral issue that dramatized most clearly the ideological divergence between socialism and the newly acquired economic liberalism of the neo-Gaullists.

The Socialists, in the wake of their 1983 economic policy U-turn, had rehabilitated profit and private enterprise and restored to profitability many of the firms they had nationalized, so the ground had been prepared for the Right to take recourse to the newly fashionable market principles further. Tactical and pragmatic motivations were far more important than the ideological ones given propaganda prominence. Just as the Socialists had resigned themselves, because of the budget deficit, to surreptitious privatisation, so the Chirac Government, for the same expedient reason but with fewer inhibitions and much more explicitly, abandoned part of its Gaullist legacy. However, it sought to perpetuate its economic nationalism by preventing foreign takeover bids and instituting worker profit-sharing. Most important, political control was kept firmly in the hands of Balladur and the Finance Ministry, ensuring that *dirigisme* was perpetuated—provisionally—by privatisation. So, 'Neoliberalism was more preached than practiced ... a kind of slogan summarising opposition to socialism, rather than a blueprint for a genuine free-market economy.'[35]

Wishing to act with extreme expedition, Balladur chose delegated legislation rather than the parliamentary route to privatisation, leading to the first major power struggle with President Mitterrand, a confrontation over procedure. At Cabinet meetings, the President made clear that he would not sign ordinances relating to pre-1982 nationalizations, which Chirac had already promised to reprivatise in December 1981. Balladur had explained that whereas 'nationalisations are relatively simple and rapid, privatisation—if done through the market—is much slower and more complex'.[36] Reassured by the advice of ex-President Giscard d'Estaing that the

---

[33] Quoted Durupty, p. 32.

[34] M. Maclean, 'Privatisation, *dirigisme* and the global economy: an end to French Exceptionalism?', *Modern and Contemporary France*, V(2), May 1997, p. 217 and p. 227, note 30.

[35] Feigenbaum *et al.*, pp. 103, 105. See also Bauer, p. 51 and H. Dumez and A. Jeunemaître, 'Privatization in France, 1983–1993' in Wright (ed.), *Privatization in Western Europe*, p. 89.

[36] Quoted in Attali, *Verbatim*, ii, p. 51; cf. 52.

President could not refuse to sign ordinances, Chirac decided to proceed by ordinance, authorized by law on 2 July 1986. However, in the traditional 14 July TV interview, Mitterrand gave as his reason for refusing to sign his duty to guarantee national independence from foreign takeovers, leaving it to parliament to take responsibility. Although most of Chirac's advice impelled him to resign, Balladur—an early advocate of cohabitation—was in favour of avoiding a trial of strength on this issue. Mitterrand could not legally be forced to sign and his resistance could be quickly bypassed by legislation—as he demonstrated, the 6 August 1986 Law offering 'proof of our speed, our cohesion and our determination'.[37] The UDF ministers were also against a confrontation, while Interior Minister Pasqua warned that until the PR electoral system was abolished, the Right might lose a precipitate election.[38] Having successfully called Chirac's threatened resignation bluff, Mitterrand avoided being reduced to a rubber stamp.[39] Thereafter, despite the cohabitension that continued until the 1988 presidential election, the crisis that the privatisation procedure had threatened to precipitate was avoided by a prime ministerial climbdown.

Balladur recalled that, thanks to Chirac's confidence and the 1986 Law, appending the list of the sixty-five firms to be denationalized, he had 'built a simple and flexible set of legal arrangements, applicable to all cases without needing to return to Parliament for the authorisation of each privatisation'.[40]

With more to privatize and a Stock Exchange with less capacity than London to absorb large amounts of capital, careful planning was necessary. This was done by a steering committee chaired by a member of his *cabinet*, meeting at least weekly at the Finance Ministry. Balladur estimated that each privatisation required the close coordination of more than a hundred people, working full time for many months. The main actors to be coordinated were, first and foremost, 'the Treasury Division, secular arm of the Shareholder State, which as such played a fundamental role in the technical preparation and supervision of the process'.[41] Second, the head of each firm to be privatised played a crucial part, so many of those in firms scheduled for privatisation were replaced with heads who were favourable to the change and could continue to run the firms after privatisation.[42] Third, the French and foreign merchant banks, the legal, financial, and auditing consultants, as well as the advertisers who would launch a mass publicity campaign on the British model, played a crucial role in fixing the price and the right moment for each privatisation and then selling it to investors. Lastly, there was the Privatisation Commission.

Although, as we shall see, the revived Privatisation Commission was given wider powers by Balladur in 1993, in 1986 it was a rather weak body, imposed on Balladur by the CC, intended to lend respectability and an appearance of independence to the privatisation process. Typical of the seven-man commission was its President,

---

[37] Balladur, *Je crois*, p. 102; cf. Attali, *Verbatim*, ii, pp. 150–1.
[38] Favier and Martin-Roland, ii, pp. 635–6; cf. 631–7.
[39] Ibid., pp. 637–43; cf. Attali, *Verbatim*, ii, pp. 152–7.
[40] Balladur, *Je crois*, p. 93; cf. 94–6, 128–9, 167.   [41] Ibid., p. 152; cf. 149–53.
[42] Zahariadis, *Markets*, pp. 131–2.

a former Gaullist minister who had promoted the idea of worker profit-sharing, former member of the CC and former President of the Stock Exchange Operations Commission, who could be relied upon not to create difficulties.[43] When the Commission's advice was sought on a proposed privatisation by the Finance Minister, it examined the firm's balance sheet. 'It listened to the comments and advice of bankers chosen by both the government and the firm, and then fixed a minimum price below which a share could not be sold', but the minister could freely fix a price subject to this restriction.[44] 'In general, this price was 5 to 10 per cent higher than the minimum price fixed by the Commission. But, compared with market forces, it represented a discount of 5 to 30 per cent.'[45] The deliberate and consistent underpricing of the shares surpassed the expectation of Balladur, his associates, and an increased number of French shareholders at the expense of maximizing state revenues. In the event, this rose about 1.5 to over 7 million in 1986–87.[46] However, more important than making one in eight French citizens a shareholder was the *dirigiste* and partisan way in which the core of stable shareholders was personally constituted by Balladur.

The Finance and Privatisation Minister revealingly protested that he had not 'reconstituted . . . an archaic capitalism, with its comfortable cross-shareholdings, based upon mutual favours, conniving between interests and family ties of the leaders'.[47] He more plausibly claimed (given the lack of French pension funds and large institutional investors) that there were too few French candidates to choose between, so while avoiding foreign control he pressed those French firms selected to include European firms as partners. In the exercise of creating minority control without ownership ('capitalism without capital') Balladur picked permutations and combinations of fifty-two firms, with fourteen firms having been chosen twice.[48] He always spread the controlling shareholdings among a dozen or so firms, who had to pay about 5 per cent above the price to ordinary shareholders and were required to retain their shares for at least two years in return for the privilege of being represented on the board of the company. As a result, Balladur had virtually appointed these boards which, despite his denials, were composed largely of his political friends, amounting to a politico-economic spoils system.

Cross-shareholdings abounded, notably between the Société Générale bank and the Compagnie Générale d'Electricité (CGE), the investment bank Suez and Saint-Gobain, which 'strengthened the existing establishment network'.[49] So, in the name of preventing foreign takeovers, the old oligopolized interlocking directorates were reinforced and repopulated with political allies (who could not be sacked by an

---

[43] Durupty, p. 51 note gives the membership of the 1986 Privatisation Commission.

[44] Bauer, p. 55.   [45] Ibid., p. 56.

[46] Estimates vary. See ibid., p. 58; cf. Feigenbaum *et al.*, pp. 101–2 and M. Maclean, 'Privatisation in France 1993–94: New departures or a case of *plus ça change*?' in *West European Politics*, XVII(2), April 1995, pp. 274–5.   [47] Balladur, *Je crois*, p. 134.

[48] Ibid., p. 133. See also C. Graham and T. Prosser, *Privatizing Public Enterprises. Constitutions, the State and Regulation in Comparative Perspective*, Oxford, Clarendon Press, 1991, pp. 155–7.

[49] Ibid., pp. 127–31; cf. Bauer, pp. 55, 59.

incoming government) into three networks based on CGE–Société Générale, Paribas, and Saint Gobain–Suez.[50] By 1988, there was an incestuous interlocking corporate interdependence between thirty-three private firms, sixteen privatised firms, and eight public enterprises.[51] The links with banks and insurance companies—some still public at that stage—were to lead to a spectacular disaster in the case of Crédit Lyonnais in the 1990s.

The CC had in June 1986 rapidly recognized the constitutionality of privatisation but required that the property rights of the state should be protected, just as it had previously required that the private owners of nationalized firms be correctly compensated. The Balladur Bill was significantly amended in other respects. 'The Council insisted, for instance, that a panel of independent experts carry out an assessment of the value of the company to be privatized and that this panel—the Privatisation Commission—should fix a minimum price for the shares at the point of flotation. Overall, the reaction—real or anticipated—of the Council led the Chirac Government to amend five of the eight articles of the initial text—even though the underlying principles and major thrust of the programme were left intact. It may even be the case that the Council provided some legitimacy for the programme by meeting some of the objections of the political opposition.'[52]

The privatisation programme was launched cautiously with the sale of 11 per cent of ELF–Aquitaine, which meant that the state retained majority control and could consequently add the proceeds as budget revenue. The choice of ELF was partly a result of the 'Chalandon affair', in which the former Gaullist minister, who had clashed with Industry Minister Fabius in 1983 over a matter involving its French rival Total, was dismissed.[53] Due to its role in both France's African and energy policy, a full sale of ELF was not proceeded with and when the Cresson Government sold a further 2.3 per cent of ELF shares in March 1992, the state still retained 51.5 per cent ownership.[54] In 1994, Balladur was to complete the sale of what was then France's largest company, although the state retained 10 per cent of the equity and a golden share.[55] However, the latter did not enable the French government in 1999 to exercise a decisive influence in the Total takeover of ELF. As in Britain, there was no logical pattern distinguishing French firms, for example ELF, Bull, Matra, and Havas, where the state had retained a golden share, from those where it had not. It reflected the fact that both governments were not prepared to accept to the full their 'free market rhetoric by permitting an unhindered operation of the market for corporate control'.[56]

---

[50] See F. Morin in *Le Monde*, 17 September 1987, reproduced in Durupty, p. 130; cf. 117–20, 129–31 and Feigenbaum *et al.*, pp. 106–8.

[51] A. Hamdouch, *L'Etat d'influence: Nationalisations et Privatisations in France*, Presses du CNRS, 1989, pp. 206–9.

[52] Wright, 'Industrial Privatisation', in Jones (ed.), p. 115.

[53] Zahariadis, *Markets*, pp. 141–3; cf. A. Chalandon, *Quitte ou Double?* Paris, Grasset, 1986 and J.-M. Lévêque, *Dénationalisations: Mode d'Emploi*, Paris, A. Michel, 1985.   [54] Zahariadis, *Markets*, p. 145.

[55] Ibid., pp. 146–7.   [56] Graham and Prosser, p. 148; cf. 149–53.

The stock market crash of October 1987[57] temporarily halted the breakneck impetus of the Balladur programme of sixty-five privatisations which he had planned to complete by 1991. Followed by the defeat of Chirac by Mitterrand in the May 1988 presidential election, at which the victor had quietistically promised 'neither privatisation nor nationalisation', it appeared that there would be at least a pause in the hyper-personalized and centralized privatisation process masterminded by Balladur. However, his successor as Finance Minister, Bérégovoy, adopted a controversial interpretation of Mitterrand's economically unrealistic but electorally astute 'ni, ni' formula of 1988, purporting to substitute an ambiguous consensus for the adversarial clarity of his first seven-year presidency. Bérégovoy was encouraged by Mitterrand to break up the core central groups of shareholders hand-picked by Balladur. The President declared at the Cabinet meeting on 27 June 1988 that they embodied 'the confiscation by a political party of all the economic feudalisms' and should be destroyed. 'I take responsibility for this decision, I declare that this is a political decision.'[58]

The problem was how was this to be done? Bérégovoy's suggestion that legislation ending the stability of the core groups be passed was rejected by Mitterrand and his adviser Attali, who wanted to avoid the ensuing political controversy. This forced Bérégovoy to work through the market by persuading business allies to buy enough shares to win control over the privatised firms; a solution that led to discreditable failure without avoiding political controversy. The initial target was the Société Générale and Bérégovoy's agent was Georges Pébereau. Having been replaced by Balladur as the head of CGE in 1986 (in circumstances to be discussed later), he had a score to settle and the cross-shareholdings between privatised CGE and the Société Générale meant that he could hope to retrieve his control of the former through taking control of the latter.[59] However, this failed after a discreditable insider trading scandal.[60]

Rocard, who had not been in favour of 100 per cent nationalization in 1981, now signalled a policy switch to partial privatisation as part of the need for national champions to develop European alliances. Of the partial privatisations that took place in 1992, before the 1993 return to power of the Right, while ELF respected the state majority control requirement, that of Total did not, although increased holdings by two state insurance companies and of Crédit Lyonnais preserved a veneer of state control.[61] Having begun as a mask for an attempt at dismembering the 1986–87 privatisations, Mitterrand's 'ni, ni' policy had become a staging post to further

---

[57] Durupty, p. 117; cf. 123–6, quoting estimates from the *Notes bleues du ministère des Finances*, No. 376.

[58] Favier and Martin-Roland, iii, p. 85; cf. 84. More generally see articles in *Le Figaro*, 17 May 1988 by P. Robin, 'Pierre Bérégovoy s'attaque aux noyaux durs' and C. Blandin, 'La casse-tête de Bérégovoy', *Le Monde*, 28 May 1988.

[59] Favier and Martin-Roland, iii, pp. 85–6. Prime Minister Rocard's staff had discouraged a direct attack on CGE. For the whole of this affair we have relied on the well-informed account of Favier and Martin-Roland. [60] Ibid., pp. 87–102.

[61] Maclean, 'Privatisation in France', pp. 279–80 and Maclean, 'Privatisation, *Dirigisme* and the Global Economy', p. 221.

Table 7.1 *French Privatisation Programme 1986–93*

1986 List implemented	1986 List not implemented on 1993 list	1993 List additions
Saint-Gobain	AGF	Aerospatiale
Paribas	GAN	Air France
CGCT	UAP	Caisse Centrale de Réassurance
Banque BTP	Bull	Caisse Nationale de Prévoyance
BIMPT	Thomson	Compagnie Générale Maritime
Havas	Banque Hervet	Renault
CGE	Crédit Lyonnais	SEITA
Mutuelle Générale	BNP	SNECMA
CIC	Péchiney	Usinor–Sacilor
Suez	Rhône-Poulenc	
Matra	ELF–Aquitaine	
	Société Marseillaise de Crédit	

Source: Wright, 'Industrial Privatisation' in Jones (ed.), p. 105.

privatisations under budget-motivated pressures, via a further loosening of restrictions on state enterprises during the brief Cresson and Bérégovoy premierships of 1991–93.

Balladur came to power in 1993 with a massive parliamentary majority, a demoralized Opposition, and an enfeebled President. He took full advantage of this favourable political context but the economic situation was much less propitious. Budgetary pressures dominated the advent of his government, leading him to launch in July 1993 a highly successful Privatisation Bond to be redeemed against shares in programmed privatisations. It attracted 1.4 million investors and raised 110 billion francs, three times expectations.[62] Table 7.1 details the firms added to the 1986 programme, only half of which had been implemented.

The 1986 list contained 12 major groups, comprising 65 major companies with a total of 1,454 subsidiaries, employing some 755,000 employees. It included 19 insurance companies (with over 200,000 employees) and almost 350 companies in the industrial sector (with some 350,000 employees). The list included some of the flagships of French industry . . . Almost half the 1986 privatisation programme was implemented in about eighteen months. A total of 30 (of the 65 envisaged) and 138 subsidiaries were transferred to the private sector, and the capital raised amounted to 71 billion francs (more than twice the amount projected for the entire programme) . . . Nearly 300,000 employees were moved from the public industrial groups to the private sector, and in the banking sector over 100,000 were transferred.[63]

The 19 July 1993 Privatisation Law, adopted in an 'extraordinary session' of parliament, involved concessions by the government, including the presentation of an annual report to parliament on the implementation of the programme. There

[62] Maclean, 'Privatisation in France', p. 281.
[63] Wright, 'Industrial Privatisation', in Jones (ed.), p. 104.

were other 'notable differences between the 1986 programme and that of 1993': these include a more market-oriented approach to pricing, a change of the rules concerning the state's golden share, a decision to sell some groups by instalments and not in their entirety as in 1986, and a strengthening of the role of the Privatisation Commission. But the biggest difference lay in the scope and scale of the new programme. It included defence-related industries such as Aerospatiale, the politically sensitive Renault car company, and even the national flag carrier Air France. The radical nature of the programme may be judged not only by its scale and scope or the inclusion of certain sacred cows of French industry, but also by the speed of implementation. Within six months of the promulgation of the 1993 Law, four major privatisations had taken place, including 'the highly successful flotation of the BNP which raised FF 28 billion and attracted 2.8 million shareholders (a figure beaten only by the Paribas privatisation of 1986); the no less successful sale of the state's 43 per cent stake in Rhône-Poulenc which raised FF 13 billion; the flotation of most of the 54 per cent of the state's equity holding in Elf–Aquitaine for FF 33 billion in February 1994—France's biggest ever financial market operation'.[64]

However, the use to which the proceeds were to be put changed dramatically between 1986 and 1993. In 1986, as we have seen, 55 per cent of the money raised was used to pay off the national debt, through a revival of Poincaré's 1926 Amortization of Public Debt Fund. Balladur virtuously explained that his intention was not to squander state assets but to make 'clear in the eyes of everyone that the State, in selling off its companies, is not using the money in order to spend more but . . . to pay off its debts'.[65] In the recession-ridden France of the early 1990s—unemployment had exceeded 12 per cent by 1994—Balladur, faced by a 1993 budget deficit double that projected pre-electorally by the Bérégovoy Government, now had quite different priorities. The proceeds were to be used to finance current expenditure to reduce unemployment and to prepare the loss-making Air France, Bull, and Crédit Lyonnais for privatisation.[66] Nevertheless, despite freezing some public expenditure, the budget deficit remained stubbornly at 6 per cent of GDP in 1993–94.[67]

Although Balladur was Prime Minister, he still ensured that he, rather than the colourless Finance Minister, controlled the privatisation process. Despite some restrictions on his power, notably through a strengthened Privatisation Commission, the latter did not make its impact until after he had left office. Balladur ensured that his close collaborators in privatisation were appointed to head ELF–Aquitaine (Philippe Jaffré) and the UAP insurance company (Jacques Friedmann). UAP was described as 'the centrepiece of French capitalism, the spider at the heart of a corporate web of cross shareholdings . . . virtually impossible to unpick'.[68] UAP and the BNP bank—both privatised in Balladur's second round—were interlocked in ownership and on a smaller scale UAP and Suez investment bank were also reciprocal

[64] Ibid., pp. 105–6. For a more detailed list of the differences between the 1986 and 1993 privatisation legislation, see Maclean, 'Privatisation in France', pp. 281–2.   [65] Balladur, *Je crois*, p. 88.

[66] Maclean, 'Privatisation in France', pp. 282–4.

[67] Maclean, 'Privatisation, *Dirigisme* and the Global Economy', p. 224.

[68] Maclean, 'Privatisation in France', p. 286; cf. 287 and Hamdouch, pp. 220–2.

shareholders. In the hands of loyal supporters of Balladur, a partisan-oriented privatisation ensured that the 'state bourgeoisie' he had condemned had been transmuted into a privatised business elite.[69] On this score, 1993–95 simply took the 1986–88 process further, the calculated reshuffling of an old elite to constitute a new one, drawn socially from the same source but with a partisan complexion and intended to confer immunity from the swings of political fortune.

Balladur having sold off the best assets, the Juppé Government engaged in fewer privatisations and was compelled to negotiate sales of loss-making firms directly to selected buyers. The sale of the Usinor–Sacilor steel and the Pechiney aluminium and packaging firms ran into difficulties in a depressed stock market in 1995. The banks which underwrote the steel flotation were compelled to make up for the public's lack of enthusiasm and in desperation recourse was had to public sector firms and the Caisse des Dépôts, an ironic outcome.[70] Usinor shares lost 16 per cent of their value in a few months, discouraging investors. Furthermore, 'Under the accounting rules of the European Union, adopted by France in June (1995), neither the tens of billions of francs that have been poured into loss-making firms, nor the proceeds of selling them, have any effect on the government's budget deficit. (They are, it is argued, investments, not continuing spending or revenues.) For a country whose first priority is to cut its deficit in order to qualify for membership of a single European currency, this removes one of the main motives for selling firms rapidly.'[71]

The rapid sacking of the ardent privatiser Alain Madelin as Finance Minister and the fear of the industrial unrest (additional to that occasioned by Juppé's social security reforms, discussed previously) that might follow mass redundancies when loss-making firms were prepared for sale, slowed down the impetus to further privatisations. While the AGF insurance company (subsequently taken over by the German Allianz) and a second instalment of Renault shares were sold in 1996, the fiasco of the attempt to sell defence electronics Thomson–CSF directly, which was successfully undertaken by the Socialist Finance Minister in 1998, meant that Juppé's 'hands on' approach had demonstrated the dangers of over-personalized and centralized decision-making. Privatisation was still not either depoliticized or routine.

The break-up and rearrangement of the stable control core of shareholders, that Balladur had hoped would stem the impact of market forces, became an increasing feature of French business after he left office. His close friend and ally Friedmann was not able in November 1996 to prevent what became an 'amicable' takeover by AXA, a merger that had been proposed a decade earlier by AXA's head Claude Bébéar in 1986 and rejected... by Friedmann, then in Balladur's *cabinet*.[72] Friedmann's partner in the 1986–88 privatisation programme preparations was Philippe Jaffré, then a senior Treasury official, who was appointed by Balladur head

[69] Zahariadis, *Markets*, p. 134; cf. Balladur, *Je crois*, p. 48.

[70] Maclean, 'Privatisation, *Dirigisme* and the Global Economy', pp. 224–6.

[71] 'Privatisation takes French leave', *Economist*, 9 December 1995, p. 80; cf. 79.

[72] P. Santi, 'Claude Bébéar', *Le Monde*, 20 January 2000, p. 13. For an analysis of the implications of the AXA takeover of UAP, see C. Blandin, 'Capitalisme, la fin de l'exception française', *Le Monde*, 29 November 1996, pp. 1, 76.

of ELF–Aquitaine in 1993. After a bitter battle in 1999, Jaffré—having lost an earlier contest with Total to take over the Belgian Petrofina—was forced to accept a bid by Total Fina. A potent factor in his defeat was that the worker shareholders supported the merger, whereas in the case of the BNP attempt to take over Société Générale that failed in August 1999, the worker shareholders—with 8.5 per cent of the shares and 12 per cent of the votes—fearing redundancies, resisted the proposed takeover. BNP had to be content with an 'unfriendly' takeover of Paribas, which had previously agreed to a merger with Société Générale.

However, in both cases, the decisive factor was the role of foreign shareholders who supported the Total Fina bid for ELF–Aquitaine but were more divided over the BNP bid. The Socialist government was largely an observer rather than an effective player in a game where market forces predominated, while the intervention of the Governor of the Bank of France, Trichet, failed to secure a peaceful arrangement of the BNP–Société Générale battle. (His effort at mediation was not helped by the fact that, as Balladur's *directeur de cabinet* in 1986, Trichet was involved in the conflicts with Budget Minister Juppé, whose *directeur de cabinet* was none other than Daniel Bouton, the head in 1999 of Société Générale.[73]) The market logic of privatisation asserted itself over the attempt to preserve old-style statist interventionism, with its old boy collusions and animosities that asserted themselves as the core control groups were destabilized by market forces.

The supreme irony was that Jospin's Finance Minister, Dominique Strauss-Kahn, deftly completed in large measure the partial or total privatisation of the rest of the state's competitive enterprises between 1997 and 1999. To avoid unnecessarily upsetting the Left, he semantically referred to 'opening their capital' rather than privatisation, but no one was deceived, least of all the Communist members of the parliamentary majority, the most ardent advocates of the 1982 nationalization programme. Strauss-Kahn had to buy off trade union hostility—notably in the case of Air France—and contain the pressures of the European Commission (notably in the cases of the Crédit Lyonnais[74] and Renault) but in two years the proceeds of state asset sales amounted to 175 billion francs, compared with 77 billion francs in 1986–88, 13 billion francs in 1988–93, and 123 billion francs between 1993 and 1997.

Although a profit of 116 billion francs was claimed over their cost, this neglects the fact that several times this surplus had been ploughed into them to meet their losses, notably of the steel and computer firms, Crédit Lyonnais, Air France, Renault, and Thomson Multimedia (TMM). In the case of the electronics TMM, the renamed Privatisation Commission—now euphemistically called Participations and Transfers Commission—valued it at 4.2 billion francs, its predecessor having blocked its sale when the Juppé Government sought to dispose of it to Daewoo for 1 franc![75]

---

[73] T. Bréhier, 'Une lecture politique de la guerre des banques', *Le Monde*, 25 August 1999, pp. 1, 14.

[74] For a succinct but pitiless analysis of the Crédit Lyonnais systemic fiasco in the EU context, see E. Cohen, *La Tentation Hexagonale. La souveraineté à l'épreuve de la mondialisation*, Paris, Fayard, 1996, pp. 243–54.

[75] *Le Monde*, 17 July 1999, pp. 1, 15, which includes an interview with the Participations and Transfers Commission chairman, François Lagrange.

However, by the time the state two-thirds holding in TMM went on sale in October 1999, its estimated value had risen to between 14.6 and 17.5 billion francs and, by September 2000, what had been regarded in 1996 as worthless was valued at 100 billion francs! (Meanwhile Daewoo had gone bankrupt.) The biggest revenues from asset sales came from France Télécom (20 per cent in 1997) which had in previous years been used as a milch cow for the ailing state sector firms, while the resuscitated Crédit Lyonnais also proved an attractive investment to the Stock Exchange. By the end of the millennium, the Left had smoothly accomplished the privatisation programme that the Right had promoted but was finding difficult to complete.

The Jospin Government—and notably Finance Minister Strauss-Kahn—fits our characterization of French privatisation as pragmatic and tactical. While the 1997 Socialist party manifesto had been committed to halt privatisation, the financial and industrial policy pursued by the Jospin Government had much continuity with its right-wing predecessors, aimed at facilitating international links and cross-shareholdings inside and outside France. In the defence sector, Thomson–CSF was partially privatised and linked with Alcatel—not Juppé's choice of Matra—itself linked with Aerospatiale and Dassault. (Matra in 1999 merged with Aerospatiale, thanks to government encouragement, to create a French champion capable of negotiating a future European merger from a position of strength.) An apparently less statist but more socialist-style strategy was reflected in the priority given to friendly society financial bodies in the off-market privatisation of CIC to Crédit Mutuel and GAN to Groupama. However, the Finance Ministry had the power to prevent decisions against the public interest taken by these bodies, which had public service obligations.[76] So, Jospin–Strauss-Kahn pragmatism was different from Balladur–Juppé pragmatism, underlining the politicized diversity underlying the continuity between Right and Left.

FRANCE TÉLÉCOM: PARTIALLY PRIVATISING A PUBLIC UTILITY AND REREGULATING A NATIONAL CHAMPION

Just as the context of privatisation has been one of accelerated liberalization, globalization, and deregulation, so the transformation of telecommunications has been part of a communications technological revolution that has elevated it into a matter requiring the attention of the core executives. Pivotal to resulting changes has been the fact that 'Markets are frequently not a physical location but rather a set of telecommunications links' between the main business users.[77] The 'Common Market' became a natural focus for pressure on governments to end the isolation of their national champion monopoly providers of telecommunication services, unable to meet the needs of 'Large firms with extensive cross-national transactions within Europe, as well as multinationals needing to coordinate subsidiaries and facilities in

[76] A. Cole, 'The *Service Public* under stress', *West European Politics*, XXII(4), October 1999, pp. 175–8.
[77] W. Sandholtz, 'The Emergence of a Supranational Telecommunications Regime' in W. Sandholtz and A. Stone Sweet (eds.), *European Integration and Supranational Governance*, OUP, Oxford, 1998, p. 134.

different EC countries'.[78] As the new services being introduced were not coordinated they were incompatible, leading to complaints from the Roundtable of European Industrialists in 1986, while 'major telecommunications users went to the Commission to push for both liberalization and EC-wide coordination'.[79] Sandholtz convincingly argues that 'The Commission had defined the key elements of its plan for EU-level liberalization and coordination as early as 1979, before states really knew what they wanted.'[80] In that year the Industrial Policy Commissioner established the Senior Officials Group for Telecommunications to coordinate the planning of future networks as well as common standards and rules of public procurement, preparing the ground for EC-led liberalization.

France was particularly subject to 'the tension between the pursuit of European collaboration and national particularism' which it sought to resolve by 'taking the lead for a co-ordinated European initiative' in technological collaboration programmes such as ESPRIT and RACE.[81] This meant disrupting the monopolistic and exclusive public service policy communities between chosen national champion firms and public administrations in the supply of telecommunications equipment. In the new competitive context, 'multinational corporations were always seeking to speed up and improve their internal data communications and coordination'[82] and would not tolerate the nation-centred compartmentalization that had previously been taken for granted. Dyson poses the question: 'what sovereignty over communications can West European states claim when corporations are closely coordinating their activities so that international scale can be used as a strategic weapon against competitors and governments?'[83] He replies that attempts to perpetuate past privileged and predictable relations between states and telecommunication authorities are 'doomed to frustration and failure'.[84] How did France seek to avoid this fate?

To overcome the US competitive advantage, reliance should be placed on state initiative and organization in the shape of the Ministry of Post's General Direction of Telecommunications (DGT), to follow up its conspicuous success in modernizing the French telephone system. Unfortunately, 'what the DGT did not sufficiently appreciate was that the telematics project did not lend itself to a state-led strategy in the way that network modernisation in the 1970s so manifestly did'.[85] What the French were to discover to their cost was that 'Heroic technocratic initiatives are not compatible with key features of the communications revolution: the sheer breadth and speed of technological and economic change, the complex convergence and collision' of many rival actors in a field where 'Co-ordination within government

[78] W. Sandholtz, pp. 141–2; cf. 149.　　　[79] Ibid., p. 142.　　　[80] Ibid., p. 146; cf. 147, 149–50, 162.

[81] K. Dyson, 'West European States and the Communication Revolution', in *West European Politics*, IX(4), October 1986, p. 16. On EU high technology collaboration, such as the European Strategic Programme for Research and Development in Information Technology (ESPRIT) and Research for Advanced Communication in Europe (RACE), see C. Shearman, 'European Collaboration in Computing and Telecommunications: A Policy Approach', in the same special issue of *West European Politics*, pp. 148, 155–7.　　　[82] Dyson, 'West European States', p. 13; cf. 11–18.

[83] Ibid., p. 24; cf. 25–31.　　　[84] Ibid., p. 31.

[85] K. Morgan and D. Webber, 'Divergent Paths: Political Strategies for Telecommunications in Britain, France and West Germany', *West European Politics*, IX(4), October 1986, p. 64; cf. 63.

and partnership of public and private actors was increasingly seen as essential' but difficult to achieve in practice.[86]

When they came to power in 1981, 'the French Socialists had not developed a single coherent strategy for communications; rather, they had stumbled into a situation where . . . they were actually pursuing different strategies'.[87] There were conflicts between cultural and industrial objectives, leading to clashes about programming policies for cable between Culture Minister Lang and Communications Minister Fillioud and over communication satellites between DGT and the Industry Ministry.[88] 'The French cable plan was initially presented as a form of Cultural Maginot Line, to provide cultural protection from US invasion.[89] DGT took charge of the Cable Plan's application but it quickly ran into institutional, industrial, and technical difficulties, so that although the Mitterrand presidency carried forward his predecessor's strategy—when 'many decisions were taken in informal negotiations between the DGT and the Elysée'[90]—it demonstrated the limitations of heroic technocratic action by one country.

Majone has pointed out that privatisation through the 'clear separation of regulatory and operational responsibilities' has reinforced public regulation.[91] Wright had argued earlier that 'regulation was not organized in a hierarchical style but by multiple ill-coordinated agencies with overlapping and often imprecise jurisdictions', so that 'far from providing a relatively stable and predictable set of policy objectives for regulators, politicians put them under cross-pressure and obfuscate their objectives'.[92] Coupled with 'a growing mismatch between national modes of regulation and the internationalised and European actors to be regulated', the ground was prepared for a combination of privatisation and reregulation.[93] Even earlier, Dyson had explained the particular need for reregulation in telecommunication, because traditional regulation 'will either be ineffective, in which case the law and the state come into disrepute, or too effective, in which case major new industries will suffer in fiercely competitive markets'.[94] Attempts at controlled deregulation within a single country were proving increasingly ineffective, as were audacious state-sponsored modernization schemes like the Cable Plan, a desperate high technology attempt to preserve national independence.

[86] Dyson, 'West European States', pp. 40–1.

[87] K. Dyson and P. Humphreys, 'Policies for New Media in Western Europe: Deregulation of Broadcasting and Multimedia Diversification', *West European Politics*, IX(4), October 1986, p. 112.

[88] Dyson, 'West European States', pp. 35–6.

[89] The point is repeatedly made in the special issue of *West European Politics*, IX(4), October 1986, pp. 19, 107, 116.

[90] M. Thatcher, *The Politics of Telecommunications. National Institutions, Convergence and Change*, OUP, Oxford, 1999, p. 126; cf. 125–30, 136. On the Cable Plan, see E. Cohen, *Le Colbertisme 'High Tech'. Economie des Télécom et du Grand Projet*, Paris, Hachette, 1992, pp. 138–46.

[91] G. Majone, 'Paradoxes of Privatization and Deregulation', *Journal of European Public Policy*, I(1), June 1994, pp. 61–2.

[92] V. Wright, 'The Administrative System and Market Regulation in Western Europe: Continuities, Exceptionalism and Convergence', *Rivista trimestrale di diritto pubblico*, 1992, 4, 1033; cf. 1032–4.

[93] Ibid., p. 1039; cf. 1035–41.　　[94] Dyson, 'West European States', p. 46; cf. 45.

A consequent shift from heroic to brokerage politics is detected by Dyson. After an initial ambitious venture, core executives learn to adopt a more circumspect approach. Political leaders become less assertive. 'They trade off loss of the substance of sovereignty for the prospects of gains in wealth, the calculation being that in this way the effective political power of the state will be better safeguarded. Thus, governments begin to give serious consideration to regulatory revision, joint ventures and licensing deals and even to the possibility of threatening once cherished "national champions" with new exposure to the rigours of the international market.'[95] However, in doing so, they discovered how weak they were in dealing with the champion firms they had protected and promoted.

Whilst impressed by the British combination of liberalization and privatisation, the Chirac Government decided that although the manufacture of telecommunications equipment could be privatised, PTT should remain a public service. It would have been tempting to privatise the very profitable DGT, which had been used heavily to subsidize loss-making nationalized firms (such as Thomson), demand for whose services was rapidly expanding. However, the DGT's image as a highly successful state administration was a deterrent, as were the hostility of both management and employees, the latter fearing a loss of their civil service status. While the PTT Minister, advised by his new head of DGT, favoured an initial change from government department to public corporation, Chirac overruled him, wishing to avoid a confrontation with the trade unions (especially *Force Ouvrière*) and urged by the Budget Division not to sacrifice a lucrative annual source of funds.[96]

Ironically, it was the Socialist PTT Minister Paul Quilès, with the encouragement of Prime Minister Rocard, who carried through a split between the postal and telecommunications arms of his ministry, which divided trade union opposition to the change of status. He cunningly asked a former planning commissioner of Socialist sympathies to provide a reassuring report on the change to greater autonomy. Aware that Chirac had overestimated the capacity of the unions to block reform, the minister overcame Mitterrand's objections. A well-judged publicity campaign, combined with various financial concessions to the unions, ensured the safe passage of his 2 July and 29 December 1990 Laws.[97] Concerned to avoid damaging claims that he was preparing the way for privatisation, Quilès ensured that the Finance Ministry would continue to receive funds until 1993 and retained control over monopoly prices, while the new France Télécom was to remain an instrument of government industrial policy. So, until the 1993 return of the Right to power, the policy of liberalization and increased regulation without privatisation continued.[98] European Community

---

[95] Ibid., p. 49; cf. 48–51.

[96] Zahariadis (1992), pp. 148–55. See also his earlier 'To Sell or Not to Sell? Telecommunications Policy in Britain and France', *Journal of Public Policy*, XII(4), 367–72 and Cohen, *Le Colbertisme*, pp. 259–66, 292–3.

[97] Cohen, *Le Colbertisme*, pp. 266–72. Quilès overcame a presidential attempt to block publication of the Prévot Report by declaring it was too late to stop it: a *fait accompli*. See Favier and Martin-Roland, iii, p. 145; cf. 142–7. See also Thatcher, pp. 155–6.

[98] Zahariadis, *Markets, States and Public Policy*, pp. 155–7; Thatcher, *Telecommunications*, pp. 156–7.

arguments were used to justify the reforms pursued, even while resisting increasing EC pressure pointing the way to the full deregulation of a single telecommunications market in 1998.

The Balladur Government was now emboldened to consider partial privatisation, returning to a 1985 suggestion for a mixed majority public/minority private enterprise that had been rejected at the time.[99] This proposal, about which the Finance Ministry was unenthusiastic, unleashed a major strike by France Télécom workers in October 1993, fearing a repeat of the major redundancies that had occurred after British Telecom's privatisation. This coincided with a strike in Air France against restructuring and the minister was forced to suspend his planned partial privatisation.[100] The argument used to justify the proposal was the need to develop transnational alliances and this, combined with continuing EU pressure and the need to acquire funds, led the Jospin Government to carry through the partial (20 per cent) privatisation of France Télécom, the Socialists steering safely the adoption of a telecom reform over which the Right had faltered.

France Télécom management were infuriated by being forced to take stakes in public sector industrial firms and insurance companies in the 1980s and early 1990s which encouraged their impatience for privatisation because their minister was too weak to protect them from the Finance Minister's depredations.[101] EU monetary union considerations also had their indirect impact, the Juppé Government used 37 billion francs from France Télécom to reduce the budget deficit to meet the 3 per cent convergence criterion in the run-up to the Euro, showing that the budget figures could be manipulated not just by debudgetizing expenditure but also by including exceptional items of revenue! By the turn of the millennium, the general case for privatising public utilities—pioneered by France Télécom—could now be debated on the Right, with not merely a Madelin but a Balladur being a protagonist.

With trade union opposition now weaker, the Juppé Government pushed through two laws in July 1996 comprehensively reforming 'France Télécom's organizational positions, established new regulatory bodies, defined the functions, powers, and duties of operators, regulatory bodies and the government and established rules governing licensing, competition and *service public*'.[102] While proclaiming that France Télécom was to provide a universal service, it formally lost its remaining monopoly powers over voice telephony and the infrastructure. To meet its short-term EMU budget deficit commitment, the Juppé Government took over responsibility for more than half of the France Télécom pension obligations (a long-term burden) in return for 37.5 billion francs, which reduced the budget deficit by 0.45 per cent. The

---

[99] Ibid., pp. 157–8; cf. 151–2 and J. Darmon, *Le Grand Dérangement*, J.-C. Lattès, 1985. Darman's prototype was ELF–Aquitaine. More generally, see J. Chevallier, 'La Nouvelle Réforme des télécommunications: ruptures et continuités', *Revue Française de Droit Administratif*, XN(5), 1996, 909–51.

[100] Zahariadis, *Markets*, p. 158.

[101] Thatcher, *Telecommunications*, pp. 191–3, 197–8, 215–16, 220. The Post and Telecommunications Ministry was actually directly under the Finance Ministry in 1990–91 and from 1997.

[102] Ibid., p. 163; cf. 161–8. More generally on public service, see J.-L. Bodiguel *et al.*, *Servir l'intérêt general*, PUF, 2000.

Juppé Government decision to sell 30 per cent of its shares was overtaken by the general election but the Jospin Government continued with partial privatisation. The state's share fell to some 62 per cent, the rest being sold to private shareholders (initially 3.8 million in October 1997, falling to 1.8 million by July 2000), exchanged with Deutsche Telekom (a cross-shareholding to promote an international alliance), or accounted for by an increase in capital.

Although 'institutional change in France was a slow and tortuous process', by the end of the century greater autonomy had been achieved, although the state was committed by law to retain at least 51 per cent of France Télécom.[103] The EU Commission challenged in 2000 the French use of its objective of universal service provision to protect France Télécom from competition as part of its attempt to enforce EU rules to avoid connection fees becoming a barrier to new entrants. Promoting interconnection was an ongoing task of achieving EU coordination in telecommunications.

If French governments were being elbowed aside by their privatised creations, they had partly themselves to blame. We earlier quoted the President of France Télécom, Michel Bon, who had bluntly declared in 1997 that he had turned in vain for guidance to ministers and their staffs.[104] As the public sector had failed to coordinate, no less control would result from the decision to privatise ownership. While the mix in the mixed economy was shifting ever further in favour of its private component, this amounted to less of a change than it seemed because core executives had primarily used their power for piecemeal short-term intervention rather than a sustained and consistent overall strategy. Nevertheless, the perception of France as a distinctive country, where the public sector was the senior partner in the mixed economy, operating in a *dirigiste* way, was now blurred. With state actors retreating openly to a junior partner status more in conformity with the realities of an international market economy, competition increasingly precluded pretensions to a coordinated industrial policy. However, the French Finance Ministry did not follow the British model of auctioning mobile telephone licences, preferring to share them out, so piecemeal state intervention remains important.

WHAT LESSONS EMERGE FROM FRENCH PRIVATISATION?

Starting with the categories used to select our case studies, it is clear that our examples shifted over the two decades between routine and non-routine coordination. While privatisation was always at the start non-routine, clear routinized aspects about many of them (selling by instalments or many off-market sales of subsidiaries) begin to be established. Routinization covered four different phenomena: stable constellation of actors, institutionalization, bureaucratization, and critical duration

---

[103] Thatcher, *Telecommunications*, p. 170; cf. ch. 7 passim and pp. 218–21, 241, 259.

[104] M. Bon in ENA, *La Réforme de l'Etat*, p. 28, quoted at the end of Chapter 3. Bon's appointment as the new head of France Télécom (he was Prime Minister Juppé's candidate) in 1995 led to this exchange. Bon to Chirac: 'I have no confidence in politicians', to which Chirac replied: 'And I have no confidence in Inspectors of Finance' (Ottenheimer, p. 204).

(redefining the legal status of France Télécom personnel was an *ad hoc* operation, but a prolonged one). A further complication is that even an emergency may be dealt with in 'routine fashion', with well-defined rules and actors for coordinating a response. The stock market crash in October 1987 provides such an example.

Similarly, when we turn to our other distinction, politicization is equally problem-ridden, since it, too, involves very different phenomena: a privatisation could be politicized because it was (1) inherently so, given its sector or cultural significance. This was the case with ELF–Aquitaine, Renault, and Havas; (2) exploited for partisan purposes or for patronage (BNP, ELF, and UAP); (3) linked with other politically charged policies (Paribas and Société Générale); (4) 'Europeanized' (Crédit Lyonnais, France Télécom).[105] As the result of (2), (3), and (4), a non-politicized policy could quickly become a politicized one. While the constellations of core executive actors are sectorally specific, they also involve political and policy externalities that require horizontal communication that may facilitate or inhibit coordination.

Although pursued in a pragmatic and tactical fashion, the pervasive impact of privatisation is difficult to separate from an ideological context when, at the start of the 1980s, the Mitterrand presidency proclaimed its ambition to 'break with capitalism'. The new economic orthodoxy, implemented and legitimized by the Socialists, and enthusiastically embraced by the Right, subsequently involved imposing fiscal discipline, public expenditure squeezes, and priority definition, tax reform, financial market modernization and liberalization, prudent exchange rate policy, the dismantling of trade barriers, the encouragement of foreign direct inward invest-ment, deregulation, redefining property rights, greater autonomy for public sector managers, and introducing greater flexibility into the labour market.[106] Coordin-ating all this was a tall order.

The fiasco of the state bank Crédit Lyonnais, which lost over 100 billion francs when it was presided over from 1988 to 1993 by former Treasury Director Jean-Yves Haberer, revealed a system of collective irresponsibility. Apart from Haberer, key roles were played by the Treasury Director from 1987 to 1993, Trichet, and by Larosière, the Governor of the Bank of France from 1987 to 1993 (and as such President of the Banking Commission) as well as by successive Finance Ministers, who should have maintained an oversight of the bank's speculative ventures. The question of whether its accounts were falsified in 1992 on instructions from Larosière and Trichet, as alleged by Haberer, was being judicially investigated in September 2000. What their transactions revealed was 'a system of collusion and confusion of interests between the government, the state shareholder, senior civil servants, the

---

[105] On the Europeanization of French telecommunications, see M. Thatcher, 'Regulatory Reform and Internationalization in Telecommunications', in J. Hayward (ed.), *Industrial Enterprise and European Integration*, Oxford, OUP, 1995, especially pp. 246–8, 253–60, 263–5; M. Thatcher, 'High Technology' in H. Kassim and A. Menon (eds.), *The European Union and National Industrial Policy*, Routledge, 1996, pp. 188–92.

[106] This enumeration comes from V. Wright, 'France in the 1990s: The End of *Dirigisme*?', versions of which were published in *Stato e Mercato*, 54, 1998, pp. 351–87 and as 'Dirigisme: Myth and Reality' in E. Bort and R. Keat (eds.), *The Boundaries of Understanding*, University of Edinburgh, Social Sciences Institute, pp. 9–28.

ex-civil servant heads of firms and supervisory bodies closely linked to the selfsame civil service'.[107] They collectively underestimated the foolhardy risks taken by the Crédit Lyonnais management, trusting to the old boy network rather than enforcing strict control. Such slackness cannot be dealt with by coordination and it was only when Finance Minister Arthuis formally laid the charge of presenting false accounts in 1996 that an attempt to pin responsibility on those guilty of this financial fiasco was finally made as a prelude to the bank's privatisation.

As a more general conclusion, the experience of French privatisation suggests that core executive coordinating capacity cannot be divorced from the wider political environment, from the heritage of cultural predispositions, of the legacies of collective action and the traditions of party competition. Institutions, interpreted in the widest sense, produce 'stickiness'—the source of policy lags. The density of French institutional structures impedes coordination as decisions work their way through an elaborate maze of actors. However, the French privatisation experience also underlines the limits of institutional constraint in a policy environment radically reshaped by technological, international, EU, ideological, and budgetary pressures.

The frequent linkages between our privatisation study with those of the budget and the EU illustrate the need for coordination rather than its actual practice in a highly sectorized and verticalized ministerial system. In fact, privatisation was notable for the lead role personally played by Balladur in 1986–88 and 1993–95, which, together with Strauss-Kahn's 1997–99 tenure of the Finance Ministry, were the periods of most effective privatisation. Minimizing the need for core executive coordination was a decisive contribution to the success achieved. The scale and pace of the programme point to the resulting capacity to carry out a very far-reaching policy reversal.

[107] E. Leser, 'Une affaire qui met en accusation l'appareil d'Etat', *Le Monde*, 12 September 2000, p. 12; cf. *Le Monde*, 14 September 2000, p. 12.

8

Coordinating the Response to Immigration Pressures: An Unending Quest

In the early 1980s, the issues of nationalization versus privatisation of France's major firms and banks, and of national integration or repressive exclusion of immigrants in the name of 'national preference', came to the fore as the main ways of distinguishing ideologically the Left and Right in France. By the late 1990s, both these issues were much more depoliticized than they had been. Part of the reason that this proved possible has been that there was a perverse contradiction between the assertive rhetoric of imperative principle and the embarrassed reality of inconsistent practice. We have already examined this in the case of privatisation, with the Left shamefacedly coming to accept the retreat from public ownership it had earlier espoused with enthusiasm. Immigration policy, which had not been a controversial party issue in a country that had for a century been accustomed to accept massive foreign inward migration without demur, became so in a context of increasing unemployment.

However, the mainstream parties were confronted by the glaring contradiction between the claim after 1974 that immigration had officially ceased, when both legal and illegal immigrants continued to enter France in large numbers, which the National Front polemically exploited to its electoral advantage. By 1997, when Interior Minister Chevènement was presenting legislation on the subject, he declared that 'The immigration question should cease to occupy a central position in the French political debate.'[1] How far were core executives able to coordinate a consensual rescue of immigrants from their unenviable position of hostages to the populist temptations and the calculated passions of adversary politics? The difficulties they encountered arose in part from the way in which immigration issues aroused fundamental normative and intense emotive dissensions, as well as from the dispersed politico-administrative institutions responsible for dealing with these symbolic and substantive sensitivities.

Three specific features mark off this policy sector from the others examined in this study. First, while the President, Prime Minister, and Finance Minister do intervene influentially from time to time, these top level core executives do not play as centralizing, sustained, and pivotal role in coordinating immigration policy as one would

---

[1] Interview in *Le Monde*, 25 September 1997, p. 10.

expect from its politicized nature. Second, despite the efforts of Interior to acquire the status of lead ministry, assisted by the territorial dimension and importance of local authorities and police, especially in policy implementation and repression, its ambitions are usually frustrated because of the high degree of spill-over into other policy areas and the multi-dimensional character of immigration, extending both horizontally and vertically among domestic, EU, and international actors. Third, although there are a mass of non-governmental organizations (NGOs) that seek to move from outsider to insider policy status, there is a lack of institutionalized interest groups, so that the politico-administrative policy community is predominantly bureaucratic and juridical, with the intrusion of politicians and their private staffs from time to time in response to crises or to exploit electoral advantage.

IDEOLOGICAL AND ORGANIZATIONAL TENSIONS

The meaning of the term 'immigrant' is itself infused with an ambiguity between first and second generation arrivals, who are assumed to be insufficiently assimilated into French culture. Even when they have acquired French nationality, those of North African extraction in particular are regarded as foreign elements within the body politic, while Portuguese immigrants, almost as numerous, are not so regarded. Despite the pride France has generally taken in its long traditions of integration, the combination of a pluri-ethnic with a uni-cultural society creates normative and practical tensions, which become exacerbated when demographic and economic imperatives cease to favour immigration. This occurs when unemployment rises as it did from the mid-1970s to the mid-1990s, ending the 'Thirty Glorious Years' of rapid economic growth and full employment.

From the mid-nineteenth century, falling birth rates and rapid industrialization, combined with the loss of manpower due to the First World War casualties, resulted in acceptance of the sustained need for immigration, assisted by the fact that the immigrants attracted were mainly of European origin, particularly Portuguese in the 1960s and 1970s. Over time, it was possible for the immigrant, 'seen as a peasant aiming at becoming a "petit bourgeois" after training as a proletarian', to be assimilated especially after second generation socialization through education, although this was always going to be more difficult for the would-be 'beurgeoisie' from North Africa.[2] Once severe restrictions were placed on worker immigration in 1974, the tendency by the mainstream parties to treat authorized, assimilated incomers indiscriminately as though they were 'clandestine', illegal immigrants has caused a confusion with serious consequences. This confusion has been damaging to the simultaneously proclaimed policy of full integration into equal citizenship, as well as allowing the xenophobic National Front both to exaggerate the dimensions of the 'invasion' (an expression used by Giscard d'Estaing in 1991 and publicized by the

[2] C. Wihtol de Wenden, 'Immigrants as Political Actors in France', *West European Politics*, XVII(2), April 1994, 96; cf. 94–5, 105. This is a special issue on 'The Politics of Immigration in Western Europe.'

media) and to engage in stigmatizing the legal by amalgamation with the illegal immigrants.[3]

French core executives, even more than French public opinion, are torn between France's multicultural reality and their monocultural aspirations, a superimposition of a secular and republican state upon a religiously diverse communitarian society, a concern to protect national identity while respecting universal human rights. At a political level, one can distinguish between: a mainstream Left whose humanism, secularism, and republicanism are tempered by the defence of national interest; a mainstream Right whose national preference is tempered by the ideals it has not rejected; an extreme Right whose national preference excludes humanist ideals; and an extreme Left that champions immigrants' rights as human rights without concessions to national preference.

The most recent attempt, in 1997–98, to achieve a prudent and judicious compromise by recourse to a piecemeal pragmatism, based upon an inductive approach, proceeding from the practical realities which yet remains committed to basic humanitarian values, has been the Jospin Government's legislation inspired by the proposals commissioned from a working party (to which we shall return). However, we must first probe more deeply into the problems posed by the French 'republican' commitment to a post-revolutionary assertion of a universalist and secularist urge to assimilate all incomers into a uniform model of citizen integration. To do so, we shall briefly consider the Muslim headscarf affair of autumn 1989, which exemplified the challenge to national identity and secularism no longer coming from the Roman Catholic Church but from a much more alien Islamic fundamentalism.

On 8 October 1989, three female pupils at a secondary school were threatened with exclusion if they did not take off their *hidjab*. After initially removing their headscarves, they attempted to return with them but were excluded on 19 October by the headmaster, who later resurfaced as an Rassemblement Pour le République (RPR) deputy. As these headscarves were seen as symbolic of fundamentalist feminine subordination, challenging the sacrosanct secular educational system's commitment to integration and equality, school teacher and public hostility presented the Rocard Government—seeking on 25 October to reduce public controversy over issues related to immigration—with a predicament. Education Minister Jospin, seeking to dedramatize the issue by an emollient appeal to dialogue not exclusion, provoked the hostility of several ministers, while the President maintained an evasive silence and Prime Minister Rocard rallied to the support of Jospin. Opinion polls in October and November showed that over half the French opposed the wearing of the headscarf at school, seeing it as an infringement of secularism, while a third did not.

Jospin sought to gain time by asking the Council of State for its advice. When this came on 27 November 1989, it declared that wearing religious insignia was not incompatible with secularist state education and it was up to the headmasters to deal

---

[3] P. Weil, *Pour Une Nouvelle Politique d'Immigration*, Notes de la Fondation Saint-Simon, November 1995, p. 10; cf. 11, 18. See also Y. Gastaut, *L'immigration et l'opinion en France sous la Ve République*, Paris, Seuil, 2000, pp. 463–5. On the role of the car strikes of 1981–84 and the 'spectre of Islam', see ibid., pp. 391–401 and 492–518.

with the issue case by case. A year later, about 400 pupils were wearing the *hidjab* in a calmer atmosphere and on 2 November 1992, the Council of State annulled a school regulation excluding three pupils on the grounds that it infringed in an 'excessive way the freedom to show one's religious affiliation'.[4] Education Minister Jospin had defused an explosive situation by his tolerance of religious pluralism.

However, this did not prevent the outbreak of a prolonged intellectual controversy that reached hysterical proportions, helpfully summarized by Jeremy Jennings.[5] Nevertheless, these ideological storms in the Parisian intellectual milieu had little impact upon the core executive decision-makers, who were responding to a changing organizational context related to the management of the divergence between the demand and supply of immigrants.

Between the era of consensus extending from the two 1945 Liberation ordinances on the conditions for acquiring French nationality and of entry and residence of foreigners and the passage of the 1980 Bonnet Law restricting entry and residence, a depoliticized immigration policy had been dealt with by administrative discretion (in both senses of discretion) by decree, circular, or memo, not by statute. Thereafter, immigration became a prominent, politicized issue. 'Until 1981, emphasis was put on laws dealing with labour, and later with legislation fostering the equal treatment of foreigner and national. In contrast, during the first years of the socialist period [1981–83] the emphasis shifted to human rights'[6] as envisaged in the propositions (numbers 79–81) Mitterrand had put to the electorate.

This watershed, between the insulation of immigration policy-makers and the intrusion of electoral and political factors in the period we are considering, marks the arena shift from predominantly closed, consensual, routine administrative decision processes to open, conflictual, non-routine political processes. As well as the general shift between before and after the 1980s, one may detect an 'election-migration policy cycle' whereby 'governments inflate anti-foreigner rhetoric before elections and then deflate the rhetoric and produce liberal reforms soon after they occur'.[7]

---

[4] Quoted in Favier and Martin-Roland, iii, p. 339; cf. 334–8. For Jospin's own views on the controversy, see his *L'Invention du possible*, Paris, Flammarion, 1991, pp. 238–95.

[5] For an informative review of this literature see Jeremy Jennings, 'Citizenship, Republicanism and Multiculturalism in Contemporary France', *British Journal of Political Science*, XXX, Part 4, October 2000, 575–98. For a review of the academic literature, see R. Hansen, 'Migration, Citizenship and Race in Europe: Between Incorporation and Exclusion', *European Journal of Political Research*, XXXV, 1999, 415–44. On the debate, see R. Debray, *Que Vive la République*, Odile Jacob, 1989; E. Todd, *Le Destin des immigrés: assimilation et ségrégation dans les démocraties occidentales*, Paris, Seuil, 1994; C. Jelen, *Les casseurs de la République*, Paris, Plon, 1997; D. Schnapper, *La Communauté des citoyens: sur l'ideé moderne de nation*, Paris, Gallimard, 1994; J. Roman, *La Démocratie des individus*, Paris, Calmann-Lévy, 1998; F. Gaspard and F. Khrosrokhavar, *Le Foulard et la République*, Paris, La Découverte, 1995; A. Touraine, *Pourrons-nous vivre ensemble: égaux et différents*, Paris, Fayard, 1997.

[6] C. Wihtol de Wenden, 'Immigrants as Political Actors in France', p. 100; cf. 98. See also D. Lochak, *Etrangers, de quel droit?*, Paris, PUF, 1985, pp. 205–32. P. Weil, *La France et ses étrangers, L'aventure d'une politique de l'immigration de 1938 à nos jours*, Paris, Gallimard, 1995, pp. 88–90.

[7] V. Giraudon, 'Citizenship Rights for Non-Citizens: France, Germany and the Netherlands' in C. Joppke (ed.), *Challenge to the Nation-State. Immigration in Western Europe and the United States*, Oxford, OUP, 1998, p. 291; cf. 289–93.

While this policy cycle would have predicted accurately the 1981 election and its aftermath, and that of 1997, when the Left won, it did not hold in 1993 when the Right won. Furthermore, we shall see that, despite the overt shift from a depoliticized and elitist juridico-executive focus prior to 1981 to a politicized and populist partisan and mass media emphasis afterwards, there was a substantial measure of covert continuity between the mainstream parties *vis-à-vis* the National Front, despite the adversarial rhetoric. Having considered the deep-seated tensions, we must now turn to the changing circumstances.

THE ROAD TO NON-ROUTINE POLITICIZATION

While there is much truth in the assertion that 'the two dimensions of cross-national variation that affect the likelihood that debate on alien rights will spill over in the electoral sphere are the level of coordination of policy-making and the degree of competitiveness of political elites',[8] there is no doubt that the reduction in the demand for labour and rising unemployment after 1974 curtailed the routine administration and increased the politicization of immigration policy. The time had passed when Prime Minister Pompidou could declare in 1963 that 'Immigration is a way of easing pressure in the labour market and resisting social pressure.'[9] However, 'As long as immigration policy was portrayed in terms of labour recruitment there was little conflict among the diverse administrative agencies responsible for developing and monitoring this recruitment.'[10] Once the strategy of party competition expanded the portrayal of the immigration issue to matters such as problems of urban housing, education and crime, before moving on to the preservation of national identity, immigration occupied an inescapably conspicuous place on the political agenda, to be exploited for partisan electoral advantage. This polarized overt party disagreement exaggerated the differences in the actual content of the policies pursued, whilst widening the arena of conflict compounded coordination difficulties.

Before 1981, the salience of immigration in electoral campaigns, in media coverage, and its ranking in public opinion polls, were modest, reflecting the insulated way it was handled by government as well as the 'strategy of stealth' pursued by proponents of the immigrant cause.[11] There was a contrast between entry and integration immigration policies. 'Policy-making on entry was dominated by a small, mostly non-political group of decision-makers in Paris. Policy-making on integration was more complicated. It frequently involved several ministries and several levels of government and administration, but the process tended to be focused on the local level. Decisions about both aspects of immigration policy were generally made by small groups of decision-makers in isolation from decisions about other government

---

[8] Ibid., p. 297.   [9] Quoted in Weil, *La France*, p. 103.
[10] M. Schain, 'The Immigration Debate and the National Front' in John T. S. Keeler and Martin A. Schain (eds.), *Chirac's Challenge*, New York, St. Martin's Press, 1996, p. 172; cf. 170–1.
[11] V. Giraudon, *Policy Change Behind Gilded Doors: Explaining the Evolution of Aliens' Rights in Contemporary Western Europe, 1974–1994*, Harvard University doctoral thesis, April 1997, p. 12; cf. 14, 194.

activities',[12] achieving consensus without coordination. From the 1970s but accelerating in the 1980s, 'As this consensus broke down...the network itself was transformed, and was increasingly centralised', while 'At the same time, the arena of participation expanded dramatically, and decision-making became more visible and more dominant on the political agenda.'[13]

The depoliticized, low-intensity, administrative character of immigrant integration policy was facilitated by its local management, insulating it from adversarial party polemics and restricting access to decision-making, thereby precluding conflict. However, moving the immigration issues from the periphery to the centre was also facilitated by the large numbers of legislators and ministers who were mayors and by the centralized administrative system. Ironically, it was particularly the Communist mayors in towns with disproportionately large immigrant populations who politicized the immigration issue in the run-up to the 1981 elections, which was exacerbated by the urban riots in the Lyon area in the following summer. Thereafter the opportunity existed for the National Front to portray immigrants as an ethnic threat to the French nation.[14]

However, the 1974 French formal suspension of non-EU immigration, coupled with newly elected President Giscard d'Estaing's appointment of a Junior Minister for Immigrant Workers, located in the Ministry of Labour but answerable to the Elysée, meant that the issue had already become a core executive preoccupation.[15] We shall later consider the role of the Council of State in striking down circulars by the Interior and Labour Ministries, coming directly to Bonnet Act of 1980 that was declared unconstitutional by the Constitutional Council (CC). The legislation was prompted by President Giscard's 1979 decision to reduce the number of immigrants by all possible means. Numerous draft bills were prepared by several ministries, with the Junior Immigration Minister taking the lead in coordination. The task proved difficult because many senior officials considered the drastic proposals neither desirable nor feasible. This was especially true of Institut National de la Statistique et des Etudes (INSEE), which argued that the necessary statistical information was not available; the Foreign Ministry, which objected to the legislation in principle; and the Social Affairs Population and Migration Division, which raised objections of cost, numerous exemptions (Algerians and EC citizens), and legal difficulties. The main clash was between the Immigration and Interior Ministers, the latter overruling the former's proposals as too weak.[16] In the event, the President's wishes were vetoed by the CC, the herald of future battles, notably over the 1993 Pasqua Law that was in turn overruled by a constitutional amendment.

The three proposals concerning immigration in Mitterrand's 1981 electoral programme were based on a 1978 PS bill, some of whose provisions they simply

[12] M. Schain, 'Policy-making and Defining Ethnic Minorities: The Case of Immigration in France', *New Community*, XX(1), October 1993, 61.   [13] Ibid.

[14] Ibid., pp. 63–6. See also M. Schain, *French Communism and Local Power*, New York, St. Martin's Press, 1985.   [15] Giraudon, *Policy Change*, pp. 204–5.

[16] Ibid., pp. 207–8, drawing on the Archives Patrick Weil at the Fondation Nationale des Sciences Politiques. See also Weil, *La France*, pp. 158–204.

incorporated. What were Mitterrand's explicit electoral commitments? Proposal 79 promised to end discrimination against immigrant workers. Proposal 80, as well as promising equal social welfare rights for immigrant workers and their right of association, included the right to vote in local elections after five years' residence in France—a controversial subject to which we shall return. Proposal 81 stated that the number of immigrant workers admitted would be fixed annually by the National Plan and the repression of illegal immigration reinforced.[17] The contradiction of the human rights ideological inspiration of this reaction against the Giscard policy, simultaneously seeking to assimilate and to exclude, derived from the ambivalent nature of the conception of integration, exacerbated by the responsive pragmatism adopted in practice. The 'republican model' of a universal and indiscriminate national integration came under intense strain from the pressures of immigration.[18]

The Communist mayors having prepared the way, the National Front (NF) exploited the issue to the full. Le Pen's 1974 presidential election programme had not even mentioned the immigration issue, but in the 1983–84 local elections the NF's breakthrough was associated with differentiating itself not merely from the Left but from the mainstream Right by its radical proposals to reverse the immigrant 'invasion'.[19] This reflected the broadening of public concern but also contributed to raising the salience of the issue, associated with insecurity, unemployment, and national identity. The general stigmatization of the immigrants, linked with the sense that government was incapable of controlling the phenomenon, not only helps explain the increase in the NF vote, especially among workers (30 per cent in the 1995 presidential election). It also promoted the immigration issue to second place after unemployment in French voter motivation.

The mainstream Right had tried to steal some of the NF thunder in the 1986 and 1993 parliamentary elections, with Interior Minister Pasqua taking the lead in proposing legislation and enforcing repression. The most spectacular incident was the deportation of 101 Mali illegal immigrants by charter plane in October 1986. The outcry, echoed within the Chirac Government by Culture Minister Léotard and the Junior Minister for Human Rights, Claude Malhuret, led the Prime Minister not to repeat this type of expulsion, which was supported only by the NF.[20] The Justice Minister Albin Chalandon reformed the Nationality Code, notably through the symbolic requirement that foreigners between the ages of 16 and 23 should deliberately seek French nationality rather than acquire it automatically. However, neither this legislation nor that of 1993, which we shall consider later, stemmed the NF tide. For that to occur, the party had to split, as it did in January 1999, enabling a more consensual, lower key approach to be adopted towards immigration. However,

---

[17] Weil, *La France*, pp. 213–16.

[18] P. Weil and J. Crawley, 'Integration in Theory and Practice: A Comparison of France and Britain', *West European Politics*, XVII(2), April 1994, 113–15 and D. Schnapper, 'The Debate on Immigration and the Crisis of National Identity', ibid., pp. 134–5.

[19] P.-A. Taguieff, 'Un programme "révolutionnaire"', ch. 10 in N. Meyer and P. Perrineau (eds.), *Le Front National à Découvert*, Paris, Presses de Sciences Po, 1996 and H. Lagrange and P. Perrineau, 'Le Syndrome Le Pen', ibid., ch. 11. [20] Favier and Martin-Roland, ii, pp. 714–17.

before this was achieved, there was much turbulence in the attempt to contain the conflicts it provoked.

THE MINISTERIAL CRISIS MANAGEMENT OF MIGRATION POLICY

While immigration easily became the focus of intense and wide-ranging controversy, those responsible for deciding policy are exceptionally numerous and dispersed.[21] Thus the issue strongly needs coordination as well as posies great difficulties in achieving it. It was an approach by four senior Council of State and Finance Inspectorate officials that led to the appointment in January 1974 of one of them as Director General of Population and Migration with the task of coordination. André Postel-Vinay was then made Junior Minister responsible for coordinating immigration policy by the incoming President Giscard in June 1974. But whereas the minister proposed to deal with the long-term problems of integrating immigrants, the Cabinet meeting of 3 July 1974 only decided to suspend immigration, while his other proposals were rejected by Prime Minister Chirac, leading to Postel-Vinay's resignation.[22]

His successor in a post not much sought after, Paul Dijoud, was able to take advantage of the fact that immigration was not coordinated at the summit by Prime Minister Chirac but by President Giscard, who gave him personal support when necessary. Initially backed up by a weak Directorate of Population and Migration attached to the Ministry of Labour, Dijoud was able to extend his coordinating duties to cover the foreign sources of immigration, as well as organizing the administrative basis for an immigration policy by 1977 when he left office.[23] This coincided with a tougher strategy as unemployment became an increasing obsession, with the new minister being expected to organize—in conjunction with the Interior Minister— the expulsion of foreign workers, among whom Algerians were particularly numerous. However, as we have seen, this policy failed and ministers of quite a different stamp took over responsibility for immigration policy in the 1981 Mauroy Government.

There was no specific junior minister for immigration in the initial Mauroy Government—an oversight—but the need for a coordinator led to the appointment of François Autain as minister 'in charge of immigrants' attached, significantly, not as hitherto to the Minister of Labour but to the Solidarity Minister, Nicole Questiaux. A member of the Council of State, she was determined to pursue a policy based on strict respect for immigrant rights, in contrast with the Giscardian inclination to give expedition priority over legality.[24] However, uncomfortable in her ministerial post, she was no match for Minister of the Interior Defferre, with whom her junior minister had to do unequal battle. An early conflict occurred over the Interior Ministry's powers of deportation, when Autain secured the support of the PS Parliamentary Group only to be outmanoeuvred by Defferre. This was the start of

---

[21] Weil, *La France*, p. 23; cf. 24–5.　　　[22] Ibid., pp. 117–30.　　　[23] Ibid., pp. 133–5, 157.
[24] Ibid., p. 218; cf. 217.

a long guerrilla war.[25] Despite Mitterrand's improvised commitment to regularize illegal immigrants, the Junior Minister (supported by the *cabinets* of the Interior, Foreign, and Labour Ministers) tried in vain to prevent this 'symbolic necessity'.[26] Nevertheless, the President and Prime Minister's staff saw to it that the President's promise was honoured. In the event, 132,000 were 'regularized', providing ammunition for the NF, used to punishing effect in the 1983 local elections.

However, by 1983, just as there was a U-turn in economic policy, so in immigration policy the emphasis switched from regularizing illegals to restricting entry and expulsion. Following a Cabinet meeting adopting the change in priorities, Mitterrand declared that to avoid the growth of xenophobia, 'I must protect the employment of French people'.[27] To carry out this new policy, Georgina Dufoix replaced François Autain. We shall see that she achieved variable results before the adoption in 1984 of the ten-year Green Card, which simplified the task of French administration, improved contacts with the emigrant countries, and satisfied a demand of the immigrant rights movements. However, before we discuss the case studies dealing with the attempted coordination of specific policies, we must describe the administrative and political framework within which they were formulated.

The core of the administrative immigration policy community in France consisted of the Population and Migration Division in the Social Affairs Ministry, the Public Liberties and Regulation Division—especially the sub-division dealing with the expulsion of foreigners—of the Interior Ministry, and the Division of French Citizens Abroad and Foreigners in France of the Foreign Affairs Ministry. Other divisions of these ministries are also involved in the broader immigration policy network, for example the Labour Division and Social Action Division of Social Affairs, and the frontier police for the Interior Ministry. Some fifteen ministries are part of this wider network to be coordinated, notably Justice (dealing with nationality matters), Labour, Housing, Agriculture, Defence (which controls the gendarmerie), Finance, and Cooperation.

The lead coordinator is the Director of the Population and Migration Division, who has substantial freedom of action in the Social Affairs Ministry. He controls the Fund for Social Action that supports immigrant housing and worker training (as well as subsidizing organizations like SOS Racism), the International Migration Office dealing with regularization, as well as the decentralized Social Service for Aid to Immigrants and Refugees. The Prime Minister's *cabinet* provides oversight, while the General Secretariat of the Interministerial Committee (SGCI) deals with EU regulatory harmonization. In the early 1990s, the administrative coordination of immigration policy necessitated weekly meetings of the senior officials concerned, who were more effective at sustaining medium-term policy continuity, despite the propensity of politicians to make changes in response to circumstantial pressures.[28]

The major locus of interdepartmental conflict is between the Social Affairs, Health, and Labour Ministries, concerned primarily with the integration of migrants,

---

[25] Weil, *La France*, pp. 222–4.   [26] Ibid., pp. 226–8; cf. 234–41.   [27] Ibid., p. 263.
[28] Schain, 'Policy-making and defining', pp. 71–2 and Weil, *La France*, Appendix 2.

and the Interior, preoccupied with law and order, supported by Finance, concerned with cost. The Justice Ministry is more ambivalent, torn between the Civil Affairs Division, concerned with nationality issues, and the Criminal and Prisons Divisions, dealing with delinquency. Foreign Affairs tends to side with the Social Affairs-led group because it wishes to promote amicable relations with the countries of origin. As long as there was consensus on the need to recruit foreign workers, the demarcation between Interior (that handled residence permits) and Labour (that issued work permits) did not pose coordination problems. Once this consensus ceased in the late 1970s, ensuing policy inconsistencies led to interdepartmental conflicts that exacerbated those inconsistencies.[29] Coupled with the contrasting background of lower ranking officials—former police officials in Interior and ex-trade unionists in Labour—and the ministerial pecking order choices of senior officials who have graduated from Ecole Nationale d'Administration (ENA), along with their contrasting clienteles, it is not surprising that the administrative immigration policy community finds it difficult to maintain cohesion. Migration control tends to be dominated by Interior, integration by Social Affairs, and international matters, notably according visas, by Foreign Affairs and Cooperation.

The clash between Interior Minister Gaston Defferre and Social Affairs Minister Nicole Questiaux in 1981–82 owed at least as much to the fact that he was Mayor of Marseille (especially exposed to immigration from North Africa) and she was from the Council of State, as to their ministerial portfolios. However, with the Right in power, Interior Minister Charles Pasqua—not distracted as Defferre had been by his pet decentralization reforms, and given a free hand by Prime Minister Chirac—assumed much more uninhibited control, using legislation in 1986 and especially its implementation to enforce strictness. However, he was forced to abandon the provocative Nationality Code Bill in 1987 after an 'immigrant' student was killed by police during the student unrest of November–December 1986. Those most opposed to persisting with the Pasqua proposals included Finance Minister Balladur and Education Minister Monory. Pierre Joxe, his Socialist successor in 1988, was not disposed to repeal the Pasqua legislation, being content to administer it in a more liberal manner. Under pressure from SOS Racism, Mitterrand promised to do so. However, Joxe ensured that the changes in his 1989 Law were in practice minor, despite the President's injunctions, demonstrating a determined minister's power in practice.[30]

Pasqua's return to the Interior Ministry in 1993 was characterized by a spectacular reassertion of repression, with four laws and a constitutional reform being enacted within nine months. Any hope that Simone Veil as Minister of Social and Urban Affairs and Justice Minister Pierre Méhaignerie (who had opposed persisting with the Nationality Code in 1986–87) would exercise a liberal restraint upon Pasqua proved vain. On the pretext of deterring illegal immigration, Pasqua in fact was

---

[29] Giraudon, *Policy Change*, pp. 210–11; cf. 214–15.

[30] Weil, *La France*, pp. 252–4, 294–8, 302–3; cf. Favier and Martin-Roland, iii, pp. 329–34. See also, on the clash between Defferre and Questiaux at the 28 April 1982 Cabinet meeting, Attali, *Verbatim*, i, pp. 323–4. On the 1986–87 battle over the Nationality Code, see Gastaut, pp. 546–59.

seeking to reduce legal immigration by family reunification for foreign students, based upon proposals by senior Interior officials to deal with examples of fraud. There was a modest fall in legal immigration masking an increase in illegal immigration.

There was public opposition to the Pasqua proposal that immigrant children should explicitly declare their wish to acquire French nationality, which was widely regarded as treating 'foreigners' with suspicion and even hostility, reflecting an exclusive rather than inclusive predisposition. The churches' hostility to his legislation prompted him to call on them to stay out of politics.[31] We shall discuss later the 1993 clash with the CC of this stormy petrel, who was to break with the RPR and found his own party in 1998, although the main motive for the split was over EU integration, not French integration policy. By then, Pasqua, the arch protagonist of 'zero immigration', had come around to advocating a mass regularizing of illegal immigrants.

The Interior and Foreign Ministries sometimes clashed over the granting of visas—the latter's responsibility. The Interior officials, considering that French embassies and consulates were too lax in issuing visas, especially to North Africans on family visits to France, tightened up restrictions even on those with visas, requiring an accommodation certificate (grudgingly accorded) from the mayor of the town where visitors would be staying. As a result, in 1988 a third of visitors from the Maghreb holding visas were denied entry. With Joxe as Interior Minister, coordination between Interior and Foreign Affairs improved, the certificates being required before visas were granted, avoiding recourse to turning large numbers back on arrival in France. Joxe had wanted to continue having the right to refuse entry for those with visas but both Rocard and Mitterrand supported Foreign Minister Dumas's objections to giving the police view priority over the consular service.[32] Matters of asylum—discussed later—are largely left by the Foreign Ministry to the French Office for the Protection of Refugees and Stateless Persons (OFPRA).

Cooperation—an independent ministry until 1998—handled local development assistance in the countries of emigration. Thus, in 1992 an interdepartmental group, jointly led by the Development Division in Cooperation and the Population and Migration Division in Social Affairs, promoted a programme in three African countries (Mali, Mauritania, and Senegal), supporting a large number of local micro-projects, linked with aiding immigrants to return to their country of origin. The 1997 Weil Report urged improved coordination with non-governmental bodies and local authorities in development of such cooperation projects.[33]

The Role of the President and Prime Minister

Mitterrand deliberately used the immigration issue to split the Right by provoking the NF Extreme Right, notably by repeatedly proposing giving immigrants the vote in local elections, the subject of one of our case studies. He also, through his *cabinet*,

[31] Gastaut, p. 178; cf. 177–88, 561–7.
[32] Weil, *La France*, p. 342; cf. 337–46; Favier and Martin-Roland, iii, pp. 330–1.
[33] Weil, *Pour une Nouvelle Politique*, pp. 140–4.

encouraged the creation of a predominantly immigrant organization, SOS Racism, in autumn 1984, despite the reservations of the Immigration Minister and more generally of the Socialist Party (PS).[34] Otherwise, Mitterrand was usually content to take a back seat. His successor, Chirac, worried by the NF's success in the presidential and local elections of 1995, left it to his Interior Minister, Jean-Louis Debré, to pursue the repressive Pasqua policies of 1986–88 and 1993–95 with redoubled fervour.

Prime Minister Rocard, in the wake of the Muslim headscarf uproar, sought in vain to promote a cross-party consensus by calling a meeting of all parties other than the NF in 1990, having appointed in December 1989 as head of a High Commission on Integration Marceau Long, who had prepared a moderate and influential report for the Chirac Government on behalf of the Nationality Commission. After envisaging the appointment of an Integration Minister and retreating in the face of the Interior and Education Ministers who feared a loss of power, Rocard appointed an official in Matignon, Hubert Prévot, as secretary general of the Integration Commission.[35] Unfortunately, the two principally concerned detested each other ideologically, Prévot being an advocate of multiculturalism while Long was a traditional champion of the indivisible Republic. So, despite Rocard's good intentions, little was achieved by his attempt to take control and coordinate from Matignon, although seventy pilot urban areas were designated for deconcentrated coordination of government action in locations of extreme deprivation.[36]

However, the tough enforcement of asylum claims under Rocard meant that some 100,000 were in illegal residence and, in May 1991, hundreds of them went on hunger strike. Edith Cresson, who had just replaced Rocard as Prime Minister, appointed the former Secretary General of the Elysée, Jean-Louis Bianco, as Minister of Social Affairs and Integration, with a Junior Minister of Togolese origin, Kofi Yamgnane, who took over Prévot's coordinating role but was too weak to do so effectively. Bianco resolved the immediate problem in the habitual fashion: mass regularization. Meanwhile, Chirac adopted NF language by saying that there was an immigration 'overdose', with their noise and smell. Under pressure to appear tough, Prime Minister Cresson—in a response to a journalist's question on whether she would use charter flights to deport illegal immigrants as Pasqua had done—unwisely said that she would and then stuck obstinately to her remarks despite the uproar at her gaffe. Her ministers refused to support her and at an interministerial meeting on 9 July 1991 she was forced to backtrack. Thereafter, it was downhill all the way. Following this incident, Cresson's unpopularity reached record levels for a Fifth Republic Prime Minister: a satisfaction rate of 18 per cent, with 35 per cent expressing confidence in an opinion poll.[37]

---

[34] Weil, *La France*, p. 292.
[35] Schain, 'The Immigration Debate', p. 186; cf. Favier and Martin-Roland, iii, pp. 340–1, 343–5, 348–50. The Long Report's full title was *Etre Français aujourd'hui et demain: Rapport de la Commission de la Nationalité*, La Documentation Française, 1988, 2 vols.
[36] Wihtol de Wenden, 'Immigrants as Political Actors', p. 92.
[37] Favier and Martin-Roland, iv, pp. 37–45; Schain, 'The Immigration Debate', p. 187.

Balladur was content to leave immigration matters to Pasqua and Juppé to Jean-Louis Debré, so the Ministry of the Interior became the uncontested lead department from 1993 to 1997. There was no longer a junior minister for immigration in the Bérégovoy, Balladur, and Juppé Governments, while Jospin turned to his ministers of the Interior and Justice—Chevènement and Guigou—to legislate along the lines proposed in the Weil Report. We shall discuss the tensions between them later.

Judicial Constraints

Core executives' capacity to impose their will, even when they were able to coordinate their policy intentions, was subject to judicial censure, first from the administrative lawyers of the Council of State and then, less systematically but more decisively, from the CC. During the Giscard presidency, the Council of State struck down a number of administrative decisions inspired by a more restrictive immigration policy. In 1978, 'The Council of State annulled all or part of the measures that it considered most detrimental to human rights in four landmark decisions. By the 1990s alien-related cases made up about 15 per cent of the now more than 10,000 cases a year before the Council', being backed up (when legislation was challenged) by the CC, culminating in the latter's ruling as unconstitutional eight of the 1993 Pasqua provisions on the entry and stay of foreigners.[38] 'Politicization and judicialization coincided, usually sparked by government initiatives to restrict flows.'[39]

The Council of State also had to be consulted on legislation for advice both on its legality and suitability to achieve the objectives pursued. Thus, in 1979 it advanced virtual wrecking amendments to the proposed Bonnet Law, regarded as against Republican tradition (of which it esteemed itself the guardian) and violating international agreements, whose political and diplomatic costs exceeded its purported employment benefits. Although the Council of State's advice is confidential, it is usually leaked to senior officials and parliamentarians and on this—as on other occasions—contributed to a retreat by President Giscard and his ministers. It 'demonstrated the ability of the Rule of Law State (*l'Etat de droit*) to resist the orders and decisions of the republican monarch . . . even when he can, in principle, rely upon the partial support of public opinion. Obstruction by internal (administrative) decision-makers, mobilised by the values of the Rule of Law State and the Council of State's supervisory role, were decisive.'[40]

President Mitterrand had in 1985 appointed Justice Minister Robert Badinter to preside over the CC as a watchdog on the actions of a future right-wing government. In 1993 (the PS and Communist members of parliament having referred the law to it) the Council's adverse decision on the Pasqua legislation restricting the rights of

[38] Giraudon, 'Citizenship Rights', pp. 298–9.   [39] Ibid., p. 300.

[40] Weil, *La France*, p. 210; cf. 184–93, 195–6, 311, 448–50, 485. More generally, see V. Wright, 'The Fifth Republic: From the *Droit de l'Etat* to the *Etat de droit*?', in Robert Elgie (ed.), *The Changing French Political System*, London, Cass, 2000, pp. 92–119.

immigrants led to a politico-juridical trial of strength that confronted the core executives with a major crisis. The most controversial of the eight annulments concerned the restriction on the right of asylum, recognized by the Preamble to the 1946 Constitution which declared that 'any person persecuted for action in support of freedom has the right of asylum on the Republic's territory'. Pasqua's immediate response was to attack the CC's 6:3 left-wing majority for preventing the Balladur Government from implementing its policy.[41] The pretext for a constitutional amendment (ironic, coming from the 'sovereignist' Pasqua) was that the Schengen agreement (to be discussed later) precluded the possibility of France granting asylum if one of the other signatory countries had rejected the request.

For three months President Mitterrand and Prime Minister Balladur sought to resolve the conflict between them amicably, the President rejecting the proposed constitutional amendment, which Interior Minister Pasqua wanted to organize by referendum to further politicize the issue. Informal consultations with Badinter established that the CC stood firm. Mitterrand decided—perhaps wrongly—that he could not refuse outright the request for a constitutional amendment. Concerned that neither of them should emerge as the victor over the other from the affair, the President and Prime Minister agreed to ask the Council of State for its view on a proposed one article constitutional amendment, whose formulation required two weeks of hard bargaining. Finally, they settled on 'The authorities of the Republic still have the right to grant asylum to any persecuted foreigner', as suggested by Mitterrand.

To placate his supporters, Balladur criticized the CC for basing its judgements anachronistically on general philosophical and political principles of earlier periods, rather than legal principles. Badinter regarded this as a challenge to the very principle of constitutional review and responded with an article in *Le Monde* on 22 November entitled 'Power and Countervailing Power'. The Prime Minister's *directeur de cabinet* then complained to his presidential opposite number that Badinter had overstepped his duty of discretion. After meetings with Balladur and Badinter, Mitterrand issued a communiqué calling on both of them to cease polemics on the CC's role and decisions, privately dismissing their remarks as gesticulations aimed at public opinion.[42] The preservation of cohabitation had been achieved by close coordination between the staffs of President and Prime Minister at the price of a presidential concession and the reassertion of the democratic principle that a government backed by a large parliamentary majority could have the last word in confrontation with an unelected CC.

The European Court of Human Rights has had a real but limited legal basis for protecting non-nationals, notably in considering family ties in deportations and residence permit cases, as well as expulsion or extradition to countries guilty of

---

[41] Favier and Martin-Roland, iv, p. 434. See also A. Stone, 'Constitutional Politics and Malaise in France' in Keeler and Schain (eds.), *Chirac's Challenge*, pp. 71–3, 76–7.

[42] Favier and Martin-Roland, iv, p. 433–9 on this whole episode. See also G. Carcassonne, 'Amendments to the French Constitution: One Surprise After Another', in Elgie (ed.), *The Changing French Political System*, p. 80.

inhuman treatment. France did not allow individual petition until 1981 and only in 1988 did the Council of State—jealous of its own role in defending foreigner rights— recognize the applicability of the European Convention of Human Rights. However, in France as elsewhere, 'national policy-makers do not consider all provisions for foreigners as rights *per se* but simply as benefits. Their decisions thus obey a different logic, based on economic calculation, interest group pressure, or a desire to diminish the attractiveness of immigration.'[43] However, the October 1997 Amsterdam Treaty's article 6, by proclaiming that the EU is 'founded' *inter alia* on 'respect for human rights', opened the way for frequent legal proceedings relating to the application of migration policies, a prospect that was probably not foreseen by its signatory states.

The Constraints of Group Pressures and Public Opinion

The core executives in the 1980s no longer decided immigration policy in seclusion but were confronted by external minority social movements and mass public opinion, both of which were responding in no small measure to NF propaganda. While the active minorities—whether idealistic cause groups or immigrant interest groups— were particularly conspicuous phenomena in France, they were arguably far less important as a contextual constraint than the passive views of the mass public as recorded by the opinion polls. This may have been due to the fact that the largest of them, SOS Racism, was in the mid-1980s coopted by the PS, in its effort to control the propensity to urban violence of some of the local associations of second gen- eration immigrants. It was feared that this would shift voters towards the Extreme Right, although it would have the advantage of splitting the right-wing vote. However, by the mid-1990s, the NF was the party winning the largest number of working-class votes, so it was also hurting the Left as it exploited the contradictions in an immigration policy that sought to be both restrictive and integrative.

The Mauroy Government having granted freedom of association to the immig- rant communities, President Mitterrand and two PS factions covertly promoted both SOS Racism and France Plus, which were active from 1985. SOS Racism (in whose creation the former *gauchiste* and future PS deputy Julien Dray played a key role, although the leader was Harlem Désir) was the most successful at organizing anti-NF mass demonstrations, especially of the young. It attracted estimated crowds of 500,000 in 1985, 200,000 in 1986, 250,000 in 1987, and 300,000 in 1988 to meetings in Paris. It was particularly effective in the use of the mass media, pop- ularizing the slogan 'Hands off my mate' to emphasize the solidarity between the heterogeneous movements that it sought to mobilize, as well as reaching those that did not attend mass meetings. France Plus concentrated more upon promoting immigrant assimilation by persuading them to apply for naturalization and then to vote and stand as candidates.

---

[43] Giraudon, 'Citizenship Rights', p. 285; cf. 283–4. However, there is an increasing realization that the implications of a commitment to human rights will require a less pragmatic approach. See the Quermonne Report, *The European Union in pursuit of legitimate and effective institutions*, National Planning Office, 1999, ch. 4, especially pp. 90–1, 116.

Both organizations relied upon substantial public subsidies from the Fund for Social Action, as did some 5,000 local immigrant associations (e.g. in 1997 over half the income of SOS Racism came from government sources). However, the attempt by Dray to unite these movements under the leadership of SOS Racism failed and they remained an 'informal network of associations, committees, and voluntary groupings', coming together in response to particular events, such as the repressive 1996 Debré Bill which promised to criminalize anyone accommodating an illegal immigrant.[44] More generally, the appeal to human rights and active citizenship, recalling the aspirations of the French Revolution, drew into the pro-immigrant campaigns organizations such as the League of the Rights of Man and the Movement against Racism and for Friendship between Peoples, which were aligned with the Left on issues like voting rights for immigrants in local elections (discussed later).

While public sympathy could be aroused by hunger strikers violently dislodged from a church by police in 1996 on the orders of Interior Minister Debré, public opinion on immigration issues was much more divided and often hostile to foreigners. This led left-wing governments to adopt equivocal attitudes, both in their policy declarations and actions, as ideological predispositions and electoral considerations collided. However, the 1986–88 Chirac Government's effort to placate the xenophobes were received with scepticism. From June 1986, when opinion on its immigrant policy was almost equally divided between approval (35 per cent), disapproval (34 per cent), and no view (31 per cent), support had declined by October 1987 to 28 per cent approval, 47 per cent disapproval, and 25 per cent with no view. When asked to compare the previous Socialist government's policy on immigration with that of the Chirac Government, 20 per cent preferred that of the Fabius Government, 24 per cent the Chirac Government, 41 per cent neither, with 15 per cent expressing no view.[45] So, the advantage of the mainstream Right was not great.

The annual opinion surveys on behalf of the National Consultative Commission of the Rights of Man (a body officially attached to the Prime Minister's Office) show a significant decline in racism over the 1990s, but 38 per cent of the French were second only to the Belgians in willingness to admit being racist in 1998. Although the numbers of those who said that there were too many Arabs in France declined from 76 per cent in 1990 to 56 per cent in 1997, while hostility to blacks fell from 46 to 27 per cent, these attitudes clearly extended well beyond support for the NF. Thus, 88 per cent rejected allowing the Muslim headscarf to be worn in school. Those totally opposed to giving asylum to refugees fell between 1990 and 1997 from 40 to

---

[44] S. Waters, 'New Social Movement Politics in France: The Rise of Civic Forms of Mobilisation', *West European Politics*, XXI(3), July 1998, p. 182; cf. 170–86. See also P. Fysh, 'The Failure of Anti-Racist Movements in France, 1981–1995' in M. Maclean (ed.), *The Mitterrand Years*, Macmillan, 1998, pp. 201–4. On SOS Racism see the contrasting accounts by H. Désir, *Touche pas à mon pote*, Paris, Grasset, 1985; J. Dray, *SOS génération*, Paris, Ramsay, 1987 and S. Malik, *Histoire secrète de SOS Racisme*, Paris, A. Michel, 1990.

[45] SOFRES, *L'Etat de l'Opinion*, Paris, Seuil, 1988, pp. 147, 154. When asked in May 1987 whether they were shocked at the idea of sending away all immigrant workers because of unemployment, 57 per cent said they were not shocked as against 35 per cent who were. Even among PS voters, opinions were equally divided (ibid., p. 180).

24 per cent, while those willing to give the vote in local elections rose from 35 to 52 per cent.[46] However, the 1999 survey showed a partial reversal of the earlier trend, with a hardening of anti-immigrant attitudes, 32 per cent calling for a complete end to asylum for refugees.[47] While most French people thought that immigration was motivated primarily by economic considerations, the gap between those who believed that immigrant workers were more of a burden than a benefit for the French economy fell from 20 per cent (54 to 34) in 1990 to 3 per cent (45 to 42) in 1998.[48] Such were the changing constraints of public opinion for which core executives had to make allowance in taking decisions on immigration policy. We turn now to the case studies to assess the efforts at coordination of core executive attempts to grapple with the issues raised by immigration policy.

CONTROLLING ILLEGAL IMMIGRATION: THE CASE OF ASYLUM POLICY

In November 1989, Prime Minister Rocard declared in a TV interview that while France should continue to offer 'political asylum . . . it could not be a haven for all the world's misery', so it would reinforce its attempts to control illegal immigration.[49] These had proved ineffective for the previous fifteen years, since the door had been formally closed to immigrant workers. Asylum requests escalated because they were a way of legally entering France, peaking in 1989 when the number was thirty times higher than in 1974.

After 1974, the increase of applicants often resulted in procedural delays of three to four years. The French authorities were often reluctant to expel an asylum seeker who had lived and worked for years in France. Also, children born in France while the asylum request was processed rendered very sensitive any prospect of deportation. The status of asylum seeker had become de facto a popular channel for labour immigration, since it entailed privileges never granted to illegal immigrants who had not applied for refugee status. Moreover, employers were aware of loopholes in the system and informed potential immigrants about the possibility to work legally as long as their asylum application was not rejected.

To prevent the abuse of the 1951 Geneva Convention (intended to protect those suffering persecution) for economic motives and to avoid the resulting costs, the Rocard Government speeded up the examination of applications for refugee

---

[46] R. Cayrol, 'La société française reste taraudée par le racisme', *Le Monde*, 2 July 1998, p. 14; cf. 15 for European comparisons and also *Le Monde*, 3 April 1996, showing 33 per cent approving the NF's immigration views.

[47] *Le Monde*, 16 March 2000, report based on *La lutte contre le racisme et la xénophobie*, La Documentation française, 2000.

[48] *Le Monde*, 25 March 1999, p. 12, summarizing the 1999 report of National Consultative Commission of the Rights of Man. In May 2000, 59 per cent of the French thought there were 'too many immigrants in France', the same in as May 1997 but far fewer than the 74 per cent in May 1995. N. Meyer, 'Les idées de l'extrême droite progressent-elles vraiment'?, *Le Monde*, 2 June 2000.

[49] Quoted in Favier and Martin-Roland, iii, p. 340.

status by the OFPRA and deprived applicants of the right to work. As a result, asylum applications fell from some 61,000 in 1989 to 27,564 in 1993 and 17,405 in 1996.[50]

The ground for the 1989 changes had been prepared by a circular in November 1983, with the establishment of twenty-three priority coordinating committees in *départements* to facilitate the detection and punishment of illegal alien employment because of the ineffectiveness of employer sanctions. 'In the late 1970s a lack of coordination among various agencies charged with enforcement responsibilities against illegal alien employment constituted an important barrier. Information gathered by one service would not or could not be shared with another concerned service, and the limited personnel and other resources committed to enforcement of laws prohibiting illegal employment of aliens were thus ineffectively utilised.'[51] So a March 1986 decree created interagency committees to facilitate enforcement and by 1987 two-thirds of French *départements* had established them, while most of the rest had set up informal committees. In 1989, the Interministry Liaison Committee to Combat Manpower Trafficking had its remit widened to cover the whole underground economy and was renamed to include undeclared employment.[52] However, unauthorized entry was being inexorably stimulated by forces beyond the French government's control: demographic pressures, great disparities in wages and life chances, ethnic and political conflicts. They engendered a supply to meet French employer demand.

The 1989–90 reforms speeded up the procedure for dealing with would-be political refugees by nearly tripling the budget of OFPRA and the appeals body, the former dealing with eligibility within two months, plus a further six months for appeal. A fast-track procedure ensures that 'manifestly unfounded' applications are quickly rejected. In 1988, OFPRA processed 25,000 applications and 78,000 in 1991. While in 1976 only 4 per cent of applications were rejected, by 1990 the figure had increased to 85 per cent.[53] A September 1991 circular abolished work permits for asylum seekers, who were no longer entitled to receive welfare benefits, while reception centres thereafter provided only immediate help.

All this marked a reversal of policy: asylum seekers were no longer so much potential *bona fide* refugees as surreptitious seekers of employment, a policy enforced by the Cresson Government and extended by the Pasqua Law of 1993. The Bérégovoy Government had, in compliance with the Schengen Agreement (discussed later), meanwhile created transit areas in airports and seaports to detain asylum seekers while their applications were being processed. As part of this restrictive policy, the number of visas granted to Algerians fell from about 800,000 in 1989 to 100,000 in

[50] Information from a working paper by Patrick Weil. More generally, see C. Norek and F. Doumic-Doublet, *Le Droit d'Asile en France*, Paris, PUF, 1989.

[51] M. Miller, 'Towards Understanding State Capacity to Prevent Unwanted Migrations: Employer Sanctions Enforcement in France, 1975–1990', *West European Politics*, XVII(2), April 1994, pp. 161–2.

[52] Ibid., p. 146.

[53] C. Wihtol de Wenden, 'The French Response to the Asylum Seeker Influx, 1980–93', *The Annals of the American Academy of Political and Social Sciences*, 534, July 1994, p. 85.

1994, with less spectacular falls for Moroccans and Tunisians.[54] In the wake of the Kosovo crisis of 1999, French public opinion became more sympathetic towards asylum seekers generally but preferred the persecuted to be welcomed only as a last resort. However, as we shall see, far more significant was the decision of the Jospin Government to implement the 1997 Weil Report by adopting a more liberal and selective visa policy.

In an influential 1995 paper calling 'For a New Immigration Policy', Patrick Weil had earlier argued that the number of illegal immigrants was always overestimated. This was partly because they could not, by definition, be counted. Furthermore, many left whilst others arrived. In 1981, whereas the number of illegals was estimated at 300,000, only 132,000 were eventually identified and regularized. Public perception, which conflated legal and illegal immigration, exaggerated the few hundred fraudulent marriages and non-deported foreign delinquents; when added to the concentration in certain urban areas of high unemployment and a distinctive ethnic character, the scale of hostility to immigrants bore little relation to reality.[55] The statistics collected by the Interior Ministry of residential permits granted far exceeded those of the International Migration Office (90,000 compared to 50,000 in 1995) because it included EU citizens. Such disparities encouraged confused polemics. A statistical working party of the High Council of Integration, chaired by Patrick Weil, recommended in its report for 1998 that all ministries should calculate on the same basis, excluding the naturalized and evaluating the numbers who had left France.[56]

A FALTERING STEP TOWARDS FULL CITIZENSHIP STATUS: THE RIGHT TO VOTE IN LOCAL ELECTIONS

While granting welfare benefits to non-citizens may be politically controversial, according the right to vote—even in local elections—necessitates constitutional reform. Both of these rights were promised in his presidential election proposal 80 by Mitterrand in 1981, the PS having (anticipated by the splinter PSU) championed immigrant voting rights from 1977, while the Parti Communiste Français (PCF) opposed them until 1985.[57] As local residents, immigrants paid taxes and were entitled to expect local authorities to attend to their needs, so the Left argued. Raising the issue when such reform was either not possible or intended smacked either of gesture politics or Machiavellian manoeuvre. Since 1978, the French Left has repeatedly sought to place the matter on the political agenda but it has never been a Socialist-led government priority. This became clear in July 1981 when it was necessary to select and sometimes redefine the 110 pre-electoral promises made by the presidential candidate. However, an incautious impromptu allusion in a speech by External

---

[54] *Le Monde*, 3 February 1995, p. 11. [55] Weil, *Pour une Nouvelle Politique*, p. 18.
[56] *Le Monde*, 13 January 2000; cf. *Le Monde*, 24 October 1996.
[57] Gastaut, pp. 166, 234–7, 525. In December 1978 the PS proposed a private member's bill suggesting local immigrant suffrage prior to incorporating it into the PS electoral programme.

Affairs Minister Cheysson on 9 August 1981, on returning from an official visit to Algeria, propelled the issue onto the government's agenda.

'The French Government is very seriously considering giving immigrants the right to vote in local elections.... Their participation in the 1983 local elections will definitely have an impact on the results in the large towns and their suburbs, especially in Paris.'[58] (This proved prophetic, not in increasing the PS vote but that of the NF!) It was immediately rejected by Chirac (who had in 1979 supported the idea but he frequently changed his views as circumstances required) on the ground that voting rights were restricted to French citizens. The hostility of public opinion, reflected in letters and telephone calls, as well as in an opinion poll which showed 35 per cent in favour, 58 per cent against, and 7 per cent of no opinion, led President Mitterrand to beat a tactical retreat. It was left to Immigration Junior Minister Autain to announce on 12 August 1981 that the reform was not among the Mauroy Government's priorities.[59]

However, Autain went beyond his remit by declaring that the local voting rights reform was 'a very long term objective' and would certainly not be adopted before the 1983 local elections. While it achieved the purpose of calming public opinion, he was curtly asked for an explanation by Prime Minister Mauroy. He replied that, apart from the political fallout of the proposal, it would require amendment of article 3 of the Constitution which restricted the exercise of national sovereignty to French citizens. Furthermore, as the Senate was indirectly elected by local councillors (articles 24 and 72) and as the hostile Senate's agreement would be necessary for constitutional amendments, defeat was certain.[60] Thus, both the Foreign Minister initially and the Immigration Minister a few days later in August 1981 had presented the President and Prime Minister with a *fait accompli*...and got away with it, although the Elysée and Matignon staff were both annoyed at having been unable to coordinate communication of a collective view on the issue.

Public opinion remained clearly opposed to dissociating even local voting from full membership of the national community. Table 8.1 shows consistent opposition of French public opinion to according voting rights to immigrants even in local elections, much less parliamentary or presidential elections. The NF, thanks to the communication political skills of its leader Le Pen, had made a breakthrough in the 1983 local and 1984 European elections by concentrating upon the immigration issue. To promote a division on the Right, Mitterrand deliberately encouraged its most anti-immigrant and nationalist supporters to swing to the NF by returning to the issue in April 1985. He declared at a Congress of the League of the Rights of Man that, while he favoured giving immigrants a local vote, the time was not ripe to implement it.[61] In his *Letter to All the French* prior to the 1988 presidential election,

---

[58] Quoted in Weil, *La France*, pp. 243–4. This case study draws on a paper by Patrick Weil.
[59] Ibid., pp. 245–7. The BVA poll of 12–13 August 1981 was published in *Paris Match*, No. 1863 of 26 August 1981. See also Favier and Martin-Roland, i, p. 171 for Mauroy's testimony.
[60] Weil, *La France*, pp. 247–50.
[61] Weil, *La France*, pp. 292–3; cf. 302, 473 and *Libération*, 22 April 1985, p. 3.

Table 8.1 *Public attitudes towards immigrant voting rights in local elections, 1981–94 (%)*

	January 1981	November 1984	January 1988	March 1990	June 1994
For	32	21	32	33	34
Against	60	74	60	59	61
No opinion	8	5	8	8	5

Source: adapted and translated from Y. Gastaut, *L'immigration et l'opinion*, op. cit., pp. 531–2, which gives details of twenty-eight polls taken in this period. All those quoted here are from SOFRES.

he repeated both his personal support for the principle and regret that a large majority of public opinion was opposed, preventing him enacting it.

In May 1989, when Prime Minister Rocard was seeking to achieve a cross-party consensus on immigration policy, he proposed abandoning the proposal of local voting rights in exchange for the Right dropping its intention to reform the Nationality Code. He did so despite the bitter opposition of the immigrant rights movements and of PS leaders such as Pierre Mauroy.[62] Mitterrand was furious at this 'ideological retreat' and insisted that the commitment should not last beyond the duration of the legislature.[63] In the event, as we have seen, the attempt at a compromise fell through. Ten years later, with the Left back in power, the 'Red Rag' issue was raised once again, this time by the Communist and Green components of the 'Plural Left'. It received the support of the former Prime Minister, then President of the National Assembly and future Finance Minister, Laurent Fabius, while Interior Minister Chevènement agreed that, after ten years' residence, holders of a residence permit should have the right to vote locally. Prime Minister Jospin, knowing that the necessary constitutional amendment would not then be carried, played down the issue, which could not become a realistic prospect until and if he was elected President in 2002. However, the Green Party-sponsored private member's bill to give the local vote to an estimated two million non-EU foreigners was adopted in the National Assembly in May 2000, without any hope of going further. Prime Minister Jospin had already declared in January 2000: 'I do not play with words. All that is over. So, although I have long since regarded this reform as logical, I will only advocate it when it is feasible.'[64] However, public opinion was being prepared in advance.

The whole issue has been complicated by citizenship rights, involving voting and standing for election to the European Parliament. In 1989 the French government began working out its position at a meeting of the SGCI on 24 March.[65] The Justice and European Affairs representatives favoured this change, with Interior opposed and the Foreign Ministry anxious that EU citizens should not be entitled to become mayors because of their state administrative functions. European Affairs Minister

[62] Gastaut, pp. 541–4.
[63] Testimony of SGP Bianco, quoted in Favier and Martin-Roland, iii, pp. 348–9.
[64] Reports in *Le Monde*, 30 April 2000, p. 7, cf. 25 and 27 November 1999.
[65] This paragraph is largely based on the Mitterrand Archives, Holleville file.

Guigou wrote to Mitterrand that she had been coordinating the views of the ministries concerned and all but Justice agreed that article 3 of the French Constitution would need to be amended, although the CC should be unofficially consulted in advance. While Justice argued that local elections did not affect national sovereignty, the Interior and Foreign Ministries were more worried about public opinion. To meet this latter problem, a Committee for the Extension of the Right to Vote to Europeans was launched on 22 November 1989 by a Club 92.

The February 1992 Maastricht Treaty of European Union added a new article 8 to the Rome Treaty giving EU citizens the right to vote and stand in local and EU elections. This required amendment of the French Constitution (article 88-3) in June 1992 which contradicted articles 3, 24, and 72 of the Constitution. However, Maastricht, by restricting local voting to EU citizens, rendered more difficult rather than easier its extension to non-EU immigrants. Meanwhile, in France EU citizens were only able to exercise their vote for the first time in the 1999 European elections and the 2001 local elections but few bothered to do so.

THE PARTIAL EUROPEANIZATION OF IMMIGRANT POLICY

Initially, the European Economic Community only provided for the free movement of workers and it was solely as a consequence of the mid-1980s creation of a single market that the need to coordinate immigration policy was officially acknowledged. Member state reluctance to consider the implications of European integration for nationality and immigration policy was also partly overcome by decisions of the European Court of Justice.

The initial response was intergovernmental, with the creation of an *ad hoc* Working Group on Immigration in 1986, following the 1985 Schengen Agreement to speed up scrapping border controls, to which we shall turn shortly. More generally, the demise of the Communist regimes of central and eastern Europe augmented the worldwide immigration pressures, compelling EU governments 'to inch their way towards an ever closer union of their immigration policies'.[66] In 1988, the Council of Ministers set up a group of national coordinators which reported in 1989 that 'over 80 initiatives or pieces of legislation were needed to achieve free movement of people within the EC', four-fifths of which were still the responsibility of national governments.[67] However, the 1990 Dublin Convention on Asylum provided that, to avoid multiple applications, asylum decisions would be made by the first country to receive one.

Less success was achieved by the 1991 External Frontiers Convention because ratification was delayed owing to a Spanish–UK quarrel over Gibraltar.[68] This

[66] A. Butt Philip, 'European Union Immigration Policy: Phantom, Fantasy or Fact?', *West European Politics*, XVII(2), April 1994, 174; cf. 172–5.

[67] Ibid., p. 173. For an organization chart of the French ministries involved in EU working parties dealing with immigration—notably Interior, Justice, and Social Affairs, see ENA, *Le Travail Gouvernemental*, ii, p. 794.   [68] Butt-Philip, p. 176.

demonstration of the limitations of intergovernmentalism was compounded by increasing public suspicion that sensitive decisions were being taken by people who were not accountable to either the European Parliament or to their national parliament. The 1997 Amsterdam EU Treaty switched immigration from the intergovernmental 'third pillar' to the supranational 'first pillar', which will detach it somewhat from national control.

The gatekeeper role of national governments in deterring entry and dealing with the consequences of their failure has shifted immigration regulatory tasks not merely to the EU but externally to foreign states and airlines, as well as internally to employer organizations and non-governmental organizations. The interdependence of states in seeking to control migration has created strong incentives to coordination not merely with other governments but with private bodies who become de facto regulators. This has been dubbed '"remote control" immigration policy' in which EU member states rely on 'carriers to serve as immigration officers' in accordance with the 1990 Supplementation Agreement of the Schengen Convention.[69] In combination with recourse to local authorities, such as we have seen occurred in France when mayors decided whether housing certificates could be issued, the potential for conflict between central and local officials, the police and the judiciary is augmented, increasing the incentive to 'privatise' and externalize immigration control.

The Schengen Treaty of 14 June 1985 created a common external border between the signatory states—initially France, Germany, and the Benelux—which others subsequently joined. This required harmonization of visa and deportation policies, which was not settled until June 1990, and became operative in March 1995. However, the main problems of coordination had been interdepartmental. In France, a senior Interior Ministry official declared at the end of 1989 that ' "the interministerial conflicts were and still are considerable, terrible, especially when the political leaders totally lost interest" and attributed it [*sic*] to traditional rivalries and a different assessment of the issues at stake. The Ministry of Foreign Affairs was adamant that non-Schengen countries did not feel offended; the Ministry of Justice insisted on the legal difficulties that the agreement entailed; the Ministry of the Interior pushed for a very strict formulation on controls.'[70] Worries about laxity in the Netherlands over soft drugs led Balladur and his European Affairs Minister in 1993 to suggest indefinite postponement of the Treaty's implementation, and in July 1995 President Chirac temporarily suspended the agreement.

Surrounded as it is by other Schengen countries, France has the strongest geographical interest in 'better international coordination [which] is much more effective than police action'.[71] However, the two are related, with the development of Europol and of SIS (Schengen Information System), a computerized database facilitating consular cooperation to avoid fraudulent visa applications, as part of the EU process of shifting borders outward.

---

[69] G. Lahav, 'Immigration and the State: Devolution and Privatisation of Immigration Control in the EU', *Journal of Ethnic and Migration Studies*, XXIV(4), October 1998, 685; cf. 681–7.

[70] V. Giraudon, *Policy Change*, p. 209.   [71] P. Weil, *Pour une Nouvelle Politique*, p. 23; cf. 21–2.

THE OBSTACLE-STREWN ROAD TO CONSENSUS

The second half of the 1990s witnessed a stark contrast between the adversarial approach of Jean-Louis Debré, Interior Minister in the 1995–97 Juppé Government, and the consensual approach of the Interior Minister in the Jospin Government from 1997, Jean-Pierre Chevènement. While Debré readily responded to intense pressure from the RPR in the National Assembly, Chevènement was helped to restrain the PS pressure to reverse both the 1993 Pasqua and the 1997 Debré Immigration Laws thanks to the Weil Report which Jospin commissioned on 1 July 1997, shortly after taking office.

The National Assembly having set up a committee of inquiry into illegal immigration in autumn 1995 at the request of the most repressive elements in the RPR parliamentary party, Debré called on his officials to prepare a draft bill along the lines that his political friends were likely to recommend. When he presented his proposals to an interministerial meeting on 21 March 1996, he knew that he would have to deal with the substantive reservations of the Ministers of Justice and Social Affairs. Prime Minister Juppé preferred to adopt lower profile regulation rather than legislation and the President's staff advised against legislation.

At a meeting on 13 June 1996, Juppé decided to separate the proposals on illegal immigration from integration, confiding the latter to the Justice Minister, who had declared that he saw 'no political benefit in a new law on immigration'.[72] However, at an Elysée meeting on 15 July, at which the Prime Minister, Interior Minister, Justice Minister, and SGP were present, President Chirac ruled out a new immigration law as politically too risky, fearing a hostile demonstration from young opponents such as led to a student death ten years previously. Illegal immigration was to be dealt with by Social Affairs, signalling defeat for Debré and the apparent frustration of months of preparatory work. Secretary General of Government (SGG) Jean-Marc Sauvé, who had drafted the Pasqua Law, stressed the danger of Debré's proposals being ruled unconstitutional and advocated adapting and rigorously implementing existing legislation which had achieved widespread acceptance.

Debré was to retrieve his lead role thanks to help from an unexpected quarter. Three hundred African illegal immigrants had been occupying the St Bernard Church in the north of Paris from 28 June 1996 but President Chirac had reassured the President of SOS Racism on 1 August that their cases would be re-examined sympathetically as a way of ending a hunger strike by ten of them. However, on 23 August Debré ordered the police to break in and evacuate the church, arguing that the affair had demonstrated the ineffectiveness of the Pasqua Law and was playing into the hands of the NF. Taking advantage of reinvigorated party pressure— from the Union Pour la Démocratie Française (UDF) as well as the RPR—Debré renewed his demand for legislation. At an interministerial meeting on 11 September

---

[72] Quoted in an excellent, in-depth article in *Le Monde*, 13 May 1997, p. 10, by Philippe Bernard and Nathaniel Herzberg, on which this discussion of the gestation of the Debré Law of 1997 has drawn. See also *Le Monde*, 24 and 30 March, 4, 18, 19, and 25 April, 1996.

Juppé agreed to this because 'the political context had changed', a view endorsed by President Chirac.[73]

Ignoring a Council of State objection to his proposals on housing certificates as a threat to the liberty and private life of those offering immigrants accommodation, at the Cabinet meeting on 6 November 1996, Debré secured agreement to proposals, which were carried into law on 25 April 1997, despite a mass demonstration in Paris on 22 February. The CC struck down the provision restricting the renewal of the ten-year resident's card. However, the Debré Law was quickly overtaken by the dissolution of the Assembly and the return of a left-wing majority. Would the highly charged adversarial atmosphere surrounding the immigration issue lead to a repeal of the Pasqua and Debré Laws?

In his letter of 1 July 1997, asking Patrick Weil to report within a month on French immigration and integration policy, Prime Minister Jospin stated that too many successive improvisations—the Debré Law being the twenty-fourth amendment of the basic 1945 ordinance—had made French legislation too inconsistent and incomprehensible.[74] Weil's task involved consulting the ministries concerned but he insisted on a personal mission rather than chairing a commission to give himself a strong coordinating role. Furthermore, he turned down a request from Interior Minister Chevènement to join his *cabinet*, protecting the independence of his supraministerial role from attempts to control him, but Chevènement's support was crucial to his appointment by Jospin. (Weil had once led the young branch of Chevènement's CERES faction of the PS.) He had been chosen not merely because of his expertise and previous PS links but because Pierre Moscovici, in charge of research for the PS, had asked him to undertake a general study of the immigration issue prior to the 1997 election, his Saint-Simon Foundation Paper of November 1995 being highly regarded. He was informally told that he need not adopt the PS line of abrogating the Pasqua and Debré Laws in his pursuit of a new consensus that would avoid the mainstream Right aligning itself with the NF.[75]

In his 1995 'For a New Immigration Policy' paper, Weil indicated that four state strategies had been available in the attempt to control immigration: discouragement, notably by the selective granting of visas; international cooperation with the countries from which immigrants came; police repression and expulsion; economic prevention by labour market action to dissuade employers from employing illegal immigrants. In the vain pursuit of entirely halting immigration, repression had been emphasized at the expense of the other strategies, dealing with its effects rather than its causes.[76] He concluded his paper by stating the political need to seize the opportunity

[73] Ibid., 13 May 1997, p. 11; cf. *Le Monde*, 18 December 1996. President Chirac, irritated by what he regarded as the Council of State's excessively conciliatory attitude towards the wearing of the Islamic headscarf in school, favoured legislation to prohibit it but nothing was done. *Le Monde*, 5 December 1996, p. 10.

[74] Preface to P. Weil, *Mission d'étude*. Twenty of these amendments had occurred in the previous twenty-three years (ibid., p. 46).

[75] The background information on his appointment is based on an interview with Patrick Weil.

[76] Weil, *Pour une Nouvelle Politique*, p. 19.

afforded by the recognition of the problems and the availability of policy solutions to the problems. 'When a window opens, often after an election, it is necessary for one or more entrepreneurs to show that they can link problems and solutions', without which there would be no reform and 'the window of opportunity will close for an indefinite period'.[77]

What was missing in 1995 was a suitable political decision-maker. 'To carry out a policy adapted to the complexity of the immigration problem, it is necessary to coordinate and activate those responsible in the dispersed Foreign, Cooperation, Justice, Interior, Social Affairs and Labour, Finance ministries and others. Since no ministry has sufficient legitimacy to undertake this, it is the Prime Minister or a ministry or body directly linked to him, that should take it on.'[78] The pertinence of his diagnosis was acknowledged twenty months later when Prime Minister Jospin designated him to coordinate an immigration policy linking problems and solutions. Weil (who had been appointed a member of the High Council on Immigration in December 1996) was to prove equal to this entrepreneurial challenge: achieving a 'republican synthesis' capable of winning the support of both the political class and public opinion.

Although he had recruited to his *Mission* twelve senior officials and six experts to help him (some of the younger ones former students of his at Sciences Po), it was very much a personal report. While he appealed to traditional principles, such as nationality based upon place of birth (*jus soli*) against that of blood (*jus sanguinis*), his approach was inductive, bottom-up, based upon practical realities. It was this that allowed him to win over those who dealt with immigration on a day-to-day basis, because they appreciated that he had understood their problems and was not seeking to impose a priori, ideological nostrums. However, the Prime Minister's support was vital and Weil kept in close touch with the Interior and Immigration members of Jospin's *cabinet*. He also received constitutional advice from Sauvé, who had prepared the Pasqua Law and was now SGG. In the event, neither of the Chevènement and Guigou Laws inspired by Weil's Report encountered CC censure.

Promptly, on 31 July 1997, Weil presented two joint reports: 'On the application of the principle of place of birth for the attribution of French nationality' and 'For a just and effective immigration policy'. Recalling the two centuries of French nationality history, in which socialization through education and military service (for men) assimilated those that a low birth rate additionally rendered desirable acquisitions, Weil fixed upon the 1889 Law, which restored place of birth as the main criterion, which it had already been before the Revolution. What had been accorded to those who were subject to the monarch's authority by virtue of living in his kingdom had become the touchstone of the republican tradition in deciding nationality.[79] However, while recommending implicitly a return to the pre-1993 automatic acquisition of French

---

[77] Ibid., p. 25.　　　[78] Ibid., p. 26.

[79] Weil, *Mission d'étude*, p. 19; cf. 13–20, 24–5. More generally, see W. R. Brubaker, *Citizenship and Nationhood in France and Germany*, Harvard University Press, London, 1992.

nationality subject to residential conditions, he added in a modified form the 'expression of will' to be French requirement instituted in 1993. It became optional, with the right to reject it at 18 years. 'Thus one can no longer be French either unwillingly or unknowingly.'[80] Despite the fears that the Weil proposal would unleash polemics,[81] the shaky previous consensus was reinforced by the Guigou Law. Pragmatism had worked when deftly applied.

Weil's Report on immigration started by placing the issue in historical perspective. 'France has been a country of immigration since the second half of the nineteenth century but until 1945 it did not have an immigration policy.'[82] This raised profound normative issues of national identity and human rights, as well as administrative problems of coordination. 'It involves all ministries, even if four of them have particularly important responsibilities: Interior, Foreign Affairs, Social Affairs, and Justice.'[83] Although there was mainstream agreement not to select migrants by ethnic or national quotas and to integrate them, partisan rhetoric had been adversarial even when claims to reverse policies or achieve zero immigration created confusion and exacerbated rather than satisfying public anxieties. French policy had asserted generous general principles and then enforced so many controls that potentially legal immigrants were transformed by this controlitis into 'paperless' people pursued by the police but infrequently expelled. As Weil said at the end of an interview on his reports: 'within the framework of a few principles . . . a link must be forged between principles and practice. This clarification of approach would make consensus possible.'[84]

Weil's Report stressed that, after 200 interviews, what was striking, in contrast to the acrimonious political debate, was 'the convergence in analysis of all the actors when it was a matter of establishing what did not work and what could be changed to improve French immigration policy'.[85] There was a consensus, ranging from the police, via civil servants, to humanitarian associations, that a repressive control of migratory flows, far from reducing unemployment, would be a threat to French workers. On political asylum, Weil suggested that in conformity with the Preamble to the 1946 Constitution, constitutional asylum should be extended to 'those who had fought for freedom', while for other persecuted people and their families, one year's renewable 'territorial asylum' would be granted, with the right to work. All asylum matters would be concentrated in the hands of OFPRA, working with the Interior Ministry.[86] While keeping the door firmly closed on unskilled immigrant workers, he was scathing about the visa difficulties placed in the way of foreign students—treated as potential illegal immigrants—foreign academics, and researchers, suggesting ways of restoring France's international cultural standing.[87]

---

[80] Weil, *Mission d'étude*, p. 32; cf. 26–35. It was Le Pen's influential denunciation of the automatic acquisition of French nationality without knowing it that prompted Weil's comment.
[81] See Dominique Schnapper interview in *Le Monde*, 1 August 1997, p. 7. More generally see D. Schnapper, *La France de l'intégration: sociologie de la nation en 1990*, Paris, Gallimard, 1991, and D. Schnapper, *La Communauté des citoyens: sur l'idée moderne de nation*, Paris, Gallimard, 1994.
[82] Weil, *Mission d'étude*, p. 45.　　[83] Ibid.　　[84] *Le Monde*, 8 August 1997, p. 6.
[85] Weil, *Mission d'étude*, p. 48; cf. 49.　　[86] Ibid., pp. 51–6.　　[87] Ibid., pp. 125–34.

More generally, it was necessary to reinforce the freedom of movement between the Schengen countries.[88]

The reception of Weil's liberal but firm recommendations was mixed but encouraging. The NF helpfully declared that 'this report is precisely at the opposite pole to the programme advocated by the National Front'. While Pasqua remained silent, suggesting implicit acquiescence, Debré asserted that his legislation would largely remain intact. Jospin welcomed the Weil Report at its appearance and promised bills by Chevènement and Guigou in the autumn. While SOS Racism and the Confédération Française Démocratique du Travel (CFDT) trade union were favourable, the Green Party was critical and the Information and Support Group for Immigrant Workers (GISTI) condemned the recommendations as 'a legitimisation of the Pasqua Law: Weil is more intelligent than Pasqua but stays on his ground'.[89]

Weil's prudent tactic of dismembering the objectionable parts of the Right's legislation, rather than abrogating them, was formally endorsed at a Cabinet 'seminar' on 21 August 1997. Prime Minister Jospin explicitly approved of this piecemeal and incremental approach, calculated to take the passion out of immigration policy, despite the symbolic promise to repeal them in the PS 1997 electoral programme. He declared: 'There has been too much play with symbols in immigration matters. What counts are the facts.'[90] Chevènement (inclined to add 'republican' to anything of which he approves) in adopting, often word for word, many of the Weil recommendations in his draft bill, proclaimed the objective of 'republican consensus', capable of enduring swings of the political pendulum. While the Communist and Green ministers did not follow their party line in criticizing the Weil Report in general terms, a prior meeting of the *directeurs de cabinet* of the nine ministers principally concerned, chaired by Schrameck for the Prime Minister, agreed to certain detailed deviations from the Weil proposals in the legislation.[91]

Circulated on 22 August to the nine ministries dealing with immigrants, the draft Chevènement Bill was discussed at an interdepartmental meeting on 25 August 1997. While twenty-five out of its thirty articles were directly derived from the Weil Report, involving a substantial measure of procedural simplification, there was an ongoing disagreement between the Interior and Foreign Ministries over which of them would be in charge of asylum, that would be resolved by leaving territorial asylum to the former and constitutional asylum to the latter operating through OFPRA. Matignon was particularly concerned about arrangements for expelling illegal immigrants, fearing possible censure by the CC, as had occurred in relation to the Pasqua Law in 1993. After a long discussion between Jospin, Chevènement, Schrameck, and SGG Sauvé, it was decided to follow the Weil Report's recommendation of fourteen days' maximum 'administrative retention' by the police.[92]

---

[88] Ibid., pp. 61–3, 132. In 1999 territorial asylum was being accorded parsimoniously, only 6.1 per cent of applications being accepted. *Le Monde*, 26 May 2000.

[89] *Le Monde*, 2 August 1997, p. 24. See the GISTI President Danièle Lochak's debate with Weil. Ibid., September 1997, pp. 16–17.   [90] Ibid., 28 August 1997.

[91] Ibid., 23 August 1997, p. 5.   [92] Ibid., 27 August 1997, p. 8, and 5 September 1997, p. 11.

Jospin settled the ten outstanding disagreements, which lower level discussions had not resolved, at an interministerial meeting on 3 September 1997. In addition to the asylum decision mentioned earlier, the Prime Minister sometimes sided with the Justice Minister Guigou against the Interior Minister or vice versa, sometimes with the Solidarity Minister Aubry against the Interior Minister or vice versa. Jospin generally opted for the tough rather than the permissive options. Against the Justice Minister's proposal to reduce the age of acquisition of French nationality to 13 years, Jospin chose 16 with automatic entitlement at 18 years.[93] The bills were then sent to the National Consultative Commission on Human Rights, the High Council on Immigration, and then the Council of State before being submitted to parliament, the serenity of whose debates contrasted with the virulent denunciations of the pro-immigrant lobbies. The High Council's much more favourable opinion of the legislation than that of the Human Rights Commission was explicitly influenced by the explanations provided by Patrick Weil, one of its members.[94]

Interior Minister Chevènement declared that although his department was 'the ministry par excellence of republican integration', other ministries would also be involved in the delegated legislation application of the immigration reforms: Foreign Affairs, Justice, Education, and Finance in particular. 'Two interministerial bodies will deal, one with the implementation of these measures, the other with the implementation of a co-development aid policy.[95] When the Chevènement Law was adopted in May 1998, after an animated parliamentary debate (1,720 amendments—1,300 from the Opposition—were tabled), Weil cautiously welcomed it. A final judgement depended on the detailed regulations because, predictably, 'The difficulty is that certain ministries are keener for reform by their neighbours than in their own department'.[96] Public opinion had supported the reforms which took the wind out of the Opposition sails. Fifty-eight per cent supported easing conditions on the spouses of French citizens, 57 per cent favoured political asylum for those who had fought for freedom in their country, and 52 per cent approved granting French nationality automatically to children born in France of foreign parents at 18 years.[97] Although referred to the CC, the Chevènement Law was validated by it in April 1998.[98]

The Guigou Nationality Law had a rougher passage through parliament, with greater polarization between those who thought it did not go far enough (the Communists and Greens abstained) and those who thought it went too far. The opposition from the Right was strongest in the Senate, which urged President Chirac

---

[93] Ibid., 5 September 1997, pp. 1 and 11.

[94] Ibid., 3 and 5 October 1997. The Human Rights Commission's President Jean Kahn, had been President Mitterrand's adviser on legal matters.

[95] See interview in *Le Monde*, 25 September 1997, p. 10.

[96] Ibid., 14 May 1998, p. 10; cf. ibid., 4 December 1997, p. 6, 14, and 17 December 1997 and 10 April 1998. The Left secured the abolition of housing certificates, returning to Chevènement's original proposal (ibid., 13 December 1997, p. 6). See also *Le Monde*, 27 August 1997.

[97] Ibid., 13 December 1997, p. 6, quoting a SOFRES poll of September 1997, published in *Figaro Magazine*, 13 December 1997.   [98] *Le Monde*, 18 April and 7 May 1998.

to call a referendum but as this could only be done constitutionally on the proposal of the government or jointly by both chambers, it got nowhere.[99] In any case, the President and Opposition were in a particularly weak position following Chirac's disastrous dissolution, so the Guigou and Chevènement legislation had a smoother passage than would have occurred in a less propitious context.

SYMBOLIC AND SUBSTANTIVE POLICY: NATIONALITY AND IMMIGRATION

As the two Weil Reports showed, nationality and immigration policies, although distinct, were closely related and revolved around the idea of restoring a consensus around values as well as decisions, of both symbolic principles and substantive practices. The Guigou and Chevènement Laws reflected in part this duality, the more liberal nationality legislation being counterbalanced by immigration provisions that retained much of the Pasqua and Debré concern to reduce the attraction of the National Front. It also reflected the differing preoccupations of the Justice and Interior Ministries—human rights and public security—to which had to be added the priorities of other ministries: Foreign Affairs and Cooperation, Social Affairs and Labour, Education and Urban Affairs. All this continued to make the task of coordination hazardous, despite the efforts of Interior to play a hegemonic lead role. It resulted in tensions, with the Justice Ministry, for example, complaining about not being informed about a circular issued by Interior mentioning its wish to secure greater severity and consistency by the judiciary in the expulsion of illegal immigrants.[100]

The Left had hoped that the 1998 reforms would stop the immigration–nationality polemics that had divided them from the mainstream Right. Evidence for this came from former Prime Minister Juppé, who devoted the first issue of *France Moderne* (the journal of his think tank) to an 'Analysis of Immigration'. In an interview in *Le Monde*, Juppé explained that while 'mentalities had evolved' since his government's 1997 legislation, the problems were still unresolved. Both illegal immigration and racial discrimination in education and employment continue. He proposed improving coordination in both spheres by setting up a new national agency against illegal employment and combining all the existing bodies for which the Interior and Social Affairs Ministries were responsible into a single agency. He had been prompted to take up the issue particularly because of 'unacceptable discriminations that threaten our national cohesion' and because of the imminent EU follow-up to the Amsterdam Treaty's commitment to a common immigration policy. With 'zero immigration' dismissed as a meaningless slogan and fifteen separate policies being unacceptable, it was necessary to recognize that Europe would need foreign labour. Acknowledging that the Jospin Government had succeeded in 'reducing the tension in immigration matters by drawing its inspiration

---

[99] *Le Monde*, 19 December 1997. See also ibid., 14, 26, and 29 November, 1997.
[100] Ibid., 29 October 1999.

from Patrick Weil Report's proposals', it was time for the Right to end the ideological altercation. 'European integration will perhaps allow us to overcome our Franco-French debates and seek a common European model.'[101] His views were not generally welcomed on the Right, Debré in particular deploring that a predominantly European worker immigration had been succeeded by African migrants in search of welfare benefits.[102]

Under article 73K of the Amsterdam Treaty, within five years a common policy on conditions of entry and residence of immigrants, as well as long-term visa and family reunification matters, illegal immigration and repatriation, was to be implemented. Furthermore, under article 73O, after five years, decisions would not be taken unanimously but by qualified majority and jointly with the European Parliament. In October 1999, a meeting of EU Interior and Justice Ministers received a joint report from France, Germany, and the UK, preparing the ground for the European Council in Finland later that month. Rejecting both zero immigration and total freedom of migration as unrealistic, it clearly separated asylum for the persecuted from economically motivated migration and championed non-discrimination in matters of education, employment, and welfare rights. However, at the Tampere European Council, both President Chirac and Prime Minister Jospin stressed that asylum decisions should remain a national responsibility.[103] The continuing rejection of economic migration—not by Juppé but he was out of office—flew in the face of reports, such as that from the United Nations, that falling birth rates in Europe would require, between 2000 and 2025, 159 million immigrants (760,000 per year in France alone) to correct the imbalance between its active and inactive population.[104]

Despite its undoubted good intentions, the Jospin Government struggled to coordinate its various efforts to promote the integration of the naturalized and regularized immigrants. The task of dealing with illegal migrants is increasingly shifting to the EU and to the Schengen coordination arrangements but national governments are still held responsible by their voters for the influx. During the French EU presidency in the latter half of 2000, Interior Minister Chevènement made harmonizing the fight against illegal immigration and the timing of short- and long-term visas a priority issue. Anticipating that the EU would have to accept an influx of fifty million immigrants in the next fifty years, he nevertheless advocated an EU directive to increase penalties on those transporting illegal migrants in the wake of a single incident of fifty-eight Chinese deaths at Dover in June 2000. Regarding it as one of the major challenges facing this century, Chevènement (shortly to resign in defence of the indivisible Republic against the prospect of conceding some autonomy to Corsica) pressed for a long-term and anticipatory rather than a reactive and incremental approach to migration within the EU.[105]

---

[101] Ibid., 1 October 1999, p. 6. Consult the first issue of *Les Cahiers de la France Moderne* on the internet: http://www.france-moderne.asso.fr
[102] *Le Monde*, 7 October 1999, p. 7; cf. ibid., 2 October 1999, p. 6.
[103] Ibid., 7 and 17 October 1999.
[104] Ibid., 6 January 2000, p. 2, summarizing a preliminary UN Report entitled 'Replacement Migration: a solution for declining and ageing populations'.   [105] Ibid., 20, 22, 29 July 2000.

It has been possible for the core executives to delegate more to administrative and local action, without being able fully to return to the pre-1974 depoliticized reliance upon peripheral consensus without coordination. Greater centralization and political monitoring of the way in which immigration problems are handled is a necessary precaution against being taken unawares by unpredictable 'events' for the foreseeable future. National Front pressure receded until 2002 but the fall in unemployment has ensured a more hospitable economic as well as political context for the conduct of immigration policy. While a provisional consensus on principles has largely been achieved, thanks to the Weil Report and the Chevènement and Guigou Laws being the reference point for all ministries, it would be an illusion to believe that this has more than eased the usual coordination difficulties. So, dealing with the practical problems continues to provoke interdepartmental conflicts which the Prime Minister endeavours to contain but cannot definitively resolve.

PART III

CONCLUSIONS

9

Overall Coordination: The Impracticable Imperative

At the outset, we explored the problems raised by our key concepts: 'core executive' and 'coordination'. We anticipated that empirical evidence would demonstrate that the core executive was a rather elastic and pluralistic entity in practice, so that it was better to use the term 'core executives' preparatory to showing how a different cluster or constellation of office-holders was involved at particular times in relation to particular issues and how this changed with the context over time. We should now be in a position to contrast our initial French model core executive with the complex and contingent character of what constitutes the core executive in actuality.

'Coordination' raised comparable problems, revealing itself on closer inspection to be a multi-dimensional activity involving both process and objectives, taking many forms. Despite making some use of habitual dichotomous categories of coordination—hierarchical/non-hierarchical, formal/informal, routine/crisis, inter-/intra-organizational coordination, administrative/political, negative/positive, institutionalized/ad hoc—each of these categories proved problematic. For example, the distinction between administrative and political coordination is very blurred in France, with cabinets ministériels composed of civil servants who are politically sympathetic to the government and a patronage network which enables the government to place administrative friends in key coordinating positions.

We shall organize our findings in two parts, dealing first with the general results of our investigations and then with the sectoral specificities that emerged from our case studies. Some were predictable, confirming the conventional wisdom, but others were unanticipated. It is only then that we can succinctly impart the full ironic significance of our title: governing from the centre. Despite its cultural and institutional distinctiveness, France has responded to the coordination predicament by reluctantly becoming much more like other European states.

COORDINATING FROM THE CENTRE[1]

First, core executives everywhere are locked into a plurality of interdependent forms of coordinative exchange, mixing both processes of unilateral adjustment and

---

[1] Much of the section of general findings was reported in the cross-national comparative chapter on 'Governing from the Centre' that was published in R. A. W. Rhodes (ed.), *Transforming British Government: Changing Roles and Relationships*, Basingstoke, Macmillan, 2000, ch. 2. We have chosen to rework and repeat rather than contradict ourselves.

interactive modalities of coordination, of hierarchy and network. This coordination mainly takes place internally at the centre: within the core executive itself; inter-departmentally; within individual departments or organizations. There is also external coordination: between the centre and state officials of implementation; between the political and bureaucratic elements of policy-making; between the state machine and outside functional and territorial interests. Whilst recognizing that multiple and complex feedbacks may increase and complicate core executive coordination require-ments, we focused largely on *internal* coordination because of our concentration on the initiation, agenda-setting, and formalization stages of state decision-making. These core executive coordination requirements related to systemic management, political management, governmental management, and administrative management; requirements which are distinct yet interrelated.

Since the 1980s, a set of eleven interrelated factors have both increased and *complicated* coordination requirements and objectives:

(1) the internationalization and transnationalization particularly of financial and industrial sectors and of decision-making;

(2) the Europeanization of actors, structures, arenas, and processes;

(3) the weakening of a general policy frame based on the state-centred approach, which has dismembered to a greater or lesser extent internal and external policy networks;

(4) the weakening of some of the traditional props of governance (contested authority and legitimacy of state elites, political parties, and peak organiza-tions of organized interests) often as the result of government policies;

(5) a changing policy agenda, with new and complicated demands to coordinate (European Union (EU), environmental concerns, law and order issues, immigration, long-term unemployment, women's rights), which have created greater interdepartmental interdependencies, political tensions, greater costs, greater national–transnational–international interdependencies;

(6) more extended territorial policy chains to manage (EU and international regulatory agencies);

(7) the emergence of new actors and new networks (outsiders acquiring uneasy insider status), policy activists and advocates, think tanks, to mention the most important ones;

(8) the collapse or reshaping of traditional sectoral networks (the increased role of financial institutions, central banks, courts; multinationalization; and public/private hybridization);

(9) new decision-making processes (more decentralized or diffused, occasionally more participative and consultative, seldom more transparent);

(10) further fragmentation of the central state apparatus (increased sectoraliza-tion, administrative deconcentration and certain aspects of new public management);

(11) the privatisation of the public domain (a multi-dimensional phenomenon involving ethos, sectors, finance, and personnel) which has led to complex issues of hybridization and regulation.

In short, some pressures (budgetary, EU) clearly require increased coordination efforts whilst the same pressures and new ones (the weakening of the traditional bases of coordination such as cost reduction, the destabilizing of the policy environment, the increased balkanization, and budgetary squeeze) are generally rendering an already difficult task much more difficult.

The second major finding is that there appears to be an increasing need for positive coordination orchestrated by a core executive more centralized around the President, Prime Minister, and Finance Minister. This places an additional responsibility upon their staffs, both in terms of internal coordination and the relations between those who can claim a general oversight over the activities of government. To a lesser extent, Foreign and Internal (and increasingly European) Affairs Ministers may compete for a share in such centralized coordinating capacity. The factors feeding this need are well known: the personalization of politics; the electoral sanctions imposed on disunity; the impact of EU policy-making which, increasingly, is seen to require a country to speak with one voice; the zero or even negative sum games involved in budgetary rectitude; the heightening political salience of issues (such as long-term unemployment, immigration, EU policy-making, law and order) which create new budgetary demands, new requirements for regulation, and increasing interdependencies and externalities. Repeated attempts at strengthening of the inter-locking politico-administrative superstructure is a response to the need for greater positive coordination, whose reiteration implies their frequent failure.

Third, whilst there are strong and convergent pressures for a more pro-active and positive core executive coordination, our evidence suggest that this is in practice modest. Coordination remains characterized by four features:

(1) it is *largely negative*, based on persistent compartmentalization, mutual avoidance, friction-reduction between powerful bureaux or ministries, which remain formidable inertial obstacles;

(2) even *when cooperative, it is anchored at the lower levels of the state machine* and organized by specific established networks. It is sustained by a culture of dialogue in vertical relations and of integration at the horizontal level;

(3) it is *rarely strategic*, so attempts to create pro-active strategic capacity for long-term planning, such as the Planning Commissariat, have been marginalized in the public policy process;

(4) coordination is *intermittent and selective* in any one sector, improvised late in the policy process, politicized, issue-oriented, and reactive.

On the whole, therefore, despite their pretensions and public perception, core executives continue principally to be arenas for actors.

The desire and/or the need to restrict the span of core executive control remain dictated by seven factors:

1. *The lack of political will*, the price of coordination being too high if it threatens to destabilize delicate political balances. 'Fudge' and slack are often essential ingredients for systemic, governmental, and bureaucratic harmony.

2. *The lack of time,* because the core executive is absorbed in many activities not directly related to policy coordination. A surprising amount of even core executive activity is taken up by managing routine affairs, as well as by symbolic representational and partisan political activity. The core executives are in the business of providing democratic legitimacy for government as well as furnishing a focus for political activity.
3. *The lack of information* or inability to manage too much information results in overload, which desperately needs to be lightened.
4. *The lack of cohesion,* arising from the fact that governments being large and complex organizations, core executives are often arenas of squabbling chieftains, each frequently representing a departmental viewpoint.
5. *The lack of effective instruments* is discussed later.
6. *The weight of 'urgent' politicized issues requiring attention* usually takes priority over important issues.
7. Lastly, there is the *presence of multiple politico-administrative constraints.* Departmental autonomy is enhanced when it is underpinned by unwritten constitutional norms and when the departments have been headed by a minister of standing and durability or when they have been in the hands of the same party for lengthy periods of time.

Our fourth finding suggests that successive French governments have resorted to a variety of measures to reduce the coordination burden, both externally and internally, but with little success. At the external level, there have been (a) an attempt to displace policy-making responsibilities (and costs) to the European level and to the sub-national level; (b) an attempt to transfer policy responsibilities (and costs) to third sector or consultative/advisory bodies; (c) radical programmes of privatisation and, in some sectors, the creation of regulatory agencies; (d) the pursuit of 'decorporatization', denoting the partial dismantling of the collusive relationships between state and major groups. However, our evidence suggests that such attempts have not reduced the coordination burden, but merely reshaped and complicated it. Moreover, there are other factors at work, such as the demands for greater transparency and participation, the increasing role of courts in public policy-making, which further complicate coordination requirements.

In terms of easing *internal* coordination requirements, French governments have resorted to a mix of eight techniques:

(1) devolving coordination responsibility lower down the hierarchy to a clearly identifiable lead ministry, to a senior civil servant, to an interdepartmental council or committee or to regional prefects;
(2) appointing coordinating ministers for political or policy purposes;
(3) improving 'pre-cooking' arrangements at the political level;
(4) reducing the size of the arena to be coordinated, through cutting the number of departments; or by the creation of superministries charged with the task of coordinating its component departments, in the hope of socializing the superministers into a culture of compromise and enabling them to appreciate

the problems of coordination (the role of the Finance and Social Affairs super-ministers in the 1997 Jospin Government are cases in point);

(5) improving contact and information flows amongst bureaux officials working in the same area;

(6) placing politically sympathetic officials in strategic positions in an issue network;

(7) mobilizing vertical and horizontal networks of the politically sympathetic;

(8) constructing a consensus or policy frame around a set of central ideas ('Europe', 'modernization', 'public service reform') and insisting that 'there is no alternative', in the hope of exerting pressure which constrains all actors.

Let us elaborate the last two techniques a little further. By entrenching 'norms', 'assumptive worlds', 'policy no-go areas', 'implicit property rights', policy frames restrict the autonomy of actors, thus reducing coordination costs. We identified five such frames:

(1) *ideological*: the prevailing economic climate of opinion, despite resistance against the 'Washington Consensus' (trade liberalization not protectionism, privatisation not nationalization, anti-inflation not full employment, fiscal rectitude not expansion, deregulation not regulation) by old *dirigistes*, reinforced by the exigencies of the Maastricht convergence criteria and the stability pact;

(2) *political systemic*: the internalization of EU policy needs and constraints, the acceptance of the legitimacy of the established constitutional order and values, often defined through the process of judicial review, as well as greater respect for due process;

(3) *organizational*: through the recognition of 'standard operating procedures' and 'routines' (discussed in Chapter 1) which, combined with other policy framing, induce 'discernible and ritualized patterns of behaviour'. These reduce coordination costs by (a) dictating the presence and position of the major actors; (b) determining the timetable involved; (c) restricting the span of the game by limiting the range of conceivable possibilities; (d) providing rewards for compliance and sanctions for non-compliance;

(4) *overall policy-framing* by electoral mandates, coalition agreements, prior budgetary commitments, and path dependencies;

(5) *sectoral policy-framing*, which are the 'givens' in a particular sector (especially defence and foreign policy), as well as the weight of prior statutory and budgeting commitments which set policy-makers on 'autopilot'.

We fully recognize the significance of the multiple processes of framing and maintain that such processes introduce continuity, stability, and predictability into the behaviour of actors. They produce institutional 'stickiness' which constrains behaviour in a way which reduces the requirements of coordination. However, our case studies also indicate the limits to the impact of such framing as an instrument for reducing coordination costs, notably because of the yawning gap between rhetoric and reality. In the first place, the combined pressure of ideological, political, organizational, and sectoral policy frames has never prevented traditional conflicts within the state machine (which might revolve around protecting turf, or maintaining corps prestige, or generalist versus specialist squabbles). Second, there is a mismatch between the generalized impact of policy-framing and the most common need for core executive coordination, which involves reacting to conflict-ridden emergencies. Finally, as a result of a set of exogenous shocks (technology, new ideological and policy fashions, developments in the labour market, membership of the EU, internal political change) and of deliberate reframing by the executives, many of the traditional frames have been unsettled, producing greater cognitive variation. Our case studies in immigration, privatisation, budget-making, and EU policy-making indicated that new perspectives are having to be learnt and processed. In this unsettled policy environment, new policy frames are only imperfectly absorbed, since they are the source of contention and division, thus heightening the need for coordination. Arguments about 'framing' still hold good for routine, heavily bureaucratized, non-politicized coordination activity involving non-zero games. It is much less effective for many of the issues that core executives are called upon to coordinate.

If we turn to networks as instruments of core executive positive coordination, we are driven to the same conclusion: they are indispensable yet inadequate. As Heclo and Wildavsky pointed out a quarter of a century ago, networks are vital for the understanding of core executive coordination capacity; they are the lubricant of the coordination system.[2] They are crucial for both external and internal coordination. We have concentrated on internal networks and analysed them according to composition, status, span, function, linkages, degree of stability and institutionalization, frequency, and mode of interaction (bargained or cooperative), notably in relation to *grands corps* networks. Our research also underlines six limits to the coordinating capacity of many of these networks.

1. Networks are often devoted to the organizational survival of the agents rather than to the wishes of the principal.
2. Paradoxically, some networks are so effective in coordinating a lower level of the ministerial chain that they inhibit effective coordination at a higher level (a point to which we shall return). They may, by a process of collusion, reinforce the processes of negative coordination, thus provoking, on occasions, the need for *enhanced* positive coordination.
3. Apparently effective networks may be internally divided, which is true of some of the French networks based on the *grandes écoles* and the *grands corps*.
4. The efficacy of a network can be diluted by the presence of members with multiple loyalties, since they may belong to other overlapping networks. Senior officials invariably are in this situation.
5. As interdependence increases, many networks become less effective because of their inadequate span.

[2] H. Heclo and A. Wildavsky, *The Private Government of Public Money*, Berkeley, University of California Press, 1974.

6. Horizontal self-coordination through networking depends on a free exchange of information and cooperation. If competitive or hostile orientations prevail, coordination becomes highly problematic. Trust within the network is crucial for its effective functioning as an instrument of core executive coordination. Yet, several of our case studies show that in France such trust is not present. One of our conclusions is that *networks function best when they are least needed.*

Fifth, what is distinctive about French core executive coordination practices, given the problem of functional equivalence of core executives?

1. The same sector or issue mobilizes *different constellations of actors.* Thus, coordinating privatisation in Austria is left to the lead ministry responsible for the enterprise to be privatised, to the Interior Ministry in the Netherlands, to the Finance Ministry in France and Spain, whilst in Italy the Industry Ministry as well as the Finance Ministry play a key role. In France, the courts (the Constitutional Council (CC) and the Council of State) and an independent privatisation commission also play important roles, which is not the case elsewhere. European Union policy coordination displays similar national variations. France has a centralized interdepartmental coordinating mechanism like the UK but unlike most EU countries. Problems relating to Schengen go to the Chancellery in Germany but to the Interior Ministry in France. Immigration issues are dealt with primarily by the Interior Ministry in France, Social Affairs in Italy, and Justice in the Netherlands. The choice of lead ministry is not politically neutral, since the ideological and cultural propensities as well as the clientele of ministries differ widely. The outcomes are likely to differ significantly as a result.

2. *The mechanisms of coordination differ* cross-nationally at both the political and bureaucratic levels. Hence, in France brief coalition agreements are generally hammered out *before* a general election, constitute a common alliance platform for second ballot contests, and a loose policy frame in the event of victory. In the Netherlands and Austria prolonged and detailed negotiations between potential coalition partners take place *after* the election. The resulting coalition agreement between the parties provides the agenda for their future collaboration in government. In Germany there is a coalition committee which meets regularly under the chairmanship of the Chancellor. As in France, these meetings bring together core executive and party bosses. Similar differences may be seen in the mechanisms of policy and bureaucratic coordination, where the French have powerful centralizing mechanisms in the form of the Secretariat General of the Government, the Prime Minister's *cabinet*, and bodies such as the General Secretariat for the Interministerial Committee (SGCI) for EU affairs, absent from most EU countries.

3. There are also significant cross- and intra-national variations in *coordinating styles*, ranging from the coercive and authoritarian (France in some cases) to the bargained and consensual (the general picture in Germany and the Netherlands). These are not mutually exclusive categories, and in the

coordination of any particular policy, governments may be forced or may choose different styles to suit changing circumstances. To complicate matters, personality often plays an important role, irrespective of partisan affiliation. The individual ministers' styles reflect the way they work and who they work with, as well as their personal policy and political ambitions. These make collective coordination inherently problematic because the national and sectoral structures and personal proclivities of the coordinators collide with the aims and personalities of those to be coordinated. Thus, in the French privatisation programmes there was a striking contrast between the conciliatory and pragmatic style of Balladur (even though he insisted on personal control) and the authoritarian and uncompromising style of Juppé, both Rassemblement Pour le République (RPR) leaders.

In attempting to explain the persistence of these differences relating to actors, mechanisms, functions, types and styles, three major factors—ambitions, needs, and capacity—emerge. Clearly, all three factors are determined by France's unique political and administrative opportunity structures. In describing these structures, our research underlines the significance for coordination of familiar features of the political process: the scope and substance of central state activity; the nature of centre–periphery relations; the relationship between executive and parliament; the nature of the party system (majoritarian or coalition, and if the latter, symmetrical or asymmetrical, stable or unstable); the degree of inter- and intra-party cohesion and discipline; the structure of state–group relations (variably corporatist, pluralist, *dirigiste*; 'hands on' or self-regulation across sectors and cases); the role of courts in public policy-making; the policy-making style (consensual, bargained, or impositional). In France, a long *dirigiste* tradition, executive-dominated politics, weak parliaments, a developing culture under the Fifth Republic of political leadership, and relatively strong party discipline exert an overall influence.

In terms of the administrative opportunity structure, we had to assess the significance for coordination of seven factors:

- the size and shape of the central state administration
- its structure (*cabinets*, corps, networks)
- the type and degree of expertise
- the extent of its partisan politicization (notably through patronage)
- its links, if any, with outside interests
- its internal organizational culture (compartmentalization or integration; cooperative or confrontational)
- its policy style.

Our sixth general finding relates to the concept of coordination effectiveness which proves to be highly problematic, there being *no single best way of coordinating policies*. Our research raised issues relating to the outcomes as well as the conditions which are required to achieve effective positive coordination. The first of the four major lessons concerning effectiveness to emerge from this study of core executive coordination is not only that there is no one best way of achieving policy coordination but that tight coordination is not necessarily always desirable. On the contrary, 'optimal' coordination will depend on a host of variables such as the nature of coordination ambitions and constitutional, institutional, political, and administrative opportunity structures.

A second major lesson on effectiveness is that reliance on tight vertical coordination, at the expense of horizontal coordination, may be dysfunctional. It may lead to a vicious circle: demands for central coordination increase so the centre is strengthened, which weakens the horizontal structures, which results in further demands upon the centre... France perfectly illustrates this feature of vertical decision-making; squabbling factions lower down the hierarchy have a tendency to refer thorny problems to the summit which becomes overloaded. There are strong propensities to avoid risk and there are few incentives to resolve problems at the lower level or to build a culture of consultation, free information exchange, integration, and compromise. Where the resources of hierarchical control and the capacity to manipulate a network are not available, notably because of the weakness of central authority or because there is no effective policy network to facilitate coordination, the policy actors will have to manage their relationships as best they can without recourse to it.

Lesson three is that 'effective' coordination may be detrimental to good decision-making both down-stream and up-stream. Loose coordination at the formalization stage may allow flexibility at critical junctures elsewhere—at street-level implementation or in other policy arenas. For example, the more efficient a ministry is in achieving internal coordination, the more difficult is interministerial coordination likely to be. Thus, a loosely coordinated position at the domestic level may be highly desirable when negotiating in Brussels, exemplified by the British approach, in contrast to that of France.

Finally, 'effective' vertical and positive coordination may clash with other highly desirable goals: participation and consultation (to ensure better implementation), transparency, organizational harmony, personal managerial entrepreneurship, and accountability.

SECTORAL SPECIFICITIES AND CORE EXECUTIVE COORDINATION

The Sectoral Specificities of EU policy-making[3]

The coordination of EU policy incorporates four elements. First is the need effectively to ensure not only a degree of complementarity across the range of national positions in the various EU negotiations under way at any time but also, ideally, to facilitate the striking of cross-sectoral trade-offs between member states across issues. Second is the necessity of arriving at national positions on each individual issue, which meet, as far as is possible, the often conflicting needs of the ministries involved.

---

[3] This summary of EU specificities draws heavily on a working paper by Anand Menon.

Third, there needs to be effective coordination of all those actors involved in and affected by the transcription and street-level implementation of EC law. Finally, there should be the ability to formulate positions for high level polity-building negotiations in the EU during Intergovernmental Conferences (IGCs). As French governments seek to play a constructive and pioneering role within the EU, they adopt a particularly active and ambitious style of comprehensive coordination, sustained by the salience of the EU dimension for both domestic and international policies.

1. *Limited control over the policy agenda* by the French government because the EU develops according to its own integrative logic. Perhaps most striking in comparison with the other sectors being studied, core executives lack control over the agenda in this policy area. First, this relates to an inability to control those issues that appear on the agenda in both routine and policy-building matters. Second, it applies to an inability effectively to determine how particular issues will be treated. Environmental issues are not a high political priority in France and yet the French position on the exhaust emission directive was eventually resolved between the French President and German Chancellor because of its high political salience in Germany.

2. *The instability of policy processes.* Since the SEA, regular IGCs have altered policy-making processes at the European level, so that national structures for ensuring coordination must be continually adjusted. Quite apart from procedural instability, the need to deal with crises, for example bovine spongiform encephalopathy (BSE), creates problems of rapid coordination with member states in 'fire-fighting' unpredictable events that take them all by surprise.

3. *Administrative mismatch* exists in two main forms: first, in terms of coordination, issues raised on the EU agenda may not fit neatly into national administrative divisions, leading to second, ambiguity, and potentially to turf wars between departments, increasing the problems of coordination. The rivalry of the French Foreign and Finance Ministries for the role of lead EU coordinator and the uncertain role of the Minister for EU Affairs, working for the Prime Minister or President, exemplifies this problem of achieving vertical coordination, especially because of presidential self-assertive improvisations.

4. *The need for network- and coalition-building.* The increasing use of qualified majority voting at the Community level means that, even if national coordination proves effective, policy outcomes may not match national preferences. Thus, one central aspect of coordination, less frequent in other sectors, is the need for bargaining and networking to occur between as well as within the national executives. Indeed, insofar as implementation of EC law is concerned, the national executives are the objects of coordination by the Commission rather than its masters.

5. *Extra-territoriality.* Particularly because of the importance of the Brussels-based Committee of Permanent Representation (COREPER) negotiations and specialist working groups, the Paris-based core executives only exert control with great difficulty over on-the-spot compromises. The influence of experts

and powerful organized interests, for example major firms, can be especially great as a result of their access.

6. *Sectorization.* The highly sectorized nature of the European Commission (EC) system at the EU level makes it very difficult for national executives to ensure effective coordination, not least because of the temptation for ministers to strike deals within their own sectoral 'Council' irrespective of the need for cross-sectoral coordination or even consultation. Hence, the importance of the SGCI's counter-sectoral pressures against ministries that deliberately promote the Europeanization of policy to evade the centralized French coordination system. In Common Agricultural Policy and Economic and Monetary Union matters, the French lead ministries have created an insulated network that largely escapes overall coordination.

7. *Decreasing bifurcation.* This refers to the relationship between purely technical matters and 'polity-building' negotiations within IGCs. Detailed specialist knowledge is needed in order to negotiate successfully. Thus, as even 'high politics' becomes technical, there is a need to ensure coordination between the two kinds of policy-making system existing within the member states.

8. *Increasing judicialization.* This has meant that legal expertise is becoming a hugely important part of effective coordination. This reinforces the wider point that the EU system is in a state of almost perpetual flux, to which national systems must adapt. France has done so with reluctance.

The Sectoral Specificity of Budget-Making

The budgetary process involves converging multi-level coordination downwards and upwards within core executive government. It is necessary to reconcile the overall ceiling and the major priorities of public expenditure fixed at the dual leadership Prime Minister–Finance Minister level with the limited scope for detailed reallocation above the floor of unavoidable past commitments based upon the demands made by ministerial advocates. It is at the intersection of these top-down and bottom-up pressures, through a nominally junior budget minister, formal inter-departmental and interministerial committees, and information discussions, that the reconciliation is largely achieved, subject to high level arbitration to settle the remaining disputes.

What is Distinctive about Budget-Making?

1. By contrast with immigration and privatisation, budget-making is a *permanent annual process*, with well-established administrative, ministerial, and parliamentary routine procedures, with occasional non-routine improvisations intruding into what is mainly an incrementalist process.

2. *It involves all spending ministries*—notably their budget bureaux—often in bilateral negotiations, with budgetary bilateralism complicating overall coordination. The Budget Minister plays a leading role, although his or her relationship with the Finance Minister is important, as well as with the Prime

Minister. The Prime Minister usually plays a prominent part, setting priorities with political sensitivity, subject to being overridden by the President. The coalition character of French governments adds further coordination problems. Demands by the spending ministries can usually be defeated, especially if the Prime Minister supports the Budget/Finance Minister. Finance Ministers may be too busy with other aspects of economic policy, leaving budgetary matters largely to the Budget Minister.

3. The preparation of *the budget cannot be divorced from monetary policy*, involving intra-Finance Ministry coordination between the Budget and Treasury divisions and extra-Finance Ministry coordination with the Bank of France and the institutions constituting the inner financial, national and international policy community and the outer national and international financial policy network. Compared to the Bundesbank, the standing of the French Central Bank had been relatively weak but was provisionally strengthened in the 1990s run-up to the creation of the European Central Bank (ECB).

4. *The inertial weight of pre-budget expenditure commitments* is so large that there is annual discretion only to make marginal adjustments. The pressure to make the total smaller (and thereby allow the electorally popular reduction of taxation) whilst making its components larger (for the electoral satisfaction of lobbies whose support needs to be attracted or whose demands cannot be resisted) presents the coordinators with a major conjuring problem that requires sleight of figures skills, especially when European Monetary Union (EMU) convergence criteria also need to be satisfied on public debt and budget deficit. The propensity and capacity of spending ministries to resist coordination is thereby constrained.

5. The 'sound finance' norm of the *balanced budget*, which pre-dated the modestly Keynesian approach to French public finance, has been revived. In combination with past expenditure commitments and EMU criteria, it has been used to contain the demands from the spending ministries. While there has been a tendency to make budgets more comprehensive, there has also been a countervailing tendency: a cosmetic device increasingly employed to ease the financial constraint is to de-budgetize major public expenditures.

6. *The problem of budget annuality*, when public investment expenditures, for example in Transport, require medium/long-term expenditure planning are influenced by medium-term forward looks. Even in its heyday, French national planning never succeeded in fitting annual budgets into a five-year framework, the political and administrative spending community reserving the right to improvise as circumstances required. Defence expenditure is a particularly spectacular example of programming investment twenty or more years ahead, yet using the same item as an 'adjustment variable of the general budget' as a French defence specialist put it.[4] So true is this of other current and capital public expenditure in France that while 'annuality is budgetary law, budgetary

---

[4] Christian Schmidt's remark at a November 1997 ENA colloquium on 'La Réforme de l'Etat', *Les Cahiers de l'Ecole Nationale d'Administration*, No. 3, 1998, p. 151. It is worth noting that defence capital

reality is today often a matter of infra-annual regulation and, dare one say, the budgetary dream would be pluriannuality'.[5] With the 1994 Quinquennial Law on Controlling Public Deficits, France linked the annual budget with 'rolling' targets for the main budgetary aggregates to accommodate the Maastricht Treaty requirements. Recourse to supplementary budgets each year result in substantial disparities between budget estimates and expenditures. Thus, far from guaranteeing predictability, budgets may increase uncertainty and give the Finance Ministry power to make abrupt and arbitrary changes in previously agreed decisions. The National Assembly has sought to retrieve some of its post-1959 financial control in 2000, hoping for more understanding by its former President, Finance Minister Laurent Fabius, who would have to overcome strong Budget Division resistance.

7. While *evaluation of policies* is more than a budgetary and financial process, there has been a reluctance of spending ministries to cooperate because the evaluated consider that they are being accused of incompetence, low productivity, and waste. However, what such evaluation reveals is the pursuit of blurred and even contradictory objectives and discontinuity of policy (particularly in a context of multi-level government), which reduce effectiveness. These are only some of the reasons why evaluation has generally not lived up to the hopes placed in it. Financial assistance to national firms and to poor countries both seek to meet a plurality of objectives delivered by several different arms of government, which complicates evaluation. For example, the evaluation of foreign aid endeavours to measure the promotion of influence and prestige in the development of assisted countries when results are a symbolic matter,[6] not merely the encouragement of trade. This presents particular constraints in countries with a former colonial empire such as France, which for long sought to retain privileged ties with it.

8. French and EU budgeting are now so interrelated as to be virtually part of a single process, under the dual impact of compliance with the Maastricht Treaty constraints and a hybridization owing to the entanglement of both levels of expenditure decisions. Procedures and actors overlap, leading to both formal and informal integration. However, this is fragmented into separate ministerial negotiations, which has reduced the Finance Ministry's capacity to retain overall control.

The Sectoral Specificity of Privatisation

Pressures for privatisation have emanated from a variety of sources: new technology which is transforming the nature of certain public sectors, the ideologues of

---

expenditure is the largest French industrial budget. French 1990s defence cuts were the more brutal for being made late. Ibid., p. 152.

[5] Didier Casas, ibid., p. 77. Other speakers complained of massive cuts at the start of the financial year or, in the case of the 1995 French defence budget, 20 per cent during the year. Ibid., p. 150; cf. pp. 85, 95.

[6] B. Perret and J. Leca, ibid., pp. 47–9; M.-C. Kessler, ibid., p. 160.

right-wing think tanks who point to the alleged intrinsic inefficiencies of public enterprises, public sector managers who yearn for easier access to the capital markets and for greater operational autonomy, governments strapped for money and bereft of new ideas, the international financial markets in search of rich pickings, the EU which sees public ownership as an impediment to the construction of an open market, and international organizations such as the Organization for Economic Cooperation and Development (OECD), the International Monetary Fund (IMF), and the World Bank which have become the remorseless apostles of neo-liberalism.

In spite of internationally convergent ambitions, privatisation policies remain different in timing, phasing, scale, and scope, so one should not generalize from the French case. The *type* of privatisation being pursued encompasses a wide range of policies: from the outright sale of a major public utility, to the sale of subsidiaries, recapitalization on the financial markets, and the sale of a percentage of the equity of a public company; some privatisations are through public flotation, others are off-market. Core executives have been intimately involved in the initiation, agenda-setting, and formalization and, even in some respects, the implementation and monitoring stages of decision-making.

1. *Institutional innovation* is much greater in privatisation than in our other three sectors. There, policy changes occur within reasonably predictable parameters: path dependencies are discernible, as are the principal agents of coordination, guided by embedded cognitive maps. All three are also increasingly heavily institutionalized and bureaucratized, and structured by identifiable actors and core networks. Privatisation, on the other hand, is relatively new on the policy agenda, is a process involving a series of discrete measures, with no set time-table, no path dependency which lowers coordination costs, and little insti-tutionalization. It shows institutions to be more malleable to far-reaching policy reversal than is often thought.

2. *The sporadic nature of privatisation* as well as its varied character has an important consequence: there are no stable networks which are an important coordinating instrument in some other policy areas. Indeed, privatisation in some sectors requires the dismantlement of the comfortable and collusive networks which existed in the public sector. While many of these decisions are internal, in the privatisation process government is extremely dependent on the outside expertise (banks, stock exchange dealers, advertising agencies), and the success of major flotations critically hinges on the cooperation of private and often foreign actors (notably American institutional investors). Privatisa-tion involves not only supply but also demand, and judging that demand is seldom easy.

3. Privatisation processes are peculiarly *vulnerable to outside pressures*, notably the state of the financial stock markets: the market crash in October 1987 had a disastrous impact in France. Several privatisations have been delayed as the

result of adverse market conditions, or become more ambitious (the 1997 Jospin Government's partial privatisation of France Télécom) as markets suddenly become bullish. The other major outside pressure has been the EU, since the Commission has often insisted on privatisation as a prior condition for recapitalizing national lame ducks. Emulation, in part, of the British experience was less a pressure than a model offering positive and negative lessons.

4. The obsessive *concern to avoid foreign control* led to deliberate avoidance of the British method of selling off state enterprises to ensure predominant French control, over and above the adoption of the 'golden share' instrument.

5. The constellation of core executive actors is clearly sectorally specific, but it tends also to be policy specific: the key actors are Finance and the sponsoring ministry, with *Finance playing the role of lead ministry*. It is especially concerned to ease budgetary problems.

6. The distinction between routinized and non-routinized coordination was difficult to establish in practice. Any *privatisation is, by definition, non-routine*, but clear routinized aspects about many of them (selling by instalments, or many off-market sales of subsidiaries) begin to be established. Routinization appears to cover four different phenomena: mobilization of a stable constellation of actors, institutionalization, bureaucratization, and critical duration (redefining the legal status of France Télécom personnel is an *ad hoc* operation but a prolonged one). A further complication: even an emergency may be dealt with in 'routine fashion' with well-defined rules and actors for coordinating a response. The stock market crash in October 1987 provides such an example.

7. *Politicization is equally problem-ridden*, since it, too, involves very different phenomena: a privatisation could be politicized because it was inherently so, given its sectoral or cultural significance; exploited for partisan purposes or for patronage; linked with other politically charged policies; used by opponents as a political instrument; or 'Europeanized'. Despite initial partisan polarization, there has been actual cross-party continuity in France as elsewhere. This was assisted sometimes by the circulation of expert elites. In the case of telecommunications, engineers from the same corps were omnipresent.

The Sectoral Specificity of Immigration Policy-Making

This sector was the one in which it was most difficult to separate the analysis of policy-making from its implementation. In the 1980s and 1990s, it was characterized by 'fire-fighting' political reactions to externally generated events. Failures in terms of implementation were imperfectly masked by frequent recourse to symbolic policy-making aimed at responding to or influencing public opinion rather than resolving the problems of sudden influx. Being unwilling or unable to deal with clandestine immigration, the issue became engulfed in a debate about national identity and the integration of foreigners, with the attendant political exploitation of xenophobia.

However, the political polarization of even technical issues, if managed with deftness as was done by the Jospin Government, can achieve a large measure of consensus.

1. The *inability to impose an ideologically motivated, radical solution* (by contrast with privatisation) leads to a disjuncture between gesture politics by political core executives and the administrative and judicial core executives who have to deal with the practicalities, for example deportation of illegal immigrants, and do so by pragmatic, piecemeal improvisation.

2. The *multiplicity and contradictory objectives of public policy*—deterrence, exclusion, restriction, assimilation—result in conflicts between the (parts of) ministries with prime responsibilities for furthering each objective. This puts a premium on intradepartmental and interdepartmental bargaining to reconcile these divergences and conflicts, of which whether one ceases to be treated as an immigrant when naturalized or second generation French-born is only the most pervasive.

3. The usual *core executive arbiters*—President, Prime Minister, Finance Minister—*play an episodic role in this sector,* preferring to leave this hot potato to others, although they are often compelled to intervene at the later stages of the coordination process. These arbiters introduce an arbitrary, personalized factor that substitutes centralization for coordination.

4. Although the *Interior Ministry has striven to take the lead* in interdepartmental coordination, assisted by its police and local authority powers, its role is strongly contested. While the Labour Ministry's role receded, with the decline of worker shortages in a period of high unemployment, that of Justice, Social Affairs, and the Foreign Ministries increased; intensified repression led to conflicts between Interior and Justice; Social Affairs was particularly involved in dealing with asylum seekers and family reunification problems; while the Foreign Ministry dealt with the international aspects of immigration policy, notably short and long-term visas.

5. The *increasing importance of the EU and international dimensions* of migration has led to an attempt to harmonize immigration and asylum policy, with France taking a lead in the EU. The need to go beyond police cooperation through Interpol and Europol in seeking—vainly—to stem the tide of illegal migration, led to the Schengen agreement which has de facto extended France's borders.

6. The *vociferousness of non-governmental organizations* (NGOs) is particularly great in this sector, with religious and caring organizations, as well as champions of human rights being active in seeking to protect those whom they regard as oppressed. These cause groups are more significant than the interest groups of 'recent' immigrants such as SOS Racism in mobilizing public sympathy, exerting moral pressure which the core executives find it difficult to shrug off without embarrassment.

7. Although hyper-politicized by the Extreme Right, which exerts even stronger pressure than the NGOs, *policy decisions*—in contrast to policy debates—tend

to *cut across the Left–Right dichotomy*. This adds to the general confusion surrounding immigration policy, posing problems of party cohesion both nationally, for example in parliament, and in local government.

REQUIEM FOR INCAUTIOUS COORDINATORS

The French conception of monocratic authority, imposing its central state will on all and sundry after having coordinated itself, proves on closer inspection to reflect rhetoric rather than reality. The executive coordinating mechanisms reveal themselves to be rival centres, with cross-cutting networks of an intricate complexity, which we have been at pains to delineate in detail, at the risk of exhausting the patience of our readers. This imposition was unavoidable if we were to demonstrate convincingly and by comparison across contrasting policy sectors the shifting and fragmented character of a soft core executive. The search for a single, central, uncontested core executive led instead to a proliferation of less rather than more effective attempts at resolving conflicts through arbitration in pursuit of elusive consensus. When analysed, the flattering image of an integrated state disintegrates. The reality is a disparate and partially paralysed institutional structure reflected in fragmented policy outcomes.

To the extent that it was formerly exceptional, France has increasingly ceased to be so, as is evident from many of the general and specific findings we have reported. Poor coordination has arisen from many directions, including internal organizational logic, conflicts of objectives, inadequate programme design (either excessive centralization or diffusion), defective information flows, and an inability to cope with unexpected events or the unintended consequences of decisions. Polycentric complexity has come to predominate over centralized simplicity, both within government and in its enfeebled attempts to control the market economy and civil society. Anachronistic symbolic shibboleths are being remorselessly prised apart by intrusive substantive pressures.

The need to overcome tendencies to political, administrative, and policy fragmentation requires sustained effort in support of institutionalized procedures calculated to prevent contradictory personal, ministerial, and policy priorities from frustrating the creation and preservation of political cohesion. As Glyn Davis has put it: 'An elective executive confronted with a state which simultaneously encompasses internal conflicts, competing external imperatives, contested boundaries, unclear jurisdictions, policy lacunae and interest capture is likely to desire some form of coordination.'[7] However, all too often it is a case of 'I coordinate, you coordinate, he coordinates, we coordinate', but each entity goes its own way, and things fall apart under the pressure of circumstances and forces beyond both core executive control and self-control. It is a lesson which the Blair Government, with its assertive tight

---

[7] G. Davis, 'Executive Co-ordination Mechanisms' in P. Weller, H. Bakvis, and R. Rhodes (eds.), *The Hollow Crown. Countervailing Trends in Core Executives*, Basingstoke, Macmillan, 1997, p. 131.

coordination ambitions,[8] should take to heart. Governing from the centre(s) should not be confused with obsessively integrated government. It may correspond more closely to Lindblom's characterization: 'Still muddling, not yet through',[9] recognized by so many of those involved in government as their everyday experience.

[8] D. Kavanagh and A. Seldon, 'Support for the Prime Minister: the Hidden Influence of No. 10', ch. 4 of R. A. W. Rhodes (ed.), *Transforming British Government*, pp. 68–76 particularly. More generally, see D. Kavanagh and A. Seldon, *The Powers Behind the Throne*, London, Harper Collins, 2000.

[9] C. Lindblom, 'Still muddling, not yet through', *Public Administration Review*, November–December 1979.

Bibliography

Albert-Roulhac, C., 'The Influence of EU Membership on Methods and Processes of Budgeting in Britain and France, 1970–1995', *Governance* 11/2 (April 1998).

Andréani, J.-L., *Le Mystère Rocard* (Paris, Laffont, 1993).

Ardagh, J., *France in the New Century: Portrait of a Changing Society* (London, Viking, 1999).

Arthuis, Jean, *Dans les Coulisses de Bercy: Le Cinquième pouvoir* (Paris, A. Michel, 1998).

Ashford, D., *British Dogmatism and French Pragmatism* (London, Allen & Unwin, 1982).

Attali, J., *Verbatim, i: 1983–86* (Paris, Fayard, 1993).

—— *Verbatim, ii: 1986–88* (Paris, Fayard, 1995).

Avril, P., 'Diriger le Gouvernement', *Pouvoirs*, 83 (November 1997).

Bacqué, R. and Van Renterghem, M., 'La Santé Paralysé', *Le Monde* (10 March 1999).

Bakema, W. E., 'The Ministerial Career', in J. Blondel and J.-L. Thiébault (eds.), *The Profession of Government Minister in Western Europe* (Basingstoke, Macmillan, 1991).

Balladur, Edouard, *Je crois en l'homme plus qu'en l'Etat* (Paris, Flammarion, 1987).

—— *Deux ans à Matignon* (Paris, Plon, 1995).

Balleix-Banerjee, Corinne, *La France et la Banque Centrale Européenne: Débats Politiques et Elaboration de la Décision* (doctoral thesis, Paris II, 1997).

Bancaud, Alain, *Changer la Vie: Les Années Mitterrand, 1981–1984.* Paper presented to the colloquium of the Institut François Mitterrand, 14–16 January. Reported in *Le Monde* (23 June 1999).

Bauchard, P., *Deux ministres trop tranquilles* (Paris, Belfond, 1994).

Bauer, M., 'The Politics of State-Directed Privatisation: The Case of France, 1986–88', *West European Politics*, 11/4 (October 1988).

Bazire, N., *Journal de Matignon* (Paris, Plon, 1996).

'Bercy: un ministère pré-visible', *Le Nouvel Observateur* (29 May 1987).

Bergeron, C., 'Où en sont les grands chantiers de Paris?', *Le Point*, 753 (23 February 1987).

Blandin, C., 'Capitalisme, la fin de l'exception française', *Le Monde* (29 November 1996).

Bloch-Lainé, F., *A la Recherche d'une Economie Concertée* (Editions de l'Epargne, 1964).

—— *Profession: Fonctionnaire* (Paris, Seuil, 1976).

Blondel, J. and Thiébault, J.-L. (eds.), *The Profession of Government Minister in Western Europe* (Basingstoke, Macmillan, 1991).

Bodiguel, J.-L. *et al.*, *Servir l'intérêt général* (PUF, 2000).

Bonini, F., *L'Histoire d'une institution coutumière: le Secrétariat Général de la République Française (1934–1986)* (Doctoral thesis, Institut d'Etudes Politiques de Paris, 1987).

Bréhier, T., 'Une lecture politique de la guerre des banques', *Le Monde* (25 August 1999).

Brigouleix, B., *Histoire indiscrète des Années Balladur: Matignon durant la seconde cohabitation* (Paris, A. Michel, 1995).

Brubaker, W. R., *Citizenship and Nationhood in France and Germany* (London, Harvard University Press, 1992).

Le Budget de l'Etat: De la préparation à l'exécution (Les Editions de Bercy, 1995).

Butt Philip, A., 'European Union Immigration Policy: Phantom, Fantasy or Fact?', *West European Politics*, 17/2 (April 1994).

Cahm, E., 'Mitterrand's *Grands Projets*: Monuments to a Man or Monuments to an Age?', in M. Maclean (ed.), *The Mitterrand Years: Legacy and Evaluation* (Basingstoke, Macmillan, 1998).

Cameron, David R., 'From Barre to Balladur: Economic Policy in the Era of the EMS', in Gregory Flynn (ed.), *Remaking the Hexagon* (Boulder, Colorado, Westview Press, 1995).

—— 'National Interest, the Dilemmas of European Integration and Malaise', in J. Keeler and M. Schain (eds.), *Chirac's Challenge: Liberalization, Europeanization and Malaise in France* (New York, St. Martin's Press, 1996).

Carcassonne, G., 'Typologie des cabinets', *Pouvoirs*, 36 (1986).

—— *La Constitution* (Paris, Seuil, 1996).

—— 'Les rapports du président français et du premier ministre', *Revue Française d'Administration Publique*, 83 (July–September 1997).

—— 'Le Premier Ministre et le domaine dit réservé', *Pouvoirs*, 83 (November 1997).

—— 'Amendments to the French Constitution: One Surprise after Another', in Robert Elgie (ed.), *The Changing French Political System* (London, Cass, 2000).

Catala, Nicole and Ameline, Nicole, *Quelles Réformes pour l'Europe de Demain?'* (Assemblée Nationale, Rapport d'information 1939, 8 February 1995).

Cayrol, R., 'La Société française reste taraudée par le racisme', *Le Monde* (2 July 1998).

Chabal, Pierre, *Des conditions de l'efficacité ministérielle dans le changement des politiques publiques*, III, Appendix. Unpublished doctoral thesis, Grenoble, University of Grenoble, 1999.

Chagnollaud, D. and Quermonne, J.-L., *Le Gouvernement de la France sous le Ve République* (Paris, Fayard, 1996).

Chalandon, A., *Quitte ou Double?* (Paris, Grasset, 1986).

Challis, L. *et al.*, *Joint Approaches to Social Policy, Rationality and Practice* (Cambridge, CUP, 1988).

Charasse, M., *55 Faubourg St. Honoré: Entretiens avec Robert Schneider* (Paris, Grasset, 1996).

Chaslin, F., *Les Paris de François Mitterrand: Histoire des grands projets architecturaux* (Paris, Gallimard, 1985).

Chevallier, J., 'La Nouvelle Réforme des télécommunications: ruptures et continuités', *Revue Française de Droit Administratif*, 12/5 (1996).

Cohen, S., *Les Conseillers du Président: De Charles de Gaulle à Valéry Giscard d'Estaing* (Paris, PUF, 1980).

—— *Le Colbertisme 'High Tech': Economie des Télécom et du Grand Projet* (Paris, Hachette, 1992).

—— *La défaite des généraux: Le pouvoir politique el l'armée sous la Ve République* (Paris, Fayard, 1994).

—— *La Tentation Hexagonale: La souveraineté à l'épreuve de la mondialisation* (Paris, Fayard, 1996).

Cohendet, M.-A., *La Cohabitation: Leçons d'une expérience* (Paris, PUF, 1993).

Cole, A., 'The *Service Public* under stress', *West European Politics*, 22/4 (October 1999).

—— and Drake, H., 'The Europeanization of the French Polity: Continuity, Change and Adaptation', *Journal of European Public Policy*, 7/1 (March 2000).

Collard, Sue, 'Mission Impossible: les chantiers du Président', *French Cultural Studies*, 2 1992).

Costa, Jean-Paul, *Le Conseil d'Etat dans la société contemporaine* (Paris, Economica, 1993).

Cotta, M., 'Conclusion', in J. Blondel and J.-L. Thiébault (eds.), *The Profession of Government Minister in Western Europe* (Basingstoke, Macmillan, 1991).

de Clausade, J., *L'Adaptation de l'administration française à l'Europe* (La Documentation Française, 1991).

de Gaulle, C., *Discours et Messages*, iv (Paris, Plon, 1970).

de Romanet, A., *Le fonctionnement de l'institution présidentielle: la communication et les méthodes de travail à l'Elysée durant la Première année du septennant de M. Mitterrand* (Mémoire IEP de Paris, n.d.).

Darmon, J., *Le Grand Dérangement* (J.-C. Lattès, 1985).

Davis, G., *A Government of Routines: Executive Coordination in an Australian State* (Melbourne, Macmillan Australia, 1995).

—— 'Executive Coordination Mechanisms', in P. Weller, H. Bakvis, and R. Rhodes (eds.), *The Hollow Crown: Countervailing Trends in Core Executives* (Basingstoke, Macmillan, 1997).

Debray, R., *Que vive la République* (Paris, Odile Jacob, 1989).

Delion, A. G. and Durupty, M., *Les Nationalisations 1982* (Paris, Economica, 1982).

Désir, H., *Touche pas à mon pote* (Paris, Grasset, 1985).

Dinan, Desmond, *Ever Closer Union? An Introduction to the European Community* (Basingstoke, Macmillan, 1994).

Dobry, M., *Sociologie des crises politiques* (Paris, Presses de la Fondation nationale des sciences politiques, 1986).

Domenach, N. and Szafran, M., *Le Roman d'un Président* (Paris, Plon, 1997).

—— and ——, *Le Miraculé: Le Roman d'un Président*, ii (Paris, Plon, 2000).

Dray, J., *SOS génération* (Paris, Ramsay, 1987).

Dufourcq, B., 'La réforme du quai d'Orsay', *Revue Française d'Administration Publique*, 77 (January–March, 1996).

Dumez, H. and Jeunemaître, A., 'Privatization in France, 1983–1993', in V. Wright (ed.), *Privatization in Western Europe: Pressures, Problems and Paradoxes* (London, Pinter, 1994).

Durupty, M., *Les Privatisations en France*, La Documentation Française, Notes et Etudes Documentaires, No. 4857, 1988.

Duverger, M., *Breviaire de la cohabitation* (Paris, PUF, 1986).

Dyson, K., 'West European States and the Communication Revolution', *West European Politics*, 9/4 (October 1986).

—— *Elusive Union: The Process of Economic and Monetary Union in Europe* (London, Longman, 1994).

—— 'EMU, Political Discourse and the Fifth French Republic: Historical Institutionalism, Path Dependency and "Craftsmen of Discourse"', *Modern and Contemporary France*, 7/2 (1999).

—— and Featherstone, K., 'EMU and Presidential Leadership under François Mitterrand', in M. Maclean (ed.), *The Mitterrand Years: Legacy and Evaluation* (Basingstoke, Macmillan, 1998).

—— and Featherstone, K., *The Road to Maastricht: Negotiating Economic and Monetary Union* (Oxford, OUP, 1999).

—— and Humphreys, P., 'Policies for New Media in Western Europe: Deregulation of Broadcasting and Multimedia Diversification', *West European Politics*, 9/4 (October 1986).

Ecole Nationale d'Administration, *Le Travail Gouvernemental*, i (La Documentation Française, 1996).

—— *Le Travail Gouvernemental*, ii (La Documentation Française, 1996).

—— 'La Réforme de l'Etat', *Les Cahiers de l'ENA*, 3 (March 1998).

Elgie, Robert, *The Role of the Prime Minister, 1981–91* (Basingstoke, Macmillan, 1993).

—— and Thompson, Helen, *The Politics of Central Banks* (London, Routledge, 1998).

Endo, Ken, *The Presidency of the European Commission under Jacques Delors: The Politics of Shared Leadership* (Basingstoke, Macmillan, 1999).

Etudes et Documents du Conseil d'Etat, no. 44 (La Documentation Française, 1992).

Fabius, L., *Les Blessures de la Vérité* (Paris, Flammarion, 1995).

Favier, P. and Martin-Roland, M., *La Décennie Mitterrand, i: 1981–84* (Paris, Seuil, 1990).

——and—— *La Décennie Mitterrand, ii: 1984–88* (Points edn., Paris, Seuil, 1991).

——and—— *La Décennie Mitterrand, iii: 1988–91* (Points edn., Paris, Seuil, 1996).

——and—— Roland, M., *La Décennie Mitterrand, iv: 1991–95* (Paris, Seuil, 1999).

Feigenbaum, H., Henig, J., and Hamnett, C., *Shrinking the State: The Political Underpinnings of Privatization* (Cambridge, CUP, 1999).

Finer, S. E., *The History of Government from the Earliest Times* (Oxford, OUP, 1997).

——Bogdanor, V., and Rudden, B., *Comparing Constitutions* (Oxford, Clarendon Press, 1995).

Fournier, J., *Le Travail Gouvernemental* (Paris, Dalloz, 1987).

Fourquet, F., *Les Comptes de la Puissance: Histoire de la Comptabilité Nationale et du Plan* (Paris, Encres/Recherches, 1980).

Freeman, Gary P., 'Financial Crisis and Policy Continuity in the Welfare State', in P. Hall *et al.* (eds.), *Developments in French Politics* (Basingstoke, Macmillan, 1994).

Fulda, A., *Un Président très entouré* (Paris, Grasset, 1997).

Fumaroli, M., *L'Etat Culturel: Essai sur une religion moderne*, Livre de Poche edn. (Editions de Fallois, 1992).

Fysh, P., 'The Failure of Anti-Racist Movements in France, 1981–1995', in M. Maclean (ed.), *The Mitterrand Years* (Basingstoke, Macmillan, 1998).

Gaspard, F. and Khrosrokhavar, F., *Le Foulard et la République* (Paris, La Découverte, 1995).

Gastaut, Y., *L'immigration et l'opinion en France sous la Ve République* (Paris, Seuil, 2000).

Gaudin, J.-P., *Gouverner par Contrat: L'Action publique en question* (Paris, Presses de Sciences Po, 1999).

Giesbert, F.-O., *François Mitterrand ou la tentation de l'histoire* (Paris, Seuil, 1977).

Giraudon, V., *Policy Change Behind Gilded Doors: Explaining the Evolution of Aliens' Rights in Contemporary Western Europe, 1974–1994* (doctoral thesis, Harvard University, April 1997).

——'Citizenship Rights for Non-Citizens: France, Germany and the Netherlands', in C. Joppke (ed.), *Challenge to the Nation-State: Immigration in Western Europe and the United States* (Oxford, OUP, 1998).

Giscard d'Estaing, V., *Le Pouvoir et la Vie*, i (Livre de Poche, 1989).

——*Le Pouvoir et la Vie*, ii (Livre de Poche, 1991).

Graham, C., and Prosser, T., *Privatizing Public Enterprises: Constitutions, the State and Regulation in Comparative Perspective* (Oxford, Clarendon Press, 1991).

Gravier, J.-F., *Paris et le désert français* (Paris, Le Portulan, 1947).

Greilsamer, L., 'Le gardien du président', *Le Monde* (28 August 1982).

Grémion, C., *Profession: décideurs. Pouvoir des hauts fonctionnaires et réforme de l'Etat* (Paris, Gauthier-Villars, 1979).

Guigou, E., *Pour les Européens* (Paris, Flammarion, 1994).

Guyomarch, Alain, 'The European Effect: Imposing French Policy Coordination', *Staatswissenschaften und Staatspraxis*, 3 (1993).

——*et al.*, *France in the European Union* (Basingstoke, Macmillan, 1998).

Hamdouch, A., *L'Etat d'influence: Nationalisations et Privatisations in France* (Paris, Presses du CNRS, 1989).

Hanf, K., in K. Hanf and F. W. Scharpf (eds.), *Interorganizational Policy Making: Limits to Coordination and Central Control* (London, Sage, 1978).

Hansen, R., 'Migration, citizenship and race in Europe: Between incorporation and exclusion', *European Journal of Political Research*, 35 (1999).

Hardin, R., *Liberalism, Constitutionalism, and Democracy* (Oxford, OUP, 2000).

Harrison, M., 'The President, Cultural Projects and Broadcasting Policy', in J. Hayward (ed.), *De Gaulle to Mitterrand: Presidential Power in France* (London, Hurst, 1993).

Hayes-Renshaw, F. and Wallace, H., *The Council of Ministers* (Basingstoke, Macmillan, 1997).

Hayward, J., *The One and Indivisible French Republic* (London, Weidenfeld & Nicolson, 1973).

—— *Governing France: The One and Indivisible Republic* (London, Weidenfeld & Nicolson, 1983).

—— *The State and the Market Economy: Industrial Patriotism and Economic Intervention in France* (Brighton, Harvester, 1986).

—— (ed.), *De Gaulle to Mitterrand: Presidential Power in France* (London, Hurst, 1993).

—— 'France and the United Kingdom: The Dilemmas of Integration and National Democracy', in J. Anderson (ed.), *Regional Integration and Democracy: Expanding on the European Experience* (Boulder, Colorado, Rowman and Littlefield, 1999).

Heald, D., 'The United Kingdom: Privatisation and its Political Context', *West European Politics*, 11/4 (October 1988).

Heclo, H. and Wildavsky, A., *The Private Government of Public Money* (Berkeley, University of California Press, 1974).

Hirschman, A., *Shifting Involvements: Private Interest and Public Policy* (Oxford, Blackwell, 1982).

Howarth, D., 'The French State in the Euro Zone', in K. Dyson (ed.), *European States and the Euro: Playing the Semi-Sovereignty Game* (Oxford, OUP, 2001).

Howorth, J., 'The President's Special Role in Foreign and Defence Policy', in J. Hayward (ed.), *De Gaulle to Mitterrand: Presidential Power in France* (London, Hurst, 1993).

Huber, J. D., *Rationalizing Parliament: Legislative Institutions and Party Politics in France* (Cambridge, CUP, 1996).

Huchon, J.-P., *Jours Tranquilles à Matignon* (Paris, Grasset, 1993).

IFSA, *Le Secrétariat Général du Gouvernement* (Paris, Economica, 1986).

Isnard, J., 'Une armée Française "otanisée"', *Le Monde* (3 July 1988).

Jelen, C., *Les casseurs de la République* (Paris, Plon, 1997).

Jennings, Jeremy, 'Citizenship, Republicanism and Multiculturalism in Contemporary France', *British Journal of Political Science*, 30/4 (October 2000).

Jospin, L., *L'Invention du possible* (Paris, Flammarion, 1991).

Joxe, P., *A propos de la France: Itinéraire I. Entretiens avec Michel Sarrazin* (Paris, Flammarion, 1998).

Kassim, H. *et al.* (eds.), *The National Coordination of EU Policy: The Domestic Level* (Oxford, OUP, 2000).

Kay, J., Mayer, C., and Thompson, D. (eds.), *Privatization and Regulation* (Oxford, Clarendon Press, 1986).

Kessler, M.-C., *La Politique Etrangère de la France: Acteurs et Processus* (Paris, Presses de Sciences Po, 1999).

Kolodziej, E. A., *Making and Marketing Arms: The French Experience and the Implications for the International System* (Princeton, Princeton University Press, 1987).

Kuhn, R., *The Media in France* (London, Routledge, 1995).

Labro, P., 'Le Hussar et l'Horloger', *Le Monde* (19 September 2000).

Laffan, B. and Shackleton, M., 'The Budget', in H. Wallace and W. Wallace (eds.), *Policy-Making in the European Union* (Oxford, OUP, 1996).

Lagrange, H. and Perrineau, P., 'Le Syndrome Le Pen', in H. Lagrange and P. Perrineau (eds.), *Le Front National à Découvert* (Paris, Presses de Sciences Po, 1996).

Lahav, G., 'Immigration and the State: Devolution and Privatisation of Immigration Control in the EU', *Journal of Ethnic and Migration Studies*, 24/4 (October 1998).

Lamassoure, A., *Rapport d'information au nom de la délégation du Sénat pour les Communautés européennes sur la procédure budgétaire communautaire*, Appendix to Senate proceedings of 12 June, 377 (1991).

Landau, M., 'Redundancy, Rationality and the Problem of Duplication and Overlap', *Public Administration Review*, 29 (July 1969).

Lequesne, C., *Paris–Bruxelles: Comment se fait la politique européenne de la France* (Paris, Presses de la Fondation Nationale des Sciences Politiques, 1993).

—— 'Union européenne et coordination gouvernemental: *quid novi* en Francé', in F. d'Arcy and L. Rouban (eds.), *De la Ve République à l'Europe* (Paris, Presses de Sciences Po, 1996).

Lévêque, J.-M., *Dénationalisations: Mode d'Emploi* (Paris, A. Michel, 1985).

Lion, R., *L'Etat Passion* (Paris, Plon, 1992).

Lochak, D., *Etrangers, de quel droit?* (Paris, PUF, 1985).

Long Report, *Etre Français aujourd'hui et demain: Rapport de la Commission de la Nationalité*, La Documentation Française, 1988.

Looseley, D., *The Politics of Fun: Cultural Policy and Debate in Contemporary France* (Oxford, Berg, 1995).

Lord, G., *The French Budgetary Process* (Berkeley, University of California Press, 1973).

La Lutte contre le racisme et la xénophobie, La Documentation Française, 2000.

Maclean, M., 'Privatisation in France 1993–94: New departures or a case of plus ça change?', *West European Politics*, 17/2 (April 1995).

—— 'Privatisation, *Dirigisme* and the Global Economy: An End to French Exceptionalism?', *Modern and Contemporary France*, 2 (May 1997).

Majone, G., 'Paradoxes of privatization and deregulation', *Journal of European Public Policy*, 1/1 (June 1994).

Malik, S., *Histoire secrète de SOS Racisme* (Paris, A. Michel, 1990).

Marchat, P., *L'Economie Mixte* (Paris, PUF, 1971).

Massot, J., *L'Arbitre et le Capitaine: Essai sur la Responsabilité Présidentielle* (Paris, Flammarion, 1987).

Mauroy, P., *C'est ici le chemin* (Paris, Flammarion, 1982).

Médard, J.-F., 'France-Afrique: des affaires de famille', in D. della Porta and Y. Mény (eds.), *Démocratie et corruption en Europe* (Paris, La Découverte, 1995).

Ménage, G., *L'Oeil du Pouvoir: Les affaires de l'Etat, 1981–86* (Paris, Fayard, 1999).

Menon, A., *The Ambivalent Ally: France, NATO and the Limits of Independence, 1981–97* (Basingstoke, Macmillan, 1999).

Metcalfe, L., 'International Policy Coordination and Public Management Reform', *International Review of Administrative Sciences*, 60 (1994).

Miller, M., 'Towards Understanding State Capacity to Prevent Unwanted Migrations: Employer Sanctions Enforcement in France, 1975–1990', *West European Politics*, 17/2 (April 1994).

Mopin, M., 'Diriger le Parlement', *Pouvoirs*, 83 (November 1997).

Moravcsik, A., *The Choice for Europe: Social Purpose and State Power from Messina to Maastricht* (Ithaca, Cornell University Press, 1998).

Morgan, K. and Webber, D., 'Divergent Paths: Political Strategies for Telecommunications in Britain, France and West Germany', *West European Politics*, 9/4 (October 1986).

National Planning Office, *The European Union in pursuit of legitimate and effective institutions* (Commissariat Général du Plan, Paris, November 1999).

Newhouse, J., 'One Against Nine', *The New Yorker* (22 October 1984).

Nicolas, V., 'Le Désordre Normatif', in *Pouvoirs*, 69 (April 1994).

Norek, C. and Doumic-Doublet, F., *Le Droit d'Asile en France* (Paris, PUF, 1989).

Ollitrault, S., 'Edith Cresson, the First Woman Prime Minister in France', ECPR Workshop paper, Warwick, March 1998.

Ottenheimer, G., *Le Fiasco* (Paris, A. Michel, 1996).

Papadopoulos, Y., *Démocratie Directe* (Paris, Economica, 1998).

Perret, B. and Leca, J., Oral interventions reported in *Les Cahiers de l'Ecole Nationale d'Administration*, 3 (1998).

Peters, B. G., Rhodes, R. A. W., and Wright, V., *Administering the Summit: Administration of the Core Executive in Developed Countries* (Basingstoke, Macmillan, 2000).

Petot, J., 'L'Europe, la France et son Président', *La Revue du Droit Public* (March–April 1993).

Pfister, T., *A Matignon au Temps de l'Union de la Gauche* (Paris, Hachette, 1985).

—— 'L'usurpation du pouvoir des cabinets ministériels', *Le Débat*, 52 (November–December 1988).

Picq Report, *L'Etat en France: Servir une nation ouverte sur le monde: Rapport au Premier ministre* (La Documentation Française, 1995).

Pierson, P., 'The Path to European Integration: A Historical Institutionalist Analysis', in W. Sandholtz and A. Stone Sweet (eds.), *European Integration and Supranational Governance* (Oxford, OUP, 1998).

Pougnaud, P., *Les Rouages de l'Etat: Voyage à l'intérieure de l'exécutif français* (Paris, Eska, 1994).

Prada, M., 'La préparation du budget vue par la direction du budget', in *Le Budget de l'Etat* (Paris, Economica, 1988).

Quermonne Report, *The European Union in pursuit of legitimate and effective institutions* (Paris, National Planning Office, 1999).

Qui fait quoi? Direction des Transports Terrestres (Paris, Ministère de l'Equipement, du Logement, des Transports et du Tourisme, 1995).

Rhodes, R. A. W., 'From Prime Ministerial Power to Core Executive', in R. A. W. Rhodes and P. Dunleavy (eds.), *Prime Minister, Cabinet and Core Executive* (Basingstoke, Macmillan, 1995).

—— (ed.), *Transforming British Government: Changing Roles and Relationships* (Basingstoke, Macmillan, 2000).

Roman, J., *La Démocratie des individus* (Paris, Calmann-Lévy, 1998).

Rometsch, D. and Wessels, W. (eds.), *The European Union and member states: Towards institutional fusion?* (Manchester, Manchester University Press, 1996).

Ross, George, *Jacques Delors and European Integration* (Oxford, Polity Press, 1995).

Rouban, L., 'Les Enarques en Cabinet: 1984–1996', *Les Cahiers du CEVIPOF*, no. 17 (Centre d'Etudes de la Vie Politique Française, 1997).

Sandholtz, W., 'The Emergence of a Supranational Telecommunications Regime', in W. Sandholtz and A. Stone Sweet (eds.), *European Integration and Supranational Governance* (Oxford, OUP, 1998).

Santi, P., 'Claude Bébéar', *Le Monde* (20 January 2000).

Savary, A., *En toute liberté* (Paris, Hachette, 1985).

Schain, M. A., *French Communism and Local Power* (New York, St. Martin's Press, 1985).

—— 'Policy-making and Defining Ethnic Minorities: The Case of Immigration in France', *New Community*, 20/1 (October 1993).

—— 'The Immigration Debate and the National Front', in J. Keeler and M. A. Schain (eds.), *Chirac's Challenge: Liberalization, Europeanization and Malaise in France* (New York, St. Martin's Press, 1996).

Schemla, I., *Edith Cresson: la femme piégée* (Paris, Flammarion, 1993).

Schifres, M. and Sarrazin, M., *L'Elysée de Mitterrand: Secrets de la Maison du Prince* (Paris, A. Moreau, 1985).

Schnapper, D., *La France de l'intégration: sociologie de la nation en 1990* (Paris, Gallimard, 1991).

—— *La Communauté des citoyens: sur l'idée moderne de nation* (Paris, Gallimard, 1994).

—— 'The Debate on Immigration and the Crisis of National Identity', *West European Politics*, 17/2 (April 1994).

Schrameck, O., *Les cabinets ministériels* (Paris, Dalloz, 1995).

—— *Matignon Rive Gauche* (Paris, Seuil, 2001).

Seidman, H., *Politics, Position, and Power: The Dynamics of Federal Organization* [1970], third edn. (Oxford, OUP, 1980).

Sharkansky, I., *The Routines of Politics* (New York, Van Nostrand Reinhold, 1970).

Shearman, C., 'European Collaboration in Computing and Telecommunications: A Policy Approach', *West European Politics*, 9/4 (October 1986).

SOFRES, *L'Etat de l'Opinion* (Paris, Seuil, 1988).

Stevens, A., 'The President and his Staff', in J. Hayward (ed.), *De Gaulle to Mitterrand: Presidential Power in France* (London, Hurst, 1993).

Stone, A., *The Birth of Judicial Politics in France: The Constitutional Council in Comparative Perspective* (Oxford, OUP, 1992).

—— 'Constitutional Politics and Malaise in France', in J. Keeler and M. Schain (eds.), *Chirac's Challenge: Liberalization, Europeanization and Malaise in France* (New York, St. Martin's Press, 1996).

Stone Sweet, A. and Sandholtz, W. (eds.), *European Integration and Supranational Governance* (Oxford, OUP, 1998).

Taguieff, P.-A., 'Un programme "révolutionnaire"', in N. Meyer and P. Perrineau (eds.), *Le Front National à Découvert* (Paris, Presses de Sciences Po, 1996).

Tétu, M., *La francophonie: Histoire, problématique, perspectives* (Paris, Hachette, 1988).

Thatcher, M., 'Regulatory Reform and Internationalization in Telecommunications', in J. Hayward (ed.), *Industrial Enterprise and European Integration* (Oxford, OUP, 1995).

—— 'High Technology', in H. Kassim and A. Menon (eds.), *The European Union and National Industrial Policy* (London, Routledge, 1996).

—— *The Politics of Telecommunications: National Institutions, Convergence and Change* (Oxford, OUP, 1999).

Todd, E., *Le Destin des immigrés: assimilation et ségregation dans les démocraties occidentales* (Paris, Seuil, 1994).

Touraine, A., *Pourrons-nous vivre ensemble: égaux et différents* (Paris, Fayard, 1997).

Vedel, G., 'Variations et cohabitations', *Pouvoirs*, 83 (November 1997).

Védrine, H., *Les Mondes de François Mitterrand: A l'Elysée, 1981–95* (Paris, Fayard, 1996).

Victor, B., *Le Matignon de Jospin* (Paris, Flammarion, 1999).

Walzenbach, G. P. E., 'Convergent Co-ordination Patterns in the French and German Core Executive: the case of the BSE crisis', *West European Politics*, 22/3 (July 1999).

Waters, S., 'New Social Movement Politics in France: The Rise of Civic Forms of Mobilisation', *West European Politics*, 21/3 (July 1998).

Webber, D., 'High Midnight in Brussels: An Analysis of the September 1993 Council meeting on the GATT Uruguay Round', *Journal of European Public Policy*, 5/4 (December 1998).

—— *The Franco-German Relationship in the European Union* (London, Routledge, 1999).

Weber, E., *Peasants into Frenchmen: The Modernization of Rural France, 1870–1914* (London, Chatto & Windus, 1977).

Weil, P., *La France et ses étrangers: L'aventure d'une politique de l'immigration de 1938 à nos jours* (Paris, Gallimard, 1995).

—— *Pour Une Nouvelle Politique d'Immigration*, Notes de la Fondation Saint-Simon, November 1995.

—— *Mission d'études des législations de la nationalité et de l'immigration*, La Documentation Française, 1997.

—— and Crawley, J., 'Integration in Theory and Practice: A Comparison of France and Britain', *West European Politics*, 17/2 (April 1994).

Wihtol de Wenden, C., 'Immigrants as Political Actors in France', *West European Politics*, 17/2 (April 1994).

—— 'The French Response to the Asylum Seeker Influx, 1980–93', *The Annals of the American Academy of Political and Social Sciences* (July 1994).

Wildavsky, A., 'If Planning is Everything, Maybe it's Nothing', *Policy Science*, 4 (1973).

Wilsford, David, 'Reforming French Health Care Policy', in J. Keeler and M. Schain (eds.), *Chirac's Challenge: Liberalization, Europeanization and Malaise in France* (New York, St. Martin's Press, 1996).

Woolcock, S. and Hodges, M., 'EU policy in the Uruguay Round', in H. Wallace and W. Wallace (eds.), *Policy-Making in the European Union* (Oxford, OUP, 1996).

Wright, V., 'Politics and Administration in the Fifth French Republic', *Political Studies*, 22/1 (March 1974).

—— 'The Administrative System and Market Regulation in Western Europe: Continuities, Exceptionalism and Convergence', *Rivista trimestrale di diritto pubblico*, 4 (1992).

—— 'The President and Prime Minister: Subordination, Conflict, Symbiosis or Reciprocal Parasitism', in J. Hayward (ed.), *De Gaulle to Mitterrand: Presidential Power in France* (London, Hurst, 1993).

—— 'The Administrative Machine: Old Problems and New Dilemmas', in P. Hall *et al.* (eds.) *Development in French Politics*, revised edn. (London, Macmillan, 1994).

—— 'Industrial Privatization in Western Europe: Pressures, Problems and Paradoxes', in V. Wright (ed.), *Privatization in Western Europe: Pressures, Problems and Paradoxes* (London, Pinter, 1994).

—— 'The Industrial Privatisation Programmes of Britain and France: The Impact of Political and Institutional Factors', in P. Jones (ed.), *Party, Parliament and Personality: Essays presented to Hugh Berrington* (London, Routledge, 1995).

—— 'The National Coordination of European Policy-making: Negotiating the Quagmire', in Jeremy Richardson (ed.), *European Union: Power and Policy-making* (London, Routledge, 1996).

Wright, V., 'Introduction: la fin du dirigisme?', *Modern and Contemporary France*, 5/2 (May 1997).

—— 'France in the 1990s: The End of *Dirigisme*?', *Stato e Mercato*, 54 (1998).

—— 'The Fifth Republic: From the *Droit de l'Etat* to the *Etat de droit*', in Robert Elgie (ed.), *The Changing French Political System* (London, Cass, 2000).

Zahariadis, N., 'To Sell or Not to Sell? Telecommunications Policy in Britain and France', *Journal of Public Policy*, 12/4 (October–December 1992).

—— *Markets, States and Public Policy: Privatization in Britain and France* (Michigan, University of Michigan Press, 1995).

Index